DANCING DESIRES

STUDIES IN DANCE HISTORY

A Publication of the Society of Dance History Scholars
Joan Erdman and Carol Martin, Series Co-Editors

Titles in Print
  The Origins of the Bolero School, edited by Javier Suarez-Pajares and Xoán M.
    Carreira
  Carlo Blasis in Russia by Elizabeth Souritz, with preface by Selma Jeanne Cohen
  Of, By, and For the People: Dancing on the Left in the 1930s, edited by Lynn
    Garafola
  Dancing in Montreal: Seeds of a Choreographic History by Iro Tembeck
  The Making of a Choreographer: Ninette de Valois and "Bar aux Folies-Bergère"
    by Beth Genné
  Ned Wayburn and the Dance Routine: From Vaudeville to the "Ziegfeld Follies" by
    Barbara Stratyner
  Rethinking the Sylph: New Perspectives on the Romantic Ballet, edited by Lynn
    Garafola (available from the University Press of New England)
  Dance for Export: Cultural Diplomacy and the Cold War by Naima Prevots, with
    introduction by Eric Foner (available from the University Press of New
    England)
  José Limón: An Unfinished Memoir, edited by Lynn Garafola, with introduction
    by Deborah Jowitt, foreword by Carla Maxwell, and afterword by Norton
    Owen (available from the University Press of New England)
  Dancing Desires: Choreographing Sexualities on and off the Stage, edited by Jane
    C. Desmond

A STUDIES IN DANCE HISTORY BOOK

DANCING DESIRES

CHOREOGRAPHING SEXUALITIES
ON AND OFF THE STAGE

EDITED BY

JANE C. DESMOND

THE UNIVERSITY OF WISCONSIN PRESS

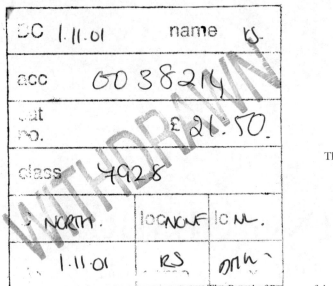
The University of Wisconsin Press
1930 Monroe Street
Madison, Wisconsin 53711

www.wisc.edu/wisconsinpress/

3 Henrietta Street
London WC2E 8LU, England

1   2   3   4   5

Printed in the United States of America

Library of Congress Cataloging-in-Publication Data
Dancing desires : choreographing sexualities
on and off the stage / Jane C. Desmond.
488 pp.   cm — (Studies in dance history)
Includes bibliographical references and index.
ISBN 0-299-17050-0 (alk. paper)
ISBN 0-299-17054-3 (pbk.: alk. paper)
1. Homosexuality in dance.   2. Homosexuality and dance.
3. Dance—Social aspects.   4. Dance—Psychological aspects.
5. Gender identity.   I. Desmond, Jane.   II. Title.
III. Studies in dance history (Unnumbered)
GV1588.6 .D43   2001
792.8—dc21   00-010661

Contents

My thanks go to all who dare to dance a different vision of life. Without your courage this book would have no reason to be. I thank all who supported this project, especially the many scholars, writers, and dancers who sent proposals, ideas, articles, and suggestions during its early phases. Although I have not been able to include all your work in this volume because of production constraints, the groundswell of interest that this book elicited bodes well for the future of dance and sexuality studies. To those whose work is presented here, my grateful appreciation for your energetic rewritings in response to my editorial suggestions and to your passionate engagement with these issues. Developing this volume with you has been tremendously rewarding.

A very special thank you must go to the Society of Dance History Scholars, which first invited me to propose an idea for an edited collection and then responded with enthusiasm and helpful critique as this idea took palpable shape. I especially want to thank Lynn Garafola, then editor of the Studies in Dance History series, who worked with me through the development phase of the proposal and who, with members of the SDHS Editorial Board, provided helpful counsel in shaping the contours of this project. Thanks too to Susan Manning and Ann Daly for early suggestions, and to SDHS board members Carol Martin and Joan Erdman for their suggestions and encouragement and for keeping this project on track. David Román deserves special thanks for his critical reading of the entire manuscript and his numerous suggestions, which helped me improve it.

Kim Marra first planted the idea several years ago, unknowingly, when she invited me to contribute a piece on dance to her coedited collection *Passing Performances* on gays and lesbians in the theater. Time constraints prevented me from taking on that piece, but even more germane were my protests to her that I knew nothing about gay and lesbian dancing or dancers. That invitation opened the issue for me and made me cognizant not only of my own ignorance but that my ignorance was symptomatic of a wider lack of engagement between gay/lesbian studies and dance studies. This book begins to bridge that chasm. Thank you, Kim, for making me think.

Finally, I must thank my dancing partner, Virginia Domínguez, for innumerable tangos, waltzes, and merengues in the kitchen and through the choreography of life.

DANCING DESIRES

Introduction
Making the Invisible Visible:
Staging Sexualities through Dance

Jane C. Desmond

This book makes a two-pronged argument. First, it suggests that to understand dance history and dance practices, we must analyze them in relation to histories of sexualities. Conversely, it suggests that the analysis of dance, as a form of material symbolic bodily practice, should be of critical importance to gay and lesbian studies and to "queer theory." Until now neither analytical approach has received much attention from dance studies scholars or from those in gay/lesbian studies.

In editing this book I hope to make clear the potential of such intersections and to suggest some preliminary answers to the following questions: What happens to the writing of dance history and criticism when issues of sexuality and sexual identity become central? And what happens to our considerations of queer theory and to gay and lesbian studies when a dancing body takes center stage? What do we see that we didn't see before? What questions do we ask that were heretofore unspeakable, unnameable, or unthinkable? What analytical tools will we need to formulate these questions and to develop provisional answers? In what ways might these initiatives reshape our readings of past histories and give rise to new ones?

This claim for the necessary intersection of sexuality studies and dance studies is based on two assertions: first, that issues of sexuality, and especially of non-normative sexuality, are not merely relevant to but play a constitutive and underrecognized role in dance history; and, second, that dance provides a privileged arena for the bodily enactment of sexuality's semiotics and should thus be positioned at the center, not the periphery, of sexuality studies.

3

These claims are grounded in the epistemological emphasis on the physical body shared by the concepts of sex, sexuality, and dancing.[1] The relationship between bodies and social categories of sexuality must always be carefully calibrated with historical specificity, and dancing provides a highly codified, widespread, especially visible, and privileged arena to investigate these changing relations. This book examines these changing relations in twentieth-century case studies drawn from the United States, Britain, and Australia. In ballet, social dance, film, club performances, and modern dance, choreographed behaviors enact notions of romance, sex, physical expressivity, and sexual identity. These motions gain their meanings in relation to dominant discourses about "male" and "female," about "masculine" and "feminine," about "heterosexual" and "homosexual." They also do so in relation to movement conventions that have their own resonant histories on the stage and in daily life.

Theatrical dance history can be seen, in many instances, as a response to, or negotiation of, the injunctions against same-sex desire and the conflation of theatrical dancing with "the feminine." In fact, we could imagine a rewritten history of twentieth-century ballet and modern dance forms (Nijinsky, Ted Shawn, Merce Cunningham, Loie Fuller, Bill T. Jones) that analyzed the works of leading figures precisely in terms of how their work staged sexuality and gender in relation to the dominant discourses of their time. Recall the visual perception exercise that posits one image when we look at the dark background and another entirely different image when we concentrate on the light-colored foreground. By focusing on the light "shape," we completely miss how the background *forms* the foreground. Homophobia, the dark background of dance history, is actually the constitutive ground of a great deal of what we know as the "canon" of dance history. Homophobia's presence has long been known in the dance world but almost never subjected to analytical scrutiny. We do not typically uncover how it has governed what dancing appeared on the stage and the interpretations of those stagings. Just as earlier work in dance studies during the 1980s and 1990s revised dance history by bringing to bear the analytic tools of feminist theory and critical race studies, so too must it be transformed again by making sexuality a central component of critical analyses.

Similar considerations emerge when we turn our attention to forms not traditionally considered theatrical. Dancing in gay pride parades, circuit parties, same-sex dancing in gay bars and at house parties, same-sex dancing in public ("heterosexual") spaces—all these instances provide sites for an analysis of what contributor Ann Cvetkovich terms "a cultural politics of movement" (chapter 10). For many cultural traditions in the United States and elsewhere, dancing is connected with romance, with enticing display, with sensuality. It is also connected to issues of spectacle, of putting one's self publicly on display. Dance lets us look at bodies for pleasure, indeed, demands that this is what we do. This has the potential to link bodies with desire and dancing with the visible manifestation, or elicitation of, desire. Because of this linkage same-sex social dancing becomes a political act of transgression, one protected as symbolic speech by law, as legal analyst Paul Siegel explains in chapter 8. In these cases dancing is explicitly politically charged precisely because it is presumed to be a public staging of desire, with "desire" a key signifier of sexuality.

Social dancing is thus an important practice for scholars of sexuality studies to understand, yet few have taken it up. And while some dance scholars have concentrated on social dance history (among them, Susan Glenn, Julie Malnig, Marta Savigliano, and Linda Tomko), overall the arena beyond professional staged dance has received less attention than its widespread practice deserves, and sexuality is rarely the focus of such studies. We can begin this work, as contributor Jonathan Bollen demonstrates in his essay about dancing at the Sydney Mardi Gras (chapter 9), by analyzing queer identifications and desires through their literal enactment on the dance floor, paying attention to movement style, spatial negotiation, or relational positioning.

If analyzing the politics of sexuality can reveal more of the constitutive framework of dance history (its allowable parameters for staging the masculine or feminine, and the moments of excess that break through those parameters) and can help us understand the ways that social dancing is a public political practice confirming, contravening, or rewriting social relations, it can also elucidate the appeal of some performers and the pleasures they provide. For example, as contributor Paul Franklin argues with regard to Charlie Chaplin (chapter 1), part of Chaplin's appeal consisted precisely of his kinesthetic manipulations—his dancing portrayed a "feminized" fellow who, as the Little Tramp, appealed to men and women alike. Similar investigations of star personas might focus on Michael Jackson's, Madonna's, or Mick Jagger's movement. For these performers and many others, dancing becomes a way of staging sexuality and a relationship to the audience that exceeds a simple heterosexual model. Dancing facilitates this staging not only because of the historically specific links drawn between body, movement, and sex, and the performers' manipulation of those signifiers, but also because the nonverbal realm is marked as one of interior expressivity, and thus often popularly regarded as revelatory of deeper emotions, feelings, and desires.

How one moves, and how one moves in relation to others, constitutes a public enactment of sexuality and gender. This is true whether we are considering Nijinsky's leaps or dancing at the local bar. Perceptions of such enactments are always calculated in relation to the perceived biological "sex" of the mover and in relation to the dominant codes for such signs. Norms of subcultural groups, and racial, age, and class differences, inflect these kinesthetic renderings (or "citations," in Judith Butler's sense). These renderings are especially critical in understanding sexualities because sexualities are not immediately readable from the biological body, as categories of gender and race are most often presumed to be, yet they are tightly tied to notions of physicality—of what one does with one's body. Sexualities must be rendered visible through performative markers of speech, movement, fashion, or subcultural cues. They must, in a sense, be declared. This declaration can be made or rendered mute through dance as an embodied practice. The "swish" of a male wrist or the strong strides of a female can, in certain contexts and for certain viewers, be kinesthetic "speech-acts" that declare antinormative sexuality.

Dancing, perhaps the most highly complex and codified of kinesthetic practices, is one of the most important arenas of public physical enactment. With its linkage to sex, sexiness, and sexuality, dance provides a dense and fecund field for investigating how sexualities are inscribed, learned, rendered, and continually resignified through bodily actions. Analyzing dance can help us understand how sexuality is literally inhabited, embodied, and experienced. It can open the way to the new arena of investigations this book seeks to promote: a kinesthetics of sexuality.

ANALYZING A KINESTHETICS OF SEXUALITY

Neither dance scholarship nor work on gay and lesbian lives nor queer theory has seriously investigated these linkages in any sustained way. The few instances of such scholarship reflect both the richness of this terrain and the remarkable paucity of such work. Among the pioneering works in dance studies are Mark Franko's discussion of Cocteau, Barbette, and Butoh artist Kazuo Ohno, in his *Dancing Modernism/Performing Politics;* Gay Morris's consideration of Mark Morris's gender-bending version of *The Nutcracker;* Michael Moon's discussion of *Schéhérazade;* and Gaylyn Studlar's "Douglas Fairbanks: Thief of the Ballets Russes."

Some dance history writing has discussed the sexual orientation of selected performers and choreographers as well, as in Jane Sherman and Barton Mumaw's *Barton Mumaw, Dancer: From Denishawn to Jacob's Pillow and Beyond*, which includes a discussion of Ted Shawn's homosexuality. In his important book *The Male Dancer: Bodies, Spectacle, Sexualities*, Ramsay Burt developed his argument that "the traditions and conventions of mainstream theatre dance are formed by and reinforce a normative heterosexual, male point of view, marginalizing and suppressing alternative sexualities," and a few very recent papers and publications are beginning to take up these issues.[2] See, for example, Bud Coleman's work on the all-male Les Ballets Trocadero and Moe Meyer's article on Harlem drag balls. The 1998 annual conference of the Society of Dance History Scholars included a panel discussion, "Dancing Queerly," chaired by Tommy DeFrantz (to my knowledge the first such panel devoted entirely to such issues at a major dance conference), and including papers by Valerie Briginshaw, Susan Manning, and Ramsay Burt. For an important early piece (originally published in 1979), see Richard Dyer, "In Defense of Disco," and his very brief but suggestive "Classical Ballet: A Bit of Uplift," (originally published in 1986).

Similarly, among some of the most widely circulating texts on gay/lesbian history and/or queer theory, dance receives only the scantest mention, despite an emphasis on the body and on popular culture. The massive 1993 collection, *The Lesbian and Gay Studies Reader*, edited by Henry Abelove, Michele Aina Barale, and David M. Halperin, includes among its forty-two articles none devoted to dance. The more recent *Out in Culture: Gay, Lesbian, and Queer Essays on Popular Culture* (1995), edited by Corey K. Creekmur and Alexander Doty, reprints three articles that discuss dance: the Michael Moon and Richard Dyer pieces cited earlier, and Anthony Thomas's essay, "The House the Kids Built: The Gay Black Imprint on American Dance Music," which, while concentrating on music in dance clubs, includes a brief discussion of the dancing that takes place there. The historian George Chauncey's *Gay New York: Gender, Urban Culture, and the Making of the Gay Male World, 1890–1940*, includes brief mentions of gay male dance halls but does not discuss dance in detail. Only Deborah P. Amory's "Club Q: Dancing with (a) Difference," in *Inventing Lesbian Cultures in America*, edited by Ellen Lewin, provides an extended treatment of a dance club. Amory emphasizes the broadly performative and sociospatial aspects of the club but gives little attention to the dancing per se— what people actually *do* with their bodies. Even these isolated examples point to the unmined possibilities.[3] The absence is all the more remarkable considering the dramatic growth in both dance studies and gay/lesbian/queer studies during the 1990s and the emphasis in both fields on body issues.[4]

Given the relative absence of models for this type of scholarship, I really had no idea what to expect when I began to solicit essay proposals for this book. I deliberately tried to lure dance scholars into thinking about issues of sexuality and to entice queer studies scholars to take on dance, often for the first time. This book reflects that effort; it includes both those who work primarily in gay/lesbian/queer studies and those who regard themselves primarily as dance or theater specialists. The resulting varieties of terminology and of approach bear the marks of a range of disciplinary specialties and of conversations very much under construction.

"QUEER" CAVEATS

Obviously, scholarly work in gay/lesbian/transgender studies, sexuality studies, and queer theory provide part of the matrix of these discussions, but what exactly is such work, and what might it offer dance studies? Already apparent in the opening paragraphs of this essay is the slippage among terms—*gay/lesbian studies, queer theory, sexuality studies*. Contributors to this book use these terms in a variety of ways. I should note at the outset that terms like *gay*, *lesbian*, and *queer* are not to be taken as unitary references or reifications but rather as provisional designations of ideas, communities, and political positionings. Expanding the definitions of these terms allows me and the other authors to address current public and scholarly discourse about non-normative sexualities. As in current discourse, I use the term *sexualities* primarily but not always to mean 'nonheteronormativity,' a realm that can include *gay*, *lesbian*, and *queer* and may refer to a whole variety of other non-normative positions, including trangendered subjects. In addition, such discussions of sexuality have relevance for our understanding of the construction of heterosexuality as well, because that category is usually the unmarked yet dominant Other in relation to which these other terms and lived experiences gain their meaning while they in turn help define the boundaries of heterosexuality. The particular meanings of these terms for various contributors can only be determined by the specific contextual instances in which they appear throughout this book.

In current scholarly discussions queer theory and gay/lesbian studies sometimes share overlapping concerns and at other times conflict. Some have criticized the term *queer* and the notion of community to which it refers as "ignoring the specificities of sexed bodies." Elizabeth Grosz elaborates: "Even if we are all composed of a myriad of sexual possibilities, of fluid, changeable forms of sexuality, nevertheless these still conform to the configurations of the two sexes . . . . It *does* make a difference which kind of sexed body enacts the various modes of performance."[5] The notion of queer can also undercut the material experience of those who define themselves as gay, lesbian, bisexual, or transgendered and who often pay a high social (and material) cost for doing so.

Some theorists characterize queer theory as white male homosexuality by another name. As David Eng and Alice Hom have argued, although *queer* can be shorthand for an oppositional politics, it can also erase racial and gendered differences in the process.[6] Eng develops this further, insisting on the necessity and analytical potential of our understanding the mutually constitutive racializing of sexuality and the gendering of race. The naturalization of the normativity of heterosexuality and whiteness go hand in hand. "We must," argues Eng, "begin to consider the multiple ways in which this universalizing of whiteness works to authorize at one and the same time the naturalizing power of heterosexuality."[7] To date, most investigations of race in dance studies have concentrated on the work of African American dancers and choreographers. The works of other "nonwhite" choreographers have received little attention overall, and the linkages between predominantly "white" dance practices and forms and the implicit production of "whiteness" as a social category through dance have received little emphasis.[8] Several contributions in this book take up this issue.

With these caveats in mind, *queer* could offer a more inclusive and more flexible concept of oppositionality.[9] As Michael Warner notes, lesbian/gay studies assumes in its very name the existence of a relatively stable and recognizable object of study: those who identify themselves as lesbians and gays. Of course, not all work done under this rubric unproblematically accepts such a definition. Indeed, one contribution of leading gay history scholars is to trace the emergence of such a social category in particular times and places, noting its shifting meanings.[10] Still, the term has

an implied stability. This stability could prove to be effective politically, in that it "aspires to a representational politics of inclusion." However, it does so by courting an essentialism based on
what Warner terms a "drama of authentic embodiment," the result of which can be a reified notion of identity and a simplified
concept of group membership.[11]

Queer theorists challenge this potentially reductive notion, one
based in a minority equal rights model. They call instead not just
for the equal recognition of gays and lesbians but also for a fundamental rethinking of the ways in which heterosexuality is positioned as central and normative. As Warner puts it: "They assert
the necessarily and desirably queer nature of the world . . . because so much privilege lies in heterosexual culture's exclusive
ability to interpret itself as society . . . as the elemental form of
human association . . . as the indivisible basis of all community."[12]
In other words, queer commentary can do the epistemological
work of revealing the historical contingency of heterosexuality. It
can expose heterosexuality as an unmarked yet hegemonic category of social formation, one intricately and inextricably linked to
other modes of social differentiation, including race, gender, and
nationality.

Warner and other theorists thus challenge us to question the
heteronormativity of the world and to reveal its operation in symbolic practices. *Queer* in this context stands for all that is not heteronormative and is a practice of symbolic production or interpretation that anyone, whether self-identified as "gay" or
"straight," can initiate about anything, whether the subject is associated with gay subculture or not. Alexander Doty puts it well
when he proposes that, as a reception practice, queerness is
"shared by all sorts of people in varying degrees of intensity and
consistency."[13] Queer approaches not only make these issues
central to gay- and lesbian-identified people but also invite us to
consider ideologies of sexuality as central to all social formations.

When adopting these notions of *queer* as an analytical framework, however, we must be attentive to the potential for misleading simplifications. While anyone may, in theory, occupy queer
positions, not all do, and all who do necessarily do so differently

and in relation to dominant social formations.[14] Acute historical and material analyses of lived experience as well as of highly marked symbolic practices and their interpretations (and the relationships between these symbolic practices and other dimensions of daily life) are crucial.

REVISIONING DANCE HISTORY QUEERLY

So far, much of the intellectual work of responding to Eve Kosofsky Sedgwick's call "to make invisible possibilities and desires visible [and] to make the tacit things explicit" has been taking place primarily in the fields of literature and mass culture studies.[15] However useful for our analyses such models may be, they are not sufficient for our purposes here. Many writings on performativity in general and sexualities in particular have drawn heavily on text-based or speech-act theories of interpretation, such as those generated by theorists like Sedgwick or Butler.[16] Much of this work (heavily cited in this book) has shaped gay studies or performance studies in crucial ways. Yet, as Sue-Ellen Case reminds us, "the critical discourses of speech-act theory and deconstruction ultimately bring the notion of performativity back to their own mode of production: print. It is confounding to observe how a lesbian/gay movement about sexual, bodily practices and the lethal effects of a virus . . . would have as its critical operation a notion of performativity that circles back to written texts, abandoning historical traditions of performance."[17]

Case's frustration is not easily dismissed but neither is text-derived theory inapplicable. Many performance theorists are drawn to Butler's work precisely because it seems to offer a way of understanding the dailiness of sexual and gendered life. Despite many misreadings of her work and her cautioning against them, in the end Butler's notion of reiteration is useful—she defines it as the practice through which social identities are communicated in relation to extant meaning systems, and that allows for change through misperformances. When adapting this notion to the stage, we must include the additional factor of theatrical history and semiotic practices. Butler points to the bodily practices that (along with speech, fashion, etc.) mark gendered and sexed positionings. This latching on to the realm of physicality has been especially pertinent for dance/sexuality analyses. But the complex semiotic possibilities for rendering such positionings must always be taken into account, and these vary with historical circumstances, community of origin, and context of reception. That so few commentators on performativity actually talk about bodily enactment in detail reflects the continuing legacy of its word-bound origins and of a lack of training in analyzing movement.

To do this work we must keep the palpable presence of dancing, sweating, moving bodies very much alive. We must be able to see and analyze movement with precision. This level of kinesthetic detail is absolutely crucial. It allows us to take bodily motion as specific evidence, not as general referent. These theoretical and historical investigations must analyze dancing as an embodied social practice, with equal emphasis on the last three words: *embodied*, meaning lived physically, not just musings on the "idea" of dance; *social*, meaning embedded in specific material and ideological conditions of possibility; and *practice*, meaning a process in time and space, one of enactment, an articulation and materialization of meanings and relationships. As scholars we must grapple with all these dimensions simultaneously. Contributor Jonathan Bollen's discussion of gay dancing at the Sydney Mardi Gras is a good example of what can happen when movement analysis meets with concepts of performativity, combined with a methodology derived from fieldwork. The result is a richly textured kinesthetic analysis of social/sexual relations.

If much of the current work on sexuality is rooted in literature and thus words, not motion, so too is it limited in its scope by the emphasis on literary texts and the muting of social history. Not only is dance history generally absent from these discussions but history in general has taken a backseat, despite the salience of key works by authors such as George Chauncey, David Greenberg, John D'Emilio, Elizabeth Lapovsky Kennedy and Madeline D. Davis, and Lillian Faderman.[18] As Lisa Duggan has recently pointed out, queer theorists rarely cite historians, dismissing them for naively accepting notions of "fact" as transparent.[19]

On the other hand, historians rarely take up the challenges of queer theory, noting its paucity of historical work. Duggan astutely notes the limitations of some queer theory work that confines itself to textual analysis of literary and media products of the twentieth century. "There has been a progressive impoverishment of the empirical, historical grounding for textual analyses of various sorts," she argues. "The impressive expansion of increasingly sophisticated analyses is balanced precariously atop a stunted archive. [For example], we get yet another article on Gertrude Stein, without any accompanying expansion of the research base for analyzing the changing discursive context for her writing at the turn of the century."[20]

By proposing this book as part of the Studies in Dance History series, I am emphasizing a commitment to historically informed theoretical excursions and to theoretically self-reflexive historical work. Of course, history and theory are inseparable enterprises, but often this interdependence goes unmarked and overlooked. It remains tacit. By not questioning the theoretical bases for what we count as historical studies, or by not bringing to prominence the theories of knowledge production (i.e., the epistemological bases) of "doing" history, we can lose sight of the necessity each has for the other, reifying into distinct realms something called history and something called theory. The aim of this book is to do neither but to consciously cross-pollinate those twin axes of intellectual work, taking as our object of investigation dance in its historically variable manifestations and meanings and focusing our investigations on issues of sexuality, queerness, and heteronormativity. In doing so, these essays offer grounded, historically specific analyses rooted in the experience of the body as an instrument of social signification.

Making History Dance

What would dance history look like if we were to emphasize these issues, to "make the tacit things explicit"? And what would gay/lesbian history look like if we analyzed its embodied practices, if we made gay history dance?

In the call for articles, I'd given the book the provisional title of *Queer Theory and the Dancing Body*, mostly as a shorthand to show that I was interested in works that focused on theoretical issues and to reflect an expansive notion of sexualities. But, to my surprise, few submissions explicitly set out to engage, first and foremost, issues relating to queer theory, or in Berlant and Warner's more appropriate phrase, "queer commentary."[21] Many authors (male and female) were most interested in analyzing work *by* gay or lesbian choreographers (most often gay men), either to ask how their work closeted their "gayness" or how more oppositional contemporary work staged their gayness in an outright manner. This was not so much an attempt at recovery scholarship—to write gay men and lesbians into dance history—as it was an effort to begin analyzing the ways sexualities shaped both product and meanings (for choreographers, audiences, and performers). While canonical dance history had omitted the contributions of other marginalized groups, such as African American choreographers and performers, it did not write out the presence of gay and lesbian dancers. Rather, it wrote out—made invisible or at least unspeakable—their gayness, through what Susan Foster, in chapter 5, terms "one of the most remarkably open closets of any profession."[22]

For example, few texts on twentieth-century U.S. and European dance history would note the sexualities of Merce Cunningham, Ted Shawn, Nijinsky, or Loie Fuller, much less analyze their works in relation to it, yet almost all such texts would canonize these choreographers. Julia Foulkes's essay on Shawn in chapter 4, and Susan Foster's extended consideration of Shawn, Cunningham, and others in chapter 5, break new ground by analyzing how social restrictions on sexuality at particular historical moments profoundly shaped the dances that got put on the stage. They point to the incalculable power of homophobia in producing what we now know as canonical modern dance history.

On the other hand, we need to consider the very recent canonization of some leading and publicly gay male modern dance choreographers, like Bill T. Jones or Michael Clark. In what ways does their acknowledged homosexuality and their choreography (engaging explicitly with issues of same-sex relationships) support a public sphere of visible queerness? How did their acceptance, even celebration, happen? For Jones, his being an artist, and a dance artist, is related to his visibility as an African American, gay, HIV-positive male. We need to explore the ways each of these positionings enables or constricts his public presence. How are they intricately intertwined? Analyzing in chapter 7 the interplay of race, gender, and sexuality in Jones's early work, Gay Morris helps us understand how Jones's current high regard is related to earlier strategies in his choreography. This too is part of dance history and of queer commentary.[23]

If many authors were not intent on engaging something they identified as queer theory per se, several did argue that dance is a way of "queering" masculinity, of stepping outside heteronormativity. Kevin Kopelson in chapter 3, for example, discusses Nijinsky's 1910 performance of the ballet *Schéhérazade* as both homoerotic and heteroerotic, and David Gere, in a discussion in chapter 11 of Joe Goode's contemporary piece *29 Effeminate Gestures*, coins the term *heroic effeminacy* to discuss the gestural limits to gender signification. In a related piece Paul Franklin argues in chapter 1 that Charlie Chaplin's success rested in part on his use of dance as a way of queering Chaplin's masculinity. In chapter 6 Ramsay Burt takes up what he terms the "discourse of the queer male dancing body," suggesting that contemporary radical dance artists have created "new configurations . . . of resistance against . . . normative heterosexuality . . . [which] have the potential to explore a radically revised imagination of the body's capacity for pleasure," a potential both straight and gay male viewers can embrace.

In each of these cases the meanings of dancing male bodies, or of males who dance, are shaped by the history of theatrical dance as well as the positioning of theatrical dance as a predominately female, and feminizing, occupation and spectacle. This historical discourse of feminization creates the ground that gives meaning to such contemporary queerings. In other words, to better understand the linkage of sexuality and dance, we must be always attentive to the variable status of "dance" as a social practice for particular populations and in particular times and places.[24]

Where Are the Women?

As this quick overview suggests, many scholars, male and female, are deeply engaged in issues involving men as dancers, choreographers, or audience. What surprised me greatly was how few scholars took up the challenge of relating issues of non-heteronormativity to women.

I did not want this to be a book just about men, but as proposals came rolling in, female choreographers, dancers, and spectators were nearly invisible.[25] In addition to forming at least half (and probably more) of the audience for theatrical dance, women predominate in performance and are, overall, more involved in social dance than men. So where were the women? Once again lesbians would be rendered invisible both on stage and now in scholarly discourse. In addition, what about bisexual or heterosexual women as spectators of dance performances featuring gay men or lesbians or their depictions? Whenever appropriate in terms of their scholarly projects, I urged the writers in this collection to consider not just men but women, lesbian, straight, or queer, as producers and consumers of dancing.

This relative absence of discussion and of representation could be due to many reasons. Some possibilities include that lesbians don't dance, that lesbians don't make "lesbian dances," that lesbians don't dance in public, that sexuality studies, like most studies, still focus on men, or that men are just more interesting (just kidding). Several feminist critics have discussed the problems of lesbian representation and the lack thereof. In a discussion of contemporary U.S. politics, Judith Butler writes,

> There are a vast number of ways in which lesbianism in particular is understood as precisely that which cannot or dare not *be*. . . . Here oppression works through the production of a domain of unthinkability and unnameability. Lesbianism is not explicitly prohibited in part because it has not even made its way into the thinkable, the imaginable. . . . How then to "be" a lesbian in a political context in which the lesbian does not exist?[26]

Esther Newton examines this problem of invisibility less in terms of the unnameable and more in terms of gendered institutional histories. Arguing that "gay men belong to the dominant gender," she notes that "holding race and class constant, gay men have more power and money than lesbians do. Their history as a distinct social entity is longer, their institutions are more numerous and developed, and they take up much more symbolic and actual public space, both in relation to dominant society and within most, if not all, institutions termed 'gay and lesbian.' "27

In the United States at least, there are no acknowledged lesbian choreographers of Bill T. Jones's or Mark Morris's stature in terms of public visibility, foundation funding, and critical acclaim. Of course, few female choreographers in general are of similar visibility. Twyla Tharp is one exception. And it is hard to imagine a scenario in which Tharp, for example, were she to suddenly begin making queer dances, or to "be" lesbian, could retain the same widespread acclaim that Jones has following his public coming out. Imagine, for a moment, a hypothetical Tharpian staging of a lesbian *Swan Lake*, parallel to the Matthew Bourne gay male staging discussed by Susan Foster in chapter 5. Who would be the audience? The same people who went to see Mark Morris's gender-bending version of *The Nutcracker* called *The Hard Nut*? Of course, maybe we need a better parallel to think this issue through. *Swan Lake* and *The Nutcracker* are full of (femme) female roles (snowflakes, swans) that support a vision of heterosexual romance. We lack many dance works of parallel "canonicity" that are populated by platoons of men whose parts could then be played by women. Still, it is possible to imagine drag kings fighting the mice and hyperfemme snowflakes flitting in *The Nutcracker*. Can we then imagine this broadcast on PBS, widely acclaimed, and widely attended? No. The reasons for this are doubtless complex, and I can only speculate here.

The feminization of spectacle, of putting oneself on display (without the cover of sport's masculinity-authorizing violence), feminizes male dancers (thus enabling a representation of homosexuality as the "specter" come true?), but female dancers are already feminized, already positioned as spectacle. Representations of lesbianism must work against or rework this feminization and thus the heteronormative pleasures of spectacle that posit a male viewing position and a female object. The modern dance world boasts strong antecedents of this refusal of spectacle, as Yvonne Rainer's famous late 1960s manifesto, "No to Spectacle," reminds us.[28] Indeed, much of the work coming out of the Judson Church period of the 1960s and continuing into the 1970s was based on everyday movement or task choreography and actively worked against traditions of sexualized spectacle; such work, although it rarely explicitly posited a lesbian sexuality or viewing position, could certainly be examined from the viewpoint of the refusal of feminine spectacle. And no matter what spectator positionings are idealized on the stage, actual spectatorial practices can always go against the grain, as more recent scholarship on spectatorship has argued. Despite these possibilities, explicitly lesbian representations have so far found a more visible home in experimental theater, like that produced at the WOW Cafe in New York City, than in the dance world per se.[29] This may suggest that we need to investigate the relationship of verbal narrative, bodily presence, and action and how these components can constrict or enable representations of lesbian desire.

These issues of presence and visibility/invisibility need a great deal more work. It may be useful to consider how the suspicion of the dancing male of being homosexual works as a sort of enabling discourse for the visibility of gay men as choreographers, whereas associations of femininity with dance (even with the presence of strong female choreographers as canonical leaders in modern dance) may work against this visibility. For some women, this invisibility may even provide a chosen haven, unlike the arena of women's sports, where athletic competence is still sometimes tinged with the suspicion of lesbianism. A host of other factors may also include women's overall lesser access to funding, which could make it less likely that professional female choreographers would take the risk of staging explicitly queer work.

STRATEGIES FOR STAGING A "LESBIAN" PRESENCE

For some female choreographers and dancers who have taken this risk, one strategy seems to be to withdraw the body from heterosexual frameworks of pleasure by depicting a spectral, grotesque, or wacky performer/body. These strategies are similar to earlier feminist interventions in representation in performance art and experimental film. The always-present body of the dancer presents special challenges and offers unique possibilities, different from those in film, painting, and literature, where the body may be represented but does not at the same time represent itself. Ann Cvetkovich, writing in chapter 10 about her experiences as a go-go dancer, notes the careful boundaries she maintains "even in lesbian clubs, in order to distinguish between a sexual performance oriented toward lesbians and a sexualized performance that caters to men." In a mixed crowd of men and women she queers the performance, aiming for wackiness rather than sexiness, to make sure she cannot be construed as male entertainment.

Contributor Julie Townsend, writing about turn-of-the-century dancer Loie Fuller in chapter 2, analyzes a related strategy of removal from heterosexual discourse. Townsend argues that Fuller, experimenting with light and fabric, removed herself from the realm of gender altogether, creating "a hallucination of infinite mutability and transformability through technology," as she portrayed images of butterflies, insects, and representations of female sexual morphology through her flowing silks and flickering lights.

Other contemporary choreographers use related approaches. In her unpublished work in progress, the British scholar Petra Kuppers is developing a theoretical framework for understanding issues of lesbian embodiment and representation in dance. Finding work to talk about hasn't been easy, though. Noting the presence of gay men and the apparent absence of lesbians, she asserts that this form of "queer visibility has more to do with what dance means in western culture—displaying oneself, being consumed as a body by the audience—than with progressive politics and spaces for alternative desire." Her active searching in the United Kingdom for lesbian dance performers who portray same-sex desire on the stage yielded only a few names: Emilyn Claid, Yael Flexer, and Kate Lawrence. These choreographers explore a variety of strategies, including staging a vision of the female grotesque body and focusing on notions of the private or spectral.[30]

Valerie Briginshaw also notes other strategies of representation used by British choreographers, including Claid, Sarah Spanton, and Gabi Agasi. These strategies she terms *disruption, interruption, eruption,* and *corruption,* each a practice of rendering lesbian desire visible and making lesbian dance political. Attentive to the difficulties in identifying "lesbians" and "lesbian content," Briginshaw notes that the term " 'lesbian dance' problematically implies a lesbian dancing body which in turn implies a lesbian body with suggestions of identity rooted and fixed in the body." This difficulty, noted in the discussion of queer theory, can imply a problematic fixity, "authenticity, normalization and essentialism," which Briginshaw seeks to avoid.

A more fluid (postmodern) notion of identities is called for, asserts Briginshaw. For theatrical performers, this fluidity can be staged by producing performances that are disruptive, which continually shift between representations of the feminine as both desiring subject and object of desire. By appropriating and rewriting traditional narratives of heterosexual desire, Briginshaw argues, lesbian dances have the "potential to dissolve constraining binaries."[31]

Here is where we can see the importance of the theater and choreography as a space and action explicitly made, denaturalized (even at times when conventions of realism prevail), and socially recognized and sanctioned as such. Dancing on the stage (and even in the sanctioned spaces of gay/lesbian clubs) can provide a liminal space, a safe in-between where the immediate material consequences of non-normative sexuality (such as danger, gay bashing, economic and psychic discrimination) are held in abeyance. In these safe spaces varieties of sexuality and desire can be symbolically rendered through the play of the imagination combined with the articulation of the body—the staging of looks, movement, sound, touch, and spatial manipulation—using the variety of choreographic strategies that Kuppers and Briginshaw suggest.

When we consider nontheatrical dance, other issues emerge. Although Paul Siegel's essay on legal injunctions against same-sex dancing (chapter 8) and Jonathan Bollen's piece on same-sex dancing and the Sydney Mardi Gras (chapter 9) both refer to men and women, little explicit work on women's same-sex social dancing exists, and that which does concentrates more on the larger social context than on the dancing per se. Again, we can speculate on a variety of reasons for this absence: lesbians don't dance together, lesbians don't dance together in public, relatively few sites exist for women's same-sex dancing (women in general own fewer bars than men, or lesbians spend less money socializing in public, or . . .). In addition, the meanings of same-sex dancing for women may be constructed differently than for men, given the greater social latitude that adolescent girls or women have for dancing together (women dancing together are not always assumed to be lesbian, whereas men dancing together in most communities in the United States may be suspected of homosexuality). When analyzing same-sex social dancing, we must also be attentive to the ways in which racial difference can shape the sites in which such dancing occurs. For example, as Rochella Thorpe has argued, for some, African American lesbians' rent parties or house parties offer a safer alternative than more public and predominately white bars, so a history of lesbian social dancing that concentrates on bars would omit many African American practices. Analyzing social dance requires ethnographic work and oral history approaches because such activities generally leave few written traces and often occur in private or semiprivate spaces.[32]

Although in the end only two essays (Anne Cvetkovich's on lesbian go-go dancing in chapter 10 and Julie Townsend's on early modern dancer Loie Fuller in chapter 2) focus exclusively on women, lesbian erotics and viewing practices receive extended consideration in three of the five essays in the final third of the book, those by Feuer, Manning, and Phelan (chapters 12, 14, and 15). Indeed, these considerations open up new theoretical territory on spectatorship.

REFLECTIONS AND EXTENSIONS

The final third of the book, called "Reflections and Extensions," has an explicit goal of extending the theoretical issues raised in the longer articles in parts 1 and 2. In each case I invited scholars to speculate on the implications of some of the longer essays, to open questions relevant to their own work and their own varying disciplinary locations. These are "think pieces," critical musings that take off on the work of authors in parts 1 and 2. Each essayist in this section received one, two, or three essays by other contributors. Rather than request a formal critique of each, I urged the commentators to use them as a springboard for their own thinking.

Like the articles, each think piece is passionate. Some even rise to poetry. Jane Feuer opens up the question of lesbian spectatorship for "straight" ballets, wondering why many gay *men* have become balletomanes. Lesbians, she tells us, sometimes read these ballets against the grain as narratives of their own desire.[33] Susan Manning offers a related model of cross-sexual identification, with dance providing a space for *both* gay and straight readings against the grain. Considering the relationship of race and sexuality in chapter 13, Jennifer DeVere Brody investigates how queerness is always about disrupting the "lily white is right" canon and static notions of the subject. But, she asks, "in reading the performance itself, where does one 'mark' queerness *exactly?*" She, like Phelan, Feuer, and Manning, takes up questions of spectatorship, suggesting that queerness often resides in reception. For Phelan, the shaping force of sexuality in perceiving, remembering, and writing about dance is key. Dance, she tells us, "opens up an inquiry that passes through [it] in search of something else." Part of that something else is a memory of desire embodied in dance. How, Phelan asks, can we account for this linkage in our writing?

In an extended response that ends the book, José Estéban Muñoz takes up several issues in chapter 16 that reverberate throughout the book: memory, gestural signification, political resistance, and the racialization of desire. In an analysis of performance by Kevin Aviance, a gay African American performer in New York City's gay club scene, Muñoz meditates on the power of gesture to connote a "cohabitation of traditional female and male traits," a hybrid gender. He focuses on Aviance's difference from, and attraction for, hypermasculine gay males, tracking his power precisely in his refusal of the troubling "femmephobic" gender logic within gay male spaces that valorizes the gymsculpted muscle of his audience. Aviance dances on a platform above the gyrating crowds, forming the "bridge" between theatricality and everynight life. In this space his vogueing gestures of applying makeup or quivering with emotion take on a multivalent force, screaming the pleasure and pain of being a "gender outlaw" far outside the conventions of heteronormativity and affirming blackness in a white world. This multivalence and the force of gesture remembered can transmit, Muñoz argues, "ephemeral knowledge of lost queer histories and possibilities within a phobic majoritarian public culture." Aviance stands as a beacon of resistance made visible through the choreography of gesture.

LOOKING OUTWARD

These are some of the key issues that have emerged in this collection, but by no means do they exhaust the relevant initiatives for research or the frameworks for investigation. Indeed, as David Román and others have cautioned, any discussion of gay, lesbian, or queer runs the risk of being taken as prescriptive, of offering a vision of what such positionings, aesthetics, or practices "should" be or even of what they "are." On the other hand, any act of symbolic speech requires the situation of an "I," a "we," no matter how provisionally declared. In that spirit this book represents a starting place, the beginning of a conversation. Paraphrasing Dinshaw and Halperin, I hope this new work will stimulate further analyses of how sexual and social meanings are articulated through (and constituted by) dance—its forms, practices, institutions, and aesthetics.[34] The results can yield a history of sexuality's kinesthetics.

Tracking this kinesthetic history will lead us in two directions simultaneously. As Foucault has argued in his articulation of the "repressive hypothesis," restrictions are not only repressive. They do not merely exclude. They are productive as well.[35] Therefore we could investigate not only how strictures *against* homosexuality have shaped dance history and dance practices (what's thinkable, doable, sayable, and by whom) but also how dance has functioned (on the stage, in the studio, in the streets, and in clubs) as an expressive mode for the articulation of gay desire and a mode of enacting gay, lesbian, or queer identity. A wide variety of questions emerges from this approach.

We might ask, for instance, if there is a "gay dance criticism"—a particular mode of aesthetic appreciation or of writing style that is extant in either a gay subcultural press or in mainstream writing. If the latter, how has that gayness permeated dance criticism in particular historical periods or places? And how has that criticism in turn influenced audience perceptions, box office, a choreographer's responses, and historians' analyses? More provocatively, should we ask, given the large presence of gay males in the professional dance world (as dancers, choreographers, critics) if in fact modern dance and ballet in the United States *is* a gay history? Imagine if, following Brenda Dixon-Gottschild's analysis of African American legacies as central to (white) concert dance in the United States, we put gayness at the center of an analysis of (supposedly) heterosexual dance history.[36]

We might ask similar questions about social dance styles and theatrical dance styles. Are there ways in which dominant aesthetic styles and valuations are saturated with gay-derived aesthetics? How would we know it if we saw it? And what would a category like "gay/lesbian/queer aesthetics" mean? When does the marking and unmarking of subcultural production occur? For instance, if, as Richard Dyer notes, disco drew heavily on African American musical styles and had a special relevance in gay male subculture akin to camp, exactly how did John Travolta's white, straight character become the heartthrob of *Saturday Night Fever*?[37] In what ways did disco's origins permeate the mainstreamed, commodified style that emerged, ultimately shaping the white heterosexuality of the Travolta character and the disco rage spawned by the movie?

These are only a few examples of the types of questions that might proceed from making issues of nonheteronormativity the starting point for our analyses. Especially urgent is more work on lesbian performers and viewers, on dance and dancers that exceed the black/white racial binary, and on dance outside the United States, a dimension represented in only a limited way in this book, which includes contributions from England and Australia. Such work must, of course, critically situate the production of non-heteronormativity in the specifics of its own geopolitics. The potential for important work on social dance, and on other public forms such as dancing in political parades, in ritualized ceremonies, as "camp" protest, on fashion runways, in drag queen and drag king shows, and so on, is huge. And the linkages between sexual economies of everyday gesture and posture and that of theatrical dance need to be investigated further too.

Methodologically, the range of approaches is broad. Reception studies, histories of criticism, analyses of staging conventions, labor histories of employment and employment discrimination, legal studies, analyses of pedagogical practices, explorations of "style," and ethnographic community-based studies of dancing and dancers are all potentially productive (and by no means exhaustive) ways of approaching some of these issues, and others still to be imagined.

A prime problem is how to investigate these issues when the costs of contravening heteronormativity have been so high that few arenas exist that allow free and public validation of such expressions and representations. The organizational and infrastructural bases of gay/lesbian/queer life are few in comparison to those of other nonhegemonic groups. Consider the long-standing power and resilience of African American churches, for instance. With few exceptions, it is really only recently that highly visible organizational structures have emerged to help support movements away from public invisibility. As Anne Cvetkovich's piece makes clear, archival and ethnographic research will be required to begin to make the traces of what was usually meant to be invisible to all but insiders readily available for scholarly analysis. And given the costs of visibility, such work will have to proceed with extreme attentiveness to issues of privacy and risk as we endeavor to "make the tacit things explicit." Only by encountering those risks, intellectually, emotionally, and institutionally, can we as scholars work toward the obliteration of homophobia. My hope is that a decade from now we will find such considerations of sexualities a commonplace part of our dance investigations, just as the explosions of feminist scholarship and critical race theory have made it impossible now to think about dance without considering those trajectories. I hope as well that sexuality studies will move off the text-based considerations of film and literature to embrace dance, and bodily movement more generally, as a crucial arena of investigation. This book charts a beginning for those future explorations and issues an invitation to explore an historical kinesthetics of sexuality.

NOTES

My thanks to David Román for his helpful critiques of an early draft of this piece, to Kim Marra for stimulating discussions, and to Virginia Domínguez and Carol Martin for insightful conceptual and editorial suggestions.

1. I want to limit the scope of such a generalization to the period and places under consideration in this book, that is, the twentieth-century United States and selected traditions in Europe and Australia.

2. See Mark Franko, "Where He Danced," *Dancing Modernism/Performing Politics* (Bloomington: Indiana University Press, 1995), 93–107; Gay Morris, "Subversive Strategies in *The Hard Nut*," in *Proceedings of the Seventeenth Annual Conference of the Society of Dance History Scholars* (Riverside, Calif.: Society of Dance History Scholars, 1994), 237–44; Michael Moon, "Flaming Closets," in Ellen W. Goellner and Jacqueline Shea Murphy, eds., *Bodies of the Text: Dance as Theory, Literature as Dance* (New Brunswick, N.J.: Rutgers University Press, 1995), 57–80; and Gaylyn Studlar, "Douglas Fairbanks: Thief of the Ballets Russes," in Goellner and Murphy, *Bodies of the Text*, 107–24 (Murphy's own piece in that book, "Unrest and Uncle Tom: Bill T. Jones/Arnie Zane Dance Company's Last Supper at Uncle Tom's Cabin/The Promised Land," 81–106, touches on issues of homosexuality but does not develop that theme extensively); Jane Sherman and Barton Mumaw, *Barton Mumaw, Dancer: From Denishawn to Jacob's Pillow and Beyond* (New York: Dance Horizons, 1986); Ramsay Burt, *The Male Dancer: Bodies, Spectacle, Sexualities* (New York: Routledge, 1995), 8.

3. Bud Coleman, "Ballerinos en Pointe: Les Ballets Trocadero de Monte Carlo," in Kim Grover-Haskin, ed., *Choreography and Dance: An International Journal*, vol. 5, pt. 1 (Amsterdam: Harwood Academic, 1998), 9–23; Moe Meyer, "Rethinking *Paris Is Burning*: Performing Social Geography in Harlem Drag Balls," *Theatre Annual* 50 (1997): 40–71; Valerie A. Briginshaw, "Theorizing the Performativity of Lesbian Dance," and Ramsay Burt, "Interpreting Jean Borlin's Dervishes: Masculine Subjectivity and the Queer Male Dancing Body," both in Linda Tomko, comp., *Proceedings of the Twenty-first Annual*

Conference of the Society of Dance History Scholars (Riverside, Calif.: Society of Dance History Scholars, 1998), 269–78 and 279–84, respectively; Susan Manning's "Coding the Message," in *Dance Theatre Journal* 14, no. 1 (1998): 34–37; Richard Dyer, "In Defense of Disco," and his "Classical Ballet: A Bit of Uplift," (originally published in 1986)—both are reprinted in his *Only Entertainment* (New York: Routledge, 1992), 149–58 and 41–44, respectively; Henry Abelove, Michele Aina Barale, and David M. Halperin, eds., *The Lesbian and Gay Studies Reader* (New York: Routledge, 1993); Corey K. Creekmur and Alexander Doty, eds., *Out in Culture: Gay, Lesbian, and Queer Essays on Popular Culture* (Durham, N.C.: Duke University Press, 1995); Anthony Thomas, "The House the Kids Built: The Gay Black Imprint on American Dance Music," in Creekmur and Doty, *Out in Culture*, 437–45; George Chauncey, *Gay New York: Gender, Urban Culture, and the Making of the Gay Male World, 1890–1940* (New York: Basic, 1994); and Deborah P. Amory's "Club Q: Dancing with (a) Difference," in Ellen Lewin, ed., *Inventing Lesbian Cultures in America* (Boston: Beacon, 1996), 145–60. Judith Lynne Hanna's *Dance, Sex, and Gender: Signs of Identity, Dominance, Defiance, and Desire* (Chicago: University of Chicago Press, 1988) began to open up some of these issues more than a decade ago.

See also Coleman, "The Electric Fairy: The Woman behind the Apparition of Loie Fuller," in Kim Marra and Robert Shanke, eds., *Staging Desire: Queer Readings of American Theater History* (Ann Arbor: University of Michigan Press, in press); a hopeful sign is the number of as-yet unpublished studies underway that address these issues. During the next few years a number of relevant dissertations should appear. Keep an eye out for new work by Tirza True Latimer, Leanne Trapedo Sims, David Lugowski, Rebekah Kowal, Carol Burbank, Paul Scolieri, and Elizabeth Claire, among others. See also David Gere's unpublished doctoral dissertation, "How to Make Dance during an Epidemic" (University of California at Riverside, 1998). I thank all who shared their works in progress with me.

I first formulated some of the questions that drive this book in my essay "Engendering Dance: Feminist Inquiry and Dance Research," in Sondra Fraleigh and Penelope Hanstein, eds., *Researching Dance: Evolving Modes of Inquiry* (Pittsburgh: University of Pittsburgh Press, 1999), 309–33, esp. 319–24, the section called "Sexuality Studies: A Deafening Silence in Dance Scholarship."

4. For scholars who may be unfamiliar with recent developments in dance studies, several collections give a good sense of key issues and debates. See, for example, Gay Morris, ed., *Moving Words: Re-Writing Dance* (New York: Routledge, 1996); Susan Leigh Foster, ed., *Corporealities: Dancing, Knowledge, Culture, and Power* (New York: Routledge, 1996); Goellner and Murphy, *Bodies of the Text;* and my edited collection, *Meaning in Motion: New Cultural Studies of Dance* (Durham, N.C.: Duke University Press, 1997).

5. Elizabeth Grosz, "Bodies and Pleasures in Queer Theory," in Judith Roof and Robyn Wiegman, eds., *Who Can Speak? Authority and Critical Identity* (Urbana: University of Illinois Press, 1995), 224.

6. David L. Eng and Alice Y. Hom, "Introduction: Q&A: Notes on a Queer Asian America," in their edited collection, *Q&A: Queer in Asian America* (Philadelphia: Temple University Press, 1998), 17. See also Yvonne Yarbro-Be-

jarano, "Expanding the Categories of Race and Sexuality in Lesbian and Gay Studies," in George Haggerty and Bonnie Zimmerman, eds., *Professions of Desire: Lesbian and Gay Studies in Literature* (New York: Modern Language Association, 1995), 124–35.

7. David L. Eng, "Heterosexuality in the Face of Whiteness: Divided Belief in *M. Butterfly*," in Eng and Hom, *Q&A*, 339; also see Jane Feuer, chap. 12.

8. Some exceptions include Randy Martin's discussion of hip-hop classes in his *Critical Moves: Dance Studies in Theory and Politics* (Durham, N.C.: Duke University Press, 1998). Brenda Dixon-Gottschild's *Digging the Africanist Presence in American Performance: Dance and Other Contexts* (Westport, Conn.: Praeger, 1996) examines not only African American dance but Euro-American dance's production of whiteness, which is dependent on a refusal to acknowledge syncretism and hybridity even in that "whitest" of forms, classical ballet. See also Susan Manning, "Black Voices, White Bodies: The Performance of Race and Gender in *How Long Brethren*," *American Quarterly* 50, no. 1 (March 1998): 24–46.

9. We must also be attentive to the differences in usage of the terms *queer*, *gay*, and *lesbian* inside and outside the academy and among various groups. A recent extended discussion of these terms took place on the listserv of the Society of Gay and Lesbian Anthropologists. One scholar noted that minority youths in San Francisco use *queer* to refer to themselves because *gay* connotes what seems to them to be the white middle-class culture of the Castro District <*SOLGA-L@AMERICAN.EDU*> (May 27, 1999).

10. For just one such example, see David F. Greenberg, *The Construction of Homosexuality* (Chicago: University of Chicago Press, 1988).

11. Michael Warner, introduction to *Fear of a Queer Planet: Queer Politics and Social Theory* (Minneapolis: University of Minnesota Press, 1993), xix.

12. Ibid., xxi.

13. Alexander Doty, "There's Something Queer Here," in Creekmur and Doty, *Out in Culture*, 72.

14. Sue-Ellen Case cautions against the evacuation of meaning that she sees in the use of the term *queer*. "Identifying as a woman," she writes, "removes me from any major identificatory relationship with queer and aligns me with the concerns of gender as a woman, in coalition with other women whose oppression may be differently or similarly configured by operations of class and ethnicity" (Case, *The Domain-Matrix: Performing Lesbian at the End of Print Culture* [Bloomington: Indiana University Press, 1996], 237).

15. Eve Kosofsky Sedgwick, "Queer and Now," in *Tendencies* (Durham, N.C.: Duke University Press, 1993), 3. For an example of the literary and mass culture emphasis, see Creekmur and Doty's *Out in Culture*, and Sedgwick's enormously influential *Epistemology of the Closet* (Berkeley: University of California Press, 1990). Readers unfamiliar with these works may find helpful Annamarie Jagose's *Queer Theory: An Introduction* (New York: New York University Press, 1996), which includes an historical sketch of the development of notions of queer theory.

16. See Sedgwick, *Tendencies*. Among Judith Butler's works, her *Gender Trouble: Feminism and the Subversion of Identity* (New York: Routledge, 1990),

and *Bodies That Matter: On the Discursive Limits of "Sex"* (New York: Routledge, 1993), have been most influential among performance studies scholars.

17. Case, *Domain-Matrix*, 17.

18. See Chauncey, *Gay New York*, and Greenberg, *Construction of Homosexuality*. See also John D'Emilio, *Sexual Politics, Sexual Communities: The Making of a Homosexual Minority in the United States, 1940–1970* (Chicago: University of Chicago Press, 1983); Elizabeth Lapovsky Kennedy and Madeline D. Davis, *Boots of Leather, Slippers of Gold: The History of a Lesbian Community* (New York: Routledge, 1993); and Lillian Faderman, *Odd Girls and Twilight Lovers: A History of Lesbian Life in Twentieth-Century America* (New York: Columbia University Press, 1991).

19. Lisa Duggan, "The Discipline Problem: Queer Theory Meets Lesbian and Gay History," *GLQ: A Journal of Lesbian and Gay Studies* 2, no. 3 (1995): 179–91. Duggan quotes Joan Scott's critique of historians for whom "history is a chronology that makes experience visible, but in which categories appear as nonetheless ahistorical: desire, homosexuality, heterosexuality . . . become so many fixed entities being played out over time, but not themselves historicized."

20. Ibid., 181.

21. See Lauren Berlant and Michael Warner, "What Does Queer Theory Teach Us about X?" *PMLA* 110 (May 1995): 343–49. They argue against the use of the term *queer theory*, suggesting instead *queer commentary*. Rejecting the seeming limitation of *theory* to academic circles, they seek to maintain links to extra-academic queer attitudes, practices, and publics and not to reduce a multifarious blossoming of such to a unitary designation.

22. The masking of gay/lesbian/queer identities in dance history is parallel to that in theater history. See Robert A. Schanke and Kim Marra, eds., *Passing Performances: Queer Readings of Leading Players in American Theater History* (Ann Arbor: University of Michigan Press, 1998). Their book puts more emphasis on the lives of performers and less on specific theatrical events than do most of the essays here.

23. For an important discussion of performance and gay life, especially as it relates to the AIDS epidemic, see David Román, *Acts of Intervention: Performance, Gay Culture, and AIDS* (Bloomington: Indiana University Press, 1998). Román takes up issues of dance choreography and AIDS discourse in the works of Bill T. Jones and David Greenberg in his article "Not-about-AIDS," *GLQ: A Journal of Lesbian and Gay Studies* 6, no. 1 (2000): 1–28. I thank him for sharing this work with me. See also Maurice Wallace, "The Autochoreography of an Ex-Snow Queen: Dance, Desire, and the Black Masculine in Melvin Dixon's *Vanishing Rooms*," in Eve Kosofsky Sedgwick, ed., *Novel-Gazing: Queer Readings in Fiction* (Durham, N.C.: Duke University Press, 1997), 379–440.

24. I use the term *dance* in quotes here to show that it designates a variable set of practices and that the criteria for inclusion and exclusion of certain forms of movement from this domain are subject to change. In addition, the boundaries between dance, theater, and performance art, as well as other styles of ritualized or choreographed movement, are provisional. However, the denotation of a certain practice as dance (as opposed to stripping, for example) can influ-

ence how it and its practitioners are perceived and even, at times, its legal protections as free speech.

25. This is in sharp contrast to the recent strength of feminist writings about dance, a majority of which deal with female dancers, viewers, choreographers.

26. Judith Butler, "Imitation and Gender Insubordination," in Abelove, Barale, and Halperin, *Lesbian and Gay Studies Reader*, 312.

27. Esther Newton, " 'Dick(less) Tracy' and the Homecoming Queen: Lesbian Power and Representation in Gay-Male Cherry Grove," in Lewin, *Inventing Lesbian Cultures in America*, 167. During the 1990s a key component in this visibility was the epidemic of AIDS and its devastating effect on gay men. This has served not only as a stimulus to gay men's political organizing (and alliances with lesbians) but also as a way of putting male homosexuality more fully into public discourse (either positively or negatively) than has been the case with lesbians (although they too, like all segments of the population, contract AIDS).

28. Yvonne Rainer, "No to Spectacle," in *Work: 1961–1973* (New York: New York University Press, 1974). I thank Carol Martin for urging me to consider this.

29. For a discussion of lesbian plays see, for example, Jill Dolan's *Presence and Desire: Essays on Gender, Sexuality, Performance* (Ann Arbor: University of Michigan Press, 1993). Although it is beyond the scope of this introductory essay, it will be important to think through the parallels and differences between work in dance (with its emphasis on nonverbal realms) and the representation of lesbian desire in theater, which combines words with physical actions and sometimes continues a tradition of realism.

30. I thank Petra Kuppers for sharing sections of her unpublished work, "Vanishing in Your Face: Embodiment and Representation in Lesbian Dance Performance," with me. I look forward to the completion of her project because she is one of few dance scholars investigating these issues in detail. I also thank Leanne Trapedo Sims for sharing her unpublished manuscript, "New Dance: Transsexual Narratives on the Stripped and Drag Body," with me. Although it does not explicitly focus on the details of dance in the performances of drag kings, this work makes clear the importance of considering these realms as a part of dance studies.

31. Briginshaw, "Theorizing the Performativity of Lesbian Dance," 269, 276.

32. Rochella Thorpe, " 'A House Where Queers Go': African American Lesbian Nightlife in Detroit, 1940–1975," in Lewin, *Inventing Lesbian Cultures*, 40–61. See also Amory, "Club Q."

33. Work on spectatorship and dance often builds on that developed with regard to mass media but, like writings on theater, must account for the live presence of the performer in the same space as the spectator. While social dance is different from theatrical forms, the living bodies in shared time and space remain a crucial component of the experience.

34. Carolyn Dinshaw and David Halperin argue for intellectual work that can "illuminate the complex interplay among sexual and social meanings, individual and collective practices, private fantasies and public institutions, erotics and pol-

itics" (Dinshaw and Halperin, "From the Editors," *GLQ: A Journal of Gay and Lesbian Studies* 1, no. 1 [1994]: iii).

35. Michel Foucault, *An Introduction*, vol. 1 of *The History of Sexuality* (New York: Vintage, 1980).

36. See Dixon-Gottschild, *Digging the Africanist Presence*.

37. Dyer, "In Defense of Disco."

Part 1
Theatrical Theories

1

The Terpsichorean Tramp: Unmanly Movement in the Early Films of Charlie Chaplin

Paul B. Franklin

> No sane man dances unless he is mad.
> —*Cicero*

> [W]hat woman wants a prancing, mincing, intensely correct husband? She wants a regular man and the sort that falls over everything and is always getting in the way of his own feet.
> —*Adeline Genée, 1915*

Dancing, of any and every variety, has never been a particularly effective means for a man to shore up his masculinity. Since at least the early nineteenth century, male dancers in the West have been besieged by public and private accusations regarding their gender and sexuality. Writing in 1837, Théophile Gautier, one of the most highly respected novelists, poets, and cultural critics of his day, openly denounced the male ballet dancer: "You know how hideous an ordinary male ballet dancer is—a lump of a youth with a long, red neck swollen with muscles. . . . Furthermore, with his elbows and feet at right angles and the look of Adonis and Apollo on his face, he makes sweeping, angular movements and performs *ronds de jambe*, pirouettes, and other gestures of mechanical puppets. Nothing could be more dreadful."[1] As late as 1934 Arnold Haskell, a widely recognized English balletomane, felt compelled to dispute the age-old stereotype of male dancers as unmanly and sexually perverse: "[O]f the outstanding male dancers that I know, and I know them all, not one is effeminate in manner, and very few indeed are not thoroughly normal."[2] With the demise of European court culture in the late eighteenth century and the efflorescence of the bourgeoisie during the same period, truly manly men refrained from dancing, especially in the publicly incriminating venue of the ballet stage. The trepidation with such masculine spectacle, according to Ramsay Burt in his pathbreaking book *The Male Dancer*, "suggests that what is at stake is the development of modern, middle-class attitudes towards the male body and the expressive aspects of male social behavior."[3]

Despite the contested legacy of the *le danseur*, and perhaps in homage to it, throughout his long cinematic career, Charlie Chaplin (1889–1977) repeatedly invoked Terpsichore as his artistic muse. From *Tango Tangles* (1914) and *The Rink* (1916) to *The Great Dictator* (1940) and *Limelight* (1951), the Tramp dances. Although these episodes often are fleeting and informal, frequently he performs virtual miniballets composed of sophisticated, choreographed movements executed with remarkable adroitness and aplomb. Furthermore, American and French scholars and critics writing about Chaplin in the 1910s and 1920s, as well as his friends and colleagues from this period, often noted the comedian's talent as a dancer, both on and off the screen. Few scholars, however, have done anything more than merely mention in passing the actor's veritable obsession with the dance, probably because he never claimed to be a serious dancer.[4] When he danced, Chaplin did so only in order to elicit laughs. And perhaps laughter should not be taken too seriously. On the other hand, scholars may be resistant to the idea of the Tramp as a dancer precisely because it calls into question Chaplin's masculine potency. And as the literary critic Lee Edelman maintains, "a masculinity subject to questioning is no masculinity at all." [5] Considering the comedian's three marriages, his numerous, highly publicized affairs, as well as his particular penchant for beautiful, barely pubescent young women, such an interpretation itself seems off the mark, odd, queer.[6]

But what about Chaplin's screen persona? Were the Tramp's terpsichorean tendencies more than hilarious yet awesomely executed interludes choreographed to delight and entertain movie audiences? Do such dances serve a narrative or structural function within Chaplin's films? If so, what do they reveal about the Tramp's body, his gender, his sexuality, and his social status? In this essay I investigate these leading questions by examining the various dance scenes performed by the Tramp in *The Floorwalker* (1916), *Sunnyside* (1919), and *The Gold Rush* (1925). These three films—a classic two-reel rough-and-tumble slapstick comedy, a nearly feature-length comedy, and a feature-length dramatic comedy—engender potent images of the male body, all of which resonate historically with the contested terrain surrounding dance, masculinity, and homosexuality in the 1910s and 1920s. I contend that the public fascination with Chaplin as a dancer can only be understood when situated within two interrelated cultural shifts precipitated during these decades: the social dance craze that swept the United States and the contentious rebirth of the male ballet dancer on the Western European stage. Vaslav Nijinsky, *le dieu de la danse* (the god of the dance), inaugurated and codified the latter phenomenon as the principal dancer for the Ballets Russes from 1909 until 1913 and again between 1916 and 1917. His mesmerizing and quixotic masculinity, suffused with elegance, etherealness, and fluidity, created a paradigm of male stage performance against which many critics compared "*le Dieu de l'écran*" (the god of the screen), as the biographer Édouard Ramond dubbed Chaplin in 1927.[7] In dancing, the Tramp, like Nijinsky, articulated his queerness, a constellation of discursive and somatic signs that, in the words of Eve Kosofsky Sedgwick, constitute "the open mesh of possibilities, gaps, overlaps, dissonances and resonances, lapses and excesses of meaning when the constituent elements of anyone's gender, or anyone's sexuality aren't made (or *can't be made*) to signify monolithically."[8] This open mesh of possibilities was what made the dancing Tramp the Nijinsky of the silver screen.[9] As the French film historian Pierre Leprohon wrote in his 1935 biography of the comedian: "One only needs to see his films to realize that music and dance are the very foundations of his art."[10]

Released on May 15, 1916, *The Floorwalker*, the first film Chaplin made after he signed an unprecedented yearlong contract for

$670,000 with Mutual Film Corp., promised to be a huge hit. Four days after the premiere *Variety* reported that the number of advance U.S. and Canadian bookings for the first-run release of the film totaled $1.3 million, an amount "[u]nprecedented in the annals of motion picture history."[11] The narrative of the film is sown together by a series of spectacular gags and chase scenes that take a department store escalator as their point of comic departure. Summoned by the store manager (Eric Campbell), the floorwalker (Lloyd Bacon) takes the high-speed moving staircase to the second floor and goes into the store offices. Here the two men conspire to embezzle the store's receipts, while downstairs, the Tramp, an impecunious customer, enters the establishment to browse. A male clerk (Albert Austin) immediately begins to follow the Tramp, suspicious that he might shoplift. With cane in hand the blundering Little Fellow, as the Tramp was nicknamed, visits various departments, wreaking havoc and leaving a trail of fallen boxes and overturned displays behind him. The clerk finally demands that he leave the store, but, before he does, the Tramp casually tosses twenty-five cents on the counter and tucks a wire rack under his arm. Unaware of this unofficial transaction, the clerk and an undercover store detective accuse their suspicious customer of shoplifting, a crime that several other well-dressed, bourgeois customers already have committed but whose larceny has gone undetected because of the obsessive focus on the penniless Tramp. As the Little Fellow resists arrest, the dazzling comedic mayhem commences.

Outmaneuvering his much larger male pursuers with his lightning speed and acrobatic aptitude, the Tramp hops on the escalator, escapes upstairs, and ducks into the store offices. As he enters the outer office, the floorwalker—who double-crossed his boss, knocked him unconscious, and absconded with the sack full of money—exits the inner office. The manic chaos of the preceding chase scenes, heightened by rapid-fire editing, dissipates the moment these two men face one another. In a sustained medium-long shot, the Tramp and the floorwalker stop in their tracks and mimic each other's actions, dumbfounded by their uncanny resemblance and convinced that they are gazing into a mirror. While such stunts originated as part of English music hall routines and were popular with dancers in American vaudeville in the 1910s, they were introduced into early cinema by the French comic Max Linder, an important early influence on Chaplin.[12]

Chaplin, however, conceived of his version of this gag with a slight twist. Staring intently at each other, the two men begin to register their differences. As if to confirm this visual realization, each extends a hand and presses it against the other's. The unexpected contact with warm human flesh sends a shock wave of sensation through their bodies, after which the floorwalker eyes the Tramp's physique and invites him to come nearer. Removing the Little Fellow's hat, the floorwalker cups the face of his near twin between his hands in a tender caress and closely inspects his physiognomy. The Tramp perceives this physical intimacy as a flirtation and reciprocates, eagerly kissing his mirror image on the lips. The floorwalker wipes his mouth in disgust, while the Tramp looks to the floor in shame and sheepishly does the same.[13] The former's abhorrence, however, appears to be more fiction than fact, for he remains remarkably calm and makes no attempt either to flee from the osculating Tramp or to humiliate him for his sexual transgression. The floorwalker also may be aware of the popular theory of the day, which identified homosexuality as endemic to vagabonds.[14] No matter how one explains this reaction, the kiss is nothing less than the cinematic literalization of Freud's notion of narcissism as the sine qua non of male homosexuality. The initial moment of misidentification on the Tramp's part clearly functions as a narrative cover for the expression of homosexual desire, just as the nervous laughter of the audience disguises the homosexual panic and, perhaps, the homoerotic pleasure precipitated by such a scene of seduction.[15]

The coupling of male homosexuality and narcissism in *The Floorwalker* is underscored further when the floorwalker convinces his newfound companion to swap clothing and trade identities, an idea that comes to him only in the aftermath of the momentous kiss. Behind closed doors and away from the outside world, the two disrobe and exchange outfits in a kind of displaced consummation of the homoerotic desire initiated with the kiss.

The floorwalker collects his bag of money, pays the Tramp for his cooperation, and ushers him out of the office in his new but oversized suit. Delighted by his sudden good fortune, the Little Fellow cautiously saunters past the undercover detective to the elevator, where he plants a kiss on the brow of the elderly lift operator (James Kelley) before boarding. The floorwalker tries to leave the store but is apprehended by the detective and the clerk who, in turn, present the satchel full of money to the Tramp. As kissing comrades, the floorwalker and the Little Fellow perform their masquerade so convincingly that no one detects the ruse, illustrating not only that it takes one to know one but also that it takes one to impersonate one.[16]

While the Tramp effortlessly assumes his new identity as a floorwalker, trouble looms as the store manager regains consciousness and searches for his double-crossing co-conspirator. Mistaking the Little Fellow for his thieving employee, he tries to choke him to death without being noticed by an observant female undercover store detective. After several violent yet hilarious run-ins with the manager, the Tramp again retreats upstairs to the outer store office in order to count the money. The burly bearded manager, however, barges into the outer office and knocks him to the floor with such force that his legs fly over his head, exposing his entire ass to the camera (a signature Chaplin move). This dramatic blow and fall miraculously transform the nervous, bumbling Tramp into a lissome, classical ballet dancer. In another sustained medium-long shot exactly like that used during the scene between the Tramp and the floorwalker, the Little Fellow stands up, places his feet in fourth position, and executes a nearly thirty-second solo ballet composed of pirouettes, a royale, jetés, soubresauts, numerous pas de bourrée, and toe dancing. His graceful and petite body glides around the room and springs into the air in "Nijinskite leaps," as Theodore Huff termed them, each move punctuated by a variety of precise but delicate head and hand gestures.[17] Befuddled and dismayed by this bizarre display of agility, the manager periodically lunges at the Tramp, hoping to arrest and capture him. The manager's rotund lumbering frame, however, is no match for the Little Fellow who, in the words of Ramond, "dances, as only he knows how to dance."[18] Only when the Tramp completes his program, bows, and waits for applause does the manager successfully apprehend him.

The ballet sequence in *The Floorwalker* functions as a set piece, a common component of early film comedy borrowed from the vaudeville stage and introduced into the narrative structure of motion pictures in order to feature an actor's particular talents as a performer. The film historians Henry Jenkins and Kristine Brunovska Karnick identify Chaplin's "dancelike pantomimes" as a recurrent set piece in his movies:

> Such performances are marked by frontality and direct address to the camera. These sequences are often filmed in long take and from a more distant camera position to preserve the comic performance's integrity. These performances involve highly stylized movements which call attention to *how* an act is performed more than *what* is being done. . . . Such performance sequences enjoy a semiautonomous status within the film narrative, functioning as "set pieces" pleasurable in their own right, apart from any specific plot functions they might serve.[19]

In *The Floorwalker* Chaplin integrated his dance spectacle so thoroughly into the diegetic scheme of the film that the "how" and the "what" of his awesome performance were one and the same. This episode, in effect, answered the Yeatsian question "How can we know the dancer from the dance?" by revealing the impossibility of maintaining such a distinction.[20] Physically speaking, the diminutive Tramp (five-foot-four and about 120 pounds) could not possibly confront his massive antagonist (six-foot-four and nearly three hundred pounds) fist to fist or man to man. He therefore relies on other strategies to preserve the well-being of his fragile unmanly body. Initially, he assaults the manager with kicks to his protruding stomach and vulnerable ass. Unable to inflict enough pain to incapacitate his pursuer fully, the Little Fellow resorts to dancing as a means to circumvent, diffuse, and derail this brutish display of male aggression. As he dances, he mocks the manager's masculinity by shamelessly flirting with him through a host of exaggerated grins, coquettish glances, jocular head movements, and effeminate wrist gestures. In 1921 the

French novelist, playwright, cinéaste, and film critic Louis Delluc summarized the events in *The Floorwalker*, acknowledging the strategic function of this turn: "Charlie snakes through the legs of his enemies, that is to say, everybody. Hurried along by aimed revolvers, clenched fists, [and] tightly closed doors, he takes up dancing, his fairy godmother, blending the seductive arts of Jacques Dalcroze [*sic*], Anna Pavlova or Isadora Duncan in an imponderable rhythm."[21] As his "fairy godmother," dance protects the Tramp and offers him a means of escape from the unbridled violence directed toward him by the manager. Furthermore, as Delluc suggested, Chaplin's fancy footwork distinguishes him as a dancer in his own right and thus the heir to Dalcroze, Pavlova, and Duncan. Finally, the balletic interlude in *The Floorwalker* destabilizes the power of the massive manager in its punning representation of floorwalking, the act of overseeing the operations of a department store, as a type of dance and the floorwalker as a dancer.

The diegetic and formal correspondence between the dance scene and that between the Tramp and the floorwalker imply that kissing and dancing are similar expressions of sexual desire. Havelock Ellis, the renowned British sexologist and authority on homosexuality, established such a correlation in *The Dance of Life* (1923): "[Dancing] has an equally intimate association with love. . . . It is a process of courtship and, even more than that, it is a novitiate for love, and a novitiate which was found to be an admirable training for love."[22] The French avant-garde poet Philippe Soupault offered a similar proclamation in 1928: "There is no reason to deny the fact that dance, in many cases, exerts a sexual influence, if we dare to express it this way. Said differently, the art of dance is the most erotic of all the arts."[23] The risqué sexual tenor at the heart of male-female social dancing made it a particularly popular target for religious conservatives and moral reformers.[24]

Chaplin further confirmed the specifically queer resonance of dancing and kissing in *Behind the Screen*, released six months after *The Floorwalker*. In this film an overworked assistant prop man (Chaplin) falls in love with an unemployed actress (Edna Purviance) who cross-dresses as a boy to find work as a stagehand when the regular crew goes on strike. Backstage the lovebirds pause to kiss one another. As they do so, the boss (Eric Campbell) enters, notices their flagrant display of affection, and exclaims, "Oh you naughty boys!" in an intertitle. The rotund Campbell then prances up and down the length of the room, swishing his hips, flitting his head from side to side, and fluttering his outstretched arms and hands. His mincing antics culminate when he turns his back on both "boys," bends over with the profile of his body parallel to the camera, and offers his huge ass for their erotic contemplation. Chaplin seizes the opportunity and kicks his antagonistic boss in the behind. This gesture reads both as a violent reproof of his boss's homophobic incriminations and as a confirmation of such suspicions. Furthermore, Campbell's eye-catching dance metonymically signifies male homosexuals as "fairies," common parlance in the 1910s for flamboyantly effeminate gay men.[25]

The equivalence of kissing and dancing in *The Floorwalker* is exemplified further by the occurrence of both activities in the protective seclusion of the outer store office. Such an architectural space recalls the vaudeville stage, an arena of controlled public spectacle where the male comedian could engage in otherwise socially prohibited behavior in order to elicit laughter often couched in cultural anxiety.[26] Within the mediated purview of the cinematic narrative, however, the outer office also instantiates the homosexual closet, a segregated space of personal performance in which queer individuals could explore and express, in earnest, the same socially restricted conduct parodied on the vaudeville stage. Set off from the rest of the department store, which itself is policed by an omnipotent system of male surveillance, this enclave offers the beleaguered Tramp the safety and comfort necessary to pucker his lips and kick up his feet precisely because it is a feminine domain, originally occupied by the manager's female secretary (Edna Purviance), as established at the outset of the film, and thus is untainted by the regulatory regime of heterosexual masculinity.[27] Despite its function as a liminal space through which the characters of the film hurriedly pass, it also is a site of epistemological privilege because nearly all the radical shifts and turns in the plot unfold herein—the floorwalker and the manager agree to embezzle the store receipts; the Tramp and the floorwalker meet, kiss, and exchange outfits; the Tramp dances and infuriates the manager to such a degree that he loses control, openly chases the Tramp throughout the store, and eventually is captured by the police. Behind the closed doors of the outer office, men meet and forge various alliances, all of which, in their blatant disregard for established codes of morality, are both criminal and potentially queer. Proof of this appears in the last scene of the film when the manager and the Little Fellow are apprehended simultaneously inside the jail-like elevator. The Tramp, however, probably will not remain incarcerated for long. Even though dancing is a crime against masculinity that threatens to effeminize him and highlight his social nonconformity, he willingly perpetrates this offense if only to demonstrate that the dancing male body is impossible to control or contain by traditional means.

Like *The Floorwalker*, *Sunnyside* (released June 15, 1919) features a dance set piece as a cinematic intertext. A satirical takeoff on the sentimental rural melodramas popularized by the actor Charles Ray, the three-reel dramatic comedy begins with an iris focused on the steeple of a country church that opens outward to reveal the bucolic village of Sunnyside. Inside the local hotel the proprietor (Tom Wilson) lies asleep in a bed above which hangs a plaque inscribed with the biblical adage "Love Thy Neighbor." The Tramp, employed as a jack-of-all-trades in the establishment, sleeps in the adjoining room. The owner awakens on Sunday morning and forces the Little Fellow out of bed, violently kicking him in the ass in a distinctly unneighborly manner. Antireligious in tone, *Sunnyside* exposes the pious pillar of the Christian community as nothing more than a hypocritical brutal slave driver. A beautiful young Jewish woman (Edna Purviance) provides the Tramp with romantic solace, as he runs himself ragged.[28]

The overworked and underpaid Tramp dutifully performs endless chores as his demanding boss terrorizes him with physical and verbal abuse. On Sunday afternoon the hotel owner goes to church, and the Little Fellow is left to drive the cows home from pasture. The camera follows the herd along a country lane, emphasizing the equally peculiar gait of these farm animals and their guardian. At a fork in the road the animals stray, but the Tramp, preoccupied with reading a book, does not notice. One beast finds its way into the church where the hotel owner is addressing the congregation. After several futile attempts to cajole the bovine to leave God's house, the Little Fellow finally decides to jump on its back and steer it to freedom. The camera cuts to the exterior of the church, and the bewildered heifer vacates the building as a wayward horned bucking bull. This stupefyingly comic gender transformation pokes fun at the Christian belief that inside God's house miracles of any and every kind are possible.

Charging through town with the Tramp-cum-rodeo-rider clinging to it for dear life, the beast traverses a small wooden bridge outside the village, throws him into the ravine below, and escapes into the countryside. Knocked unconscious, the Little Fellow dreams that four wood nymphs rescue him (Helen Kohn, Olive Burton, Willie Mae Carson, and Olive Acorn). Clad in sleeveless diaphanous gowns of a classical Greek style and sporting laurel wreaths atop their long flowing tresses, the nymphs materialize on the bridge and dance barefooted in circles as they clutch a long floral vine. One of them spots the unconscious Tramp and touches him with the vine, causing him to awaken immediately. The buoyant Little Fellow joins their arcadian exhibition and accompanies them to a meadow where they continue their sylvan dance, twirling harmoniously, skipping, and running after one another. In a brilliant burlesque on Nijinsky as the faun in *L'Après-midi d'un faune* (1912), the Tramp sits on a large boulder, twists his hair into the shape of two horns, and puts a daisy to his lips, as if playing a flute. With his lips pursed, hyperextended fingers fluttering, and eyes twinkling, he flirtatiously serenades the nymphs.[29] Such a picturesque moment of bucolic bliss ends abruptly when he accidentally falls backward and sits squarely on a bed of cacti. This mishap of metaphoric anal penetration ignites a mysterious transformation in the Tramp's gender. Just as the stray cow metamorphosed into a bull inside the church, the formerly flirtatious faun quite literally becomes an effeminate fairy. Having previously followed the four nymphs and imitated their every gesture, he now

Chaplin in *Sunnyside*, 1919 (Museum of Modern Art, Film Stills Archive)

leads the frolicking feminine pack around the meadow in an accelerated modern dance punctuated by grands jetés. With his arms
flapping and head swaying, he rubs his tender buttocks and, in effect, performs as the fifth nymph. The Little Fellow's small stature,
equal to that of the women, as well as the elegance and expertise
with which he executes these movements, dramatically reinforce
such a reading. Delluc focused on this very transformation in his
review of the feature: "One of his best films, *Sunnyside*, shows him
dancing and twirling about with the exquisite grace of—as we
say—an 'excentric [*sic*] girl.'"[30] This visually potent dream sequence is an homage *both* to Nijinsky and to the queerly all-female
spectacles staged by Duncan and her female followers. Transpiring
beyond the social, moral, and juridical boundaries of civilized
Christian society, this pagan pastoral dance suggests a utopian return to nature where femininity and effeminacy rule supreme and
where homosexuality itself may be a virtue rather than a vice. Such
idealism crumbles, however, as the four nymphs return to the

bridge, and, in a final episode of gender inversion, dissolve to reveal four men, who rescue the Tramp from the ravine. One of
these men is the Tramp's employer, who proceeds to kick the Little Fellow in the ass repeatedly as they return home.

Although *Sunnyside* failed miserably at the box office in the
United States, numerous critics singled out Chaplin's balletic bac-
chanal as ingenious. "The delightful sequence . . . , by itself, is
enough to make the picture memorable," claimed Huff in his
1951 biography of the filmmaker.[31] French cinéastes and critics,
in particular, praised the poetic lyricism of this episode. The art
historian and film theorist Élie Faure described Chaplin in *Sunnyside* as a "sly elf-like figure" and an "imp of humanity" and compared his dancing to the paintings of Watteau and Corot.[32] Leprohon characterized the movie as "the most 'aerial' film he ever
made," while Ramond expressed envy for "Charlie, svelte shep-
herd of Theocritus in his bowler hat," who, despite his traumatic
run-in with a cow, "falls asleep [*sic*] at the bottom of some ditch
and dreams of nymphs in short dresses who lead him in the most
light-hearted, the most rural of ballets."[33] Released in France as
Une Idylle aux champs (An Idyll of the Fields), the title posited the
dance sequence as the film's diegetic core. Such a marketing strategy proved remarkably successful in a country steeped in a long
tradition of ballet and courtly dance.[34]

Whereas modern dance provides the Tramp a dreamlike escape
from oppressive masculine rule in *Sunnyside*, and classical ballet
offers him a means of self-defense and flirtation in the *Floorwalker*,
the Tramp's distinct *inability* to dance socially in *The Gold Rush*
(released June 26, 1925) sets him apart from other men. This dramatic comedy, the cinematic venture for which Chaplin most
wanted to be remembered, recounts the endless obstacles that be-
fall a naive tramp prospector on the arctic frontier among fortune
hunters during the 1898 Klondike gold rush. As soon as the Little Fellow appears on screen, his odd personality is immediately
apparent. The film opens with a long shot of an unending proces-
sion of weary male prospectors making their way through a snowy
pass; several die of exhaustion and hypothermia on the way. The
camera cuts to the Tramp, who parades aimlessly through the

snow in solitude, dressed in nothing but his worn undersized jacket and oblivious to either the cold or the huge black bear following him. Brandishing his signature cane and wearing a bowler hat, he skids along the mountainside with a placid smile on his face, like a dandy or flaneur. After surviving a near-fatal encounter in the snow-covered wilderness with Big Jim McKay (Mack Swain) and Black Larson (Tom Murray)—two, tall, beefy, bearded prospectors—the Tramp happens upon a lively boomtown with a dance hall. He enters the establishment timorously and tries to mix with the boisterous, festive crowd of drinking and smoking townspeople, none of whom, however, notices the downtrodden interloper. The band strikes up a tune and male–female couples flood the dance floor. A long shot frames the timid motionless Tramp from behind as he surveys the spectacle of heterosexual courtship before him and leans on his cane, suggesting that he has been stricken by some disability that precludes him from participating in the revelry. The Tramp, in fact, is the victim of a disability of both a physical and an emotional nature. Not only is his right foot wrapped in a mass of cloth, hampering his movement, but he also suffers from loneliness after a recent separation from his would-be dance partner, Big Jim McKay.

Just before he wanders into town, the Tramp waits out a blizzard with McKay and Larson in an isolated cabin. Without food, they cut cards and Larson is drafted to battle the storm and scavenge for rations. Thanksgiving arrives and the resourceful Tramp prepares an impromptu feast, with his boiled right shoe as the main course. In this ingenious scene he slaves over the hot stove like a culinary queen as McKay looks on in wide-eyed disbelief at his companion's finesse in the feminine sphere of the kitchen. Like a loving wife or mother, the Little Fellow sets the table, artfully divides his shoe, and presents McKay with the "meatier" sole. Both men consume their portions and, despite indigestion, survive until the next day when they part ways after a heartfelt farewell. The fraternity and fidelity celebrated during this meal amplify the Tramp's alienation and awkwardness upon entering the convivial dance hall.

When the Tramp finally does venture onto the dance floor, his status as a social misfit, a queer category visually signified by his missing shoe, is dramatically reiterated. Georgia (Georgia Hale), a beautiful, free-spirited, saucy dance hall girl who has otherwise ignored the Tramp, unexpectedly invites him to dance but only to spite Jack Cameron (Malcolm Waite), a macho, muscled, mustachioed suitor who arrogantly demands she dance with him. Nervous and self-conscious, the Little Fellow accepts her invitation. As they waltz, he loses his belt, and his oversized trousers begin to sag and fall off his waist. He hastily grabs a piece of rope lying on a table and fastens it around his slender waist, which lacks the necessary masculine girth to support such a capacious garment naturally. The other end of the rope, however, is attached to a large dog that follows the couple around the floor in an amusing triangulated dance and brings the Tramp's happiness to an abrupt end when it spies a stray cat. The force of the canine's pull causes the Tramp to tumble to the floor as Georgia and the rest of the onlookers laugh uproariously. Ashamed and embarrassed, the Little Fellow laughs at himself and coyly follows Georgia off the dance floor. He then encounters Cameron, who is ready to pummel the Tramp but teases him mercilessly instead, pulling his derby down over his eyes. The frightened and defenseless Tramp prodigiously outwits his attacker by accidentally striking a post that he mistakes for Cameron. This flailing gesture causes a precariously positioned clock to fall from the post and knock the brute unconscious. Proud of his victory, which onlookers realize is the result of sheer luck, the Little Fellow confidently struts out of the dance hall, deluded that he owns the place. Unlike in the remote cabin where his ingenuity and deftness saved him and McKay from starvation, in the erotically charged public domain of the dance hall where size, strength, and self-confidence are measures of a man's status and determine his success with women, the Tramp is out of his element.

From the dangerous and humiliating dance hall the Tramp retreats to the safe and comfortable cabin of a fellow bachelor prospector (Henry Bergman), who invites him to look after his home while he is away on an expedition. Ensconced in this intimate abode, the Little Fellow tends to his domestic chores, only to be interrupted by Georgia and three other dance hall girls romping outside in the snow. He asks them in and, while he is outside collecting firewood, Georgia discovers a photograph of herself hidden beneath his pillow. Aghast yet touched by his romantic interest in her, she decides to flirt with her secret admirer, who cannot hide his nervousness. In a final moment of cruelty the four women lie and promise to return for dinner on New Year's Eve. As they walk away laughing at the Tramp's gullibility, he gleefully dances around the cabin, jumping on the bed and swinging from the rafters. His illusions of heterosexual bliss, however, are soon shattered.

The Tramp occupies himself anew with the household preparations for a holiday feast. He cleverly unfolds a piece of newspaper to be used as a tablecloth, sets the table, arranges place cards and party favors, and tends to the chicken roasting in the oven. Meanwhile, at the dance hall the townspeople have congregated to dance in the New Year. As echoes of their merriment penetrate the cabin, the solitary Tramp sits motionless at his immaculately laid table, waiting patiently for the arrival of his guests. This pathetic scene dissolves into the imaginary festive one of a dream in which his cooking and conversation capture the hearts of the four female dancers. The mirthful women encourage their gracious host to give a speech, but even in his own fantasy he is unwilling or unable to muster the masculine courage necessary to deliver a public oratory. The Little Fellow offers instead to "speak" to the women in a different language, the feminine language of dance in which they are fluent. He proceeds to spear two large dinner rolls with forks, lowers his head toward the table top, and performs the celebrated "Dance of the Rolls."[35] Shot in close-up and lit dramatically like a vaudeville stage lined with footlights, this scene depicts the Tramp with the huge head and thin tiny body of a caricature, lacking the somatic signs of a definitive sex or gender. These queer prostheses transform the otherwise disabled Tramp into a skilled leggy dance hall "girl" who, like his guests, expertly executes the can-can, the shuffle, splits, and sideways hops. Sidling off to the wings, "she" returns to bow before an applauding audience as if to say, in the words of Nijinsky, "I am an

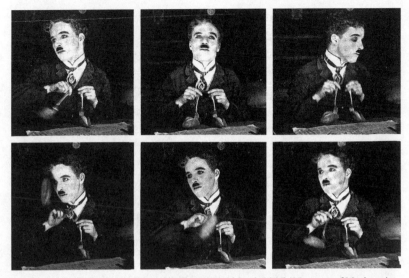

Chaplin performs "Dance of the Rolls" in *The Gold Rush,* 1925 (Museum of Modern Art, Film Stills Archive)

artist whose voice is dance." [36] Having previously exposed his ineptitude and inability to participate in the heterosexual ritual of social dancing, the Tramp performs the solo "Dance of the Rolls" in a moment of cross-gender identification with the four dance hall girls. His hopeless hunger to possess Georgia romantically is merely a displaced desire to be her—a sexy female dancer with an adoring male audience.

The Tramp's gender-bending demeanor during this vaudevillian turn captivated two of Chaplin's French admirers. The writer and journalist Jean Prévost explicitly identified this performance as a ballet and claimed that it encapsulated the very essence of the Tramp's character: "[T]he ballet of the small rolls in *The Gold Rush* is not, therefore, a random discovery [on Chaplin's part], imitable or adaptable. It is a stylization, a summary, an abstraction of Charlie [the Tramp] himself."[37] Ramond elaborated on Prévost's reading, arguing that this gag, "a veritable poem . . . without parallel in the history of silent film," disclosed the Tramp's predilection for female impersonation: "[W]ith a simple hand gesture—the hands of Charlie, it is true, are supple, eloquent [*parlant*], subtle—with sways of his shoulders and his head emerging above the edge of the table, and with the help of some facial expressions, to have suggested, realized, imitated the dance of a classic ballerina in a tutu is pure poetry and indisputably a phenomenon of a very sensitive and very great artist."[38] For many French aficionados, such perverse and peculiar practices were what identified Chaplin as an artist. And the male artist, according to Jean Cocteau, one of Chaplin's earliest French champions and himself a rather notorious homosexual, "must be partly male and partly female."[39]

The Little Fellow's desire to be a dance hall girl like Georgia, with a coterie of male admirers, becomes a reality near the end of *The Gold Rush* when his long-lost buddy, Big Jim McKay, stumbles into town after a scuffle with Larson during which he received a blow to the head. Unable to remember the location of either his cabin or his gold claim, he enters the dance hall, desperately searching for the dejected Tramp, who himself is on the lookout for Georgia. The two find one another on the dance floor amid a throng of gyrating couples. McKay sweeps the Little Fellow into his arms and hugs him tightly, demanding that he take him to his cabin. Before departing, however, the Tramp professes his love to Georgia in a moment of such bombastic melodrama that the husky McKay yanks him away. The Little Fellow utters his final farewell suspended in midair in a posture reminiscent of a sissonne soubresaut. He then leads McKay to his cabin, where they battle the elements, survive numerous mishaps, and eventually strike it rich. The final scene of the film shows the Tramp and McKay outfitted in the finery of millionaires aboard a ship bound for the States. After his repeated failures as a man in the Klondike dance hall, the Tramp confidently struts his stuff on deck, accompanied by his old mining partner and newfound mate, who saved him from ever having to dance socially again.

Critics or movie audiences during the 1910s and 1920s commonly noted the frequency with which Chaplin integrated dance performances into films like *The Floorwalker*, *Sunnyside*, and *The Gold Rush*, as well as the acumen with which he executed such choreographic programs. In 1919 one French journalist declared that, above all else, Chaplin was a danseur, and two years later another reporter heralded him as "the king of the pirouette."[40] Faure characterized Chaplin as a modern-day Descartes, who in his movies proclaimed to the world, "I dance, therefore, I am."[41] In a 1916 exposé Stanley Todd described Chaplin as "an exceedingly clever dancer" and disclosed that he employed a private chiropodist to "care for his pedal extremities," which "mean so much to himself—and the world at large."[42] Perhaps the most intriguing commentaries regarding Chaplin's talent as a dancer are those that compare him directly to Nijinsky. In the opening pages of his 1921 monograph on Chaplin, the first booklength examination of the actor's work, Delluc waxed rhapsodically, "I think of Nijinsky when I think of Chaplin. . . . Chaplin is an inventor in his art just as Nijinsky was in his."[43] Lady Ottoline Morrell, an English patron of Sergei Diaghilev's Ballets Russes during the 1910s, mused in her memoir, "I found in Charlie Chaplin something of the same intense poignancy as there was in Nijinsky. . . . Nijinsky and Charlie Chaplin certainly have much in common."[44] The French artist Jacques-Émile Blanche, a close friend of Diaghilev's who painted numerous portraits of Nijinsky, identified the same resemblance after seeing the Russian dancer perform: "His presence was magnetic, like that of Charlie Chaplin."[45]

Nijinsky appears to have crowned Chaplin as his cinematic heir. In late December 1916 the Ballets Russes arrived in Los Angeles as part of its second national tour. Although he had never seen a ballet, Chaplin attended the debut performance on Christmas Day at Clune's Auditorium. Eager to meet the movie star, the dancers in the troupe delayed the program and coaxed the comedian on stage where they lauded him.[46] Romola de Pulszky-Nijinsky, who pursued the dancer, seduced him away from Diaghilev, his lover, and married him in 1913, confirmed that "Vaslav always thought Chaplin was the genius of the cinema, a wonderful mime. They immediately became friends."[47] By the end of the evening Nijinsky's prowess totally enthralled Chaplin: "The moment he appeared [on stage] I was electrified. I have seen few geniuses in the world, and Nijinsky was one of them. He was hypnotic, godlike, his somberness suggesting moods of other worlds; every movement was poetry, every leap a flight into strange fancy."[48] Before leaving the theater, the spellbound actor invited the Russian to visit his studio. The dancer-choreographer, along with several other members of the Ballets Russes, took Chaplin up on his offer, unaware that the secretive and temperamental comedian rarely allowed anyone on the set except his cast and crew. Nijinsky and his colleagues witnessed the filming of *Easy Street* (released January 22, 1917), a slapstick comedy full of chase scenes and classic knockabout antics.[49] Impressed by what he witnessed behind as well as in front of the camera, the Russian dancer, as Chaplin recalled, complimented his host: "Your comedy is *balletique* [*sic*], you are a dancer."[50] This historic meeting was documented in a photograph, showing the artists standing with an arm around one another's shoulder and bright smiles on their faces amid their entourages.[51]

The "*balletique*" abilities that Nijinsky noticed in Chaplin stemmed from his childhood training as a dancer. Between 1899 and 1900, at the age of ten, Chaplin toured Great Britain as a member of an all-boy clog-dancing troupe known as The Eight Lancashire Lads.[52] This formative experience set Chaplin apart from most of his male contemporaries in the early cinema; his peers strategically avoided such potentially incriminating behavior in front of the camera except when securely coupled with a leading lady or squarely rooted within the comedic context of burlesque. For example, when Chaplin appeared on the set in Chicago to shoot *His New Job* in January 1915, his first film for Essanay Film Manufacturing Co., he stunned and confused the cast and crew with his gyrating body. One observer reported that he danced "so seriously that everybody wondered if he was out of his mind, because it seemed so uncalled for."[53] Francis X. Bushman, the studio's handsome heartthrob and one of the industry's first matinee idols, was a "wee-bit peeved" to see himself displaced by the puny and peculiar Chaplin.[54] W. C. Fields, who began his career in vaudeville as a tramp juggler and identified Chaplin as his professional nemesis, also despised the actor's seemingly obsessive propensity to dance, mainly because of his questionably masculine style. After watching *Easy Street*, the embittered Fields reputedly referred to the King of Comedy as a

Nijinsky and Chaplin (*upper right*) on the set of *Easy Street,* 1916 (Roger Pryor Dodge Collection, New York Public Library for the Performing Arts, Astor, Lenox, and Tilden Foundations; used with permission)

"goddamned ballet dancer" and vowed that "if I ever meet the son of a bitch I'll murder him!"[55] Conversely, several prominent members of the Ballets Russes actually named the dancing Tramp as a source of avant-garde inspiration. Igor Stravinsky, the company's principal composer, acknowledged that in the 1910s "Chaplin was an event in my life, as he was in Diaghilev's."[56] Under the tutelage of Diaghilev, Léonide Massine, the impresario's lover after Nijinsky's marriage, based two characters in his early ballets on Chaplin—Niccolo, the waiter, in *Les Femmes de bonne humeur* (1917) and the male can-can dancer in *La Boutique fantasque* (1919). The most ambitious and ingenious adaptation of the Little Fellow's persona, however, appeared in Cocteau and Massine's 1917 ballet, *Parade.*[57]

Whether viewed positively or negatively, Chaplin's pedal poise largely determined his initial cinematic fame and secured his box office success. More than his undersized derby hat, baggy trousers, cane, or mustache, the Tramp's bizarre gait entranced audiences. "Of course the walk is Chaplin so far as picture audiences are concerned. No matter what else I may do that is amusing in the course of my plays I don't believe I can ever get away from the walk," Chaplin admitted in 1916.[58] Characterized by early reviewers as everything from "funny little mincing steps" and a " 'quarter-to-three' walk" to a "characteristic French kick" and a "queer shuffle," the comedian's unique walk consisted of the jaunty and jerky movement of his legs with his feet prominently splayed.[59] Even when the Tramp was not actually dancing, his comportment echoed that of a dancer. With his legs together, heels touching, and feet turned out, his body naturally rested in first position.[60] The witty manner by which the Tramp rounded corners—pivoting on one leg while elevating the other and extending it horizontally outward—also suggested a choreographed grand battement or a demi-grand rond de jambe en l'air, two classical ballet moves. Finally, Chaplin periodically disrupted the frenetic rhythm of his waddle by bending a knee and lifting his foot toward the calf of the supporting leg, a gesture reminiscent of a sissonne.

Chaplin's uncannily balletic bearing led one journalist to allege that Mutual Film Corp. signed the star to his lucrative six-figure contract in February 1916 because of his "excruciating amble," which sent fans into "paroxysms" and guaranteed record receipts.[61] The studio willingly paid the comedian such an extraordinary sum because it was hoping to cash in on the Chaplin craze that had commenced the year before. While the *New York Times* likened Chaplin's "skipping, prancing gait" to that of "an Ariel," the *Milwaukee Journal* reported that the American National Association Masters of Dancing officially recognized a new dance called the "Charley Chaplin Waltz," which promised to be "the one novelty to be seen in ballrooms in 1916."[62] As part of the 1915 New York stage revue *Watch Your Step*, the English actor Lupino Lane crooned "That Charlie Chaplin Walk": "In London, Paris or New York/Ev'rybody does that Charlie Chaplin Walk!"[63] During the 1915 Broadway season the leggy lovelies at the Ziegfeld Follies donned Chaplin drag and dazzled audiences with their rendition of "Those Charlie Chaplin Feet."[64]

Eager to profit from the popularity of the Tramp's walk, Tin Pan Alley musicians churned out similar tunes, including "The Chaplin Waddle," "The Charlie Strut," "The Chaplin Wiggle," "The Charlie Chaplin Glide," and "The Charlie Chaplin—March Grotesque." The "Charlot One-Step" was a favorite among the French. In their titles all these songs directly acknowledged the Little Fellow as a dancer.[65]

The overwhelming recognition of the Tramp's cinematic antics as dancelike must be viewed in the context of the dance mania that swept the United States during the 1910s and 1920s. At the close of the nineteenth century, a constellation of structural shifts in modern society, including rapid urban growth, a loosening of Victorian morality, and the explosion of youth culture, led to a proliferation of legitimate commercial venues for nighttime entertainment separate from those previously found in vice districts or working-class neighborhoods. Decidedly less formal than theaters or concert halls, cabarets, cafes, and lobster palaces enabled white men and women, both married and unmarried from various class and ethnic backgrounds to congregate casually and mix promiscuously. Such venues often featured professional dance teams, like Vernon and Irene Castle or Maurice Mouvet and Florence Walton, who introduced patrons to numerous new social dances, many of which included choreography and musical rhythms appropriated from African American culture. Despite white middle-class concerns regarding the overt sexual underpinnings of dances like the turkey trot, shimmy, fox trot, cakewalk, monkey hug, and tango, thousands of such establishments, along with much larger dance halls and dance palaces, opened across the country to satiate the desires of dance-mad Americans.[66] Concomitant with the popularity of social dancing, modern "art dance" also gained increased attention from a cross-section of the population due to extensive theatrical tours by female dancers like Isadora Duncan, Loie Fuller, Ruth St. Denis, Maud Allan, and Gertrude Hoffman.[67] Finally, vaudeville programs and stage reviews consistently included serious acts by classical ballet and modern dancers as well as lighthearted burlesques of both forms of terpsichorean entertainment.[68] The Castles spoke for an entire generation when they characterized dance as "the exponent *par excellence* of the joy of living."[69]

During the initial years of Chaplin's film career, the U.S. movie industry also succumbed to the dance craze. Between 1915 and 1927 movie makers increasingly integrated both social and high art forms of dancing into the plots of motion pictures. Studio executives imported classically trained European ballet dancers, like Pavlova and Theodore Koslov, to act in films and simultaneously transformed society dancers, like Irene Castle and Rudolph Valentino, into Hollywood stars. Scores of vaudeville dancers, like Gertrude Bambrick, Blanche Sweet, and Paul Swan, also successfully made the transition from stage to screen. Encouraged by directors like D. W. Griffith (whom Bambrick taught to dance) and Cecile B. DeMille, numerous actors and actresses enrolled in dance classes to learn technique as well as to refine their comportment. Ted Shawn and Ruth St. Denis catered to such a clientele at their Los Angeles–based Denishawn School, which opened in 1915, as did Ernest Belcher at his Celeste School.[70]

As two media of nonverbal visual expression, dance and silent film encompassed several similar ideological and structural components. Both perfected and relied on an expressive vocabulary beyond that of the spoken word. The body in motion constituted the foundation of this evolving lexicon of communication. Furthermore, each strived to create a visual spectacle augmented by musical accompaniment.[71] Equally invested in redrawing the corporeal limits of the human body, dance and film were a match made in Hollywood. Rex Ingram, who directed Valentino in *Four Horsemen of the Apocalypse* (1921), attested to the fruitfulness of such a union when he professed that "a good dancer frequently makes a good screen actor."[72] By the mid-1920s, dance had become such a fundamental ingredient to the success of silent films that *The Dance* whimsically but accurately identified Tinsel Town as a veritable paradise to which "good dancers go when they die."[73]

Even though certain members of the early motion picture industry recognized the alliance of dance and film, the majority overlooked, ignored, or rejected it. Beginning in the 1910s movie executives like Adolph Zukor, founder of Famous Players

Film Co. (1912), and Harry Aitken, founder of Triangle Pictures (1915), recruited well known performers from the Broadway stage to work in Hollywood. In so doing, they hoped to legitimate their fledging industry, attract respectable middle-class audiences, and appease moral crusaders who attacked the cinema as a form of working-class vice. Photoplays, as the medium was termed, adopted drama as their narrative template and recreated numerous literary and theatrical classics for the screen. Writing in the film and arts magazine *Shadowland* in 1923, Albert Lewin lamented the continued dominance of such an aural and text-based paradigm in the silent visual medium of the movies:

> Artistically the worst pictures being made today are those which are adapted from serious plays, designed to present a theme or elucidate a problem. . . . But they should never have been done in pictures at all, because their vitality and their movement are not those of the movies. Their explosions are those of speech, untranslatable into movement. Thrown upon the screen, they become static and photographic dramas, bereft of speech, dumb, helpless, inarticulate.[74]

Lewin argued that movies could only regain their dynamism if actors and directors "realize consciously or intuitively that the art of the screen is closer to the dance than it is to the drama."[75] And, in his judgment, Chaplin was the cinematic personality who most thoroughly comprehended the aesthetic correspondence between film and dance and successfully deployed it as a creative force in his work:

> The dance at its purest expresses with a minimum of irrelevance the quintessential movement and flow of experience. In this sense Charlie Chaplin is the greatest dancer of modern times. What he does on the screen has hardly the slightest relationship to the art of the drama. . . . To call Chaplin an actor is to miss the salient point of his art. He is the great new dancer—intimate and profound, sublime and trivial, glorious and futile, magnificent and impotent.[76]

The French painter Fernand Léger corroborated Lewin's assessment of Chaplin as a dancer in his 1924 film *Ballet mécanique*, an avant-garde rumination on the poetics and erotics of mechanized motion in both machines and the human body. Composed of a series of detailed montage shots of household objects, working machines, and mostly female body parts juxtaposed through rapid-fire editing, the film begins and ends with a wooden marionette image of the Tramp, whose jerky movements are remarkably dancelike.[77]

Despite the general tolerance for social dancing, men who devoted their energy to classical ballet or modern dance, with or without a female partner, often were suspect because, in dancing, they raised doubts regarding their masculine potency. J. E. Crawford Flitch encapsulated the intensity of this cultural angst in his 1912 book, *Modern Dancing and Dancers*: "The dance, in any other sense than that of a ball-room accomplishment, is generally regarded as unsuited to the masculine character. How often has not one heard the remark that it is unpleasing to see a man dancer. And a man himself would as a rule rather be caught in the act of stealing than of dancing alone or with his fellows."[78] Ted Shawn recalled that one of his college fraternity brothers, upon hearing that Shawn intended to drop out of the University of Denver in the early 1910s in order to become a professional dancer, shockingly rejoined, "But, Ted, *men* don't dance."[79] Despite their muscularity and athleticism, male ballet dancers often raised eyebrows as they raised their legs. Throughout his career Shawn fought this stereotype. In a 1916 interview titled "A Defence [*sic*] of the Male Dancer," he distinguished himself from Nijinsky, a "feministic [*sic*] personality," and argued not only that "the male dancer can be thoroughly masculine" but that he "should create masculinity."[80] Edward Bernays, the nephew of Sigmund Freud and the father of modern public relations who also spearheaded the publicity campaign for the Ballets Russes during its U.S. tours, identified homophobia as the foundation of the cultural prejudice against the danseur: "Men who danced in ballet were an affront to America's pride in its manly, rugged pioneers. It was generally thought male dancers were likely to be deviates."[81] Unlike competitive sports, dance demanded that its practitioners mask the true physical power of their bodies as well as the brute force expended during performances and instead foster an air of effortlessness buttressed by elegant and delicate gestures. Ironically, the success of such a masquerade directly depended on a dancer's muscular prowess.

No one did more to damage irreparably the case against the male ballet dancer than Nijinsky. His peculiar and spectacular stage antics unsettled and undermined the heavily policed cultural boundaries separating male from female, masculinity from femininity, homosexuality from heterosexuality, and human from nonhuman. From the submissive Golden Slave in *Schéhérazade* (1910) and his incarnation of a rose in *Le Spectre de la rose* (1910) to the ambisexual Hindu god in *Le Dieu bleu* (1912) and the fetishistic faun in *L'Après-midi d'un faune*, Nijinsky's queer personae exposed gender as a regulatory regime imprinted on the body.[82] The provocative contradiction between the virtuosity of Nijinsky's hard body, especially his overdeveloped thighs, and his unabashed embrace of effeminacy enthralled certain theater goers, many of whom attributed his unorthodox behavior on stage to his eastern European heritage. The English balletomane Cyril Beaumont, one of Nijinsky's earliest and most passionate defenders, championed the dancer for his wholesale disavowal of traditional modern masculinity: "*Nijinsky is not a man* in the true, robust sense of the word. . . . An examination of his *roles* will show that none are allied with the physical strength and beauty of manhood."[83] Those who characterized Chaplin as a dancer or explicitly compared him to Nijinsky aligned the actor-filmmaker, whether wittingly or unwittingly, with the queer legacy of the *le dieu de la danse*.

Chaplin himself encouraged such an analogy, both on and off the silver screen. During the 1910s and 1920s the actor was especially fond of impersonating stars of both the Ballets Russes and modern "art dance." In a 1916 newspaper article Mary Pickford recounted a visit she made to Keystone Studios in 1914 during which the comedian, who was on the set and in drag, imitated Pavlova so persuasively that Pickford assumed him to be a trained ballerina.[84] Clare Sheridan, an English sculptor and writer, recalled a similar incident in 1921 during a camping trip she and her son took with Chaplin: "When the sunset sky became streaked pink and purple, Charlie kicked off his shoes, and danced with his beautiful small feet naked on the sand. He did imitations of Nijinsky and Pavlowa—he does it so well and with so much grace that one doesn't know whether to laugh or silently appreciate."[85] In her memoir Pola Negri, the sexy Polish actress who Chaplin met in Berlin and with whom he had a highly publicized affair shortly after her arrival in Hollywood in September 1922, likened her ex-lover to a ballet dancer: "One of the few physically appealing things about Chaplin was the way he moved. He had the grace, precision, and timing of somebody trained for the ballet. I never ceased to wonder at this innate gift. If he had not become the greatest clown of his day, he could certainly have become one of its foremost dancers."[86] Negri spoke with the voice of experience, having begun her career as a dancer at the Imperial Theatre in St. Petersburg. Louise Brooks, a chorus girl with the Ziegfeld Follies when Chaplin had an affair with her during the summer of 1925, also described an evening she and friends spent with the star in New York during which he "acted out countless scenes for countless films. He did imitations of everybody," including "Isadora Duncan [who] danced in a storm of toilet paper."[87] In her 1935 book, *Charlie Chaplin Intime*, May Reeves, a Czech beauty queen, dancer, and polyglot who was hired to translate the foreign mail Chaplin received during his 1931 trip around the world and with whom both he and his older brother Sydney had a sexual liaison, reported that the actor danced in order to seduce her when they first met in Nice: "[H]e performed a ballet for me alone. He rounded the tables and spun around. He swayed, rocked, and imitated the lithe acrobatics of a Pavlova with his arms and hands. . . . Everything in him danced, fluttered, undulated, and unfolded in graceful movements."[88] Playing the lissome Terpsichore worked like a charm for the diminutive Chaplin.

Concurrent with such anecdotes, friends and colleagues identified Chaplin's lack of masculine potency as a defining aspect of both his personality and his filmic persona. When Chaplin first arrived at Essanay in early 1915 to begin work on *His New Job*, he considered casting the young Gloria Swanson as his female lead. The inexperienced actress, however, failed miserably during rehearsal, and in the end she played only a minor role as a stenographer: "He kept laughing and making his eyes twinkle and talking in a light, gentle voice and encouraging me to let myself go and be silly. He reminded me of a pixie from some other world altogether, and for the life of me I couldn't get the feel of his frisky little skits. All morning I felt like a cow trying to dance with a toy poodle."[89] Recounting his meetings with Chaplin in Europe in 1921 and 1931, the English writer Thomas Burke painted a portrait of the actor as delicate and effeminate: "His movements are as piquant and precise as a ballerina's. He is as slim as a faun and as graceful; so slim and light that he seems scarcely human; and it is on recognising this that one is aware of that touch of the bizarre."[90] Sir James Barrie had a similar opinion of Chaplin. When he encountered the comedian in 1921, the writer tried to persuade the comedian to perform the role of Peter Pan in the first screen adaptation of the celebrated play.[91] Although Barrie finally decided on the Fokine-trained Betty Bronson for the 1924 film, Chaplin's diminutive stature, childlike impishness, and acrobatic alacrity would have suited him well as Peter, the boy who refused to grow up and instead sprouted fairy wings and escaped to Neverland. Chaplin did little to combat such assessments of his masculinity. Unlike his best friend, Douglas Fairbanks, whose brawn and swashbuckling heroism made him a box office sex symbol, the actor proudly embraced his boyish effeminacy and deployed it to very different filmic ends.

Whether in private or on the movie set, Chaplin danced his way into the hearts of millions and into cinematic history. As I have tried to illustrate, his consistent deployment of dance sequences in films like *The Floorwalker, Sunnyside*, and *The Gold Rush* functioned narratively to mark the Tramp as effeminate, unmanly, socially marginalized, queer. In showcasing his unconventional masculinity on film, Chaplin embodied what Marjorie Garber identifies as the inherent bisexuality of celebrity, where bisexuality signifies "gender-envy, gender crossover, cross-gender identification." According to Garber, "All great stars are bisexual in the performative mode. . . . Whether it is actualized in sexual relationships or remains on the level of elusive attraction, this heightened performative state, this state of being simultaneously all-desiring and all-desired, incarnates in the celebrity the two, sometimes apparently conflicting, definitions of bisexuality: having two genders in one body, and being sexually attracted to members of 'both' sexes."[92] The Tramp embodied both aspects of bisexuality, which explains his nearly universal appeal, a dramatic contrast to the criticism waged against the serious-minded and often questionably masculine performances of male ballet dancers like Nijinsky. "Not for the first time we can see that what is perverse in the private individual may be culturally valued in the celebrity. What is pathologized in the clinic is celebrated on the stage and at the box office," Garber acknowledges.[93] Chaplin was acutely aware of the performative potential of his petite body and harnessed its terpsichorean magic to produce some of the most sublime and comedic moments ever captured by a motion picture camera. In 1921 Wolfgang George Schleber, Pola Negri's lover at the time, asked the actor how the Tramp was born, and Chaplin responded, "Herr Schleber, if I was as tall and handsome as you, there never would have been a tramp. You see, there would have been no need to hide."[94] And, for that matter, no need to dance.

NOTES

1. Théophile Gautier, *Écrits sur la danse*, ed. Ivor Guest (Paris: Actes Sud, 1995), 31–32. Unless otherwise indicated, all translations are mine.

2. Arnold Haskell, *Balletomania* (London: Victor Gollancz, 1934), 299. On the history of the male ballet dancer and his virtual disappearance from the Western stage during the nineteenth century, see Ivor Guest, *The Romantic Ballet in Paris* (London: Dance Books, 1980), 20–22; Lynn Garafola, "The Travesty Dancer in Nineteenth-Century Ballet," in Leslie Ferris, ed., *Crossing the Stage: Controversies on Cross-Dressing*, (London: Routledge, 1993), 96–106; and Ramsay Burt, *The Male Dancer: Bodies, Spectacle, Sexualities* (London: Routledge, 1995), 10–30.

3. Burt, *The Male Dancer*, 12.

4. For two unremarkable exceptions see Arthur Knight, "Charlie Chaplin and the Dance," *Dance Magazine* 26, no. 5 (May 1925): 11–14; and Dan Kamin, *Charlie Chaplin's One-Man Show* (Methuchen, N.J.: Scarecrow, 1984), 75–92. In his exhaustive, highly acclaimed, 750-page biography of Chaplin, David Robinson concedes that the actor-filmmaker was a "brilliant if eccentric dancer" but does little to substantiate such a conclusion, either historically or

theoretically (Robinson, *Chaplin: His Life and Art* [New York: McGraw-Hill, 1985], 250).

5. Lee Edelman, *Homographesis: Essays in Gay Literary and Cultural Theory* (New York: Routledge, 1994), 164.

6. At least two biographers have attempted to explain Chaplin's screen persona by insinuating that, off screen, the actor was a practicing, if closeted, homosexual. See Gerith von Ulm, *Charlie Chaplin, King of Tragedy* (Caldwell, Id.: Caxton, 1940), 297; and Joyce Milton, *Tramp: The Life of Charlie Chaplin* (New York: HarperCollins, 1996), 181–82.

7. Édouard Ramond, *La Passion de Charlie Chaplin* (Paris: Librairie Baudinière, 1927), 195.

8. Eve Kosofsky Sedgwick, *Tendencies* (Durham, N.C.: Duke University Press, 1993), 8, emphasis in the original.

9. Extant film footage of Nijinsky dancing has yet to be found. However, rumors of its existence have circulated for years. Most recently, Peter Ostwald, citing a Russian source, claimed that a short film showing Nijinsky dancing at the Dalcroze Institute in Hellerau, Germany, in November 1912 was broadcast on Russian television in the late 1980s or early 1990s (Ostwald, *Vaslav Nijinsky: A Leap into Madness* [London: Robson, 1991], 139). Ostwald subsequently told me that this information was erroneous. For an overview of the mysterious history of Nijinsky's appearance on film, as well as the related history of him in still photography, see Daniel Gesmer, "Nijinsky and Film," *Ballet Review* 27, no. 1 (spring 1999): 77–84; Gesmer, "Re-Visioning Vaslav," *Ballet Review* 28, no. 1 (spring 2000): 82–94; and Lynn Garafola, "Dance, Film, and the Ballets Russes," *Dance Research* 16, no. 1 (summer 1998): 3–25. Florent Fels bemoaned the failure to capture Nijinsky on film (Fels, "Danseurs russes," *L'Art vivant*, no. 183 [April 1934]: 169). In her biography of her husband, Romola Nijinsky wrote: "He believed that in time it would be possible to photograph dancing; but he also believed that special dances must be composed for motion-pictures. He said that even the acting must differ from that of the theatre. He and Diaghileff had often discussed the possibilities of motion-pictures which Vaslav claimed as the future form of entertainment, which could eventually be developed into a fine art" (Romola Nijinsky, *Nijinsky* [1934; reprint, New York: Pocket Books, 1972], 282–83). In his diary, Nijinsky acknowledged: "I am familiar with cinema. I wanted to work with cinema, but I realized its significance. . . . Diaghilev often said to me that something like cinema had to be invented because its power was great. Bakst, a well-known artist and a Russian Jew, used to say that cinema was good from the money point of view" (Joan Acocella, ed., *The Diary of Vaslav Nijinsky*, trans. Kyril Fitzlyon [New York: Farrar, Straus and Giroux, 1999], 107).

10. Pierre Leprohon, *Charles Chaplin* (1935; reprint, Paris: Librairie Séguier, 1988), 142.

11. "Chaplin's 'Floorwalker' Breaks All Picture Records," *Variety* 42, no. 12 (May 19, 1916): 24.

12. Robinson, *Chaplin*, 170. On tandem work and mirroring devices in vaudeville dance routines, see Barbara Stratyner, *Ned Wayburn and the Dance Routine: From Vaudeville to the Ziegfeld Follies*, Studies in Dance History, no. 13 (n.p.: Society of Dance History Scholars, 1996), 46–47.

13. A similarly pregnant scene of male–male physical intimacy transpires between Chaplin and the cross-eyed comic Ben Turpin in *His New Job* (released February 1, 1915). Waiting outside a casting director's office, they sit in adjoining chairs. In an attempt to relax, Turpin throws his leg over the arm of Chaplin's chair and pulls out a cigarette. Offended by the smell of Turpin's foot, Chaplin gets angry and pushes his neighbor's leg away. The angry men bring their faces close together as if ready for a showdown when Chaplin suddenly snatches Turpin's cigarette with his mouth. This quick, unexpected gesture echoes the kiss between the Tramp and the floorwalker.

14. On homosexuality and other sexual pathologies among tramps, see [Josiah Flynt Willard], "Homosexuality among Tramps" in Havelock Ellis, *Sexual Inversion* in vol. 2 of *Studies in the Psychology of Sex* (1896; reprint, New York: Random House, 1942), 359–67; and Nels Anderson, *The Hobo: The Sociology of the Homeless Man* (Chicago: University of Chicago Press, 1923), 137–49.

15. From the moment they were introduced at the turn of the century, movie theaters were cruising grounds in the urban landscape where men of all sexual persuasions engaged in a variety of anonymous homosexual behavior in the safety and excitement of darkness. See George Chauncey, *Gay New York: Gender, Urban Culture, and the Making of the Gay Male World, 1890–1940* (New York: Basic, 1994), 194–95; Kevin White, *The First Sexual Revolution: The Emergence of Male Heterosexuality in Modern America* (New York: New York University Press, 1993), 95; and Willy [Henry Gauthier-Villars], *Le Troisième sexe* (Paris: Paris-Éditions, 1927), 165–71. On the general moral dangers of movies and movie theaters during this period, see Lary May, *Screening Out the Past: The Birth of Mass Culture and the Motion Picture Industry* (Chicago: University of Chicago Press, 1980), 37–59.

16. During the 1911 North American tour of the music hall sketch "A Night in a London Club," in which Chaplin played an inebriate, a Canadian critic presciently noted that "off the stage, with the paint washed off and garbed in civilized attire, he [Chaplin] looks quite harmless and even goodlooking. In fact, he might almost pass for a floor-walker in a department store" ("Only Drinks When Playing 'Drunk,'" *Winnipeg Tribune*, September 8, 1911, microfiche 1 ["1896–1913"], Margaret Herrick Library of the Academy of Motion Picture Arts and Sciences, Beverly Hills, California).

17. Theodore Huff, *Charlie Chaplin* (New York: Henry Schuman, 1951), 112.

18. Ramond, *La Passion de Charlie Chaplin*, 68.

19. Henry Jenkins and Kristine Brunovska Karnick, "Acting Funny," in Henry Jenkins and Kristine Brunovska Karnick, eds., *Classical Hollywood Comedy* (New York: Routledge, 1995), 152–53, emphasis in the original. On the influence of vaudeville aesthetics on early cinema, see Henry Jenkins, *What Made Pistachio Nuts? Early Sound Comedy and the Vaudeville Aesthetic* (New York: Columbia University Press, 1992).

20. Yeats posed this question in his poem "Among School Children." See William Butler Yeats, *The Poems* (New York: Macmillan, 1983), 215–16. On Yeats's interest in dance as a poetic trope, see Terri A. Mester, *Movement and*

Modernism: Yeats, Eliot, Lawrence, Williams, and Early Twentieth-Century Dance (Fayetteville: University of Arkansas Press, 1997), 27–65.

21. Louis Delluc, *Charlot* (Paris: Maurice de Brunoff, 1921), 44. Around the turn of the century in Geneva, Émile Jaques-Dalcroze invented a method, known as "eurythmics," for relating music to bodily movement that greatly influenced the development of modern European dance choreography during the 1910s. See Émile Jaques-Dalcroze, *Rhythm, Music, and Education* (1921; reprint, London: Dalcroze Society, 1980).

22. Havelock Ellis, *The Dance of Life* (Boston: Houghton Mifflin, 1923), 43–44. The most popular of Ellis's books, this text went through seven printings in the first six months of publication. See Phyllis Grosskurth, *Havelock Ellis: A Biography* (New York: New York University Press, 1985), 314–19.

23. Philippe Soupault, *Terpsichore* (Paris: Émile Hazan, 1928), 93–94.

24. See Ann Wagner, *Adversaries of Dance: From the Puritans to the Present* (Urbana: University of Illinois Press, 1997); and Kathy Peiss, *Cheap Amusements: Working Women and Leisure in Turn-of-the-Century New York* (Philadelphia: Temple University Press, 1986), 88–114.

25. On the term *fairy*, see Chauncey, *Gay New York*, 13–16. Surviving outtakes from *Behind the Screen* (released November 13, 1916) include a dance scene during which the Tramp and five big, buxom, unkempt cleaning women parody Mack Sennett's Bathing Beauties. The Tramp and the cleaning ladies notice a group of four long-haired lovelies on a movie set dancing à la Isadora Duncan. As the director finishes shooting, the Tramp leads his sidekicks onto the set and directs them in a hilarious ballet during which he plays the principal dancer and the women perform as the corps de ballet. These outtakes are reproduced in the documentary *Unknown Chaplin: My Happiest Years*, prod. and dir. Kevin Brownlow and David Gill, Thames Television, 1983, videocassette.

26. Cross-dressing was perhaps the most common socially restricted practice performed on the vaudeville stage at the turn of the century. Robert Toll and Marybeth Hamilton persuasively argue that this potentially controversial form of entertainment possessed a broad-based middle-class appeal precisely because it did not overtly transgress traditional bourgeois sexual norms. See Toll, *On with the Show* (New York: Oxford University Press, 1976), and Hamilton, " 'I'm the Queen of the Bitches': Female Impersonation and Mae West's *Pleasure Man*," in Ferris, ed., *Crossing the Stage*, 107–19. Also see Laurence Senelick, "Lady and the Tramp: Drag Differentials in the Progressive Era," in *Gender in Performance: The Presentation of Difference in the Performing Arts* (Hanover, N.H.: University Press of New England, 1992), 26–45. In the late 1910s Chaplin met and befriended Julian Eltinge, the most successful male cross-dresser in the U.S. entertainment industry, who arrived in Hollywood in 1917 to make movies. See Robinson, *Chaplin*, 191; and Kenneth S. Lynn, *Charlie Chaplin and His Times* (New York: Simon and Schuster, 1997), 182–83.

27. Edna Purviance was Chaplin's leading lady from 1915 to 1923 as well as his lover until 1917. Critics applauded her acting abilities, but she did not possess a distinct screen persona like the Tramp.

28. We learn near the end of the film that the Tramp's romantic interest is

Jewish; he visits her home where her father sits in a living room chair, wearing a yarmulke and reading a Hebrew newspaper.

29. The horns on Chaplin's head may also be interpreted as a burlesque on the age-old, anti-Semitic canard that Jews played a role in the crucifixion of Jesus and therefore were heathens, a reading supported by the Tramp's romantic interest in the Jewess.

30. Delluc, *Charlot*, 14.

31. Huff, *Charlie Chaplin*, 110.

32. Élie Faure, *The Art of Cineplastics*, trans. Walter Pach (Boston: Four Seas, 1923), 52–53.

33. Leprohon, *Charles Chaplin*, 77; and Ramond, *La Passion de Charlie Chaplin*, 82.

34. On the history of ballet in France, see Guest, *Romantic Ballet*; Guest, *The Empire Ballet* (London: Society for Theatre Research, 1962); and Guest, *The Ballet of the Second Empire* (Middletown, Conn.: Wesleyan University Press, 1974).

35. Chaplin added a soundtrack to the film in 1942 for its re-release, and this dance turn synchronized seamlessly with "The Oceana Roll." Robinson (*Chaplin*, 354) notes that in the 1918 film *The Cook*, Chaplin's friend and colleague, Roscoe "Fatty" Arbuckle, performed the same gag, which he may have learned from Chaplin. Edward Manson, who worked for Chaplin as a publicist during the 1920s, recalled that the "Dance of the Rolls" was "one of the Chaplin pet pastimes and he would cut this caper anywhere there was an audience, entertaining his guests at dinner, in restaurants he has performed to an audience of one individual, appreciative waiter" (Manson, "Charlie Chaplin Secrets," ca. 1964, typescript, p. 65, Special Collections, Herrick Library).

36. Nijinksy, *The Diary of Vaslav Nijinsky*, 237.

37. Jean Prévost, "Essai sur Charlot," *Le Navire d'argent* 2, no. 8 (January 1, 1926): 460.

38. Ramond, *La Passion de Charlie Chaplin*, 206–7.

39. Cocteau is quoted in Harold Acton, *Memoirs of an Aesthete* (1948; reprint, London: Hamish Hamilton, 1984), 178.

40. Georges Saverne, "L'Art de faire rire," *Filma: Revue cinématographique*, no. 55 (November 1–15, 1919): 6; and Jean Galtier-Boissière, "Charlot," *Le Crapouillot*, special issue (March 1, 1920): 13.

41. Faure is quoted in *Le Disque vert*, nos. 4–5 (1924): 28.

42. Stanley W. Todd, "The Real Charlie Chaplin," *Motion Picture Classic* 3, no. 1 (September 1916): 42, 44.

43. Delluc, *Charlot*, 10.

44. Ottoline Morrell, *Memoirs of Lady Ottoline Morrell: A Study in Friendship, 1873–1915*, ed. Robert Gathorne-Hardy (New York: Knopf, 1964), 215, 231.

45. Jacques-Émile Blanche, *Portraits of a Lifetime*, ed. and trans. Walter Clement (New York: Coward-McCann, 1938), 262.

46. For an eyewitness account of Chaplin's presence at this performance, see Otheman Stevens, "Ballet Russe Overwhelming," *Los Angeles Examiner*, December 26, 1916, sec. 1, p. 8.

47. Nijinsky, *Nijinsky*, 304. Romola Nijinksy reports that Chaplin expressed interest in making a film with Nijinsky (305).

48. Charlie Chaplin, *My Autobiography* (New York: Simon and Schuster, 1964), 192. A few years later Chaplin met and befriended Anna Pavlova, who came to Hollywood to make movies. A photograph of them appears in the comedian's autobiography.

49. Lydia Sokolova, a principal ballerina with the Ballets Russes during its U.S. tour, also recalled the visit to Chaplin's studio (Sokolova, *Dancing for Diaghilev*, ed. Richard Buckle [London: Murray, 1960], 93).

50. Chaplin, *My Autobiography*, 192. Nijinsky spoke rudimentary French and Chaplin did not speak the language at all, thus "*balletique*." In his retrospective account of the event Chaplin misidentified *The Cure*, (released April 16, 1917) as the film under production when Nijinsky visited his studio. Similarly, he erroneously remembered meeting Diaghilev, who in fact did not travel with the Ballets Russes on its second U.S. tour. Diaghilev, permanently jaded after Nijinsky left him to marry Romola, recounted a slightly different story regarding the meeting between Chaplin and Nijinsky. In an interview conducted in 1929 but not published until fifty years later, he attested: "[W]hen in Los Angeles, the whole motion picture world, of course, came to see our performances. Charlie Chaplin, who is a great admirer of the ballet, was there. He was already almost as celebrated as he is today and when our troupe was being photographed he put his arm through Nijinsky's. The latter seemed restless and, after the photographers had finished, he said to me: 'He is a dreadful fellow, this Chaplin. He does not intend to miss any opportunity to attract attention to himself.' Poor Nijinsky thought he himself was the greatest genius in the world! Charlie Chaplin was a mere nobody by comparison" ("Around the World with the Russian Ballet," *Dance Magazine* 53, no. 9 [September 1979]: 52).

51. The inscription along the bottom of the photograph reads: "Yours Truly/Charlie Chaplin/To Mr. R. H. Herndon." Richard Herndon was the company manager of the Ballets Russes during its U.S. tour.

52. Robinson, *Chaplin*, 28.

53. Charles J. McGuirk, "Chaplinitis," *Motion Picture Magazine* 10, no. 7 (August 1915): 85.

54. Ibid.

55. Fields is quoted in Carlotta Monti and Cy Rice, *W. C. Fields and Me* (Englewood Cliffs, N.J.: Prentice-Hall, 1971), 67; and Lita Grey Chaplin and Morton Cooper, *My Life with Chaplin* (New York: Bernard Geis, 1966), 159. In his first film, *Pool Sharks* (1915), Fields modeled his performance on Chaplin, and in later silent films he sported a Chaplinesque mustache. See Simon Louvish, *Man on the Flying Trapeze: The Life and Times of W. C. Fields* (New York: Norton, 1997), 186–90.

56. Igor Stravinsky and Robert Craft, *Memories and Commentaries* (London: Faber and Faber, 1981), 109.

57. Cocteau envisioned both the Horse and the Little American Girl in *Parade* as possessing characteristics reminiscent of Chaplin. See Jean Cocteau, "La Collaboration de 'Parade,'" *Nord-Sud: Revue littéraire*, nos. 4–5 (June–July 1917): 29–31.

58. Charles Chaplin, "Funny Business," *New York Sun*, November 12, 1916, p. 3.

59. Esther Hoffmann, "'How I Make Millions Laugh': Charles Chaplin," *Milwaukee Journal*, March 28, 1915, sec. 2, p. 2; Langford Reed, *The Chronicles of Charlie Chaplin* (New York: Cassell, ca. 1917), vi; E. V. Whitcomb, "Charlie Chaplin," *Photoplay Magazine* 7, no. 3 (February 1915): 35; and Fred Hamlin, "Charlie Chaplin, Tired, Turns to Simple Life," *Toledo Blade*, October 28, 1921, p. 1.

60. In this balletic pose Chaplin also resembled Nijinsky. Bronislava Nijinska, the dancer's sister and herself a member of the Ballets Russes, noted: "Even when holding a pose, Vaslav's body never stopped dancing" (Nijinska, *Early Memoirs*, ed. and trans. Irina Nijinska and Jean Rawlinson, intro. Anna Kisselgoff [New York: Holt, Reinhart and Winston, 1981], 294).

61. Edward H. Smith, "Charlie Chaplin's Million-Dollar Walk," *McClure's Magazine* 47, no. 3 (July 1916): 26.

62. Benjamin de Casseres, "The Hamlet-Like Nature of Charlie Chaplin," *New York Times Book Review and Magazine*, December 12, 1920, sec. 3, p. 5; and "Charley Chaplin Waltz 1916's Newest Novelty! Here's Way to Dance It," *Milwaukee Journal*, January 16, 1916, p. 10.

63. The lyrics are quoted in Robinson, *Chaplin*, 153.

64. Archie Gottler and Edgar Leslie, "Those Charlie Chaplin Feet" (New York: Maurice Abrahams Music Co., 1915).

65. Robinson, *Chaplin*, 152–53; and Lynn, *Charlie Chaplin and His Times*, 14–15.

66. See Lewis A. Erenberg, *Steppin' Out: New York Nightlife and the Transformation of American Culture, 1890–1930* (Westport, Conn.: Greenwood, 1981); Russel B. Nye, "Saturday Night at the Paradise Ballroom: Or, Dance Halls in the Twenties," *Journal of Popular Culture* 7, no. 1 (summer 1973): 14–21; Peiss, *Cheap Amusements*, 80–105.

67. See Sally Banes, *Dancing Women: Female Bodies on Stage* (London: Routledge, 1998), 66–93; and Mark Franko, *Dancing Modernism/Performing Politics* (Bloomington: Indiana University Press, 1995), 1–24.

68. See Barbara Naomi Cohen, "Ballet's Satire in the Early Broadway Revue," *Dance Scope* 3, nos. 2–3 (spring 1979): 44–50; and Stratyner, *Ned Wayburn*, 1–72.

69. Irene Castle and Vernon Castle, *Modern Dancing* (New York: Harper, 1914), 164.

70. Gaylyn Studlar, "Douglas Fairbanks: Thief of the Ballets Russes," in Ellen W. Goellner and Jacqueline Shea Murphy, eds., *Bodies of the Text: Dance and Theory, Literature as Dance* (New Brunswick, N.J.: Rutgers University Press, 1995), 107–8; and Elizabeth Kendall, *Where She Danced* (New York: Knopf, 1979), 134–49. For a list of American films from the silent period that included dance and dancers, see David L. Parker and Esther Siegel, eds., *Guide to Dance in Film* (Detroit, Mich.: Gale Research, 1978).

71. Studlar, "Douglas Fairbanks," 107.

72. Ingram is quoted in Kendall, *Where She Danced*, 142.

73. "A Dance Mappe [*sic*] of These United States: Culture Made Pleasant," *The Dance* 6, no. 6 (October 1926): 24.

74. Albert Lewin, "Dynamic Motion Pictures," *Shadowland* 9, no. 2 (October 1923): 46.

75. Ibid.

76. Ibid.

77. Léger first canonized the Tramp as a harbinger of the avant-garde in a series of four highly typographical drawings created to illustrate *Die Chapliniade*, a long *Kinodichtung*, or *poème cinématographique*, as it was subtitled, written by Ivan Goll and published in 1920 (Dresden: Rudolf Kaemmerer). The first French edition of the poem appeared as "La Chapliniade: ou Charlot poète; poème drame film" in *La Vie des lettres* 7, no. 5 (July 1921): 534–51. Like Léger, Chaplin explored the relationship between dancing and mechanical assembly-line production in *Modern Times* (released February 5, 1936). This politically charged satire of mass production directly contradicted Léger's wholesale embrace of this capitalistic process. The scenes in *Ballet mécanique*, which show Léger's marionette images of Chaplin, are outtakes from an unrealized film project entitled *Charlot Cubiste*. See Judi Freeman, "Bridging Purism and Surrealism: The Origins and Production of Fernand Léger's *Ballet mécanique*," in Rudolf E. Kuenzli, ed., *Dada and Surrealism* (Cambridge, Mass.: MIT Press, 1996), 28–45; and *Fernand Léger et le spectacle*, exhibition catalogue (Paris: Réunion des musées nationaux, 1995).

78. J. E. Crawford Flitch, *Modern Dancing and Dancers* (Philadelphia: Lippincott, 1912), 216.

79. Ted Shawn and Gray Poole, *One Thousand and One Night Stands* (1960; reprint, New York: Da Capo, 1979), 11, emphasis in the original.

80. F[rederick] J[ames] S[mith], "A Defence of the Male Dancer," *New York Dramatic Mirror* 75, no. 1951 (May 13, 1916): 19.

81. Edward L. Bernays, *Biography of an Idea: Memoirs of a Public Relations Counsel* (New York: Simon and Schuster, 1965), 103.

82. I am glossing the ideas of Judith Butler in *Gender Trouble: Feminism and the Subversion of Identity* (New York: Routledge, 1990). For a particularly poetic queer reading of Nijinsky's stage personae and his gay following, see Kevin Kopelson, *The Queer Afterlife of Vaslav Nijinsky* (Stanford, Calif.: Stanford University Press, 1997).

83. Cyril W. Beaumont, *Bookseller at the Ballet: Memoirs, 1891 to 1929* (London: Beaumont, 1975), 134, emphasis in the original.

84. Mary Pickford, "Daily Talks: Personalities I Have Met, Charlie Chaplin," *Buffalo Enquirer*, August 1, 1916, p. 5. Chaplin probably was filming *A Busy Day* (released May 7, 1914), in which he played an angry unrefined woman. In his memoir Harcourt Algeranoff, an English-born ballet dancer who toured with Pavlova's dance company and partnered her on several occasions, describes Pavlova's imitation of the comedian. In August 1921, while in Liverpool on a six-week tour of Great Britain, the ballerina and her troupe were warming up on stage when she suddenly began jigging around the stage in her tutu, impersonating the Tramp's gait, swinging an invisible cane, tipping a nonexistent bowler,

and sending everyone into fits of laughter (Algeranoff, *My Years with Pavlova* [London: Heinemann, 1957], 17).

85. Clare Sheridan, *My American Diary* (New York: Boni and Liveright, 1922), 347. Around 1930, during the filming of *City Lights* (released January 30, 1931), Winston Churchill, Sheridan's uncle, visited Chaplin's studio. Unable to put his guest at ease, Chaplin, dressed in all white, broke into a short ballet consisting of delicate arm gestures and several entrechats. The cigar-smoking Churchill and five other men looked on and laughed. Film footage of this episode, housed in Chaplin's private archive, appears in Brownlow and Gill's *Unknown Chaplin*. Valentino, who began his career as a tango dancer, also impersonated Nijinsky in *L'Après-midi d'un faune* for a 1921 series of photographs taken by Helen MacGregor in collaboration with Valentino's second wife, Natacha Rambova, who performed with Theodore Kosloff's dance company in the late 1910s. At least one image from the series was published in a movie magazine. See *Shadowland* 8, no. 6 (August 1923): 50; and Michael Morris, *Madam Valentino: The Many Lives of Natacha Rambova* (New York: Abbeville, 1991), 102–4.

86. Pola Negri, *Memoirs of a Star* (Garden City, N.Y.: Doubleday, 1970), 215.

87. Louise Brooks, "Charlie Chaplin Remembered," *Film Culture*, no. 40 (spring 1966): 6. Years later Brooks acknowledged her artistic debt to Chaplin, characterizing his screen persona as balletic: "I learned to act by watching Martha Graham dance, and I learned to dance by watching Charlie Chaplin act." Brooks is quoted in Barry Paris, *Louise Brooks* (New York: Knopf, 1989), 110. I thank Eric Concklin for bringing this reference to my attention.

88. May Reeves, *Charlie Chaplin Intime*, ed. Claire Goll (Paris: Gallimard, 1935), 11–12.

89. Gloria Swanson, *Swanson on Swanson* (New York: Random House, 1980), 40. Concerning Swanson, Chaplin wrote: "I couldn't get a reaction out of her. She was so unsatisfactory that I gave up and dismissed her. Gloria Swanson years later told me that she was the girl and that, having dramatic aspirations and hating slapstick comedy, she had been deliberately uncooperative." See Chaplin, *My Autobiography*, 166. Swanson later won acclaim for her screen impersonation of Chaplin in *Manhandled* (1924) and for her impersonation of that impersonation in *Sunset Boulevard* (1950).

90. Thomas Burke, *City of Encounters: A London Divertissement* (Boston: Little Brown, 1932), 135.

91. Charlie Chaplin, *My Trip Abroad* (New York: Harper, 1922), 86. On the queer tenor of *Peter Pan*, see Marjorie Garber, *Vested Interests: Cross-Dressing and Cultural Anxiety* (New York: Routledge, 1992), 165–85.

92. Marjorie Garber, *Vice Versa: Bisexuality and the Eroticism of Everyday Life* (New York: Simon and Schuster, 1995), 140.

93. Ibid., 142.

94. Negri, *Memoirs of a Star*, 180.

2

Alchemic Visions and Technological Advances: Sexual Morphology in Loie Fuller's Dance

Julie Townsend

Et ainsi s'achève sa légende.
Elle fut errante toute sa vie.
Elle ne pouvait se fixer nulle part.
[And thus her legend comes to a close.
She was errant all her life.
No where could she settle herself.
(author's translation)]
—*Yvon Novy*

In 1916 and after, Loie Fuller's company performed several permutations of the *Dance of the Great Opal*. In a magical scene, a visitor watches the nymphlike inhabitants form what Giovanni Lista describes as an "enormous jewel" of ballooning fabric, illuminated in a "suggestive way" from the inside; at once a crystallized jewel and a mutable form, this paradoxical image of solidity and fluidity is typical of Fuller's stage spectacles. The nymphs disappear inside the luminous formation as a princess looks on "filled with wonder."[1] "Strange scene," remarks Lista in his 1994 biography of Fuller. Although the scene may have appeared strange, the image of a jewel occurs frequently in descriptions of Fuller's work. The construction of an illusion that defies the morphology of objects and bodies by using theatrical prosthesis and technology is emblematic of Fuller's work.

In the 1890s, Fuller's performances in Paris disrupted and reconstructed nineteenth-century notions of dance and the limits of the body. Female sexual imagery and lesbian eroticism appear frequently in her work and the iconography inspired by it. Com-

bining knowledge of Fuller's performance, her sexual relationships with women, and representations of her as eternally feminine, acknowledged lesbian, or monstrous man-woman, I will
trace patterns of sexual identity through her performance and its
reception.[2] On the one hand, this is an historical inquiry into the
representation of sexuality in the context of dance performance
and the ways in which these spectacular images entered into literary and visual media; on the other hand, this essay is a theoretical
inquiry into the use of technology as a tool for reconceptualizing
the body and into the ways in which Fuller's artistic production
might contribute to a contemporary theorizing of lesbian and
queer sexuality.[3]

The immense body of images and texts surrounding Fuller's
dances maps a complex and contradictory site of performance,
sexuality, and technology at the turn of the twentieth century.
Her work gives rise to several questions: What are the implications of a dynamic representation of morphology in the context
of late nineteenth-century gender structures? To what extent did
Fuller's work have implications for the performer's experience of
the body as well as for representations of it? How does Fuller
combine femininity and technology to reconstruct the female
body as at once feminine and denaturalized? Is this female body,
with its transformative potential, coded as a lesbian body in
Fuller's work? If so, was that lesbian body readable by some of her
spectators? And how does the deliteralizing of femininity through
the use of metaphor function as a strategy for locating, or perhaps
relocating, desire?

I will approach these questions using a variety of texts and images from the turn of the century, including Fuller's autobiography, excerpts from reviews of her work, and some symbolist
texts on dance. Although some historians and theorists of dance,
sexuality, and performance have noted that Fuller acknowledged
her lesbianism and have inquired into the implications of her
work for the development of modern dance, none has developed a thorough reading of the connection between her lesbian
identity and her work as an artist. I argue that these two aspects
of Fuller are inextricably linked. Fuller's career spanned more

than thirty years, from the 1890s into the 1920s, and her aesthetic development parallels an evolution in the representation of sexuality. Beginning with the invention of Fuller's early dances and her advances in theatrical technology, continuing with her lover's writings about her work, then comparing those to Stéphane Mallarmé and Paul Valéry's writings on dance, and finally turning to Fuller's experimental film *Le Lys de la vie*, I explore what Yvon Novy, a French journalist, described as Fuller's "un-fixable errancy" and what might be identified as the queer aesthetic in her work.

In the 1880s Fuller began her career as an actor in New York. Particularly notable are her cross-dressing performances as Tom in *Little Tom Shepard* (1886, New York) and as Aladdin in *One Thousand and One Nights* (1887, New York). The figure of Aladdin would become an important metaphor for her later work, as she described her signature costume as the seed from which an "Aladdin's lamp would spring" for her benefit.[4] Fuller invented her *Serpentine Dance* during a rehearsal of *Dr. Quack* (1891, Boston and later New York). She was to perform as a patient in a trance who is following the suggestions of a hypnotist. She dug up a dress made of voluminous white material that surrounded her and that had been sent to her from an admirer in India. The robe "was entirely suitable for the hypnotism scene, which we did not take very seriously. . . . I endeavored to make myself as light as possible, in order to give the impression of a fluttering figure obedient to the doctor's orders. . . . At last, transfixed in a state of ecstasy, I let myself drop at his feet, completely enveloped in a cloud of light material."[5] Although Fuller may not have taken this scene seriously, for the modern theorist the idea that dance expresses hypnotic experience carries weighty implications for the conceptualization of the unconscious and its relation to the body and the ways in which representation might illuminate and transform desire.[6]

Beyond the scope of this particular performance, Fuller's invention was both a personal and an artistic revelation. In her autobiography she describes experimenting in her bedroom with this new costume and the dance it became:

> The mirror was placed just opposite the windows. The long yellow curtains were drawn and through them the sun shed into the room an amber light, which enveloped me completely and illumined my gown, giving a translucent effect. Golden reflections played in the folds of the sparkling silk, and in this light my body was vaguely revealed in shadowy contour. This was a moment of intense emotion. Unconsciously I realized that I was in the presence of a great discovery, one which was destined to open the path which I have since followed. Gently, almost religiously, I set the silk in motion, and I saw that I had obtained undulations of a character heretofore unknown. I had created a new dance. Why had I never thought of it before?[7]

The light takes on an independence and becomes the catalyst of Fuller's experience as well as the image she sees in the mirror; it is the light that envelops her and plays in the folds. From a place not consciously known to Fuller comes the "presence of a great discovery"; she locates its source both in her mind and in the sunlight. Fuller realizes her dance is a coincidence of the outside light, her own unrecognized thoughts, and her movement. She acts only at the end of the passage, and her motion combines the disparate elements into a dance. Fuller's sensual synthesis of light, her body, and the ability to create links artistic creation to the language of sexual self-discovery.

Fuller's early dances in the 1890s were a spectacle unlike any seen before. Her revolutionary costumes surrounded her entire body with mobile fabric, and her pioneer work in the use of electric rather than gas lights created prismatic effects on the stage. Rejecting story lines and traditional scenery, Fuller typically performed a series of short dances: *The Serpentine*, *The Butterfly*, and *The Violet* (all 1892), to name a few. These object-based dances removed the thing (serpent, butterfly, or flower) from any recognizable scenario or story line. The performance metaphorically conjured the image of these objects and animals but removed them from any narrative reference. Her bodily motions were hidden from view and she faced the audience only for her bow. Developing a motif, often accompanied by a waltz, Fuller would typically begin her performance in darkness and then project light

Loie Fuller in *L'Archange*. Fuller's innovative costumes often included prosthetic arms that contributed to her representation of the body as a site of metamorphosis. (Dance Division, New York Public Library for the Performing Arts, Astor, Lenox, and Tilden Foundations; used with permission)

from various positions to illuminate the fabrics that surrounded her. Some performances included colored lights projected alternately from different directions or placed on moving pedestals to produce mobility; in some instances she danced surrounded by mirrors or on a box with a clear top so that light could be projected from beneath her.

Not only did she decontextualize the object of her dance but her movements posed a problem for the definition of dance. Early theorists challenged Fuller's status as a dancer. J. E. Crawford Flicht wrote, "We do not know if this invention of Loie Fuller is a matter of dance in the proper sense of the term. The serpentine dance has no steps, gestures or poses. . . . She does not answer to any of the typical criteria by which we can judge a dance."[8]

Radically different from any other theater or dance performances, Fuller's act instantly found imitators in the United States and in Europe. She made attempts to patent her dances, but such efforts failed because her performances were not based in narrative. The judge proclaimed: "It is essential for such a composition to recount a story. The plot can be simple. It could be only a narration or a representation of a single event, but it must affirm or mime an action, story, emotion, passion or character, real or imaginary."[9] Fuller's work did not, according to the judge, fit these criteria. Her innovations in dance sent her beyond the available interpretations and definitions. No one seemed capable of defining her performance with any of the available categories. This ruling, perhaps more than writings or images of her work, reflects the disruptive and groundbreaking aspects of Fuller's work. Stonewalled by the limitations of the legal system, Fuller used protections as best she could within the confines of a system that could not recognize her work as a describable entity. She opted instead for patents of her costumes and lighting designs. Although she may have experienced these legal problems as obstacles, undefinability became precisely the most fascinating aspect of her work and the one that would establish an aesthetic break from earlier dance forms. Fuller's technological effects, the effacement of her body, and the impersonality of her performance prefigures modernist concerns with the decentered or impersonal subject, mechanization, and antinarrative strategies. Her rejection of narrative and her focus on the ideal of a mutable image became influential in symbolist circles, to modernist writers, and for avant-garde filmmakers such as Réné Clair.[10]

Unable to launch a dancing career in the United States, Fuller went to Europe—a move followed by many early modern dancers, such as Isadora Duncan and Ruth St. Denis—where venues and audiences were more open to her performances. After a series of disappointments Fuller made a smashing debut in 1892 at the Folies-Bergère in Paris. Her *Serpentine*, *Butterfly*, and *Lily* dances became the rage of Paris as she pioneered a new art form that revolutionized dance in its opposition to both classical ballet and the cabarets where she performed. As Rhonda Garelick observes: "Fuller never relied upon the motif of heterosexual seduction traditionally present in cabaret dance, especially in the popular North African and 'Oriental' style dances that dominated cabaret stages in Paris at the turn of the century."[11] These cabaret shows often included striptease and *danseuses nues* (nude dancers), either in romantic scenarios or as staged titillation for heterosexual men in the audience.[12] Until Fuller's act, the Folies-Bergère was considered exclusively men's entertainment. Fuller's performances opened the door of the Folies-Bergère for a new audience of women and children and were also attended by the most well-known artists and scientists of the period: Sarah Bernhardt, Stéphane Mallarmé, Auguste Rodin, Toulouse-Lautrec, the Flammarions, and Marie Curie, to name but a few.

The costumes and lighting of Fuller's performances were not only central but in fact an integral part of the image she produced. In a venue of striptease Fuller's dance did not exist without her all-encompassing costume. Beneath her costume Fuller used bamboo extensions for her arms. The costume was designed to close around the neck and to hang over the extensions, like a circle skirt that began at the neck rather than at the waist. When Fuller lifted her arms, the fabric, held by the arm extensions, reached far above her head. By turning or even wavering slightly, she would produce ripples and undulations in the fabric, and a movement under one area of the costume would resonate throughout the mass of

Loie Fuller, 1901. Fuller's use of light and reflective material on the stage created ethereal and prismatic effects. (Photograph by Falk; Dance Division, New York Public Library for the Performing Arts, Astor, Lenox, and Tilden Foundations; used with permission)

fabric. Added to this were Fuller's innovations in theater lighting. By projecting light from a variety of angles and even sometimes from a mobile base, Fuller was able to emphasize portions of her costume and play with shadow and reflection. The only scenery she used in her early dances was meant to further the effects of reflected light; for instance, in one set she hung crystals above her, and the reflections of the crystals created the appearance of tiny silver specks all around her dancing figure. Mirrors were another of Fuller's techniques for amplifying reflection. Although she performed alone in these early dances, the use of mirrors would sometimes multiply her image. The elements of costume and light were not simply an enhancement of the stage image, but they in fact constituted Fuller's dance. She performed a transmutation by means of covering and extending the limits of her body and illuminating that altered morphology.

Fuller made the dancing body into a three-dimensional screen that transforms itself through contact with movement and light.

Loie Fuller (Photograph by Langfier; Dance Division, New York Public Library for the Performing Arts, Astor, Lenox, and Tilden Foundations; used with permission)

She did this by projecting first white light, then colored light and images from all angles around her body and even from below it. Fuller's body became the screen rather than an image projected onto it. Her creation of an altered body prefigured the interests of avant-garde filmmakers—such as Réné Clair and Fernand Léger—in bending, cutting, speeding up, and slowing down movement. Fuller created the illusion of an impossibility: she disembodied herself through her own bodily movements. Rather than a concrete and defined entity, the body became a vehicle for its own dissolution. Fuller created a hallucination of infinite mutability and transformability through technology, which led journalists to name her the "modern Salomé."[13]

Like many of the dancers of the period, Fuller worked with orientalist themes and images, particularly the biblical story of Salome. She eschewed the already popular versions of Salome by a decadent author, including *A Rebours* (J.-K. Huysmans, 1884), on which Oscar Wilde based his *Salome* (1894).[14] Instead Fuller asked artist Georges-Antoine Rochegrosse to work with her on a new production. Rhonda Garelick notes that instead of using revealing costumes, "her veil dances relied . . . on technology, lights, and elaborate stage machinery of her own invention."[15] Fuller's *Salomé* opened at the Comédie-Parisienne in 1895. Changing the popular narrative of Salome as the bloodthirsty femme fatale, Fuller focused instead on a chaste Salome caught in a power play between her mother and stepfather, Herodiade and Herod. Instead of situating the protagonist in a traditional narrative, Fuller constructed her Salome around a series of tableau-type dances. Fuller included in her autobiography Jules Claretie's description of her 1907 *Tragedy of Salome* that he wrote for *Le Temps*:

> Fuller will show several new dances there: the dance of pearls, in which she entwines herself in strings of pearls taken from the coffin of Herodiade; the snake dance, which she performs in the midst of a wild incantation; the dance of steel, the dance of silver, and the dance of fright, which causes her to flee, panic-stricken, from the sight of John's decapitated head persistently following her and surveying her with martyred eyes. . . . Loie Fuller has made studies in a special laboratory of all the effects of light that transform the stage. . . . She has succeeded . . . in giving the actual appearance of the storm, a glimpse of the moonbeams cast upon the waves, of the horror of a sea of blood. . . . The light in a weird way changes the appearance of the picturesque country.[16]

Claretie's list of dances separated by semicolons mirrors Fuller's tableaulike performance, focusing on the idea of a series of dances rather than on a seamless narrative. As she did in earlier productions, she used scenery to create an atmosphere rather than to add realistic touches. In Fuller's distinctive version Salome dances for John the Baptist, imploring him to protect her from Herod's lascivious desires. Herod orders John's decapitation in a fit of jealousy. Salome attempts to save John by offering herself to Herod, but her efforts fail. Finally, she falls to the ground dead, as if struck by lightning.[17] This version decenters the heterosexual narrative of the myth and replaces it with Salome's strategy to escape the patriarchal structure. Whether this version is feminist, as Lista argues in his biography of Fuller, seems questionable: Salome becomes a victim rather than a perpetrator of violence. Her flight is squashed as Herod ensnares her again in his power scheme by killing the only person who can help her flee. The performance relied heavily on colored lights and the use of color symbolism to connote the narrative. Individual dances from this series became part of Fuller's repertoire, and she performed them out of the context of a full-length performance.

In his reading of Fuller's costume and performances Lista argues that she sought to hide or even efface her body behind her all-encompassing fabric, but this reading contributes to a desexualization of Fuller and her work. Fuller was not afraid to appear nude on stage, albeit behind an illuminated screen, in one of her performances of Salome, and when she was a guest at the home of the queen of Romania, Fuller asked that her bed be surrounded by mirrors. Rather than simply seeing Fuller's costumes as an attempt to hide her body, reading the imagery created by them might be more productive. During Fuller's time critics and spectators seem to have two distinct readings of her performance image: some portrayed her as a chaste ethereal spirit, and others saw her image as erotically invested. The iconography surrounding Fuller is varied in its representation of her as chaste angel, conjuring sorceress, and childish imp; notably, whether pure or demonic, each representation makes her "unavailable" to the male heterosexual viewer.

Her experience and representation of her body as transformative could instead be read as a strategy with lesbian implications. The images she created by her flowing veils express a phantasmic experience of the body—as motion, as sexuality, as metamorphoses. Sue-Ellen Case argues that lesbian identity in theater may present itself as an effacement of gender: "Ironically . . . one way of escaping gender is to so disguise erotic and sexual experience as to suppress any representation of its specificity."[18] By constructing her self as Other (insect, serpent, butterfly, etc.), Fuller removed herself from the realm of gender altogether. She highlighted the separation between her body and the limits of gender construction by questioning the relationship between the biological and the cultural through a masking of human-ness and a creation of the body as full of transformative potential.

What appears as an effacement of gender also exposes a moving, changing female sex. Fuller's costume is easily read as the folds and contours of labia. But is the suggestion or even the flagrant exposition of labial and vaginal imagery necessarily lesbian? Of course not. In fact, both Fuller's anatomical suggestion and her somewhat asexual "becoming" of insects, flowers, or patterns leave theorists at an interpretive impasse. Did some journalists and writers represent Fuller as an ideal of purity as an alibi for the sudden presence and acceptability of women and children at the Folies-Bergère? Was this a way to cover Fuller's acknowledged lesbian sexuality with yet another layer of fabric? The iconography that Fuller inspired reveals this split between a sexualized and an asexual representation of her work. Although certain aspects of the dances coincided with bourgeois modesty around women's bodies, this does not mean that Fuller's aesthetic did not also question and disrupt those values. Her masking contrasted the flesh revealed by the *danseuses nues*, but on a more complex iconographic level Fuller may have exposed the genitalia that the *danseuses nues* were forbidden by law to show on stage. I would therefore read Fuller's earlier dances as experiments in the configurations and reconfigurations of sexual morphology—a kind of searching for, or re-searching of, an artistic identity that had implications for sexual identity.

In 1899 Fuller began a lifelong relationship with her lover and collaborator Gabrielle Sorère: "I knew Gab for at least two years before it entered into my head that she was fond of me. . . . Only a supernatural personality, it seemed, would ever be able to understand her."[19] Years later Sorère wrote the following to Fuller: "I never see you as you are but as you appeared to me that day."[20] Even in the intimacy of a friendship and love affair, Fuller's identity could not be separated from her artistic production. Key in Sorère's statement is the verb *appear*. As Terry Castle has written in her book *The Apparitional Lesbian*, literary history shows lesbian love being told through ghostly apparitions, and Fuller's work participates iconographically in that history. Her upbringing was filled with late nineteenth-century spiritualism, and she maintained a deep interest in the problem of representing the spirit within the confines of the body. Certainly, her movement, costumes, and lighting all emphasized the possibility of changing form, of suddenly disappearing, and, interestingly, of changing from one type of spirit to another. The following lines, written by a fourteen-year-old Sorère after seeing Fuller perform for the first time, give us a glimpse of how a lesbian spectator might read Fuller's performance. Most telling is Sorère's response to Fuller's fire dance: "A crackling flame is kindled. It turns, twists and glows. . . . In the midst of the tumult, licked by torrent of foaming fire, a mask, also a strange flame, is outlined in the reddish air. The flames die into a single flame, which grows to immensity. You might think that human thought were rending itself in the darkness."[21] The implications of Fuller's performance for the thoughts of the spectator are key to reading Sorère's prose. Her words slip easily into the experience of passion, the kindling of a flame, its tongue licking, twisting, and finally these tongues becoming one immense entity. Sorère's identification of her own thoughts in Fuller's motion would be structurally repeated in symbolist readings of Fuller, although the content would differ.

In her autobiography Fuller reveals her relationship with Sorère as intertwined with a common artistic vision: "I wonder if her friendship, so well founded and positive, is not intimately mingled with the love of form, of colour and of light, which I interpreted synthetically before her eyes when I appeared before her for the first time."[22] Certainly, for Fuller and Sorère collaboration and creation had direct implications for their sexual relationship. This brings to light the ways that Fuller's performance and its technological transformations became the foundation for a way of viewing and of being that reconfigures gender and sexuality by altering the way we see—or do not see—Fuller's body in motion. Although Fuller emphasizes Sorère's response to her work in *Fifteen Years of a Dancer's Life*, the intellectual reader of Fuller's work would be more familiar with Stéphane Mallarmé's essay "Ballets," in *Crayonné au théâtre*, published in the *National Observer* in 1893 and then in *La Revue Franco-Americaine* in 1895. Fuller's use of light and fabric attracted the eye of Mallarmé, father of the symbolist poetry movement. He emphasized the image of Fuller in diaphanous white gauze and constructed a de-sexualized vision of her dance; for him her performance enacted the ideal of dance as "*écriture corporelle*" (corporeal writing).[23] What Mallarmé saw as the genderless impersonal ideal of poetry provides a contrast with the erotic image that Sorère saw.

For Mallarmé, Fuller became an emblem for the definition of poetry in the symbolist movement. His essays on the relationship between poetics and dance reveal parallels between Fuller's aesthetics of non-narrative image transformation and his work on poetry that would ideally reveal the nudity of ideas through language. For the purposes of a gender-based reading, Mallarmé's passage gives us a window into the possibility of Fuller's early performances as an escape from gender constraints. The often-cited phrase, *[la danseuse] n'est pas une femme . . . elle ne danse pas* (the female dancer is not a woman . . . she does not dance) breaks down the word *danseuse* (woman dancer) into its two elements and then claims that she is neither a woman nor does she dance.[24] This statement reconfigures both the idea of dance and the idea of woman. The act of dance in Mallarmé becomes linguistic rather than corporeal and performs a genderless impersonal body. In this reading, dance becomes an inversion of the performative speech-act: rather than a phrase that performs an action, Fuller's act performed a linguistic configuration.[25]

For Mallarmé, the dancer's "impersonality," figured by her use of the veil—or in Fuller's case, her costume—is the key to her performance of objects (for example, flowers).[26] For Mallarmé, this image is simultaneously literal and ideal; this ensemble is manifested in the veil, the screen that masks the body and suggests the nudity that lies behind it. That final veil, which literally covers her sex and metaphorically replaces her body, obscures the dancer so that she becomes the dance itself.[27] The veil, which both hides and suggests the possibility of her nudity, produces the potential for conceptual revelation in the spectator. This screen, like a veil, allows for a projection of the spectator's concepts and vision onto the figure of the dancer, but in this instance the dance is also a veil that reveals poetry. Her performance carries the spectator to a revelatory state through slippage and confusion of the apparently disparate elements of body, sign, dance, and spectator; a moment of clarity emerges as the sign becomes transparent and reveals or spills the viewer's secret from behind the veil. This secret, the spectator's imagined unity of the dancer and the thing she becomes, is situated in the impersonality of the dancer—"between her female appearance and the mimed object," Mallarmé wrote.[28]

In her essay "Stéphane Mallarmé, Loie Fuller, and the Theater of Femininity," Felicia McCarron explains that in Mallarmé's configuration, "Fuller is both signifier and signified. . . . The dance itself is also both a content and the act of producing that content."[29] But what makes this illusion effective is that it is a momentary fiction in the imagination of the spectator. Fuller's dancing screen is the signifier that produces the momentary illusion of being the thing itself. Mallarmé suggests that the veil, hiding the moving body, allows this illusion, but constantly pulling against and counterbalancing this illusion is the material existence of the dancer's body. In other words, the dancer covers her gendered body and her technical apparatus to become something other than what she would seem to be. The spectator believes for a moment that the dancer is not a woman but is instead the thing she performs: she is both a woman and not a woman. By radically redefining the notion of her body, Fuller becomes something outside the available system of gender. Although this illusion is only temporary, might it have implications for the configuration of femininity? Doesn't it imply that femininity is an illusion, a mask worn and an image performed?

Mallarmé's construction illustrates a coincidence between Fuller's masking and transformation. If her costumes and lighting might be read as a strategy to reconstruct her female morphology into an unrecognizable Other, Mallarmé's construction might be a window into the structure of Fuller's strategy of questioning and escaping gender constructions through dance. Fuller's performance seems to give Mallarmé access to a heretofore inaccessible consciousness. The idea is present in the mind but inaccessible except through the sensory experience of watching Fuller perform.

Valéry's response and revision of Mallarmé's poetics of dance radically reinscribe and illuminate the gender implications that lie behind the curtain of Mallarmé's essay. Valéry approaches the dancer from the direction of the thing, not accidentally a jellyfish, which in French is *méduse*. Valéry collapses the idea of the jellyfish and the figure of Medusa by capitalizing *méduse* in the following passage:

> Not women, but beings of an incomparable substance, translucent and sensitive, flesh of glass madly irritable, domes of floating silk, hyaline crowns, long lively strips all cut with rapid waves, fringe and gathers that fold and unfold . . . which deform and take flight . . . the ideal of mobility . . . not solid, either, in their bodies of elastic crystal. . . . Never a danseuse, human, heated woman, drunk with movement . . . of the presence of ardent looks charged with desire, has expressed the imperious offer of the sex, the mimicked call of the need to prostitute, like this large *Méduse*, who . . . with a strange and immodest insistence, transforms into a dream of Eros; and suddenly . . . her dress of cut lips, turns over and exposes itself, furiously open.[30]

Disengaging the dance from any intention, it becomes a transparent veil that must then be invested by the spectator. The "danseuse," broken down to be precisely a dancer and a woman, is neither; instead, Valéry proposes that the Méduse is a danseuse. In the paragraph describing the jellyfish, Valéry uses terms that connote Fuller's movement and costumes: the folding and unfolding, the undulating movement of transparent silk, the appearance of weightlessness, and the use of strips of fabric that alternately catch and elude the rays of light—all are shared by the "*Méduse*" and Fuller's early dances. However, Valéry insists that he is not speaking of women who dance. His prose alternates between what the *Méduse* is and what the dancer is not: "no woman" and "never a human dancer." The image of the jellyfish emphasizes the effacement of the body by fabrics and the use of lighting, and the jellyfish appears to consist of nothing but the translucent fluid of its phantomlike form. Particularly revealing are the images "flesh of glass" and "elastic crystal," which invoke the fluid jewel, a single entity that embodies paradox—which is neither the components of its makeup nor the sum of its parts. The tension between the static and the fluid is a repeated theme in Valéry, and the jellyfish provides an example of that which appears to be crystallized in its translucidity and reflection of light but is undulatory and flows through its own crystalline forms.

For Mallarmé, the dance functions as a metaphor for the poem. To elaborate Mallarmé's illustration of poetry through dance and go even further into the realm of the impersonal, Valéry illustrates the dance through the *Méduse* and locates all subjectivity in the spectator. However, Valéry's distant and objective description of the *Méduse* as an "ideal of mobility" reinscribes gender as it transforms into an impassioned erotic dream of feminine sexuality as viewed by desiring eyes in a dream of Eros: a heated woman, drunk in movement, in the presence of desiring eyes, offering her imperious sex in a call for prostitution. This dream, however, turns into a nightmare of cut lips, furiously open; the danseuse becomes a Medusa's head, severed from the body, exposing the female sex. Rather than remaining, as Mallarmé does, in the position of philosopher at the moment of revelation, Valéry, in a particularly uncharacteristic moment, exposes his horror at the spectacle. As the *Méduse* exposes itself, Valéry's dream is exposed to him and he in turn exposes the gender implications of this reading.

The image of the chaste ethereal feminine body seen by many poets and artists in Fuller's image is never far from collapsing into the paralyzing figure of Medusa, who exposes her unwieldy sex. Doing and undoing the codes of feminine purity and sexual difference, Fuller exposes the contours of an Other sex—one that provokes a fascinated panic in Valéry. But how does one reconcile this image with Sorère's erotic vision of a collaboration between her as a lesbian spectator and Fuller as performer? What can we assume about Fuller's spectatorship? What may seem an attractive vision of chastity slips into the image of castration, as in Freud's configuration, both exciting and horrifying the spectator. But this same image appears to the lesbian viewer as Cixous's laughing Medusa, the sex that writes itself and is beautiful.[31]

Although much of the symbolist discussion of dance is arguably neither about dance nor about gender, the terms of these writings rely heavily on the veiling and unveiling of gender structures that illuminate the representation of women's bodies, femininity, and sexuality. The secret of Mallarmé's danseuse and the unveiling that exposes the sex of Valéry's *Méduse* reveal the ways in which female sexuality, although masked, is essential to the workings of Fuller's aesthetic. Although her costumes may have given her a means by which to cover and transform herself into an ungendered figure, they may also have been a vehicle for reconfiguring a powerful sexualized identity that, through its rejection of gender structures, made available a previously unrepresentable sexuality. Valéry's moment of panic at the sight of the unwieldy sex might be an opening to the sexual implications of Fuller's performance.

In 1908 Fuller collected her students, all young women, into an official dance school that performed worldwide.[32] At this point in her career Fuller reentered the world of narrative; however, her early explorations led her to approach narrative from a position that questioned the stories traditionally portrayed in nineteenth-century full-length ballets. Although her early work may have exposed a vision of eroticism based in a new representation of women's sexuality, these dances would be more properly identified as "feministic theatre" than as lesbian.[33] But as Fuller began to develop a company and produce full-length performances, she turned back to narrative and developed an interest in imaginary worlds filled with fantastic beings. This allowed her to combine her technological skills with an exploration of spaces and figures that are not subject to the limitations of daily life. Her students often performed as sylphs, fairies, and spirits. These worlds were also exclusively female; her troupe was comprised solely of women and girls. Her performances used images from classical Greek— nymphs and bacchantes as well as witches and fairies from fairy tales. Nineteenth-century classical ballet also used such figures, but Fuller's depictions relied more on technological effects and avoided the heterosexual narratives on which classical ballets were usually based. Debussy's "L'Après-midi d'un faune" (Afternoon of a Faun, 1895), inspired by Mallarmé's poem (1865), was one of Fuller's preferred compositions. No doubt she was familiar with the poem, which figures a lesbian scenario interrupted by a Pan-like intruder:

And there, entangled at my feet (cast down
By languor in the pain of being two)
Lie sleeping nymphs, at risk in their embrace.[34]

Even back to Euripides' *The Bacchae*, these images of ethereal women in scenes of nature are a site of both lesbian sexuality and violence.

Late in her career Fuller explored the darker side of those angelic images in ways that also used and reworked culturally stereotypical images of lesbian sexuality. She associated her technological illusions with sorcery and witchcraft. Fuller modernized age-old images of magical women with the technology of light, color, and projected images. Sorère writes of Fuller's staged magic: "Her firm, precise glance penetrates the soul of things even when they have none. The inanimate becomes animate, and thinks under her magical desire."[35] Gender and science combine to attribute "desire" to things (or, people) that heretofore had none. Fuller did not participate in the turn-of-the-century campy Paris lesbos scene; although she knew some of the women in that group, her aesthetics were quite different.[36] Rather than working with parody, Fuller's strategy seems to be that of a symbolic reworking with the aid of new technical developments of performance. Novy wrote: "There is nothing that is at once so simple and complex as the alchemy from which gushes such moments of beauty. Loie Fuller poisons in the real sense of the word, bending over mixtures in which the most dangerous ingredients are mixed for the purposes of a new richness of color which haunts her."[37] This portrayal of Fuller as a magical sorceress haunted by her own creations may mask the advanced technology that lay behind her work. However, it highlights her ability to create an illusion so effective that it poisons the viewer. Again, the lines between Fuller the person and Fuller the performer and producer blur. She is haunted by her own creations just as the viewer is poisoned by them. Representations of Fuller's creative process and performance often located her in the world of magic and figure her as a channeler of mystical art; ironically, the magic of Fuller's work stems from her technological advances.

Later in her life Fuller turned increasingly to projected images and film. *Le Lys de la vie* (The Lily of Life, 1921), first a ballet and then a film, was based on a short story by Queen Marie of Romania. This film is perhaps the most explicit development of the queer in Fuller's work. An interesting counterexample to her earlier work, the fairytale is complete with two competing princesses and a prince, love and disappointment, magical lands, and a voyage in search of the lily of life. Scenes and images peripheral to the overall narrative frequently disrupt the story. The film opens in a garden where women and girls in Greek costume dance. This idyllic scene is then interrupted as we enter into an orientalist castle with a king and two princesses. The interior of the castle is a site of wandering desire and a mixture of all variety of persona and paraphernalia. The cast of the film includes African servants dressed in ancient Egyptian costumes, a pet monkey and dog, and a dwarf. The set is constructed of animal skins, statues, and golden and semitransparent draperies. Trying to reproduce the never-never land of Queen Marie's tale, Fuller combined all variety of historical and orientalist trappings. News of a prince in search of a wife reaches the castle, and the princesses both fall in love with the prince, played by the young Réné Clair (then Réné Chomette).[38] Alongside this fairytale, the general atmosphere is one of flirtation and erotic tension: the princesses and the African servants exchange loaded glances, the monkey flirts with a dog and with the head of a bearskin rug, one princess caresses the head of a dwarf in her bedchamber, and a kiss between Princess Mora and the prince is mirrored with a parallel screen of two black children kissing. This scene was constructed by mounting two images side by side, thus splitting the screen vertically in two, with half showing the children bathed in blue light. Color was painted onto the film during editing to add to the magical effects.

When the prince falls ill, Corona, the rejected princess, goes in search of the mythical lily of life that will bring happiness. This journey comprises the second half of the film, which is too fragile to view. In it the princess goes on a fantastic journey filled with fairies and nymphs that both fascinate her and help her overcome obstacles, such as a bed of snakes through which she must pass. A version of the *Dance of the Great Opal* is included as one of the scenes observed by Corona. She eventually retrieves the lily, but, alas, it brings happiness to others. The prince recovers and continues to love Mora. Corona dies of love, but Fuller rewrites her death as a rebirth as she is resurrected by the fairies from her voyage and joins their mythical world. The film ends with the opening scene, emphasizing the circular and mythic nature of the narrative.[39]

Playing on ideas of the natural and the unnatural, *Le Lys de la vie* produces erotic tension between animals of different species, across race and class, between a princess and a dwarf, and even between children, who mirror the sexual encounters of adults. Corona's final transfiguration provides a rewriting of Fuller's Salome performance; rather than being struck down by the force of patriarchy as Salome was, Corona's body is brought back to life by the fairies that fascinated and seduced her during her journey. She is the figure that both enables the success of the heterosexual love narrative and displaces it with her own journey and transfiguration. In keeping with the representation of the lesbian world as ethereal and intangible, a lesbian reading requires a leap into the world of spirits. However, taking into account the ways that Fuller represents her relationship with Sorère in *Fifteen Years of a Dancer's Life*, I do not think that this is a fatalistic rendition of lesbian love; rather, Fuller's depiction of the concrete ways that imaginary worlds enter into interpersonal relationships implies that the fantasy is ultimately achievable. The disruptive narrative elements and free-floating sexual desires that appear throughout the film emphasize how that which is outside the linear narrative and constantly disrupts the romance takes precedence over the love story. While this errant desire that becomes its own image and refuses to be fixed may be the most fully developed example of the queer in Fuller's work, its antecedents appeared in her early work as the figure who performs her own fantasy by becoming animals, flowers, and spirits.

In Fuller's aesthetic, desire, like the body, is a living, moving screen onto which any image can be projected. The story line developed in *Le Lys de la vie* can be read with her transformative theater aesthetic as a kind of mass production of queer desire insofar as it can change form at any moment, has no heterolinear goal, and seeks to escape the constraints of narrative and the limitations of physics. Through her use of technology, in costume design, lighting, and film, Fuller disrupted limitations on women's bodies and reconfigured categories of art. Although she is rarely recognized in the work of current theorists of lesbian art, Fuller's performances provide a representational precursor to women performance artists and filmmakers through intersections of technology, gender, and sexuality. At a time when women's bodies were constrained by corsets, Fuller's representations provided a vision of her body as the site of uncategorizable transformation. Responses to her work by journalists and writers reveal ways that this new vision was seen alternately as enshrining Victorian femininity and as radically overturning that limiting category. Similarly, her aesthetic redefined classical ballet's notions of dance as a well-defined and categorized system, thus providing the foundation for modern dancers such as Isadora Duncan. Fuller's costumes may have covered her body, but they are also the image of a female sex that is stimulated by Fuller's movements and that in turn caresses and envelops her body. If social restrictions on the possibilities of "body" failed to meet Fuller's needs, she managed to create a form that could not be classified—that was outside language, uncategorizable—initially, not even labeled as dance.

NOTES

1. Giovanni Lista, *Loie Fuller: Danseuse de la Belle Époque* (Paris: Stock-Editions d'Art Somogy, 1994), 529, my translation.

2. The subtle and not-so-subtle mockery of Fuller's sexual identity was often connected to her image as a dancer. Cocteau represented Fuller in her stage costume but with the face of a large, mustachioed man, and the Cirque d'Hiver performed a parody of Fuller's work in which three men donned costumes similar to hers and performed. Lista argues, and I would agree, that these images reference Fuller's sexual identity.

3. I use *technology* here in a variety of senses: scientific technology and research—particularly on color and light—were central to Fuller's aesthetic; but also, as Theresa de Lauretis has explored in *Technology and Gender* (Bloomington: Indiana University Press, 1987), gender itself is a category of technology insofar as gender, like sex and sexuality, was discursively and legally defined in the disciplines of sexology, psychology, and the law. More specifically, I argue that Fuller's experiments in lighting design and costume construction constitute an inquiry into the ways that technology might transform our experience of the human body and destabilize the relationship between sex, gender, and sexuality.

Clearly the use of *queer* in this context requires some clarification: *queer* has emerged in the context of political action as a response to the problematic of identity politics; in addition—and certainly related—*queer* has become a category of critical inquiry into the structures of gender, sexuality, and desire. My use of *queer* develops from specific images and narrative configurations that Fuller developed late in her career.

4. Loie Fuller, *Fifteen Years of a Dancer's Life* (Boston: Small, Maynard, 1913), 28.

5. Ibid., 28–31.

6. For an analysis of the *Dr. Quack* scene, see Debora Silverman's *Art Nouveau in Fin de Siècle France: Politics, Psychology, and Style* (Berkeley: University of California Press, 1989), 299–300.

7. Fuller, *Fifteen Years*, 33.

8. J. E. Crawford Flicht, *Modern Dancing and Dancers* (Philadelphia: Lippincott, 1912), 86–87, translation mine.

9. Lista, *Loie Fuller*, 105.

10. Clair worked with Fuller on her film *Le Lys de la vie* (1921); many of Fuller's aesthetic concerns can be seen in Clair's *Entre'acte* (1924).

11. Rhonda Garelick, "Electric Salomé: Loie Fuller at the Exposition Universelle of 1900," in J. Ellen Gainor, ed., *Imperialism and Theater: Essays on World Theater, Drama, and Performance* (New York: Routledge, 1995), 85.

12. *Danseuse nue* is somewhat misleading because these dancers were forbidden from dancing entirely nude; they were required to hide their genitals with a *cache-sexe*, which is something like a G-string.

13. Garelick, "Electric Salomé," 86.

14. J.-K. Huysmans, *A Rebours* (Paris: Éditions Gallimard, 1977); Oscar Wilde, *Salome* (London: Faber and Faber, 1989). I am using "decadent" aesthetics here in reference to theorists such as Eugenio Donato in *The Script of Decadence: Essays on the Fictions of Flaubert and the Poetics of Romanticism* (New York: Oxford University Press, 1993).

15. Garelick, "Electric Salomé," 86.

16. Fuller, *Fifteen Years*, 282–83.

17. Lista, *Loie Fuller*, 224.

18. Sue-Ellen Case, ed., *Performing Feminisms: Feminist Critical Theory and Theater* (Baltimore, Md.: John Hopkins University Press, 1990), 23.

19. Fuller, *Fifteen Years*, 251.

20. Ibid., 266.

21. Terry Castle, *The Apparitional Lesbian* (New York: Columbia University Press, 1993); Fuller, *Fifteen Years*, 263–64.

22. Fuller, *Fifteen Years*, 266.

23. Stéphane Mallarmé, *Oeuvres complètes* (Paris: Gallimard, 1945), 304.

24. Ibid.

25. It might be interesting to explore this concept with Judith Butler's work on gender as performative in *Gender Trouble: Feminism and the Subversion of Identity* (New York: Routledge, 1990).

26. Mallarmé, *Oeuvres complètes*, 298.

27. This parallels Yeats's configuration: "How can we know the dancer from

the dance?" (William Butler Yeats, *Selected Poems and Three Plays*, ed. M. L. Rosenthal [New York: Collier, 1986], 123).

28. Mallarmé, *Oeuvres complètes*, 296.

29. Felicia McCarron, "The Theater of Femininity," in Ellen W. Goellner and Jacqueline Shea Murphy, eds., *Bodies of the Text: Dance as Theory, Literature as Dance* (New Brunswick, N.J.: Rutgers University Press, 1995), 219.

30. "Point des femmes, mais des êtres d'une substance incomparable, translucide et sensible, chairs de verre follement irritables, dômes de soie flottante, couronnes hyalines, longues lanières vives toutes coutues d'ondes rapides, fringues et fronces qu'elles plissent, déplissent . . . se déforment, s'envolent . . . l'idéal de la mobilité. . . . Point de solides, non plus, dans leur corps de cristal elastique. . . . Jamais une danseuse humaine, femme échauffée, ivre de mouvement . . . de la présence ardente de regards chargés de désir, n'exprima l'offrande impérieuse du sexe, l'appel mimique du besoin de prostitution, comme cette grande Méduse, qui . . . avec une étrange et impudique insistance, se transforme en songe d'Eros; et tout à coup . . . ses robes de lèvres découpés, se renverse et s'expose, furieusement ouverte" (Paul Valéry, *Oeuvres*, ed. Jean Hytier [Paris: Gallimard, ca. 1957–60], 1173, my translation).

31. These images of Medusa are developed in Sigmund Freud, "Medusa's Head," in *Sexuality and the Psychology of Love* (New York: Collier Books, 1963), 212–13, and Hélène Cixous, "The Laugh of the Medusa," in Robyn R. Warhol and Diane Price Herndl, eds., *Feminisms* (New Brunswick, N.J.: Rutgers University Press, 1991), 334–49.

32. In *Paris Was Yesterday*, a collection of Janet Flanner's writings for the *New Yorker*, Flanner notes that Fuller's dancers were on a high salary whether they were performing or not and that each was guaranteed an inheritance in the event of Fuller's death (Flanner, *Paris Was Yesterday*, ed. Irving Drutman [New York: Viking, 1972], 36).

33. Claretie, cited in Fuller, *Fifteen Years*, 282.

34. Mallarmé's "L'Après-midi d'un faune" was one of a variety of heterosexual male poems and novels (Baudelaire, Loüys, etc.) that treated the subject of lesbian sexuality in the late nineteenth century. The original French reads: . . . quand, à mes pieds, s'entrejoignent (meurtries / De la langueur goûtée à ce mal d'être deux) / Des dormeuses parme leurs seuls bras hasardeux (From Mary Ann Caws, ed., *Stéphane Mallarmé: Selected Poetry and Prose* [New York: New Directions, 1982], 36).

35. Quoted in Fuller, *Fifteen Years*, 265.

36. Fuller's autobiography describes a passionate friendship with the actress Sarah Bernhardt that ends in a bitter falling out. For more on the Paris lesbos scene, see Emily Apter, "Acting Out Orientalism: Sapphic Theatricality in Turn-of-the-Century Paris," in Elin Diamond, ed., *Performance and Cultural Politics* (New York: Routledge, 1996), 15–34.

37. Yvon Novy, press clippings, Collection Rondel, Bibliothéque de l'Arsenal, Paris.

38. Clair later worked with images of dance in his film *Entre'acte* (1924) and was clearly influenced by Fuller's aesthetic.

39. Details of the second half of the film come from Lista, *Loie Fuller*.

3
Nijinsky's Golden Slave

Kevin Kopelson

The Golden Slave in *Schéhérazade* (1910) was Vaslav Nijinsky's fourth such role. He'd been the Mulatto Slave in *Le Roi Candaule* (1906) and the Favorite Slave in both *Le Pavillon d'Armide* (1909) and *Cléopâtre* (1909). People noticed the pattern. "How odd it is that Nijinsky should always be the *slave* in your ballets," Walter Nouvel told Sergey Diaghilev, "I hope one day you'll emancipate him."[1] They also noticed that *Schéhérazade* was the first time Nijinsky died on stage. Or, rather, the first time he'd been killed—slain, along with all but one of the other revelers, by the Sultan's janissaries. (The Sultana, danced by Ida Rubinstein, a notorious Salomé, kills herself.) The death of the Golden Slave, however, is no mere death. It's a tragic early gay death and as such, like Salomé's *Liebestod*—in the play by Wilde, if not the opera Strauss based upon the play—has distinctly heteroerotic, homoerotic, and homophobic overtones. To cite an erotic-minded and death-driven enthusiast, "[Nijinsky] put such beauty into [his death] that we became amorous of death."[2] To a phobic-minded and life-affirming critic, "he has to be punished . . . for being the erotic subject of the (male) spectator's gaze."[3]

But how does the death of the Golden Slave in *Schéhérazade*, a total artwork, signify synaesthetically? To what extent are these overtones musical (aural)? To what extext are they decorative (visual)? To what extent are they narrative (diegetic)? And to what extent are they gestural (kinetic)?

To Lincoln Kirstein, an erotic-minded and synaesthetic critic, the love portion of Nijinsky's *Liebestod* was fundamentally musical: "In *Schéhérazade*, Nijinsky moved in three dimensions, muscle against lurid color on top of heavy-breathing orchestration."[4]

To Edwin Denby, a like-minded critic, "The 'Slavic harmonies' of Rimsky's score dunked the orgy on stage in a bath of gold."[5] To Harold Acton, a phobic-minded enthusiast, the death portion was fundamentally musical. "To me, [*Schéhérazade*] was one of the most memorable of Diaghileff's ballets: the heavy calm before the storm in the harem: the thunder and lightning of negroes in rose and amber; the fierce orgy of clamorous caresses; the final panic and bloody retribution: death in long-drawn spasms to piercing violins."[6] The two orgy references are accurate. Diaghilev had renamed and reprogrammed the final section of Rimsky-Korsakov's symphonic suite, "Festival at Baghdad: The Sea," as "Orgy: Slaughter." Acton's reference to piercing violins, however, is somewhat misplaced insofar as it is Rubinstein, not Nijinsky, who dies with strings attached. The Golden Slave dies just after brass blare; the Sultana dies while the concertmaster plays her leitmotif one last time. The misplacement is nonetheless understandable. Not only, as we will see, do the Sultana and her Golden Slave share certain characteristics, the tune blared by the brass is a reduction of that leitmotif as well. What we hear, then, as the slave dies is the musical essence of his mistress.

Denby, "dazzled . . . by the sensual shock of [Leon Bakst's] brilliant décor," understood Nijinsky's *Liebestod* in visual terms too, a function of the fauvist color scheme Kirstein called lurid, associating it with his, Kirstein's, development of "preferences beyond . . . 'good taste,'" and of the orientalism Westerners find sexy.[7] To quote André Levinson who, insofar as *Schéhérazade* is more symbolist than naturalist and thus more or less extrapsychological, did appreciate the ballet: "This ardent and cruel magnificence of color, this effluvium of sensuality which emanates from the setting produces an action in which the very excess of passionate ecstasy can only be satiated by the spilling of blood."[8] But unlike the Mulatto Slave, the Golden Slave—for Parisians, if not Russians—was both primitive and oriental. In other words, if the Mulatto Slave seemed rather civilized to Diaghilev, reminding him of Pushkin, the Golden Slave seemed rather barbaric to Proust, or to Proust's compatriots, reminding them of full-blooded Africans.[9] To quote Glenn Watkins: "Noting the effect of the mise en scène upon those who were given to making hollow distinctions among the Russian ballets, Proust provided testimony of the natural tendency to fusion between Orientalism and Primitivism by observing that some were tempted to claim *Schéhérazade* as a kind of *art nègre*."[10] But if Proust himself never displayed that tendency to fusion, like Levinson he did appreciate the symbolic dimension of *Schéhérazade*'s orientalism. Or, rather, he appreciated its semisymbolic dimension. For if the ass Charlus thrusts outward seems "almost symbolic" to gays in the know, the one the Golden Slave thrusts upward, a description I'll soon clarify, seems so as well—although, unless every rectum is a grave, as Leo Bersani would have it, in a different sense of the symbolic.[11]

Most of us, however, find the narrative ended by "Orgy: Slaughter" remarkable. After all, tragic early death is always already literary, even when orchestrated or visualized. Tchaikovsky's *Romeo and Juliet*, for example, is based upon Shakespeare, and Michelangelo's *Pietà* is based upon Scripture. In *Schéhérazade* the Golden Slave is the last to be released from captivity (he springs to life from behind a third blue door), the only one to captivate the Sultana, the only one nearly to escape the janissaries, and the last one to be killed by them. The symbolism of this naturalist narrative, however, calls into question whether the Golden Slave is really captivated—either by being kept by the Sultana or killed by the Sultan. In other words, for anyone attuned to the symbolism, Nijinsky is a free agent, whatever his psychological motivation or final fate may be. Metaphysically speaking, he is the beleaguered individual who cannot be taken, the blithe spirit who embodies the license, including the sexual license, Westerners fantasize. Or, to quote Lynn Garafola, making the fusion Proust and Watkins deplore, "a primitive who from the moment he bolted onstage until the final spasm of his death exalted the fully liberated self and its inevitable clash with society"—a "fully actualized being" who, notwithstanding the naturalism Michel Fokine tried to attain, both "disavowed psychology" and "demarcated a psychic space where id transgressed and triumphed."[12] So is the Specter of the Rose, according to Garafola.

Needless to say, the meaning of Nijinsky's first performative death is generated by other such oppositional and primarily narrative differences. For example, in addition to signifying in between symbolic enfranchisement and naturalist disenfranchisement, a signification with little gay connotation, the Golden Slave also signifies, gayly, in between his spectacular entrance and equally spectacular exit. The entrance is a curiously immodest opening of a closet door—one Cyril Beaumont describes as "the kind of leap a tiger might make"—whereas the exit is a curiously immodest refusal to reenter the closet.[13] The Golden Slave also signifies in between savagery and civility, a semiotic situation anticipated by the Mulatto Slave and typical of Russia in general, for non-Russian orientalists, and of the Ballets Russes in particular. As Peter Wollen points out, the Diaghilev ensemble was "both 'ultra-natural' (wild, untamed, passionate, chaotic, animal) and 'ultra-artificial' (fantastic, androgynous, bejewelled, decorative, decadent)."[14] Which is to say that one of the things that makes Nijinsky, as the Golden Slave, gay makes him both balletic and Russian as well. All three orientations negotiate the ultranatural/ultra-artificial contradiction.

Another such contradiction is the oppositional difference of gender—the androgynous collapse of which Wollen mistakenly calls artificial.[15] Once again the Golden Slave signifies in between masculinity and femininity—a semiotic situation located in between *Schéhérazade* and other ballets Nijinsky starred in as well as within *Schéhérazade* itself. All the roles Nijinsky initiated while sexually involved with Diaghilev occupied both ends of the spectrum at once and thus tended to be read off one another.[16] As would also prove to be true of *Le Spectre de la rose* and *Petrushka*, *Schéhérazade*, with Nijinsky as the Golden Slave, cast him as an artistic genius—a masculine classification that, paradoxically, authorizes men to express typically feminine emotions. And as would prove to be true of the Faun, the role cast him at the other end of the homosapient spectrum: as an equally paradoxical animal. To quote Michael Moon, a critic given to hosting "Scheherazade parties" of his own: "Both subhuman and superhuman, [the Golden Slave] is simultaneously perceived as an effeminate cat and a tremendous stud, but not as 'masculine' in any ordinary sense."[17] Unless, of course, Beaumont, who describes the entrance as both feline and studly, is more on the mark. Then again, Beaumont is more likely to have denied the femininity of a performance he loved than is Moon, who unlike the Briton never saw Nijinsky live.

The androgyny of the Golden Slave and the meaning of his untimely demise are also located, narratologically, in relation to Nijinsky's previous slaves, their exits in particular.[18] Notwithstanding the manhandling or rape that I fantasize Diaghilev having fantasized in connection with the Mulatto Slave, and notwithstanding that he never seems to lay a hand on the Sultana, the Golden Slave is far more aggressive, virile, and thus masculine than his predecessors. Whereas Armida's Favorite Slave, that pearly apparition, acts like a perfect gentleman, and whereas Cleopatra's rarely goes near her, the Golden Slave, for all intents and purposes, actually enacts the male rape fantasy the Sultana's male librettists attribute to her.[19] To quote Acton again, the Sultana submits to his "clamorous caresses." To quote Carl Van Vechten, "This strange, curious, head-wagging, simian creature, scarce human, wriggled through the play, leaving a long streak of lust and terror in his wake. Never did Nijinsky as the Negro Slave touch the Sultana, but his subtle and sensuous fingers fluttered close to her flesh, clinging once or twice questioningly to a depending tassel."[20] To quote Kirstein, the slavery in *Schéhérazade* is, for the first time, "a lyric metaphor [spelling] ambiguous and provocative servility; ownership licensed willing or unwilling physical possession." And to quote Garafola: "The Golden Slave ravished rather than courted his mistress; flaunted rather than concealed his body; loosed rather than bridled his physical prowess. Sex incarnate, Fokine's exotic primitive did onstage what respectable men could only do in fantasy."[21] But even though he does not seem to touch her and even though he is aggressive, virile, and masculine, the Golden Slave, in yet another symbolic—or imaginary—dimension, does cross over, or pass, into the Sultana's feminine camp. Or, rather, into her femme-fatale and thus androgynous camp. In a bejeweled outfit more outrageous than the Favorite Slave's—the Golden Slave may not wear a skirt, but he does wear harem pants and a brassiere—and therefore more of a

Nijinsky in *Schéhérazade* (Dance Division, New York Public Library for the Performing Arts, Astor, Lenox, and Tilden Foundations; used with permission)

renunciation of the Great Masculine Renunciation (straight-laced dressing from which men have yet to recover), Nijinsky, like Rubinstein in both *Cléopâtre* and *Schéhérazade*, is Salomean. Both female captor (Rubinstein) and male captive (Nijinsky) represent phallic women, a figure typical of fin-de-siècle literature and visual art. Rubinstein, that is, subjects Nijinsky to her desire and he in turn subjects her to his—which may not be a bad prescription for the happily-ever-after these two cannot but should attain.

Within *Schéhérazade* itself, however, Nijinsky and Rubinstein do not exactly occupy the same gender position. When push comes to shove—which, given Fokine's hands-off approach, it never seems to do—Rubinstein is more of a femme fatale than Nijinsky.[22] This difference is a function of Rubinstein's biological sex, of course, but it is also a function of her unusual height, of the fact that she alone kills herself (suicide being a female malady in 1910), and of her tendency to sit still while Nijinsky runs around. The stasis/kinesis gender opposition is grounded in modern dance history. Whereas Isadora Duncan, contrary to popular belief, maintained the static orientation of classical ballet, Nijinsky emphasized its kinetic component.[23] But the opposition is not unique to dance history. As everyone in attendance must have known, and this is especially true of *Schéhérazade*'s Anglo-American audience, nice women—and neither the Sultana nor Rubinstein is very nice—were not supposed to move very much, or signify *jouissance*, during sexual intercourse.

Rubinstein, of course, gets to signify the Sultana's naughty *jouissance* otherwise. Her stasis, in fact, symbolizes antihomophobic resistance far more effectively than it symbolizes sexual repression. Nijinsky, leaping about like a maniac, simply is not "permitted to signal anything like Rubinstein's 'majestic' and overwhelming gesture of prolonged motionless resistance to the murderous violence that furiously manifests itself in the piece's last scene."[24] Yes, antihomophobic—even in the context of a heteroerotic orgy. Moon is more concerned with gay rehearsals of the final orgy—and with one performed by a friend named Mark in particular—than with the ballet itself:

I take the "Scheherazade party"—the conspicuous energies with which it is enacted as well as the phobic violence with which it is repressed, violence of either the explosive variety that Mark experienced or the corrosive kind that gradually disabled Nijinsky—as an emblematic expression of a perilously highly charged compromise, the energies of which both "sides" in the ongoing war for and against gay visibility, homophobic and homophile, have been effectively exploiting for most of this century."[25]

But setting aside Moon's problematic conflations—of Nijinsky and the Golden Slave, both disabled by homophobia, and therefore of homophobia and schizophrenia—and bracketing his important focus on gay rehearsals of *Schéhérazade*, it is nonetheless true that the eroticism of *Schéhérazade* itself is both homoerotic and heteroerotic, and the violence of the finale both homophobic and heterophobic. In this regard the ballet has as much in common with *Salomé* as it has with *Cléopâtre*, a more obvious pretext. The Sultana's homoerotic feelings for the Golden Slave correspond with Salomé's homoerotic feelings for Jokanaan as well as with Cleopatra's heteroerotic feelings for Amoun. The Sultan's homophobic murder of the Golden Slave corresponds with Herod's homophobic murder of Salomé as well as with Cleopatra's heterophobic murder of Amoun.

Given these internal differences— Rubinstein's majestic immobility as opposed to Nijinsky's manic flight in particular—it may surprise you that many gays, including Moon, think both the Golden Slave and the Sultana resist the Sultan's homophobic violence—indeed, think the Golden Slave alone, symbolically speaking, liberates himself from it even though he's the one who is killed and she's the one who takes her own life. What enables this counterintuitive and wish-fulfilling reading is Nijinsky's final gesture and the kinetic, or hyperkinetic, overtones it manages to produce. The gesture is tripartite. The Golden Slave, in closing, makes a spectacular leap (defying gravity), turns a series of somersaults (letting gravity do its thing), and then does something hard to describe and even harder to imagine. He ends his final somersault by spinning on and leaping off the back of his neck. Think of break dancing. The thrust, as noted in passing, is upward—gravity defying. The maneuver is dangerous—death defying. Think acrobatics.[26] And the beauty of this gravity-defying, death-defying, and thoroughly unballetic *Liebestod* is transcendent. Think *Tristan and Isolde*. To quote Van Vechten, "Pierced by the javelins of the Sultan's men, the Slave's death struggle might have been revolting and gruesome. Instead Nijinsky carried the eye rapidly upward with his tapering feet as they balanced for the briefest part of a second straight high in the air, only to fall inert with so brilliantly swift a movement that the aesthetic effect grappled successfully with the feeling of disgust which might have been aroused." Or, more to the point, to quote Francis de Miomandre: "The transport of his movements, the encircling giddiness, the dominance of his passion reached such heights that when the executioner's sword pierced him in the final tumult we no longer really knew whether he had succumbed to the avenging steel or to the unbearable violence of his joy in those three fierce somersaults."[27] To which there is little one can add, except that the phrase "the unbearable violence of his joy" may be the pithiest conflation of homophobia and homoeroticism ever uttered.

When I call the gesture gravity defying, I do not mean weightless. Unlike the flights of Nijinsky's Bluebird and Specter of the Rose, the weightlessness of the Golden Slave is challenged—indeed, tempered—by the downward thrust of the somersaults and by the steel of the scimitars. Oddly enough, it is *Schéhérazade*'s first straight reenactment—as opposed to its gay rehearsals, including Mark's—that tricks us into conceiving the Golden Slave, or at least into conceiving one of his reincarnations, to be weightless. In other words, it has us reimagine gay male flight, if not gay male prancing, as straight male flight. I'm referring to Douglas Fairbanks Sr., the athletic actor who in *The Thief of Baghdad* (1924) became an athletic dancer. "Watching him move" there, commented Mary Pickford, Fairbanks's wife, "was like watching the greatest of Russian dancers." In *Schéhérazade*, that is. The two texts, the film and the ballet, have similar scenic and costume design—although Fairbanks ditched the bra. And the two male leads have similar body language. As Gaylyn Studlar says, it is the orientalized and feminized body of Nijinsky, with its "grace, ges-

tural nuance, physical submission, and . . . polymorphously suggestive exhibitionism" that Fairbanks emulates in *The Thief of
Baghdad.*[28] Or, rather, it's the bearable lightness of the Golden
Slave's gay male being that he emulates—which for some reason
did not seem queer at the time. Fairbanks's gravity-defying style
of motion—bounding up stairs, bouncing through giant jars, and
in the end riding a magic carpet with the woman he loves, a far
cry from the conclusion of *Schéhérazade*—enabled his character
to scale his way into conventional masculinity and Fairbanks himself to become "the world's most famous filmic exponent of energetic, vital American masculinity."[29]

Of course, Fairbanks, in *The Thief of Baghdad*, is no sex slave.
He fails to scale the Dionysian heights of *Schéhérazade*—unprecedented heights that account for the ballet's popularity, including its gay popularity. Unprecedented in the world of dance,
that is, for who knows what went on in the privacy of late Victorian homes. Unlike the proper, measured farandole in *Sleeping
Beauty*, Fokine's bacchanals, beginning with *Schéhérazade*, "were
writhing masses of humanity, orgiastic round-dance responses to
symbolist 'communality' in a theater that united performer and
audience in dionysian ecstasy."[30] In other words, they answered
the Nietzschean call for Dionysian theater—with Ronald Fir-
bankian if not Douglas Fairbanksian consequences for queer individuals who contemplated the communal finale in the privacy
of their homes and publicity of their writing. Firbank himself, in
The Flower beneath the Foot (1923), put a campy spin on the Sultan's heteroerotic and therefore homosocial jealousy:

> "With whom," [Yousef] asked, "sweetheart, were you last danc-
> ing?"
> "Only the brother of one of the Queen's Maids, dear," Made-
> moiselle de Nazianzi replied. "After dinner, though," she tittered,
> "when he gets Arabian-Nighty, it's apt to annoy one a scrap!"
> "*Arabian-Nighty?*"
> "Oh, never mind!"
> "But (pardon me, dear) I do."
> "Don't be tiresome, Yousef! The night is too fine," she mur-
> mured, glancing absently away towards the hardly moving trees.[31]

Denby, in a review of an inferior revival, "wonders what *Schéhérazade* could have looked like when it scandalized our parents or when Parisians swooned at the lushness of [Nijinsky's bounding] about . . . like a panther in thrilling spasms that grew to a paroxysm of death at the climax." I'd like to think Denby had thrilling spasms of his own while pondering the lost production. Kirstein certainly did. He also had a seminal experience, communal rather than individual, that relates to the unconventional preferences he associates with his exposure in grammar school to *Schéhérazade*'s lurid decor. Kirstein, a young American in Fontainebleau, first learned to liberate his potential, to identify and act on personal goals, by "behaving as if something were true even if it wasn't," to push himself to "extreme situations," and to embrace the suffering necessary for growth when he witnessed a Fokine-like finale improvised by cult followers of Georgei Gurdjieff, the Armenian spiritualist:

> In one thunderous surge, the entire body of men and women went berserk, and racing, with a startling jump as from a catapult, the whole mass of bodies came hurtling straight at me. I was spared immediate annihilation only when a voice [Gurdjieff's] from the central pavillion yelled "STOP!" The amalgam of bodies froze. . . . The violent collective rush toward me, and the sourceless, shouted "STOP!" gave me a theatrical shudder to which no dance or drama that I had ever seen could compare. It seemed less of a game than a—what? An event? An inexplicable rite? A spectacle?[32]

Of course, Kirstein would have compared it with *Schéhérazade*, had he seen the ballet. And, who knows, maybe that—what? event? rite? spectacle?—would have precipitated the self-actualization later prompted by the Fontainebleau farandole. Nijinsky's Golden Slave, after all, did represent a fully actualized being whose role demarcated a psychic space where id transgressed and triumphed. And he too, even when slain, did behave as if something were true—as if he were liberated—even if it was not.

The joyous death of the Golden Slave, however, is not the last thing *Schéhérazade*'s audience, if not its imaginary audience (Denby, Kirstein), sees. The audience then sees the Sultana kill herself. And people then see, as the curtain falls in dead silence, the Sultan weep—weep, moreover, as Herod never does. What were we to think in the end? That the Sultan feels sorry for the Sultana, sorry for having let jealousy get the better of him? That the Sultan feels sorry for the Golden Slave as well, sorry for having let homophobia get the better of him? And did we identify with him? Did we too come to regret homophobia, or not?[33] Or were we to think the Sultan is sorry for himself alone—the self-pitying tears of the wife beater or gay basher—and therefore to think, with more than a little exasperation: "Men! Can't live with them; can't live with them."

Which, oddly enough, is what Michael Jackson enables us not to think. In *Remember the Time*, Jackson's heteroerotic and nostalgic reenactment of *Schéhérazade*, with *Cléopâtre* thrown in to give the video an African cast, the Gloved One, dressed as a golden slave, sings for Pharoah (Eddie Murphy, a notorious homophobe), seduces Pharoah's wife (Iman—now married to David Bowie, a gay icon), is pursued by his henchmen, and, unlike Nijinsky, manages—magically—to escape. At the last possible moment Jackson spins into a shower of gold, making an uncanny spectacle of himself (we seem to have seen this before, thanks to Diaghilev, Nijinsky, Zeus, and Danaë), of his Midas touch (something Diaghilev could appreciate), of his psychotic if not schizophrenic relation to the Other (could you see him with either Iman or Lisa Marie?), and of his antihomophobic—yes, antihomophobic—foreclosure on the death drive.

If you believe in fairies, clap your hands, for only a Peter Pan could outwit and outlive a Sultan. Only Jackson could do so synaesthetically, music videos being today's total artworks. And only he could be so pleasing—or blissful—about it. Blissful? Can there be *jouissance*, or *Liebestod*, without an implication of death? Without love? And, in Jackson's case, without sex? I suppose only his boyfriend or plastic surgeon would know for sure—Jackson is both Dorian Gray and Peter Pan—because the performer may have a *jouissance* of his own and his final spin on *Schéhérazade* in *Remember the Time* may be a gesture to which gays and queers should attend. It might be the blissful act of a pleasurable and truly liberated body, having nothing to do with the desire we have interrogated to death and having a great deal to do with the future of human sexuality.

NOTES

"Nijinsky's Golden Slave" is reprinted from *The Queer Afterlife of Vaslav Nijinsky* by Kevin Kopelson, with the permission of the publishers, Stanford University Press. Copyright © 1997 by the Board of Trustees of the Leland Stanford Junior University.

1. Richard Buckle, *Nijinsky* (New York: Simon and Schuster, 1971), 124.
2. Charles Ricketts, *Self-Portrait: Taken from the Letters and Journals*, ed. Cecil Lewis and Sturge Moore (London: Peter Davies, 1939), 175.
3. Ramsay Burt, *The Male Dancer: Bodies, Spectacle, Sexualities* (London: Routledge, 1995), 85.
4. Lincoln Kirstein, *Nijinsky Dancing* (London: Thames and Hudson, 1975), 99.
5. Edwin Denby, " 'Schéhérazade': A Foundering Warhorse," in Robert Cornfield and William MacKay, eds., *Dance Writings* (New York: Knopf, 1986), 240.
6. Harold Acton, *Memoirs of an Aesthete* (London: Methuen, 1948), 113.
7. Denby, " 'Schéhérazade,'" 240; Lincoln Kirstein, *Mosaic: Memoirs* (New York: Farrar, Straus and Giroux, 1994), 212; Bakst combined blue, green, and orange and used Turkish, Persian, and Mogul design elements.
8. André Levinson, *Bakst: The Story of the Artist's Life* (London, 1923), 158.
9. The Golden Slave wore dark blue body paint "not unlike the bloom on black grapes" (Cyril W. Beaumont, *The Diaghilev Ballet in London* [London: Putnam, 1940], 35). According to Michel Fokine, however, the Golden Slave was "a primitive savage, not by the color of his body make-up, but by his movements. Now he was a half-human, half-feline animal, softly leaping great distances, now a stallion, with distended nostrils, full of energy, overflowing with an abundance of power, his feet impatiently pawing the ground" (Michel Fokine, *Memoirs of a Ballet Master*, ed. Anatole Chujoy and trans. Vitale Fokine [Boston: Little, Brown, 1961], 156). Following Fokine's gendered imagery, Alexandre Benois called the Golden Slave "half-cat, half-snake, fiendishly agile, feminine and yet wholly terrifying" (quoted in Buckle, *Nijinsky*, 141).
10. Glenn Watkins, *Pyramids at the Louvre: Music, Culture, and Collage from Stravinsky to the Postmodernists* (Cambridge, Mass.: Harvard University Press, 1994), 67. See Proust: "Even those society people who professed to be endowed with taste and drew otiose distinctions between the various Russian ballets . . . were almost prepared to attribute [*Schéhérazade*] to the inspiration of Negro art" (Marcel Proust, *The Captive*, in vol. 3 of *Remembrance of Things Past*, trans. C. K. Scott Moncrieff and Terence Kilmartin [New York: Random House, 1982], 238).
11. Marcel Proust, *Cities of the Plain*, in vol. 2 of *Remembrance of Things Past*, trans. C. K. Scott Moncrieff and Terence Kilmartin (New York: Random

House, 1982), 890. Proust saw Charlus, a homosexual love-slave, as Diaghilev, and Morel, a bisexual violinist, as Nijinsky: "A manager modest in regard to his true merits, [Charlus] contrived to place [Morel's] virtuosity at the service of a versatile artistic sense which increased it tenfold. Imagine a purely skilful performer in the Russian Ballet, trained, taught, developed in all directions by M. Diaghilev" (941–42).

12. Lynn Garafola, *Diaghilev's Ballets Russes* (New York: Oxford University Press, 1989), 32, 34.

13. Beaumont, *Diaghilev Ballet*, 35. Most characters, even drama queens, go out the way they come in. The Specter of the Rose, for one, leaps out the open window through which he had leaped in, a more structurally satisfying because perfectly symmetrical denial of the closet thematic the Golden Slave invokes in order to enact fatal gay liberation. Of course, no orgiast slain in *Schéhérazade* goes out the way he or she comes in. Nor does the Sultana.

14. Peter Wollen, "Fashion/Orientalism/The Body," *New Formations* 1 (spring 1987): 27.

15. Both gender difference and the sexual difference presumed to naturalize gender difference are thoroughly—or "ultra"—artificial.

16. See Michael Moon, "Flaming Closets," in Ellen W. Goellner and Jacqueline Shea Murphy, eds., *Bodies of the Text: Dance as Theory, Literature as Dance* (New Brunswick, N.J.: Rutgers University Press, 1995): "At the time of *Schéhérazade*, [Nijinsky] was still successfully negotiating the powerful projections of sexual contradiction onto his performances" (62).

17. Ibid.

18. The Specter of the Rose, Petrushka, and the Faun are not slaves and hence less analogous to the Golden Slave, and because the three postdate him, the Golden Slave could not be read through them for some time.

19. This is an anticipation of *L'Après-midi d'un faune* (1912). See Lynn Garafola, "The partners never touch. They seem to touch, however, and at nearly every point the suggestion of contact is sudden and fraught with violence. Again and again the Faun turns on his prey, locking her in the vise of his powerful arms. Almost always, the throat is the locus of entrapment, as if that exposed column were the gateway to sex itself" (Garafola, "Vaslav Nijinsky," *Raritan* 8, no. 1 [summer 1988]: 9).

20. Carl Van Vechten, "The Russian Ballet and Nijinsky," in Paul Magriel, ed., *Nijinsky, Pavlova, Duncan: Three Lives in Dance* (New York: Da Capo, 1977), 9–10. The Golden Slave did, in fact, touch the Sultana in their supported adagio. Van Vechten's misimpression, however, appears to have been common. According to Francis de Miomandre, for example: "Without ever touching, his feverish hands run over her from brow to ankle with so exquisite a shudder and so deep a sense of the loveliness of desire that we are almost haunted" (Francis de Miomandre, introduction to George Barbier, *Dessins sur les danses de Vaslav Nijinsky* [Paris: Bernouard, 1912], 5).

21. Kirstein, *Nijinsky Dancing*, 95; Garafola, *Diaghilev's Ballets Russes*, 33.

22. According to Wollen, Nijinsky may approximate the "libidinal power of woman, once her desire is released," but Rubinstein, "both petrifying and petrified, castrating and castrated . . . incarnate[s] the phallic woman of the Deca-

dence" (Wollen, "Fashion/Orientalism/The Body," 18). Compare this to what Buckle says in *Nijinsky*: "In 'Schéhérazade,' though an embodiment of lust, [Nijinsky] had been in a way more feminine than Ida Rubinstein" (144).

23. Even in repose, to quote Paul Claudel, Nijinsky "seemed imperceptibly to be dancing" (quoted in Françoise Reiss, *Nijinsky: A Biography* [London: Black, 1960], 167). Nijinsky, however, would come to embrace Duncan's aesthetic, which she claimed to have based on ancient Greek art, in *L'Après-midi d'un faune*.

24. Moon, "Flaming Closets," 64. Moon is referring to Fokine's description of the Sultana's penultimate gesture: "She majestically awaits her fate—in a pose without motion" (quoted in Wollen, "Fashion/Orientalism/The Body," 20).

25. Moon, "Flaming Closets," 65.

26. At a Buenos Aires performance people thought Nijinsky had really hurt himself and "rose with a scream," according to Nijinsky's wife, Romola, when "in that final jump, Vaslav, with the briefest touch of his head on the floor, flung himself into the air by the action of his neck-muscles, quivered, and fell" (Romola Nijinsky, *Nijinsky* [New York: Simon and Schuster, 1968], 313). Londoners were less alarmist. According to Beaumont, "It was a thrilling experience to see him now darting this way and that, now doubling on his pursuers in a desperate frenzied anxiety to escape the avenging scimitars. But a blade flashed and he fell headlong, to spin on the back of his neck with his legs thrust rigid in the air. Then the body fell, rolled over, and was still. This simulated death scene invariably aroused a storm of well merited applause, for, apart from the rare skill obviously essential to its performance, it looked dangerous in the extreme" (Beaumont, *Diaghilev Ballet*, 36).

27. Vechten, "Russian Ballet and Nijinsky," 10; Miomandre, introduction, 3–4.

28. Scott Eyman, *Mary Pickford: America's Sweetheart* (New York: Donald I. Fine, 1990), 301; Gaylyn Studlar, "Douglas Fairbanks: Thief of the Ballets Russes," in Goellner and Murphy, *Bodies of the Text*, 110.

29. Studlar, "Douglas Fairbanks," 108.

30. Tim Scholl, *From Petipa to Balanchine: Classical Revival and the Modernization of Ballet* (London: Routledge, 1994), 65.

31. Ronald Firbank, *The Flower beneath the Foot*, in *Five Novels* (New York: New Directions, 1961), 14.

32. Denby, "'Schéhérazade,'" 240; Kirstein is quoted on his childhood experience in Joan Acocella, "Heroes and Hero Worship," review of Lincoln Kirstein, *Mosaic: Memoirs*, in the *New York Review of Books*, November 16, 1995, p. 32; Kirstein describes the finale in his *Mosaic*, 135.

33. The ending of *Salomé* posed a similar problem. Wilde's play enabled people to either approve or disapprove of its homoerotic heroine's execution. See Kevin Kopelson, *Love's Litany: The Writing of Modern Homoerotics* (Stanford, Calif.: Stanford University Press, 1994), 42–44.

4

Dance Is for American Men:
Ted Shawn and the Intersection of Gender,
Sexuality, and Nationalism in the 1930s

Julia L. Foulkes

In 1926 Ted Shawn, the male half of the dance pair and institution known as Denishawn, published *The American Ballet*. In the foreword Shawn conceded that he had chosen the title "as an admission of defeat." The word *ballet* was too tied to European forms of dance and Shawn predicted that "the birth of the dance in America will make new forms . . . seemingly formless" and big like Walt Whitman's *Leaves of Grass*.[1] In eschewing ballet, heralding Whitman, and naming national dance traits, Shawn allied himself with Isadora Duncan and the emerging generation of modern dancers of Martha Graham, Doris Humphrey, and others. Shawn described himself as "merely a wave carried on this tide," but his mission also differed from that of other modern dancers.[2] His dictum: "Dancing is for men, American men."[3] Shawn had promoted dancing for men at least since 1916 in an article entitled "A Defence [*sic*] of the Male Dancer" in the *New York Dramatic Mirror*. There, Shawn declared that "the decadent, the freakish, the feverish" Russian ballet dancer Vaslav Nijinsky, who appealed to Parisians, would not find such an enamored audience in the United States: "America demands masculinity more than art."[4]

Like female modern dancers, male modern dancers faced assumptions about masculine and feminine characteristics both on stage and off. While Graham and Humphrey accumulated descriptions of their dancing as masculine and ugly, accusations of effeminacy and suspicion of homosexuality dogged male dancers.[5] At this time the delineation between queer and straight signified an inversion of gender roles more than particular sexual acts or partners. Queers were men who exhibited perceived female traits and behaviors such as a high-pitched voice, a languid swivel-hipped walk—and an interest in the arts, especially dance.[6] The lack of financial security in a dance career was also more problematic for men because of their traditional roles as breadwinners. Financial instability and the gentility associated with the arts only further strengthened the conventional union of dance and femininity. Shawn challenged these notions by meshing virility with Americanism, a winning combination in the tremulous times of the Great Depression.

The 1930s was a time of gender troubles because economic hard times undermined the traditional role of the man as the breadwinner of the family. Although this had more often been an ideal than a reality for most Americans, the conditions of the 1930s challenged both the reality *and* the ideal. Women asserted new strength in holding the family together, played a larger role in the workforce and politics, and assumed this would continue—all epitomized in the towering tenacity of Eleanor Roosevelt. The gender troubles sparked new fears of gender inversion and homosexuality. More severe crackdowns began on gay bars, drag balls, and theatrical pansy acts in New York City, and legislation prohibiting the representation of homosexuality increased.[7] Obvious displays of gender reversal symbolically threatened the revival and rebirth of the nation itself. Nationalism—Shawn's strong patriotism and Americans' deep need to believe in the endurance and uniqueness of their nation during the depression—provided the foundation for Shawn's success. And, while Shawn's homosexuality molded his dances, it remained an undercurrent, an allusion most often picked up on only by other gay men. Shawn transformed his offstage homosexual inclinations to an onstage American virility, shaping the American male dancer into a near-nude Greek ideal of an athlete-artist: a heroic image that Americans heartily embraced.[8]

SHAWN'S STORY

Edwin Meyers Shawn was born in Kansas City, Missouri, on October 21, 1891, the second son of Elmer Ellsworth Shawn, a journalist for the *Kansas City Star*, and Mary Lee Booth Shawn. Shawn's mother traced her lineage back to "a nobleman serving under William the Conqueror when he invaded and conquered England"; his father came from less aristocratic German folk who had emigrated to the United States in the 1840s.[9] The Shawns moved to Denver in Ted's early childhood and there Ted decided to become a Methodist minister, attracted to the high moral ideals of a religious life. During his third year as a pretheology student at the University of Denver, Shawn contracted diphtheria, a bacterial infection that caused difficulty in breathing, high fever, weakness, and, in Shawn's case, temporary paralysis of his legs. To rebuild his stamina and physical dexterity, he sought out dance lessons.

Shawn had displayed an interest in theater before his bout with diphtheria. In 1911 for his fraternity, Sigma Phi Epsilon, he wrote a two-act play entitled *The Female of the Species*, a satirical look at women's suffrage. The play depicted a postsuffrage future (in 1933) where men dressed in "ruffled trousers, laced waists, earrings" and women wore "men's full dress coats and shirts"; women ran the government as commissioners of the "Bargain Counters" and "Manicurists and Beauty Parlors," and the only men ran the tiny department of "Municipal Affairs." "Horrified and shocked beyond expression" at this futuristic scene, the rabid feminist character swore "to renounce suffrage."[10] In reinforcing traditional roles for men and women, the play foreshadowed Shawn's own path through the dance world.

Shawn's theater experience and ballet and ballroom lessons led to his leaving the University of Denver, his forgoing a ministerial career, and his launching a lifelong career in dance.[11] Although he gave up his ideas of being a minister, Shawn, like Isadora Duncan and Ruth St. Denis at the same time, believed that dance joined mind and body in a spiritual union. Shawn found affirmation in *The Making of Personality* by the poet Bliss Carman, who described dance as "that perfect fusion of sense and spirit, without which no art is possible and no life is fortunate," a view that prompted Shawn to write him for advice about making a career in dance.[12] Carman's reply captured one of the difficulties Shawn faced, noting that the male dancers "who have made it in America have been foreigners, with all the prestige of Europe."[13] Shawn sought Carman out at the Triunian School of Personal Harmonizing in New Haven, Connecticut, in early 1914. That meeting eventually led Shawn to Ruth St. Denis, whom Carman believed best embodied the union of "sense and spirit." After a first meeting between St. Denis and Shawn in New York, their mutual admiration for each other soared as they exalted shared idols such as Ralph Waldo Emerson, Mary Baker Eddy, and François Delsarte. St. Denis asked Shawn to accompany her on an upcoming tour; he quickly accepted. Their passionate conversation continued and, after much beseeching, Shawn convinced St. Denis to marry him later that same year, in August 1914.[14] St. Denis gained a dance partner and entrepreneurial acumen; Shawn benefited from St. Denis's prominence and her devotion to and success in creating a new form of dance.

Their alliance initially prospered, with Denishawn schools sprouting nationwide and worldwide tours in the 1920s. But their personal relationship was continually fractious. Professional envy (most often, Shawn's jealousy of St. Denis) and extramarital love affairs by both riled them. By the late 1920s they were spending more and more time apart, eventually splitting personally and professionally. The Denishawn school and company ended in 1931 and, although they did not divorce, Shawn and St. Denis never lived together after 1930.

BEAUTY AND BROTHERHOOD

While St. Denis dallied with men during her marriage to Shawn, most of them younger than she, Shawn also pursued the affection and love of men. Their mutual affection for one man contributed to their permanent separation. Shawn and St. Denis met Fred Beckman in 1927 in Corpus Christi, Texas, while on tour. In early 1928 Shawn invited Beckman to become his personal representative. Beckman fulfilled that role and became Shawn's lover. Although the dissolution of St. Denis and Shawn's company and marriage was imminent, a secret liaison between St. Denis and Beckman doomed the partnership when Shawn found a romantic letter from St. Denis to Beckman.[15]

Shawn fled to solo tours in Europe. German newspapers praised his American "freshness, youth, even boyishness," which contrasted sharply with the Russian male dancers who toured in Germany and who were "sluggish, degenerate . . . [and showed the] weariness of civilization."[16] The generous flattery helped soothe Shawn's ego, bruised by the betrayal of St. Denis. Denishawn had crippling debts when it folded; because Shawn needed money, he toured the United States with a small company as "Shawn and His Dancers" from 1931 to 1932. He soon headed resolutely to the wooded retreat he had bought in 1930 near Lee, Massachusetts, named Jacob's Pillow. Jacob's Ladder was the highest mountain in the Berkshires; a large sloping rock on Shawn's property thereby became Jacob's pillow. At the restful farmhouse in the woods Shawn turned his full attention to his earlier mission: men must dance.

On his 1931–1932 tour Shawn had devised lecture-demonstrations for university and college audiences advocating dance for men. During the winter of 1932–1933, he found a way to apply his ideas. Nearby Springfield College (then named the International Young Men's Christian Association College) had a strong physical education program for men and, with the enthusiasm of the college president, Shawn offered a class in dance. Shawn was determined to overcome the charge that male dancers were sissies, so he stipulated that the class be mandatory for all, thus ensuring that all suffered the stereotype and that peer pressure would not arouse further divisions among the male students. Shawn gave them strenuous exercises the first day, pushing them to recognize the physical stamina dance required. He learned that simple descriptive active verbs—*leap*, *turn*—translated better for his class than the French ballet terms such as *ballon* and *pirouette*. By the end of the term he "had his disciples."[17] More important, he had fellow performers. In quick response to an offer to perform in Boston, Shawn pulled together men from his Springfield College classes and performers (including women) from his touring company. On March 21, 1933, at the Repertory Theatre, Shawn and his dancers debuted to rave reviews, with the all-male pieces receiving the most praise.

The success of the Boston performance inspired Shawn to arrange a formal company, called Shawn and His Men Dancers, and he immediately set about training, choreographing, and touring. From 1933 to 1940 the company of either eight or nine men (including Shawn) held 1,250 performances in more than 750 cities in the United States, Canada, and England.[18] Throughout the seven years of touring, Jacob's Pillow was home and sustenance. There each summer the troupe built cabins, a studio, and eventually a theater; took daily dance classes; refurbished older works and created new ones; and each noon hour sunbathed nude as Shawn read from Havelock Ellis, Ouspensky (a disciple of the theosophist Gurdjieff), and the philosopher Alfred North Whitehead. (A 1936 catalogue for the "Shawn School of Dance for Men" described this last daily ritual as a "required course in the principles of applied anatomy, body mechanics, corrective exercises and massage . . . held, as a rule, during the noon-hour sunbathing period."[19]) At the suggestion of F. Cowles Strickland, a friend of Shawn's and director of the Berkshire Playhouse in nearby Stockbridge, the troupe began "teas" to make a little money. Shawn invited the dowagers of western Massachusetts to the Pillow in the late afternoon. The "boys" would serve tea, then retreat to the woods and emerge, stripped to tan trunks, and perform. These teas blossomed into the Jacob's Pillow Dance Festival that continues today.

Shawn's commitment to promoting men in dance, and especially the ideal of an all-male company, encompassed his idealization of homosexual love between men. Shawn looked to the musings of Walt Whitman, and the British writers Edward Carpenter and Havelock Ellis, the standard reading list among gay men of the era, to fortify his belief in the higher ideal of love between men.[20] Shawn sought out Carpenter and Ellis during a 1924 tour to London, and Walter Terry, Shawn's friend and biographer, suggested that the meeting eased Shawn's mind about his own homosexual inclinations.[21] In his book *Love's Coming of Age*, Carpenter wrote of the "intermediate sex," which combined a balance of masculine and feminine characteristics in one person and included a same-sex love object. Love between men or be-

Students at the Shawn School of Dance for Men sunbathing after their noon meal in the Tea Garden at Jacob's Pillow, ca. 1936 (Barton Mumaw Collection, Jacob's Pillow Archives; used with permission)

tween women was not a "result of disease and degeneration" in Carpenter's view; in fact, "it is possible that in this class of men we have the love sentiment in one of its most perfect forms." Among men the "intermediate sex" man who unified masculine and feminine traits exhibited superior artistic talent, and Carpenter named as examples Michelangelo, Shakespeare, and Marlowe.[22] This was a vision of homosexuality that Shawn could heartily embrace. Shawn yearned for legitimation of his artistic talent. The idea of the "intermediate sex" also incorporated his sexual relations with both men and women. Terry argued that Shawn clung to the Greek ideal of a husband with a wife *and* a male lover.[23]

It was Plato who best captured Shawn's feelings. To Barton Mumaw, Shawn's lover from 1931 to 1948 and the principal dancer in his company, Shawn recited this passage from Plato's *Symposium*:

> The whole soul, stung in every part, rages with pain; and then again remembering the beautiful one, it rejoices. . . . It is perplexed

and maddened, and in its madness it cannot sleep at night or stay in any one place by day, but is filled with longing and hastens wherever it hopes to see the beautiful one. And when it sees him and is bathed with the waters of yearning, the passages that were sealed are opened, the soul has respite from the stings and is eased of its pain, and this pleasure which it enjoys is the sweetest of pleasures at the time.

Therefore the soul will not if it can help it, be left alone by the beautiful one, but esteems him above all others, forgets for him mother and brothers and all friends, neglects property and cares not for its loss, and despising all the customs and proprieties in which it formerly took pride, it is ready to be a slave and to sleep wherever it is allowed, as near as possible to the beloved; for it not only reveres him who possesses beauty, but finds in him the only healer of its greatest woes. Now this condition, fair boy, about which I am speaking is called Love by men.[24]

This kind of heroic physical love guided Shawn's relations with Mumaw and his next long relationship, with John Christian, which lasted from 1949 until Shawn's death in 1972. This embrace of homosexual love did not include the "fey actions" (presumably effeminate or campy gestures), as Mumaw puts it, of other homosexual men. Shawn wrote to Mumaw: "[It] makes me sick. It's all wrong. That's the kind of thing that brings discredit on what is essentially a noble thing. Our kind of love . . . must be lived on a higher plane than the other or it sinks to a lower level."[25] Shawn's vision of a higher kind of love borrowed heavily from Edward Carpenter and, especially, Havelock Ellis's *Studies in the Psychology of Sex*. In six volumes, published from 1897 to 1910, the British sexologist defended sexual passion, including homosexuality, and attributed spiritual qualities to sex. For Shawn, dance emerged from this spiritual and idealistic view of sex and love; Ellis's *Dance of Life* was "the dancers' bible" and Shawn rarely missed an occasion to extol it.[26] His group of men dancers, then, was more than a sales campaign for dancing as a career for men. It was also a philosophical ideal—which included homosexuality—in action.

This purpose was clear to other gay men. Lucien Price, the gay male music critic for the *Boston Globe* and a novelist, first saw Shawn dance his *Thunderbird* in 1931 and "was in an agony of desire to see it right over again."[27] Price also attended the 1933 Boston performance that included all-male dances and became an indefatigable champion of the troupe and a constant correspondent with Shawn throughout the 1930s. Price recognized that they "serve[d] the same dieties [*sic*]—beauty and brotherhood."[28] Price commended and emboldened Shawn's effort to recreate a Greek ideal in his group of men dancers, combining athletic grace, philosophical import, and the quest for "Beauty" in the male body: "I think the combination of high intellectual content and genuine spiritual feeling in the dances, together with almost complete nakedness of the male body, are letting people feel, if not see, for the first time that there need be no conflict between flesh and spirit, and that an ennobled sexual attraction can be a vehicle for religious feeling."[29] Price praised the combination of intellectual stimulation and physical prowess possible among men, but he also exalted the closeted nature of homosexuality: "Uncomfortable as one's position may often be, it has the comfort of not being exposed to this mass-exploitation by theater, movie, literature, and every crude device down to the roadside advertising signs."[30] For Price, gay male sexuality, unlike heterosexuality, remained free of corruption by mass culture and, in this way, also contributed to the idea that a higher love existed between men.[31]

The example of Shawn and His Men Dancers inspired Price to write *The Sacred Legion*, his series of four novels that chronicled love between men, some of whom were dancers, and that he chose to publish privately to escape censorship problems.[32] Price recalled, "In you and the boys I had watched [the ideal] being lived."[33] Other gay men were inspired to be a part of the dance world. Walter Terry took dance classes with one of Shawn's former students at the University of North Carolina and roomed with Foster Fitz-Simmons, who was to become a member of Shawn and His Men Dancers. Terry had decided on the career of a dance critic rather than dancer, and Shawn encouraged him, helping Terry gain his first post at the *Boston Herald* in 1936 (he moved to the

New York Herald Tribune in 1939). Similarly, Arthur Todd approached Shawn about writing his biography, a duty that Shawn had already promised to Terry. Todd ended up working primarily in the fashion world but photographed Shawn and wrote about dance in *Dance Observer* and the *Dancing Times*. John Lindquist, a cashier at Filene's department store in Boston, stopped by the Pillow one summer afternoon in 1938 out of curiosity.[34] An amateur photographer, Lindquist became entranced by capturing dancers on film, especially naked male dancers. Lindquist came back to the Pillow every summer from then on, becoming the official photographer of the Pillow and the unofficial photographer of male dancers posing nude in the woods outside the studio and theater areas.[35] For some gay men, Shawn and His Men Dancers was a triumphant model of a loving brotherhood that inspired involvement in the dance world.[36]

MASCULINE MOVEMENT

Shawn's vision of brotherhood relied on an emboldened masculinity. In his attempt to dispel the popular link of dancing and effeminacy and to counter the dominance of women in the American concert dance field, he embraced distinctive, essential differences between men and women and heralded "masculine" traits.

From his earliest publicized thoughts on the subject, beginning in 1916, Shawn divided movement into masculine and feminine types. Dance had "one fixed limitation that must be faced: the human body is the instrument and medium of the dancer, and human dances are either male or female."[37] Male and female bodies engendered different postures. Men's posture was "widespread, feet and legs apart, pelvis forward, chest forward, a broad stance"; women's was "the concave receptivity."[38] He pronounced that men and women had always held different roles in society that would naturally lead to different kinds of movement:

> Modern people inherit movement impulses from thousands of generations of ancestors who did all the labor of the world with hand implements. Thus the women's movements are conditioned by cooking, sewing, tending babies, sweeping, etc., small scale movements which use comparatively little stress through the trunk

Tony Charmoli, Jacob's Pillow, ca. 1940 (Photograph by John Lindquist; Harvard Theatre Collection, Houghton Library; used with permission)

of the body and a greater use of the small arm movements, with resultant greater flexibility of wrist and elbow. The executive man of today, in his office, still inherits movement impulses from forefathers who wielded scythe, axe, plough, oars, etc., and the masculine movement uses stress from the ground up through the entire body, culminating in big arm movements from the shoulder out, and with much less flexibility of elbow and wrist joints.[39]

Starting from this different base of movement, then, men's dancing was made up of broad sweeping gestures that mimicked their outdoor, adventurous, and often dangerous lives. According to Shawn, "The movement of men should project itself beyond the body of the dancer and create in the mind of the audience a sense of spaciousness, great distances and invincible strength."[40]

The emphasis on the flexibility of the wrists in this description (and the lack of it in "masculine movement") seems to be another attempt to disassociate male dancers from this sign of effeminate homosexuality. George Chauncey charts the development of coded signs that were linked to popular notions of homosexuality but that also constituted a system of divulgence and communication among gay men. Limp wrists, flamboyant dress and colors (especially a red tie), and an exaggerated walk bespoke effeminacy and perhaps homosexuality.[41] Shawn condemned men who danced "with pinked toes and wisps of white chiffon [who] writhed and skipped to our mingled amusement and disgust."[42] Similarly, "to most normal people masculine movement in a woman dancer is just as repulsive as feminine movement in a man dancer."[43] The goal was to achieve the unity between men and women dancing in their respective "anatomically, functionally, emotionally, and . . . inherited movement impulses . . . eternally different—opposed and yet complementary."[44]

Shawn also retraced the history of dance, proclaiming it an occupation originally "limited to men alone." Citing both the societies of Western civilization such as Greece and Rome and what he called the primitive societies of Native Americans and Latin America, Shawn claimed that only men had performed in theatrical works and rituals. It was the European courts that turned dance into a feminine art and removed it from its ceremonial importance.[45] To return to its proper status at the apex of the arts, dance needed men. No art form could succeed if "dominated by one sex" and, more important, "the dance in its fullness . . . demands strength, endurance, precision, perfect coordination of mind, body and emotion, clarity of thinking, all distinctly masculine qualities."[46] Men needed to study dance with men because through women teachers "unconsciously there crept into his gesture a feminine quality."[47] In fact, the best course was to isolate men thoroughly: "I wanted to get them away from all feminine influence—away from any chance to mimic feminine gestures."[48] Shawn even let go his female accompanist in favor of a male accompanist and composer, Jess Meeker. Thus the male idyll at Jacob's Pillow was born.

Dances emerged from masculine living at the Pillow. *Labor Symphony* (1934) offered four portrayals of men's work: in the fields, the forests, on the sea, and in a factory. Movement mimics actual work motions. In "Labor of the Fields," a dancer lurches forward, chest toward the ground, as if pushing a plow through the fields. Planting seeds follows with long swinging arm gestures, and the section ends in a harvest, with full knee bends and scooping motions. The next sections match this pantomimic approach: two men saw a tree with broad back-and-forth torso movements; a crew rows as one man guides a rudder and another throws out a net and hauls it in; and, circular alternating arm motions of the group in a rhythmic pattern create a human gear shift in the final section.[49]

Through Shawn's impressive publicity drive and his dances, reviewers almost always commented on the manliness of the performance; as one critic noted, "The female dancer decidedly was not imitated nor missed."[50] Another waxed profusely: "Vigor limned by restraint; furious motion controlled and balanced and suggestive of mighty harmonies; muscular orderliness and pointed grace; a hale and rugged lyricism whose line is gentle, but never effeminate or Hogarthian; energy; humility and bravura, suavity and simplicity; power; beauty. Which of these qualities apparent in Shawn's work can be called effeminate?"[51] Reviewers responded more covertly to the suggestion of homosexuality and praised Shawn's success in freeing the dance "from the purple tints which usually hover around male dancing" and commented on Shawn's "expressive hands and muscular wrists."[52]

Shawn promoted the athleticism of the men, and he preferred that his dancers have athletic training and no dance background. He believed that athletics prepared men better for "masculine movement." The 1936 application for the Jacob's Pillow summer school included these questions: "At what athletic games are you proficient?" and "List athletics for which you have received awards." Wilbur McCormack was a "former track man, wrestler and gymnast" from Springfield College; Frank Overlees was a swimmer and all-around athlete; Dennis Landers held the record for pole vaulting for northeastern Oklahoma.[53] Athletics suffused Shawn's choreographic ideas too and culminated in *Olympiad*, for which individual members of the company choreographed their own solo or group dances. Wilbur McCormack choreographed a "Boxing Dance"; Fred Hearn did "Fencing"; Foster Fitz-Simmons danced the "Decathlon." *Olympiad* ended with a basketball "dance." The offstage apparel of the troupe also gave the impression of an athletic team: terry cloth bathrobes worn immediately before and after performances, like boxers, and knit sweaters that sported a large *S*, like members of a college tennis team. Most reviews of the troupe mentioned the athletic backgrounds of the troupe members, often comparing the performance of the male dancers with that of athletes. A sportswriter for a Springfield, Massachusetts, paper compared Shawn to a wrestler and concluded that Shawn was "far more the master of a far more flexible craft [who] makes the liveliest wrestler seem like a petrified tree stump."[54]

For Shawn, athletics prepared men for masculine movement, but dancing nude best communicated such movement. While female modern dancers covered their body in long tubular dresses, in effect downplaying their curvier physical attributes with little display of the legs, Shawn and His Men Dancers most often performed as close to nude as permissible. Shawn credited Isadora Duncan and Ruth St. Denis with bringing the "almost nude body" to the stage.[55] Both women wore flowing tunics that hinted at nudity rather than revealed it (St. Denis did bare her midriff often, however, in her oriental dances). Quoting Whitman and Ellis, and noting the example of Greek civilization about the divinity of the body, Shawn protested that clothes always restricted the dancer and, more, limited what a dancer could communicate: "There is no way of representing invisible form, the idea of Man, except by the nude human body. We cannot associate the cosmic Man with clothes, because clothing suggests classification—clothes would place him as to race, nationality, period of history, social or financial status—and Man would become man."[56] His 1923 *Death of Adonis* again drew on Greek ideals in a portrayal of a Phoenician god as the epitome of human physical beauty. Shawn performed the piece in a powdered wig, powdered his body white, and wore only a fig leaf G-string. The work consisted mostly of poses, flowing from one into another, and his idea was to convey a fluid sculpture.

But it was the beauty of the *male* body that particularly interested Shawn. In describing the moderation and good health that would come about if all had to walk around naked, Shawn picked an image of a woman as the example of excess: "To look at a nude woman whose breasts are flabby and discolored, whose body is gross and fat, produces only nausea and disgust."[57] Photographs of nude male dancers taken at the Pillow by John Lindquist, the noontime nude sunbathing hours, and Shawn's later hobby of carving wood sculptures of male nudes demonstrated his continued fascination with the male body. Shawn's 1935 solo *Mouvement Naif*, inspired by a Whitman poem, personalized this fascination. The piece was a discovery of the motions of one's own body through isolated moves of shoulders, torso, ankles, arms.[58]

Shawn's reverence for the nude male body was part of a "rediscovery of the human body" common in early twentieth-century America and Europe. George Mosse argues that the search for an enduring image of strength arose to counter the artificiality of modernism and then was easily folded into nationalist and fascist movements based on eugenic ideas in Germany and Italy.[59] Nature, however, always required tuning. In Shawn's case the practicalities of performing nearly nude required a weekly all-over shave in an attempt to achieve a "sexless impersonality."[60] Homosexual desire, though, was probably always present in this Greek model of male nudity, which was resurrected by a German art historian with homosexual inclinations in the late eighteenth century and revived again in the twentieth century.[61] Lucien Price claimed that dance, in particular, allowed for a greater suggestion of homoeroticism than literature: "Its idea can be communicated to others to just that extent to which they are qualified to receive it."[62] A hairless reified "natural" body escaped censorship when dancing in the name of manliness and virtue.

While Price and other gay men picked up on a homosexual allure, women in the audience also appreciated the sexual masculinity Shawn and His Men Dancers displayed. As the wife of a friend of Lucien Price's remarked (in Price's recounting): "The show was wonderful. I tell you it was simply wonderful. Why, the young men had next to nothing on. Next to nothing on. You might say they were naked."[63] Barton Mumaw claims that often the curtain would raise to gasps and then stunned silence, the men's sexualized bodies arousing the audience into watching them.[64] Katherine Drier, in her book on Ted Shawn, may have had sexual imagery in mind when she wrote that Shawn "stands for a power of rhythm which refills one with fresh vitality."[65] After a 1940 slide show at a women's luncheon, a publicist for Jacob's Pillow commented to John Lindquist that his pictures were a "KNOCKOUT. Every time I showed a single of Barton they applauded and insisted on the film being held in the projector."[66] For these women and the dowagers who supported Jacob's Pillow, Shawn and His Men Dancers offered a rare spectacle of male sexual exhibition.

The ironies of social attitudes about male and female bodily display on stage emerge in looking at reactions to Shawn and His Men Dancers. Although the company danced close to nude, the dancers rarely received admonitions for their performances, even in Boston, where Katherine Dunham was censured in 1941 and 1944.[67] (A friend of Dunham's suggested that Boston was "more like a Clothing Convention than an Art Center."[68]) Price attributed Shawn's success there to the fact that Shawn did not accompany his performances with "frank discussions" (presumably about sex or the divinity of the body), although no other modern dancers did either.[69] Nudity was partially censored in the art projects sponsored by the Works Progress Administration (WPA)— officials allowed the use of nudity in paintings and sculptures in allegorical settings but excised it from artistic portrayals of contemporary life. Barbara Melosh suggests that this policy more pointedly targeted female nudity, ostensibly because it was more sexualized and represented a greater "affront to public decency," an idea that apparently applied to the dance world as well.[70]

Newsreels and Farm Security Administration photographs of saddened, resigned men in battered shacks and long unemployment lines were perhaps the most prominent images of men during the decade. Artistic images countered this documentation, with partial nudity of dynamic men as part of the strategy to inspire national strength. Many popular WPA murals and paintings featured the bare muscular torsos of laboring men. This celebration of manly strength in portrayals of manual laborers was reminiscent of National Socialist art in Nazi Germany and Soviet realist art of the 1930s.[71] Bernarr Macfadden, the entrepreneur behind the magazine *Physical Culture*, picked up on this trend of the 1930s and advocated the combination of virile bodybuilding and active citizenry. *Physical Culture* featured pictures of Shawn and occasional articles by Benito Mussolini, who extolled healthy "aggressive" bodies as the basis for his fascist citizen army.[72] Unlike partially nude women, partially nude men in magazines, paintings, and dancing on stage projected an inflated masculinity and strength that was accepted and even promoted if used in the cause of workers or nationhood. Bare bulging muscle men flattened images of emaciated, shrunken specters.

Although homosexuality inspired Shawn's plying of nudity in the cause of nationalism, the almost hypermasculinity of his troupe diminished the homosexual implications of the bare bodies because it did not fit into the societal framework of homosexuality as fey effeminate inversion. Ramsay Burt argues that the pressure to conform to heterosexual images of men prompted Shawn's heroic masculinity and that, in so doing, he did not challenge the "dominant heterosexual male norms."[73] Although this may be true, Shawn's visions were *also* about an idealized male homosexuality, which some audience members picked up. These manly men dancers may have conformed to heterosexual norms, but they were challenging common homosexual images of sissies. And, in this way, Shawn helped change the definition of homosexuality from gender inversion to same-sex object choice, through visual display of the male body itself. Dance abetted this change. Visual display of the body is a central component of dance, and Shawn exploited this characteristic to reveal the male body as an object of audience gazes and sexual attraction. The physicality of dance mirrored the physicality of sex; for gay men, choosing to engage in sex with a man meant choosing a male *body* over a female one. Through dance Shawn highlighted the centrality of the body in this choice.

But different audience members picked up different messages. Shawn countered notions of gender inversion and homosexuality in dance more frankly than he posited same-sex object choice for gay men. Shawn refuted the feminization of dance with gleaming muscular bravado and replaced any fluidity of gender roles that modern dance may have inspired with the rigidity of separate roles for men and women, emanating from different physical bodies. And his deliberate forgoing of any women dancers in his company assured the triumph of masculinity over femininity. This vision depended upon a heightened machismo *and* Shawn's closeting of his homosexuality. Shawn asked both St. Denis and Mumaw to remain silent about his sexual practices, because he thought the truth would cause more harm than good.[74] This silence accompanied images of hairless men dancing in tight trunks that epitomized a kind of heterosexual manliness far removed from common notions of queer effeminacy.

If Shawn's brandishing of the virile male body as object of sexual attraction for men received notice only from other gay men, its embedding at the core of images of heroic American virility demonstrated the depth of the need to believe in a triumphant masculinity and the necessity to hide any wisp of homosexuality.[75] His rigidly defined images belied the destabilizing conditions of changing economic, family, and public roles for American men and women during the depression. But the reality of Shawn's homosexuality alters this image. Not only did Shawn's dances present same-sex object choice for gay men, they detached masculinity from heterosexuality. Shawn unraveled definitions of homosexuality based on gender inversion and reconstructed another by upholding essentialist gender traits.

DANCING AMERICAN MEN: *O, LIBERTAD!*

By the mid-1930s Shawn's promotion of male dancers and masculine movement resonated throughout the dance world. In May 1935 *New Theatre* magazine and the New Dance League sponsored a dance recital of men only. Shawn and His Men Dancers did not appear, but most men active in the dance field in New York City did, including Charles Weidman, the ballet dancer William Dollar, and the African American dancer Add Bates. The second (and final) "Men in the Dance" program the following year in March featured a greater variety of dance, including African dancers (led by Momodu Johnson, who would choreograph *Bassa Moona* for the WPA Federal Theatre Project's Negro Project in December 1936), the white jazz dancer Roger Pryor Dodge, the Russian ballet dancer Vladimir Valentinoff, and a final section by modern dancers, headed by Charles Weidman and José Limón. The variety of dance styles illustrated the necessity of grouping all men dancers together for the unified cause of promoting dance as a career for men. Female dancers could afford to maintain a righteous distinction between ballet and modern dance (and even between the different groups within modern dance); male dancers recognized the bigger social barriers and, on these two occasions at least, overlooked aesthetic battles.

John Martin, the *New York Times* dance critic, deemed that the thrilling opening of the 1936 performance by the African dancers "made what followed seem a bit pale and lifeless in spots."[76] Martin's comment reinforced the trend among male dancers and critics to plunder ethnic and racial cultures and stereotypes for models of masculine movement and imagery in dance.[77] The imagery of these cultures played on preconceptions about these societies' closeness to nature and sex and reinforced the association of heterosexuality with masculine movement. Shawn portrayed Native American warriors and Spanish conquistadors, although not African tribesmen, which betrayed his prejudice against African Americans and what he considered their degenerate contributions of jazz and tap to American culture.[78] Shawn's persistent racist attitudes, more overt than those of other modern dancers,

Laboring in the Nude, Jacob's Pillow, early 1930s (Joseph Marks Collection, Harvard Theatre Collection, Houghton Library; used with permission)

demonstrated the enduring nativist elements especially apparent in the 1920s that lingered in the 1930s.

Shawn turned against Europe and Africa in his quest to promote dancing for men and re-created a mythic American manhood with his own all-male troupe. Combining athleticism, pioneering labor and courage, outdoor living, and entrepreneurial spirit, these men, according to Shawn, were the "ideal type of young representative American manhood."[79] Life at Jacob's Pillow was based on the hard physical labor and pioneer adventurousness of American men dancers. Price wrote in 1933, "Is it entirely an accident that in this homestead of an 18th century New England pioneer now dwells a cultural pioneer of the early 20th century?"[80] In addition to pioneering fortitude, Shawn and His Men Dancers had business acumen. They incorporated the group itself and shared ownership of two cars, the costumes, and sets and split profits from the tours. On tour they drove trucks, set up the stage for the day's performance, and then danced. These young American men were self-sufficient (including financially), responsible, and *active*. Their robust dynamism was a rebuttal to depression-era resignation.

Shawn also cultivated a populist basis for his American manliness by publicizing his midwestern roots. An apparent draft of a press release declared that from his Kansas City birth and Denver upbringing "no beginning could have been purer U.S.A.—just as his consequent career and entire personality is of the flavor of the hardy and staunchly patriotic early American pioneer."[81] Shawn did not rest on paeans to midwestern roots, however. He claimed that he brought the new American dance to the "hinterland of the States" where intense prejudice still existed against male dancers and against dance as an art form.[82] In a 1934 interview with the *Cornell Daily Sun* he chastised New York artists for their elitist attitude: "New York is not as American as even other big cities."[83] Shawn and His Men Dancers intended to appeal to "real" Americans outside New York City. The dances created from the back-breaking outdoor labor at Jacob's Pillow "have a quality of verity about them," Shawn argued, "that convinces audiences out in Texas and Montana and Wyoming."[84]

Reviewers around the country picked up on this populist appeal and praised Shawn for it. A writer in the *Dallas Times Herald* in 1937 commended Shawn for shunning "the glib way of the high-pressured press agent," organizing his own tours, and demonstrating tenacity in his annual long winter tours throughout the States. "His business has been to dance, and to dance, he has not been ashamed to appear in obscure halls, school auditoriums and many strange and humble places." The writer cautioned that audiences should not take him "for granted" and celebrate the "latest sensation" from Europe.[85] Walter Terry, Shawn's champion, named the populist appeal of Shawn's dance as his greatest feat: "He brings the most understandable art to the greatest number of people."[86] The mere appearance of Shawn and His Men Dancers in small towns throughout the South, Midwest, and West, to audiences that most likely had never seen much dance, gives credence to Terry's statement.

The Americana folk flavor of Shawn's works also bolstered his success. He created *Four Dances Based on American Folk Music* in 1931, a solo piece that included an American country dance, choreography to a Negro spiritual, and a dance to a Methodist revival hymn, and culminated in a patriotic finale to the "Battle Hymn of the Republic." *O, Libertad! An American Saga in Three Acts* (1937), an evening-long work, was his fullest vision of America and incorporated earlier solo and group dances. *O, Libertad!* depicted the past, present, and future in three acts. Shawn's "past" mainly consisted of dances based on those of Native Americans. "Noche Triste de Moctezuma" and "Los Hermanos Penitentes" narrated the influence of Europeans and then European Americans on Native Americans. The West of Mexico and California was the setting for the final three dances of the act, which ended with the "49ers," a rowdy square dance mimicking the celebration of the newly rich miners of 1849. Act II, "The Present (1914 to 1937)" started off on a college campus and rambled through war and the jazz decade. Its high point was "Depression," a piece composed of two parts, "Modernism" and "Recovery—Credo." A critic for the *Dancing Times* described Shawn in "Modernism" as "a hag in robes, ringlets and a frightening mask. It was comic and startling, for it proved a pitiless burlesque of the Martha Graham manner, a courageous step that made her followers gasp and sent more rational observers of the dance into hilarity."[87] Shawn's response to "Modernism" was "Recovery—Credo," his own autobiography in dance form. "Credo's" deep lunges, extended arm movements, and leaps swallowed the bent over, grave, and insistent stamping of "Modernism." "The Present" ended with the suite of dances earlier performed independently as *Olympiad*, which emphasized America's endurance and strength through the keen athleticism of its men.

The performance peaked in Act III, "The Future." Titled *Kinetic Molpai*, and originally choreographed in 1935 (and captured on film that survives from the mid-1930s), this work fused many of Shawn's ideals and hopes.[88] Shawn drew on the work of Gilbert Murray, author of *The Classical Tradition in Poetry*, for the title and idea of the piece. According to Murray, the Molpê (the singular form of Molpai) was an ancient Greek art form that included poetry, singing, drama, and rhythmic movement, but "in its essence it was only the yearning of the whole dumb body to express that emotion for which words and harps and singing were not enough."[89] Shawn's *Kinetic Molpai* begins with his entrance and circling the stage with pounding steps. Stopping center stage, he moves his torso from side to side, as if finding new possibilities of movement within his body for the first time. This leader then beckons to the four corners of the stage with a strong upswing of an arm; men enter in response. Different groupings of men move in and out of geometric patterns of circles and squares and often trade movements in a kind of bodily counterpoint. Later in the piece the leader falls to the ground, "dying." The men mourn the loss with small stoic steps and balled fists hitting their thighs. They circle aimlessly around the stage, ending in a lump of flesh, falling over one another. The piece then climbs to a crescendo with men whirling in "Surge." They create a wavy fugue with four alternating lines, falling to the floor and rising, and then repeating the pattern in side motions in three lines. In a dramatic depletion of the frenzy, the dancers dive to the floor and form a circle, each head to another's feet, as bodily links in a circular chain. Into this calm the leader comes forth from offstage, in a kind of resurrection. Holding onto one man's arm, he runs around the circle, successively pulling up all the men and creating a simple but dramatic explosion of energy. The finale, "Apotheosis," moves to a waltz and features big balletic steps of tourjetés, arabesques, and even a set of fouetté turns for Shawn. *Kinetic Molpai* finishes with a fierce run forward to the audience in a straight line spanning the stage, a drop to the knees, and broad side arms that spotlight center stage. Shawn stands there, regal, arms stretched upward and then sideways, as if in an embrace of the kneeling men.

Kinetic Molpai melded masculine movement and Greek heroism to form a triumphant vision of "the Athletic Art of the Dance as a field of creative endeavors for the American man," as it was described in the program notes. Shawn used dance and men to express this hopeful idealized vision of American civilization. In 1936 he wrote, " 'Another Athens shall arise' prophesied Shelly.

Where better than in America, with the athlete, the artist, the philosopher combined in one man—the dancer."[90] And he envisioned himself as that dancer. Shawn's idealistic, even egotistic, vision sold in small towns across America where the economic hard times of the depression had corroded hope. In a crisis of American manhood, where men lost jobs more often than women, suffered from not being the breadwinner for the family, and witnessed women successfully scrounging up jobs, the heroic masculinity Shawn and His Men Dancers portrayed and embodied soothed them. Even if the present was a time of struggle, the hope for the future of America dwelled in its kinetic heroic men.

DANCING IN THE ARMY

When the specter of a world war became a reality in the early 1940s, nationalist fervor changed from a broad movement that included interrogation of America's past and present policies to a more devout unquestioning patriotism. Although this celebratory embrace of the United States affected other modern dancers whose nationalist beliefs had been more critical than hagiographical, Shawn's brand of nationalism moved easily from theater buildings to theaters of war. Shawn's increasing age, the exhaustion of constant touring, dancers' desires to go on to something else, and the impending possibility of war all contributed to the group's demise in 1940 after seven years of performing. By 1942 many male modern dancers were serving in the armed forces, including almost all the dancers from Shawn and His Men Dancers, the accompanist and composer Jess Meeker, and the dance critic Walter Terry. Shawn, then fifty-one, escaped service because of his age. If a dearth of men had always been a problem in the dance profession, the war only heightened the shortage.

The number of modern dance performances diminished in New York City, and companies took no major tours around the country during World War II. But in the armed services some of these men found ways to dance. Mumaw was assigned to the Technical School of the Air Corps at Kessler Field in Biloxi, Mississippi, in 1942. Daniel Nagrin eventually served there and Paul Magriel, an author of books and articles on dance, was the librarian at the base. Shawn lived at the Hotel Biloxi to be near Mumaw. Within a few months Shawn and Mumaw were performing at Kessler Field and in nearby Gulfport. Performances and lecture-demonstrations at the base were benefits to raise money for a "Reception Cottage," which Shawn described as "a charming home-like place dedicated to the purpose of providing privacy for boys to say goodbye to their womenfolk when they are shipped away."[91] Shawn and Mumaw both received commendations from Col. Robert E. M. Goolrick, the commanding officer, for their efforts to raise money for the cottage.

Shawn did not comment on the irony of two gay lovers raising money for a building devoted to privacy with womenfolk, nor does Shawn's close relationship with Mumaw seem to have caused consternation for the military officers at a time when homosexuality was deemed a mental illness by the U.S. military and ground for a dishonorable discharge. In fact, the 1943 Cornell Selectee Index created by a group of doctors to simplify the initial psychiatric exams of inductees included a category of occupational choice: interior decorators, window dressers, and dancers were suspected of homosexual inclinations.[92] Allan Bérubé argues that gay men and women not only populated the wartime military but even developed a stronger sense of individual and group identity through the forced same-sex living circumstances and the military's attempts to define homosexual characteristics and behavior. While definitions tightened and prohibited some men from being admitted to the armed services, once there regulation of sexual behavior and rigid gender roles loosened. Within this intense and unusual situation female impersonators (many of them mimicking ballerinas) flourished as entertainment on bases in the well-known shows such as Irving Berlin's *This Is the Army*. Military and popular press reviews downplayed the association of female impersonation with homosexuality, which was more common to writings both before and after the war. In the exigencies of war the threat of homosexuality somewhat diminished.[93]

In this atmosphere Shawn and Mumaw's relationship and their performances of "interpretive dancing" roused only cheers.

Shawn noted that twenty-three hundred men at Kessler Field had *bought* tickets to see their performance; "they behaved like a dance fan audience at Carnegie Hall, even to bravos."[94] Mumaw performed solos when he was transferred to a base in England, to continued acclaim. And male members from the Littlefield Ballet, Ballet Theatre, Ballet Caravan, and Shawn and His Men Dancers performed in a rendition of *This Is the Army* in 1944 at an unspecified base. The reviewer noted that "Ted Shawn would probably have apoplexy if he could see one of his former dancers, trained in the uncompromising virility of the Shawn technique, swish his skirts as Betty Grable; yet on second glance he would undoubtedly take pride in the dancing of Charles Tate, for Pfc. Tate is excellent as Betty Grable and, in matters of dancing, infinitely more accomplished."[95]

The enthusiastic reaction to dance—even modern dance—in the armed forces probably had more to do with the boredom and stress of military life than with a new passion for dance. But some men may have also been interested in dance because of a sexual attraction to men, either because of the absence of women on the bases or not. Walter Terry, stationed in Egypt, wrote to Shawn that Shawn and His Men Dancers were well known among "the boys" there. The soldiers were reading Terry's recently published book, *Invitation to Dance*, which heralded Shawn's *O, Libertad!* as "the story of America with its cruelties, its greatness, its success and its failures told in terms of dance, told through the bodies of American men." And a picture Shawn sent of himself "has wound up over my bed (if you don't mind being a pin-up boy!)."[96] When Terry himself performed a Native American dance in the manner of Shawn at the Royal Opera House in Cairo, he claimed that the picture in *Stars and Stripes* was "gracing the walls of several of my buddies: one, Bill Joyce, an ex-Boston-cop has my photo sharing honors with his fiancee, and in another barracks I am flanked by Betty Grable and Ann Corio."[97]

The positive reaction to modern dance and female impersonation in the macho-minded military demonstrated the fluidity of sexual identity and behavior during wartime service. Certainly, homosexual contact flourished, from the tight sleeping quarters to the "Find-Your-Buddy-Week" that encouraged close friendships among men.[98] For gay male dancers, the war provided a way to prove their patriotism and their virility. But at least Terry recognized that Shawn had epitomized that ideal long before the war. In a letter to Mumaw in 1944 Terry upheld the vision of Shawn as reason enough to fight the war: "The dance contribution [of Shawn] has stood for the very best in America, has revealed our physical prowess, our spiritual heritage, our vision and something that I can describe only as the clean freshness of the New World. Such dances being as they are distillations of America, are worth living and fighting for."[99]

Ted Shawn expressed both his patriotism and his attraction to men through his company of, and choreography for, dancing American men. In Shawn's dancing portraits of America "masculine movement" operated in a variety of ways: as an example of America's potency, as a sign of essential differences between men and women, and as an ideal of homosexual love between men. His choreographic proclivities for near-nude male bodies nourished the need for symbols of natural vigor during the Great Depression and World War II. In fact, the attention to bodies may have attracted gay men to dance over other genres of art. With their bodies as sites of spectacle and spectatorship, gay male dancers could both flaunt and entice homosexual male desire. And Shawn's strategy of heightened virility on stage subtly changed the message, from signs of gender inversion to a hearty flaunting of male bodily display. Nationalism enabled this vision, masking homosexual urges and desires in a cloak of American masculine triumph that consoled men and women as they faced economic hardship and military battle.

NOTES

My thanks to Kathy Peiss for insights that continue to reverberate and to Jane Desmond for pushing me to think through key issues. I am also indebted to Mary Edsall for telling me about the treasure trove of materials on Ted Shawn and Jacob's Pillow at the Harvard Theatre Collection; the Houghton Library of Harvard University for its financial support; the staff of the Harvard Theatre Collection for helping me wade through the materials; and Norman Owen for access to, and insights about, the archival material at Jacob's Pillow.

1. Ted Shawn and Gray Poole, foreword to *The American Ballet* (New York: Holt, 1926), n.p.

2. Ibid.

3. Shawn is quoted in Walter Terry, "The Early Years at Jacob's Pillow," *After Dark*, August 1975, p. 30.

4. Ted Shawn, "A Defence of the Male Dancer," *New York Dramatic Mirror*, May 13, 1916, p. 19.

5. For an examination of the gendered reactions to women modern dancers at this time, see my *Modern Bodies: Dance in American Modernism*, (Chapel Hill, N.C.: University of North Carolina Press, forthcoming). Scholarship on women and gender in dance has boomed in recent years. For an overview of the literature, its influence on dance scholarship, and some of the important essays on the topic, see Jane Desmond, ed., *Meaning in Motion: New Cultural Studies of Dance* (Durham, N.C.: Duke University Press, 1997), especially her introduction. Less attention has been paid to the status of men in dance, although Ramsay Burt's book, *The Male Dancer: Bodies, Spectacle, Sexualities* (New York: Routledge, 1995), perhaps signifies a new trend.

6. For prescriptive evidence from the time period about the association of homosexuality among men interested in the arts, see Lewis M. Terman and Catherine Cox Miles, *Sex and Personality: Studies in Masculinity and Femininity* (1936; reprint, New York: Russell and Russell, 1968), and sources cited in Henry L. Minton, "Femininity in Men and Masculinity in Women: American Psychiatry and Psychology Portray Homosexuality in the 1930s," *Journal of Homosexuality* 13, no. 1 (fall 1986): 1–21. For a novel of the period that links homosexuality and dance, see Lew Levenson, *Butterfly Man* (New York: Castle, 1934). On the history of homosexuality and gay men, George Chauncey, *Gay New York: Gender, Urban Culture, and the Making of the Gay Male World, 1890–1940* (New York: Basic, 1994), is indispensable. Also helpful: Jonathan Weinberg, *Speaking for Vice: Homosexuality in the Art of Charles Demuth, Marsden Hartley, and the First American Avant-Garde* (New Haven, Conn.: Yale University Press, 1993); Allan Bérubé, *Coming Out under Fire: The History of Gay Men and Women in World War II* (New York: Free Press, 1990); John D'Emilio, *Sexual Politics, Sexual Communities: The Making of a Homosexual Minority in the United States, 1940–1970* (Chicago: University of Chicago Press, 1983); and Eve Kosofsky Sedgwick, *Epistemology of the Closet* (Berkeley: University of California Press, 1990).

7. Chauncey, *Gay New York*, chap. 11.

8. For histories of masculinity of this period, see George L. Mosse, *The Image of Man: The Creation of Modern Masculinity* (New York: Oxford University Press, 1996); Gail Bederman, *Manliness and Civilization: A Cultural History of Gender and Race in the United States, 1880–1917* (Chicago: University of Chicago Press, 1995); Michael Kimmel, *Manhood in America* (New York: Free Press, 1996); and Michael S. Kimmel and Michael A. Messner, eds., *Men's Lives* (Boston: Allyn and Bacon, 1995). On nationalism and sexuality see George L. Mosse, *Nationalism and Sexuality: Respectability and Abnormal Sexuality in Modern Europe* (New York: Howard Fertig, 1985) and Andrew Parker, Mary Russo, Doris Sommer, and Patricia Yaeger, eds., *Nationalisms and Sexualities*

(New York: Routledge, 1992). For a well-drawn study of the intersection of gender and nationalism in the case of dance, see Susan Manning, *Ecstasy and the Demon: Feminism and Nationalism in the Dances of Mary Wigman* (Berkeley: University of California Press, 1993).

9. Betty Poindexter, "Ted Shawn: His Personal Life, His Professional Career, and His Contributions to the Development of Dance in the United States of America from 1891 to 1963" (Ph.D. diss., Texas Women's University, 1963), 80, 84. See also the only published biography of Shawn, Walter Terry, *Ted Shawn: Father of American Dance* (New York: Dial, 1976).

10. Ted Shawn, *The Female of the Species,* Folder 625, Denishawn Collection, Dance Collection, New York Public Library for the Performing Arts (hereafter Dance Collection).

11. A publicity photo of Shawn with his dance teacher, Hazel Wallack, almost led to Shawn's dismissal from college. The university chancellor denounced Shawn and Wallack for their sensuous activity, evidenced in the photograph by the slit in Wallack's gown that exposed her leg almost to her hip. The chancellor would have expelled Shawn if he had not already quit school (Terry, *Ted Shawn*, 15).

12. Bliss Carman, *The Making of Personality* (1906; reprint, Boston: Page, 1929), 211.

13. Bliss Carman to Ted Shawn, November 13, 1912, quoted in Poindexter, "Ted Shawn: His Personal Life," 143.

14. Suzanne Shelton, *Divine Dancer: A Biography of Ruth St. Denis* (New York: Doubleday, 1981), 119–20; Ted Shawn and Gray Poole, *One Thousand and One Night Stands* (1960; reprint, New York: Da Capo, 1979), 25.

15. Shelton, *Divine Dancer,* 218–21. Beckman went on to marry a daughter of a wealthy investment banker (227).

16. The translation of the review in *Berner Tagblatt*, May 4, 1931, may be found in the Ted Shawn Scrapbook, Dance Collection.

17. Poindexter, "Ted Shawn: His Personal Life," 238–41; the quote is from "Shawn's Art Form for Athletes," unidentified, undated clipping [mid-1930s?], Folder 628, Ted Shawn Collection (hereafter Shawn Collection), Dance Collection.

18. Poindexter, "Ted Shawn: His Personal Life," 284; the scope of the tour is confirmed by the meticulous route lists Shawn kept, which have been preserved in the Shawn Collection.

19. Catalogue, "Shawn School of Dance For Men," Shawn Programs, Dance Collection.

20. Chauncey, *Gay New York*, 284–85.

21. Terry, *Ted Shawn*, 107.

22. Edward Carpenter, *Love's Coming of Age* (1906; reprint, New York: Michell Kennerley, 1941), 136.

23. Terry, *Ted Shawn*, 14. Shawn's eradication of feminine influence in dance may have come from a growing bitterness toward women: his hurt over the early death of his mother and the philandering of St. Denis, which he believed prompted him to turn to men for love and affection. Although Shawn acknowledged to Terry that he " 'guessed' his homosexuality was always there

'deep down,'" he never stopped believing that if St. Denis had been faithful to him, he would have been satisfied in marriage with her (130).

24. Jane Sherman and Barton Mumaw, *Barton Mumaw, Dancer: From Denishawn to Jacob's Pillow and Beyond* (New York: Dance Horizons, 1986), 72–73.

25. Ibid., 124.

26. Ted Shawn, "The Dancers' Bible: An Appreciation of Havelock Ellis's *The Dance of Life*," *Denishawn Magazine* 1, no. 1 [1924], n.p. Shawn also recommended Ellis in *The American Ballet*, and *Dance We Must* (1940; reprint, Pittsfield, Mass.: Eagle Printing, 1950), 119. Ellis accorded Shawn at least some attention; he wrote the introduction for Shawn's *The American Ballet*.

27. Lucien Price to Ted Shawn, July 10, 1962, Folder 380, Shawn Collection.

28. Price to Shawn, December 14, 1935, Folder 52, Shawn Collection.

29. Price to Shawn, February 8, 1934, Folder 39, Shawn Collection.

30. Price to Shawn, February 21, 1935, Folder 47, Shawn Collection. For another iteration of this view, see Price to Shawn, January 6, 1935, Paige Box 9, Joseph Marks Collection, Harvard Theatre Collection, Houghton Library.

31. Price to Shawn, September 1, 1963, Paige Box 9, Marks Collection. In the next paragraph of this letter, however, Price asks to see recent photographs Shawn had gotten from Denmark, most likely a reference to the Danish pornographic magazine *Eos*. Shawn corresponded with Pillow photographer John Lindquist about this magazine and strategies for getting such material through the U.S. mail during the same month (Shawn to Lindquist, September 15 and 26, 1963, Correspondence Box 3, Folder 3, John Lindquist Collection, Harvard Theatre Collection). Certain forms of sexual commodification, then, Price valued.

32. Price to Shawn, September 28, 1960, Paige Box 9, Marks Collection.

33. Price to Shawn, August 14, 1961, Folder 380, Shawn Collection. In fact, Price had been attracted to one member of Shawn's troupe, John Schubert, an interest that was apparently mutual (John Schubert to Lucien Price, October 22, 1938, Paige Box 9, Marks Collection). Schubert died in World War II, however, and his death, along with that of another lover during World War I, contributed to Price's romanticized vision of homosexual love.

34. The Harvard Theatre Collection houses the John Lindquist Collection, which includes some correspondence and a massive amount of photographic material. For a general overview of the collection and biography of Lindquist, see Amy Lucker, "The John Lindquist Collection at the Harvard Theatre Collection," *Performing Arts Resources* 20 (1996): 57–74.

35. For gay men at this time it was quite useful to have a photographer as a friend. Lindquist personally developed film that was considered criminal. He apparently distributed these photographs fairly widely, to a circle of gay men that included Shawn and other male dancers (see letter to Lindquist from unidentified man [Jon?], February 11, 1961, Correspondence Box 1, Folder 5, Lindquist Collection). Shawn and Lindquist had an understanding that Shawn would see *all* pictures taken by Lindquist before anyone else saw them. While Shawn was worried about particular pictures "falling into the wrong hands," he also built up quite a picture collection for his own use and enjoyment (Shawn to Lindquist, July 17, 1965, Correspondence Box 3, Folder 3, Lindquist Collection).

36. Neither John Martin, dance critic of the *New York Times*, nor Lincoln Kirstein, writer on dance and supporter of George Balanchine, consistently praised Shawn. Although both engaged in homosexual affairs, both were married and perhaps less inclined to glorify Shawn's fraternal ideal. They also held high artistic standards, which they may have believed Shawn did not reach.

37. Ted Shawn, "Men Must Dance," *Dance* (East Stroudsburg, Pa.) 1, no. 2 (November 1936): 10.

38. Shawn, *Dance We Must*, 119.

39. Ted Shawn, "Dancing Originally Occupation Limited to Men Alone," *Boston Herald*, May 17, 1936.

40. Shawn, "Men Must Dance," 10.

41. Chauncey, *Gay New York*, 52–55, 344.

42. Ted Shawn, "Dancing for Men," *Physical Culture*, July 1917, p. 16.

43. Shawn, "Dancing Originally."

44. Shawn, "Men Must Dance," 10.

45. Shawn, "Dancing Originally."

46. Shawn is quoted in "Found Dancing Wasn't for Sissies," unidentified, undated clipping [*Springfield Republican* or *Berkshire Eagle*? 1934?], Shawn clipping file, Dance Collection.

47. Shawn, "Dancing Originally."

48. Shawn is quoted in Barbara Busse, "Ted Shawn and Only Troupe of Male Dancers Give Program in Christian College Auditorium," *Columbia Missouri Christian College Microphone*, March 20, 1934, Shawn Clipping File, Dance Collection.

49. My analysis is based on a film of the piece, dated 1934–1940, Dance Collection.

50. Theresa J. Shier, "Ted Shawn's Male Dance Troupe Hypnotizes M.S.C. Audience," *Lansing (Michigan) State Journal*, November 6, 1936.

51. "Ted Shawn Dancers Put through Vigorous Siege," undated clipping from the *Springfield Republican*, Shawn Clipping File, Dance Collection.

52. *Dancing Times*, October 1934, p. 12; *Des Moines Register*, April 2, 1934.

53. Margaret Lloyd, "The Dance as a Manly Art," *Christian Science Monitor*, undated [1938?], clipping file of Ted Shawn and His Men Dancers, Dance Collection.

54. Edward Eddy, *News and Leader*, February 14, 1932.

55. Shawn, "Dancing Is Unique among the Arts in That Human Body Is the Medium," *Boston Herald*, May 5, 1936.

56. Shawn, *American Ballet*, 65.

57. Ibid., 81.

58. "He-Man Dances," *Now and Then*, January 1938, p. 6. Offstage, his own body preoccupied him too, and his weight bounced dramatically in response to intense periods of dieting and training followed by laxity. Shawn continued to send nude pictures of himself to a select audience throughout his life (and found in the John Lindquist Collection). Shawn included one in a letter to Barton Mumaw that was taken when Shawn was nearing his seventy-fourth birthday. Shawn kidded about his "Narcissus complex" (Sherman and Mumaw, *Barton Mumaw, Dancer*, 223).

59. Mosse, *Image of Man*, 95; Mosse, *Nationalism and Sexuality*, chap. 3. For an analysis of the natural body in dance during this period, see Ann Daly, *Done into Dance: Isadora Duncan in America* (Bloomington: Indiana University Press, 1995).

60. Sherman and Mumaw, *Image of Man*, 105.

61. Mosse discusses the influence of J. J. Winckelman in *Nationalism and Sexuality*, 11–14.

62. Price to Shawn, September 11, 1936, Paige Box 9, Marks Collection.

63. Price is quoted in Sherman and Mumaw, *Barton Mumaw, Dancer*, 129.

64. Ibid., 124–29.

65. Katherine S. Drier, *Shawn the Dancer* (New York: Barnes, 1933), n.p.

66. Harry Gribble to John Lindquist, January 18, 1940, Correspondence Box 1, Folder 1, Lindquist Collection, emphasis in original.

67. One reviewer did comment that "in the opening group of dances the particular thing reminding me of the fan dance was the absence of a fan" (*Chicago Daily News*, April 9, 1934).

68. Martin Sobelman to Katherine Dunham, April 5, 1941, Box 2, Folder 2, Katherine Dunham Collection, Southern Illinois University. Certainly, the perceived licentiousness of African American women also contributed to Dunham's problems in Boston; see chap. 3 of my forthcoming book. On censorship in Boston and elsewhere, see Paula Kane, *Separatism and Subculture: Boston Catholicism, 1900–1920* (Chapel Hill: University of North Carolina Press, 1994); Charles W. Morton, "The Censor's Double Standard," *The Reporter* 2, no. 6 (March 14, 1950): 22–24; Kaier Curtin, *"We Can Always Call Them Bulgarians": The Emergence of Lesbians and Gay Men on the American Stage* (Boston: Alyson, 1987); and Abe Laufe, *The Wicked Stage: A History of Theater Censorship and Harassment in the United States* (New York: Ungar, 1978).

69. Price to Shawn, December 28, 1935, Folder 52, Shawn Collection.

70. Barbara Melosh, *Engendering Culture: Manhood and Womanhood in New Deal Public Art and Theater* (Washington, D.C.: Smithsonian Institution Press, 1991), 205–8.

71. For a detailed account of women in Soviet iconography, see Victoria E. Bonnell, "The Peasant Woman in Stalinist Political Art of the 1930s," *American Historical Review* 98, no. 1 (February 1993): 55–82.

72. "Mussolini Writes a Signed Article Expressly for Our Readers," *Physical Culture* 65, no. 6 (June 1931): 18–20, 80–81; Benito Mussolini, "Building a Nation's Health," *Physical Culture* 68, no. 1 (July 1932): 14–15, 64, 68. Shawn appeared on the cover of the July 1917 issue of *Physical Culture* and was featured in the November 1924 issue. Shawn and Macfadden had a personal friendship as well; Shawn and his company stayed at Macfadden's Florida home and spa in 1936 (see Shawn Newsletter, January 1937, Barton Mumaw Collection, Harvard Theatre Collection). Macfadden's interest in dance was inspired by his first wife, Mary, who had studied "nature dancing" (Robert Ernst, *Weakness Is a Crime: The Life of Bernarr Macfadden* [Syracuse, N.Y.: Syracuse University Press, 1991], 83). See also Ann Fabian, "Making a Commodity of Truth: Spec-

ulations on the Career of Bernarr Macfadden," *American Literary History* 5, no. 1 (spring 1993): 51–76.

73. Burt, *Male Dancer*, 110.

74. Sherman and Mumaw, *Barton Mumaw, Dancer*, 144.

75. John Martin, the *New York Times* dance critic, seems to have picked up on the homosexual allure only partially masked by heightened masculinity. He applauded Shawn's effort to attract young men to dance but had some unease about Shawn's approach. About a 1934 performance Martin commented that "Mr. Shawn's present program . . . is highly personal and its costuming scant to the point of non-existence—a combination not conducive to comfort on the receiving side of the footlights" (*New York Times*, February 11, 1934). Perhaps Martin picked up on this because the "highly personal" approach of Shawn in finding sexual desire in male bodies paralleled Martin's own desires.

76. *New York Times*, March 16, 1936.

77. Burt, *Male Dancer*, 109. The experience of African American gay male dancers would lend a needed perspective on how they negotiated these powerful stereotypes. Unfortunately, I have come across virtually no primary materials from this period that speak to this issue. While this may mean that most African American male dancers were not gay, the difficulty of finding documentation of sexual behavior and activities is compounded in the case of racial and ethnic minorities.

78. Shawn, *American Ballet*, 20–22; Shawn, *Dance We Must*, 96–98.

79. Ted Shawn, "Shawn Trains Dancers in Berkshire Refuge," *Berkshire Evening Eagle*, June 27, 1936.

80. Lucien Price, "Mr. Ted Shawn's Significant Movement to Restore the Art of the Dance for Men to Its Rightful Place in Modern Life," *Boston Globe*, October 22, 1933.

81. "Ted Shawn: His Career as a Dancer," undated, unidentified clipping [mid-1930s?], Folder 628, Shawn Collection.

82. "Ted Shawn Today: Success of His Male Ballet," *Dancing Times*, October 1934, pp. 10–11.

83. *Cornell Daily Sun*, November 2, 1934.

84. Shawn, "Shawn Trains Dancers."

85. *Dallas Times Herald*, February 24, 1937.

86. Walter Terry, "Leader of the Dance," *New York Herald Tribune*, February 18, 1940.

87. Russell Rhodes, "Shawn and His Men Dancers at Last Reach Broadway," *Dancing Times*, April 1938, pp. 31–32.

88. The film is in the Dance Collection. For a detailed narrative of the dance, see Sherman and Mumaw, *Barton Mumaw, Dancer*, 270–77.

89. Murray is quoted in the program for the performance at the Majestic Theater in New York, February 27, 1938, Shawn Programs, Dance Collection.

90. Ted Shawn, "Asceticism of Dark Ages Almost Buried in America, Shawn Says," *Boston Herald*, June 4, 1936.

91. Shawn to Terry, May 28, 1943, Folder 521, Shawn Collection.

92. Bérubé, *Coming Out under Fire*, 20.

93. Ibid., chap. 3.

94. Shawn to Terry, November 20, 1942, Folder 520, Shawn Collection.

95. Unspecified publication [*Stars and Stripes?*], December 1944, Folder 143, Shawn Collection.

96. Terry to Shawn, January 15, 1944, Folder 143; Walter Terry, *Invitation to Dance* (New York: Barnes, 1942), 77.

97. Terry to Shawn, January 15, 1944, Folder 143, Shawn Collection.

98. Barton Mumaw discusses this from his own experience in the armed forces (Sherman and Mumaw, *Barton Mumaw, Dancer*, 161–62). See also Bérubé, *Coming Out under Fire*.

99. Terry is quoted in Sherman and Mumaw, *Barton Mumaw, Dancer*, 172.

Closets Full of Dances: Mc
Performance of Masculinity

Susan Leigh Foster

Matthew Bourne's sensationally popular "gay male" *Swan Lake* premiered in London's West End in September 1995, eventually breaking box office records for longest-running production set by Diaghilev's Ballets Russes. Using the original Tchaikovsky score and a modern dance vocabulary that only occasionally invokes ballet, Bourne has re-envisioned the famous romance between the Prince and the Swan Queen as the coming-out story of a gay prince, dominated by his mother, who finds no satisfaction in the royal regimens or underground getaways that comprise his life. On the verge of suicide he instead dreams himself into a world inhabited by magical creatures, male swans whose sensuous strength and sinuous vulnerability promise sexual and emotional satisfaction. Swan, part of this all-male corps de ballet, reciprocates his affections in a series of duets, tender, passionate, and erotic, yet their attachment is finally severed by the two separate societies to which they belong. The Prince's court cannot accept his homosexuality and condemns him first to the asylum and then to the sickbed; Swan's cohorts cannot forgive his dalliance with a mere mortal. In the final scene Swan, hounded by his fellow swans, scoops the dying prince into his arms and ascends heavenward, presumably toward a world where they might live happily ever after.

Exhilarating, epic, entertaining, the production elicits enormous sympathy for the gay male couple. The Prince's severely constrained life and inarticulate feelings resonate strongly with the closetedness of homosexuality in dance and in society. Swan's bravery and vulnerability evoke the kind of admiration reserved for the noblest of heroes. The corps de ballet, hairy chested, gangly, athletic, sweaty, and sexy, summons up an Otherness—magical, menacing, seductive, enthralling—that the female entourage in the original production must have achieved but can no longer sustain.[1] When the male swans appear, one by one, cavorting to some of Tchaikovsky's most famous phrases, they seem to burst through the closet's door. Rather than a diminution of their power, through endless duplication the addition of each swan connotes yet another celebratory coming out.

Part of the production's dazzling success is sustained by its witty references to the original ballet. Bourne's clever choreography keeps viewers in continual and delighted suspense as to how he has altered the well-known scenario. Swan, for example, reappears in Act III, not as the Black Swan but as a leather-clad bounder who puts the make on the mother. Bourne also uses to dazzling effect imaginative sets, costumes, and a movement vocabulary drawn from social, club, and folk dance traditions as well as several schools within modern dance. Beyond this impressive display of craft, the dance's greatest achievement is its synthesis of wit, spectacle, and social cause. This is a dance with a clear and timely message delivered with such deft agility and beguiling seduction as to win over the most hardened homophobe.

For all my assertions as to the gay male meaning of the piece, critical coverage in both Britain and the United States has consistently ignored its brazenly open treatment of this taboo subject. Nor does Bourne commit to a homosexual reading of his work, claiming instead a more universal significance in which Swan represents for the Prince the "freedom, the beauty and the strength . . . that he's not got in his restrictive Royal life."[2] Although Bourne, in an interview for the gay male newspaper *Edge*, happily notes the gay male interpretation, he prefers a reading of the swans as more transcendent figures:

> Well, you know, there's a lot of panic around whether it gets dubbed that. When we first announced that we were doing it—because we've got male swans and still have a prince—the actual assumption was that it's *obviously* the gay *Swan Lake*, which is true up to a point. It can be seen as that, which we're happy about as

well. But really, it's about someone, the prince, who can't be what
he wants to be. It certainly suits the story and it works completely
on that level. Gay audiences who come and see it can read it that
way and love it because of that. Obviously, it's something they can
identify with, and there isn't an enormous amount of things you
can go and see and have that kind of relationship with. So it's there.
But what I've tried to do is make it more universal.[3]

Critical reviews sustain Bourne's intent by consistently failing to
mention any homosexual references.[4]

Both the dance, in its sensuous representation of same-sex desire, and the criticism, in its uncanny neglect of obvious homosexual content, bring into sharp relief modern dance's closeting
of homosexuality throughout this century. The production's
scale and enormous popularity illuminate with astonishing clarity
just how little sexual desire, much less homosexual desire, the
modern dance tradition has ever staged. For one hundred years,
modern dancers and choreographers have resisted all allegations
that their art alluded, however discretely or remotely, to sex. Early
American luminaries in the new genre, Isadora Duncan and Ruth
St. Denis, went to enormous lengths to elaborate in and for dance
a nonsexualized corporeality. Subsequent generations of choreographers and dancers likewise cultivated the body as a muscu-
loskeletal system that responded to emotional but never sexual
impulses. Only toward the end of the century did dances begin to
elucidate clear sexual identities and desires on stage, and in large
part, this choreographic initiative has centered on gay male identity.[5] Living through the gay liberation movement and the AIDS
crisis, choreographers Bill T. Jones, David Rousseve, Nigel
Charnock, Lloyd Newson, Javier de Frutos, along with Bourne
and many others, have begun to press hard on the closet walls.

At the beginning of the century, modern dance's closet, one
that housed what studies of human sexuality had only recently
identified as the homosexual, formed a part of the very foundation of this new dance genre. In order to secure their experimental aesthetic claims, the earliest modern choreographers strategically positioned their dances as far from the sexual as possible.
Because they were women, because they were performing pub-

licly new kinds of bodily movement, the presumption of immoral, illicit, or prurient elements in their work jeopardized the entire project. Their solution, to create a chaste dancing, ensured success and at the same time offered a haven for homosexuality. Not only was homosexuality protected because the dances were never about sex but choreographers and dancers could explore movement in new ways that might simultaneously encode the sexual, whether heterosexual or homosexual, and articulate a nonsexual physicality.

Unlike ballet, a form of bodily display whose reputation could be partially salvaged through references to chivalric codes and aristocratic comportment and whose tradition extended back over generations, the new modern dance, with its emphasis on individual creativity, required new forms of justification. A company such as the Ballets Russes, in its revitalization of ballet through lavish exoticist spectacle, could feature a dancer such as Nijinsky by using as rationale the equation between deviance and artistic brilliance. In contrast, the modern dance elaborated an antisexual environment in which choreographers and dancers formulated alternative identities, both aesthetic and physical. Thus modern dance's closet, even as it allowed viewers to project a sexualized identity onto the dancers, assured them that the choreographic basis for such fantasy did not exist because dance and dancers resolutely pursued a nonsexual investigation of human movement.

This essay examines four distinct closets in the history of modern dance as exemplified in the choreographic projects of Ted Shawn, Merce Cunningham, Mangrove, and Matthew Bourne.[6] The field in which these men worked was, until recently, dominated by female choreographers and dancers, and it focused on the "woman's" work of investigating psychological interiority and cultivating the body.[7] Dismissed by many as vulgar exhibitionism or ephemeral nonsense, it was marked as a feminine pursuit and denigrated accordingly. Beginning with Shawn, male choreographers in modern dance have necessarily contributed choreographic solutions that simultaneously pioneered within the field, asserted masculinity, and closeted homosexuality. Unlike female choreographers, whose sexual orientation, immersed in the gynocentric preoccupations of the tradition, never posed an obvious problem, male choreographers have contended with the prejudice that a man dancing is unmanly, hence deviant, effeminate, and probably homosexual. Analysis of these male choreographers' initiatives thus brings the contours of modern dance's closet into focus.

In order to sharpen this focus still further, each of the four choreographic projects considered here is situated with respect to theories of homosexuality of the same historical moment. Both the research on sexuality and the choreography postulated similar kinds of subjectivities and corporealities, constructing from them explanations of homosexual behavior and a closeted version of that behavior in danced form. In the history of twentieth-century sexology the epistemological foundations for rationalizing homosexuality shifted many times, as did the closet of the homosexual. Modern dance has staged with consummate clarity the embodied version of the closet's changing epistemology.

By situating choreography and sexology side by side, I want to argue for parity of the two practices as forms of knowledge production that theorize identity and corporeality. By comparing one with the other, I hope to show how each makes similar kinds of theoretical moves. The sexologies do not provide the context within which to interpret a choreographer's motivation or intent. Rather, authors and choreographers, sexologies and dances, are evaluated as discursive sites that register a social and corporeal politics. As discourses both dances and sexologies open themselves to many spectatorships, many readings, and I have alluded to this multiplicity of interpretations by also providing one "alternative" response to each choreographic closet. Before turning to an examination of these closets, however, this essay considers the climate of concerns around the body, movement, and gender in which modern dance was founded.

CHASTE DANCING

Alongside the wide variety of movement practices that engaged turn-of-the-century Americans as participants and viewers—new

forms of physical education and expressive culture, Delsarte exhi-
bitions, pageants, folk dance performances, dances of the world
as seen at the world fairs and expositions—choreographers Isadora Duncan and Ruth St. Denis began to elaborate an entirely
new vision of dancing.[8] This new approach to dancing and dance
making, a "high" art form radically distinct from ballet, on the
one hand, and vaudeville, cabaret, or follies entertainments, on
the other, promised a glimpse of the human soul, its changing-
ness, its transcendent veracity.[9] Duncan and St. Denis, not the
first or only progenitors of this exceptional artistic initiative, stand
as monumental emblems of its success. Offering contrasting visions of the soul's corporeal manifestations, Duncan in her aus-
tere Greeklike toga and St. Denis in her ornate orientalist veils invited audiences to celebrate a body unencumbered by the artifices
of society, a body tuned to inner spiritual rhythms. An extraordinary accomplishment, especially for women, the new artistic
genre they helped to found imbued the body with a dignity and
beauty that gave life new meaning.

Responses to Duncan's dancing repeatedly betrayed the viewer's
surprise at the remarkable chasteness of her performance. Her
nearly naked body purveyed no erotic allure, no stimulation of
physical desire. Through her gaze and gestures she communicated
her conviction that the body constituted a hallowed place.
Through her shaping of and in space, she trained viewers to attend
to the sculptural potential of movement. Not only did she resem-
ble a work of classical art but she articulated a new yet classical
movement aesthetic. She did not promenade like a showgirl or
pose fetchingly like a ballerina. Instead, she commanded viewers to
focus on the way the body moved in tandem with the music, and
she persuaded them that this movement tracked that of the soul.

To buttress the claims she was making choreographically, Duncan expounded verbally and in writing on her vision of a new
American dance.[10] She drew upon the dignity of the body summoned up in Hellenistic humanism and in the poetry of Walt
Whitman.[11] She fashioned an idiosyncratic feminism, one that
championed the body's freedom from the constraints of dress and
social comportment, and she embraced Nietzschean philosophy

and its use of dance as metaphor for life and change. She also tapped the country's desire to witness a uniquely American artistic production, envisioning the lithe and healthy body of "America Dancing." At the same time she railed against ballet, with its rigid patterns and barren imagery, and she denigrated African dance, as exemplified by Negro dances, for its lascivious simplicity. Both traditions resonated with sexual connotations that Duncan was eager to avoid. The ballerina as kept woman signaled the decadent trajectory of ballet's form, the inevitable product of a stultifying society such as Europe's. The African dancer, possessed by a sexual frenzy, demonstrated a primitive and unrefined variety of bodily responsiveness against which Duncan asserted her own naturalistic cultivation of the body. Duncan used both traditions to distinguish her new danced vision, effectively organizing racist and nationalist sentiments to reinforce one another.

Whereas Duncan epitomized a white America dancing, St. Denis, an amalgam of orientalist types incarnate, bolstered nationalist and racist discourses not through her depiction of the white body as universal but through her effective appropriation of other dance traditions.[12] Tapping America's extensive interest in religious experimentation, the impetus to reevaluate spiritual practices in light of new exposure to world religions, St. Denis choreographed religious quests set in exotic Asian lands. She deployed sumptuous spectacle as the environment for her spiritual exploration, initially reinforcing viewers' expectations of standard exoticist entertainment. Yet her movement and phrasing, all uncannily dissimilar from other vaudeville performances, soon forced a different kind of attention. She paused for too long; she evinced too much concentration; the stunt never materialized. Instead, viewers witnessed the representation of spiritual awakening. And although the narrative of her quest propelled the body toward ecstatic obliviousness, St. Denis consistently subverted and sublimated any sexual connotations that her delirium might suggest.

Like Duncan's reception, St. Denis's reviews often commented on the quantity of exposed midriff but went on to stress the spiritual essence of her dancing. To portray religiosity on stage and to

vincingly provided the ultimate refutation of any sexual
. Yes, viewers might have reasoned, she danced the pil-
an Eastern and not Christian devotee, but all religions
dication to spiritual rather than carnal experience. Yes,
sne appeared in uncontrolled and uncontrollable ecstasy, but she
always retreated into solitude after communing with her god. Yes,
she assumed a foreign character, but, after all, she was a white
woman who merely represented this foreignness, demonstrating,
as one critic observed, "a universal rhythm beneath the broken
chaos of our modern industrial world which shall infuse new joy
and rhythmic harmony into our common life."[13]

The antisexual tactics developed in Duncan's and St. Denis's
choreography, infused with racist and nationalist sentiments, provided the necessary defense against the inevitable charges that
their performances purveyed only the trivial or lurid. By ensuring
the absence of sexuality, these women could display a new body-
centered endeavor, found a new genre of dancing. Yet it is worth
examining in greater detail just what kinds of assumptions Duncan and St. Denis were working with and against in their campaign to create a whole new kind of dance, a newly respectable
view of dance. Why were viewers so surprised at how chaste their
dancing was? What did they expect to see that Duncan and St.
Denis repeatedly subverted?

THE CUPIDITY OF THE FLESH

The writings of humanist, sexologist, and dance aficionado
Havelock Ellis provide an extraordinary view of the epistemological relatedness of dance and sexuality at the beginning of the
twentieth century. In his most popular and best-selling book, *The
Dance of Life*, and in his earlier sexologies, Ellis demonstrates
clearly the kinds of racist and colonialist prejudice that Duncan
and St. Denis reiterated, as well as the sexist prejudice that they
had to refute, all in an effort to create a new kind of dancing.[14]
It is worth examining his theories of dance in some detail, because many of their underlying presumptions continue to inform
the status of dance in politics, religion, and education throughout the twentieth century.

For Ellis, dancing expresses religious belief, amorous zeal, or aesthetic inquiry. The origin of all forms of dancing, however, regardless of their function, lies in the sexual impulses of animals. Of the "two primary arts," dancing and building, dancing is perhaps the first because "the nest of birds is the chief early form of building, and . . . the nest may first have arisen as an accidental result of the ecstatic sexual dance of birds."[15] Species as primitive as insects evidence the inclination to dance as part of their courtship rituals. The urge to mate, that which inspires the spastic jerks of the chimpanzee's feeble legs, is the crude motion out of which "the heavenly alchemy of evolution has created the divine movements of Pavlova," Ellis writes.[16] Not only does dancing originate in mating impulses, Ellis says, but competence at dancing facilitates the conquest of woman by man: "By his beauty, his energy, his skill, the male must win the female, so impressing the image of himself on her imagination that finally her desire is aroused to overcome her reticence. That is the task of the male throughout nature, and in innumerable species besides Man it has been found that the school in which the task may best be learnt is the dancing-school."[17] Thus dancing, according to Ellis, makes manifest the most primitive sexual urgings, heterosexual urgings, which are common across the whole evolutionary continuum from arthropods to bipeds.[18]

Yet, Ellis argues, in order to develop the facility at dancing necessary for sexual conquest, the body must be disciplined, its most unruly parts must be subjected to the rigors of measure, proportion, and rhythm.[19] Dances of the world evidence different approaches to this disciplining process, but African dance distinguishes itself as the most complete, "in which the play of all the chief muscle-groups of the body is harmoniously interwoven. When both sexes take part in such an exercise, developed into an idealized yet passionate pantomime of love, we have the complete erotic dance."[20] Desire fuels the quest for a disciplined body through which its urgent messagings might be apprehended, he reasons. Although "potent and dazzling images, all wrought by desire" have proliferated among the cultures of the world, both the mechanism of bodily cultivation and its message remain the same.[21] Thus Ellis's notion of dancing—protean, evolving—takes different forms but remains continuous with its primitive origins.

Ellis's earlier studies of the sexual impulse had likewise explored dance's role as a major form of arousal of the sexual instinct. He argued that sexual desire, that category of human experience that links animals and humankind, both primitive and civilized, is brought about by and cultivated through dance movement. In his *Analysis of the Sexual Impulse* Ellis presents an overwhelming array of ethnographic evidence in support of his theory that both civilized and savage peoples use dancing to arouse sexual excitement. After discussing the choreography of courtship practices among snails, octopi, spiders, preying mantises, cowbirds, tyrant flycatchers, "red-breasted marsh-birds," mallards, pheasants, and ostriches, Ellis proceeds with pages of anecdotal reports drawn from anthropological and travelogue literatures on the relationship between dancing and sexual activity. He quotes descriptions of lascivious dances among the Muras of Brazil who hold "a Bacchantic dance in a great circle [that includes] a pantomimic representation of sexual intercourse"; the Wolofs who perform a dance in which "the woman tucks up her clothes and convulsively agitates the lower part of her body; she alternately shows her partner her vulva and hides it from him by a regular movement, backward and forward, of the body"; and the "Australians of Dieyerie" whose "women keep time by clapping their hands between their thighs; promiscuous sexual intercourse follows after the dance; jealousy is forbidden."[22] In the Torres Strait "the young men woo girls by being good dancers as a substitute for the old days in which whoever brought home the head of someone they had killed was considered the best catch."[23] Women dancers living on the island of Nias in the Malay Archipelago perform "a lascivious undulation of the flanks while the face and breast are slowly wound round by the *sarong* held in the hands, and then again revealed,"[24] whereas the Tahitians perform dances "consisting of motions and gestures beyond imagination wanton."[25] Those who organize ritual ceremonies that begin with dancing and end with sexual intercourse include the Alfoers of Seram in the Moluccas, the Kafirs of southern Africa, the Guros of the

Ivory Coast, and the Minitari (Hidatsa) of the Three Affiliated Tribes of North Dakata. Those cultures that feature dancing at marriage ceremonies both to enhance the desire of the newly married couple and to promote feelings of courtship among unmarried attendees include people living along the Wanigela River in Papua New Guinea and in Sumatra, according to Ellis. He even includes mention of Marquesan celebrations, in which, he alleges, all the men present are invited to engage in sexual intercourse with the bride.[26]

Ellis makes several observations about dance in relation to sexual practices based on this evidence: first, that dancing develops the musculature thoroughly and effectively; second, and as a consequence, dancing produces tumescence, that biological condition that marks an essential stage in the narrative of sexual fulfillment; and third, that because dancing leads inevitably to tumescence, all species place dance in the service of the sexual instinct.[27] The link between dancing and sexual excitation may be attenuated but never severed. Indeed, the distinction between primitive and civilized societies can be established in the degree to which civilized groups prolong and abstract the fact of tumescence as evidenced in their dance practices, Ellis says. He goes further, claiming that savage societies engage in realistic pantomimes of sexual arousal and coitus, whereas civilized societies elaborate a more remote, symbolic version of sexual excitation, one that nonetheless serves in some cases as a complete substitute for sexual gratification.[28] Paradoxically, then, civilized choreography, which places sex at a great distance from dance by removing the overt sexual references, can and does stand in for the actual sexual act. As proof of this, Ellis explains that young British girls find that once sexual relations have been established, their ardor for dancing dissipates.[29]

Underpinning Ellis's vision of dance is the biological presupposition that as muscular movement increases, the higher centers of the nervous system no longer dominate. According to Ellis: "Muscular movement of which the dance is the highest and most complex expression, is undoubtedly a method of autointoxication of the very greatest potency. All energetic movement, indeed, tends to produce active congestion. In its influence on the brain violent exercise may thus result in a state of intoxication even resembling insanity."[30] As the body engages in intense physical exercise, it produces a state of congestion that reduces one's capacity to think and to control desire. Or perhaps the prolonged and repetitious use of the neuromuscular system simply diminishes brain activity. Whatever the case, dancing not only enhances heterosexual desire but when practiced alone encourages an autoerotic ecstasy, according to Ellis, working on the nervous system simultaneously as a narcotic and a stimulant.[31] Under conditions that fail to monitor dancing properly, such delirium may even approach insanity.

The act of dancing cultivates tumescence, creating either autoerotic or heterosexual fervor. But even watching the dance produces this same effect, he says.[32] At its least, the spectacle of dance induces states of well-being and a sense of increased potency. If the numerous descriptions of savage dances cited by Ellis are any indication, viewing the dance may even arouse desire to participate in sexual acts. Whether as performer or viewer, participants in dance slide backward along the continua of biological, social, and evolutionary development toward more primitive states of being. Biological notions of higher and lower centers of bodily control reinforce even as they complement evolutionist theories of complex and simple species and of civilized and primitive peoples. By dancing, participants and viewers activate lower nerve systems, revert to more primal needs, and respond to base, instinctual impulses, according to Ellis. One of the travelogue accounts on which he relied summed dance up this way: "There is, perhaps, no exercise in greater accordance with the sentiments or feelings of a barbarous people, or more fully calculated to gratify their wild and ungoverned passions."[33] According to such accounts, dancing both inspires and cultivates base desires, uncontrollable desires. Dancing thus signals barbarism and all its attendant conditions—unruliness, self-absorption, hedonistic indulgence in the sensate, and uncontrollable violence.[34]

Little wonder, then, that choreographers such as Duncan and St. Denis marshaled their forces so carefully to refute all pre-

sumptions of equivalence between sex and dance. The mere fact
of their bodily motion, female bodily motion, on stage summoned up the deviant, the savage, and the sexual.[35] In order not
to appear as fallen women—women who had degenerated from
civilization into barbarism, from mind-controlled action into
bodily determined frenzy, or from the human into the bestial—
they crafted bodily movement that insistently referenced nonsexual dimensions of human experience. In order to justify their art,
they effectively tapped the same racist and colonialist impulses
that motivated the descriptions of dance-as-sex that Ellis relied on
for his research. Unlike African dance, which simply enhanced as
it displayed stages in the sexual act, Duncan's dances embodied
civilization—noble, refined, classical. Unlike the actual dances of
Asia and the Pacific, whose ritual frenzy belied their sexual investment, St. Denis's dances gestured toward a higher spiritual
quest.

But in their resolute denial of the sexual, these choreographers
also manifested the newly imagined subject, a subject capable of
possessing a sexuality, which studies such as Ellis's had begun to
reveal. Rather than investigate taxonomies of sexual practices, Ellis
and the other turn-of-the-century sexologists had pursued sexuality as an individually distinctive coalescence of identifiable patterns
of desire, arousal, and fulfillment into a singular entity. Both sexuality and the subjectivity that surrounded it operated as bounded
autonomies, and choreographers such as Duncan and St. Denis
gave embodiment to precisely this vision of identity. Their onstage
personas, no longer trapped within the familiar romances displayed by the ballet, enacted narratives of their own design that
contoured the geography of the psyche. Even as they seemed
transported into the ecstatic space of communion with musical
and spiritual universals, their bodies responded deftly, as admirable
instruments of expression. Through their choreographic mapping
of interiority, they gave embodiment to the kind of fulsome subjectivity within which something called a sexuality might dwell.
The body served as emblem of this subjectivity, charting new ter-
ritories of the natural and also as docile vehicle for conveying the
subject's exploration of identity. It mimicked the structural in-

tegrity of sexuality, and in the very same moment demonstrated that this sexuality could be controlled, even denied.

Thus even as sexuality was achieving new status as a powerful motivating force within the individual, Duncan and St. Denis demonstrated how such a sexuality could be contained. Unlike the dancing girls of ballet and cabaret, whose identities metonymically elided with sexual practices—flirtation, promiscuity, prostitution—both on stage and off, Duncan and St. Denis possessed a sexuality over which they exerted individualized control. Duncan, the mother of three illegitimate children, remained resolutely chaste in her dances; St. Denis, who flaunted her precarious control over bodily desires on stage, performed off stage as a devoted wife. Both artists exhibited to their public an alluring independence and a spiritual purpose that ensured they would not slide into deviant or uncivilized categories of behavior.

Through these founding gestures—individual creative exploration, the display of whiteness, and chastity—these women secured a new tradition of choreographic experimentation and a place for themselves within that tradition. This new tradition challenged the politics of danced spectacle by deflecting the objectifying force of the male gaze and ennobling the dancer on whose body all eyes rested. In this aesthetic and political labor, it joined hundreds of other Progressive-era initiatives to bring women and a female presence into the public sphere.[36] Yet this labor did not challenge the conception of dance itself as feminine nor alter significantly the prejudice against men dancing. Dancing's decorous display of the body and its interest in emotional and spiritual life aligned it too strongly with the feminine ever to be considered man's work, that is, until Ted Shawn, the director and choreographer for an all-male dance company, announced his campaign to prove that dance was a manly pursuit.

A HALE AND RUGGED LYRICISM

Ted Shawn first met Havelock Ellis in 1923, just after the publication of *The Dance of Life*.[37] According to his biographer, Walter Terry, this crucial encounter helped Shawn come to terms with his homosexuality: "For the first time he was able to hear someone discuss sex easily and homosexuality without embarrassment. . . . It is likely that his readings of ancient Greek culture and the acceptance of male-for-male love were removed from myth and placed into reality for him by Ellis."[38] Shawn visited Ellis while on tour with his wife and collaborator, Ruth St. Denis. They had begun working together in 1914, fashioning programs of dances that extended St. Denis's orientalizing approach to include duets and larger group pieces, as well as her renowned solos and complementary solos for Shawn. With indefatigable dedication they proselytized for the new modern dance in thousands of performances across the United States, Asia, and Europe and in their Denishawn schools established in Los Angeles and New York. By the late 1920s, however, Shawn and St. Denis could no longer sustain their professional or personal relationships, and they separated permanently in 1931, leaving Shawn free to embark upon his life-long dream of founding an all-male dance company.[39]

At the height of the depression Shawn retreated to a rundown farm in western Massachusetts that he named Jacob's Pillow, and from there he recruited dancers he taught at Springfield College and others who had seen him dance with St. Denis. With no electricity, heat, or running water and little to eat, they set about creating a repertory of dances to be toured across the United States. In their spare time they repaired and improved upon facilities at the farm. The company, consisting of eight to ten dancers, lived communally, rehearsed in the summers, and toured in the winter for eight seasons, from 1933 to 1940. At first using contacts with physical education programs in universities, and eventually playing at such prestigious venues as the Brooklyn Academy of Music and Carnegie Hall, they gave 1,250 performances in more than 750 cities, averaging forty-two thousand miles of travel each year (see chapter 4). While on tour they did the driving, set up the theater, performed, struck the show and packed the truck, met with interested people, and then drove on to the next town. In the first year alone they offered 111 performances, and Shawn personally "talked to 150 audiences at luncheons, assemblies, and club meetings; I had given 100 newspaper interviews, and 50 radio broadcasts."[40]

Shawn's message at these gatherings, zealously delivered and easily apprehended, affirmed that "yes, men can and should dance." The organization of his arguments belied the prejudice that his company aspired to redress: that dancing was a feminine and therefore unmanly pursuit and that those men who did make dancing their vocation were probably homosexuals. In support of dancing's manliness, Shawn, like Duncan, elaborated on images of the body in Whitman and in classical Greek dancing, but rather than emphasize the healthy and unfettered female body, he focused on the athletic and virile male body. He attributed the low esteem for dance as an art form to the absence of male participation, and, insisting on dance's importance, especially for an active nation like the United States, questioned whether such a significant pursuit should be left in the hands of women.

To this masculinist line of argumentation Shawn added a racist assessment of Negro dance, expounding a complex evolutionist theory that connected the Negro to the sexual:

> The Negro brought with him all the primitive simplicity of the rhythm of the savage, the unsophistication in regard to his body and its natural functions. . . . Because Negroes are very simple in their emotional structure and in their mental and spiritual development, their attitude toward the physical body is one of great naiveté and the natural movements of the body are not sinful to them. And so their dances are innocently sensual. When one sees a Negro do a dance of Negro origin, he can do all sorts of things, such as the movements in the "shimmy" and the "Charleston," and one likes it. It is his, and it belongs to him. But when one sees a white person do these dances, it is disgusting, because the Negro mental and emotional conditions cannot be translated into the white man.[41]

Because Negro peoples were less evolved, he argued, they exhibited none of the licentiously sexual connotations that more sophisticated whites would evoke when performing Negro dances.[42] This kind of argument made use of and relied upon the presumptions about dance's relation to sexuality that Ellis had included in his anthropological and travelogue evidence. Shawn thereby reinforced stereotypic images of race and dance but at the same time distanced his own choreography and company from such "savage impulses." In this way Shawn reaffirmed the antisexual stance of modern dance and defended his work against allegations of homosexuality.

The concerts that "Ted Shawn and His Male Dancers" presented embodied this vision of virile, nonsexual, physical accomplishment even as they made use of the exotic capacities of world dances. Building on St. Denis's and Shawn's earlier approach to repertory, the concerts delivered a pleasing array of visually contrasting short works whose distinctive costuming and movement vocabulary would be rationalized by a single theme. *Olympiad*, for example, presented dances based on movement themes from the shot put, hurdling, tennis, fencing, running, boxing, and basketball. *Labor Symphony* included renditions of labors of the field, forest, and sea, as well as mechanized labor. *Primitive Rhythms* presented dances based on themes from Ponca, Hopi, Sinhalese, Dayak, and Maori dances. *Religious Dances* offered a whirling dervish in full regalia, monks, a portrait of St. Francis, and several dances performed to Negro spirituals.[43] *Dance of the Ages* grouped studies of different movement qualities into four sections, each associated with a different element—fire, water, earth, and air—and a different level of social and political organization—tribe, city-state, democracy, and beyond democracy.[44] And *Kinetic Molpai*, with its zealously performed variations of effort and rhythm and its interlocking patterns, celebrated modernism itself. A typical evening's program would combine exotic and athletic dances to ensure visual diversity while reinforcing the strenuous physical achievement.

Where the dances representing foreign lands exhibited the unusual in costuming and movement, dances based on familiar activities such as sports or work rendered those activities strangely exciting. Viewers were presented with the challenging and engaging request to decipher the activity being depicted, whether it be fencing or sawing down a tree. Typically, the most pantomime-like, and hence most recognizable, versions of activities occurred near the beginning of the section. Having identified the referent, viewers could then track the elaboration of these actions into more abstract movement phrases. By treating movement itself as material capable of being varied and transformed, Shawn, like Duncan and St. Denis before him, directed attention away from the dancing body as a preconceived source of sexual impulses and toward the spatial and temporal properties of the movement. At the same time the selection of masculine topics and the vigorous rendering of those topics imbued the body with an almost hypermasculinity.

Embodying Shawn's distinctively masculine movement style and set of procedures for moving bodies through space, dancers traveled rapidly across the stage using small rhythmic step patterns while maintaining a stiff torso, arms held rigidly in place. In many pieces dancers clenched their fists throughout in order to enhance the musculature of the upper body and to evoke images of brute strength. Never undulating or contracting but sometimes twisting in the manner of classical Greek sculpture, dancers locomoted and then posed, turned and then jumped, ran to a new place and posed again. Each pose was stated emphatically, energy surging through the dancers' limbs until they achieved the desired shape, limbs arresting abruptly yet swelled with tension as they maintained their position. The dancers' shaved armpits and chests further enhanced their resemblance to classical Greek beings in repose and in motion.

Again and again, dancers separated into two groups of four, formed columns, and crossed the stage toward each other in unison or quick succession, indicating a kind of aggressive or competitive engagement. This back-and-forth dialogue would dissolve into circular configurations, dancers running, leaping, or falling to the floor while delineating a large circle at center stage. Shawn used diagonals only occasionally, preferring a frontal display of the body moving from upstage to downstage or across stage. Almost all movement phrases were repeated two or four times to alternating sides of the body. Relentless, repetitive, symmetrical, the bodies sustained a vigorous display of motion and shape, usually culminating in massive numbers of jumps. Yet as routinized as the sequences often appeared, the bodies maintained a distinctive physicality and individuality. They never achieved a perfect unison, nor did they exhibit the classical grace imparted in ballet training. Not bodies attempting to approximate a perfect shape, they displayed themselves as bodies that had developed their inherent strength and agility.

Throughout, dancers consistently retained a three- to five-foot distance from one another. Individual bodies seldom performed contrasting actions, and they never moved closer to or farther away from one another than the prescribed distance between all bodies. Dancers never touched; they never assisted one another, leaned into one another, or moved through space arm in arm.[45] Only when dancers were assembled together to create a single design configuration did their bodies make contact, their weight merge. These designs involved the entire group, seldom four dancers and never two alone. Usually symmetrical, bodies were arranged on either side of a central figure, Shawn. Alternatively, bodies connected to suggest a single line, carried sequentially along from one to the next to create a dynamic upward gesture.

Shawn himself circulated around and through these younger bodies, exhorting, fostering, summoning their energies, commanding, or directing them. He alerted them to the drama, comforted them when they were down, revealed the future to them when kneeling, inspired them to rise and move, called them on stage, and designated their pathways through space. He appeared fatherlike, understanding, but also visionary and pioneering. In contrast, his solos elaborated a more lyrical, slow-moving, and softer style. Often in 3/4 time, he mused, deliberated, and searched, portraying a kind of interior life that the other dancers never showed. Sometimes he incorporated poses and phrases from pantomime, as graphic and stilted as those of the silent films. Crushed, desolate, without hope, he would sink to the floor, only to rise, inspired by or appealing to a higher good. Terror transformed into courage and despair into resolution. But these elegiac dramatizations of interiority were soon displaced by the return of the company, whose exhibition of dance as expressive work dissipated any lingering images of the soul-searching individual.

The overall effect of the evening's dances, with their rugged exuberance, their direct symmetrical frontal engagement with movement, convinced audiences immediately of men's vital place in the world of dance. Shawn's choreography used the abstract potential of dance movement to construct a democratic vision of individual creativity and individually developed bodies in which masculinity held a privileged place. As one critic enthusiastically explained, the concerts presented

> vigor limned by restraint; furious motion controlled and balanced and suggestive of mighty harmonies; muscular orderliness and pointed grace; a hale and rugged lyricism whose line is gentle as the contour of a mountain may be gentle; but never effeminate or Hogarthian; energy; humility and bravura, suavity and simplicity; power; beauty. Which of these qualities apparent in Shawn's work can be called effeminate?[46]

The dances exalted the male body's noble restraint, grandeur, and potency, proclaiming loudly that nothing effeminate, much less homosexual, could survive in this robust environment. This message was so powerful that even the other dancers in the group referred to lead dancer Barton Mumaw, Shawn's lover for many years, as "the best dancer in the group" or as "the only dancer with prior training and dance experience." [47]

By presenting an all-male dance company, Shawn directly confronted audience prejudices against dance and homosexuality. By showing the noble male body engaged in vital virile expressive work, he begged entirely the question of the dancers' sexual orientation. In stark contrast to the contorted repression of sexuality evident in Nijinsky's vocabulary, Shawn's dances cultivated an open direct Greek ideal. Based on his readings of Ellis, Edward Carpenter, and John Addington Symonds, Shawn's conception of the Greek included homosexual forms of love and filiation.[48] As his company performed across the United States, however, its classical cultivation of the body probably referenced high art, noble ideals, and nothing more. And unlike Nijinsky's elite aesthetic accomplishments, Shawn's able-bodied youths compounded their high ideals with a populist enthusiasm that invited everyone to celebrate dance.

In his study of homosexuality, *Sexual Inversion*, Ellis allies the homosexual with the artistic genius. Both, he argues, exhibited the same nervous predisposition, and a remarkable number of homosexuals that Ellis interviewed possessed artistic aptitude in varying degrees.[49] Where Nijinsky danced forth just this vision of the connection between sexual deviance and artistic brilliance, Shawn sought to mask the possibility of homosexual preferences and to refute any association between sexuality and creativity. Shawn's dances choreographed a closeting of the kind of homosexual desire Ellis describes.

For Ellis, homosexuality, or, as he calls it, inversion, results from an aberrant alteration in the individual's "recessive sex."[50] Events in childhood, puberty, or even adulthood that shape the sexual impulse could further influence this congenital predisposition toward inversion. Ellis found enormous variations in inversion and devoted much of his study to delineating different proclivities, preferences, and characteristics within the invert population. In contrast to Freudian-based studies that proposed a purely psychological and social basis for homosexuality, Ellis attributes a congenital cause to a significant percentage of the cases he had observed:

> Putting the matter in a purely speculative shape, it may be said that at conception the organism is provided with about 50 per cent. of male germs and about 50 per cent. of female germs, and that as development proceeds, either the male or the female germs assume the upper hand, until in the maturely developed individual only a few aborted germs of the opposite sex are left. In the homosexual, however, and in the bisexual, we may imagine that the process has not proceeded normally, on account of some peculiarity in the number or character of either the original male germs or female germs, or both, the result being that we have a person who is organically twisted into a shape that is more fitted for the exercise of the inverted than of the normal sexual impulse.[51]

Because of this "twisted shape" in the "recessive" sexual "germs" of the invert, homosexual men exhibited a general tendency to adopt feminine traits and habits, and homosexual women were more likely to take on masculine qualities. This twist, in the strictest sense of the term a degeneration or falling away from the higher developmental goal of the organism, should not, in

Ellis's liberal opinion, be viewed pejoratively but rather as a kind of "sport" or variation like color-blindness that affects all organisms.[52]

Shawn's dances depicted the kind of autonomous beings Ellis describes—their character developed from innate predispositions in interaction with social influences. His choreography championed the individual, creating a tense and dynamic relationship between each body and the larger group. Yet Shawn's dances exhibited no trace of the degenerate, no hint of the feminine. Inverting the invert, the dancers never looked soft or flexible; they never curved. They never even touched except in those rare moments when the choreography stipulated that all bodies contribute to a common design. Like Duncan and St. Denis before him, Shawn sequestered sexuality so effectively that no one in the audience could even speculate about whether the dancers, like the "savages" that Ellis discusses, might embark on other kinds of bodily explorations after their concert. Shawn's hypermasculine choreography, built with the same premises Ellis stipulates in his definition of homosexuality, closeted him effectively, if not completely.

Silenced as they were by the chastity of the dancing, some audience members saw straight past Shawn's manly ideal to the possibility of male homosexual love celebrated and honored in the noble forms of the dance. In his autobiography Mumaw reminisces about the many occasions when young men, discovering their homosexual preferences, found inspiration in the company of men dancers:

> We were constantly made aware of a more subtle response to our work by young men, students mostly, each of whom confided that his Old Man preferred him to run the risks of injuries in a football game rather than accept the challenge of an art that was equally strenuous, vowing that "I'll see you *dead* before I'll let you be a dancer!" Many of these frustrated boys were proficient in different fields of athletics. Some dared knock on stage doors, or come back to the locker rooms of college gyms to talk to us about dancing. Others approached us on campus or on small-town streets, pathetically pretending a fascination with our streamlined DeSoto in an attempt to disguise their real interest. Only a few were furtive.

The rare spats I had with Ted during periods on the road were triggered by my meeting someone who became infatuated with me.[53]

Yet these repeated incidental encounters exerted no influence on
the general reception of the work or on Shawn's sense of aesthetic
purpose. The message he hoped to disseminate concerned the respectability and vitality of men dancing, not the need for a new
understanding of homosexual love. And his approach proved
enormously successful. Shawn's immense labor, touring and introducing viewers across the United States to modern dance, was
met with understanding and great enthusiasm. Only the cata-
clysm of World War II could arrest his initiative to exalt an American form of dance and a male dancing body.

SIMPLY AN ACTIVITY OF MOVEMENT

Whatever the gains in respectability for the male dancer following Shawn's eight-year campaign, the conservative reassertion of
traditional gender roles following World War II resuscitated many
prejudices against him. Still, in the relatively protected ecology
of modern dance in New York City and with Martha Graham's
formidable reputation as legitimation and her harsh, nonlyrical
movement vocabulary as a resource, Merce Cunningham emerged
as a promising young male artist when he left her company in
1947 to pursue his own career as a choreographer. The postwar
modern dance, a field dominated by women artists, also focused
on the gynocentrically marked concerns of feeling and psychological intensity. Choreography, an introspective process, helped
to reveal and communicate innermost motivations, impulses,
and desires. As the only male choreographer to appear in many
group concerts or in a given season of programming, Cunningham would have been subject to scrutiny regarding his masculinity and his sexuality: What made him choose dance? What might
his dances reveal about the inner depths of his psyche?

Although suspicions regarding his sexual orientation undoubtedly circulated among dancers and viewers, confirmed for
those who knew him by his ardent relationship with John Cage,
Cunningham determinedly embarked on his choreographic ca-

reer, supported by the general climate of experimentation. His early repertory evidenced several distinct lines of investigation: haunting, psychologically probing solos; humorous, light-hearted, or absurdist group works; and explorations of bodies in space and time.[54] His solos conveyed the substance of interiority by using a contorted dissonant vocabulary that pushed at the limits of acceptable dance movement, as this description of *Untitled Solo* (1953) by Clive Barnes suggests: "With *Untitled Solo*, the mood changed to neurotic despair. Swift and sinuous, this solo proved pungently unpleasant—it was perhaps the nearest Cunningham got all season to choreography that was visually assaulting and unpleasant in precisely the same way that the musicians, on quite frequent occasions, made ugly and offensive noises."[55] Similarly, *Changeling* (1957), a "strange and ugly solo," yet acclaimed for its "technical brilliance" and "imaginative punch," seemed "to suggest a man climbing through a never ending tunnel."[56] In these pieces Cunningham cultivated the expressivity of bodily tension, the contrasting and dynamic oppositions that parts of that the body were capable of, that Graham had used so effectively in her work. Yet, unlike Graham, he seems to have interpolated pedestrian motifs and quixotic gestures that effaced the monumental claims to an archetypal significance made by her dances. As the music critic Peter Yates observes, "I had seen Merce Cunningham's work, a couple of times, as late as 1955, appreciating the individuality of his approach, his manner—clown, Pierrot, fantasist—still anchored to the diagonal axes and the expressive exaggeration of gesture which had made him for several years a leading dancer of the Graham company, though already freed, as I now realize in retrospect, of the mythic, monumental formality."[57]

Alongside his charismatic solos, Cunningham contrived humorous group works such as *Banjo* (1955), which he described as "an accelerated and heightened montage of familiar southern American motifs," and *Antic Meet* (1958), a dance that collaged absurd and preposterous situations involving multiple props, costumes, and well-known physical gags.[58] According to Barnes's review of *Antic Meet* from performances given in London in 1964:

Antic Meet is a projection into wispy infinity of the two archetypal American jokes. . . . Two men fight—one is killed—the other solicitously returns to drag him off . . . wearing a fur coat. A man with a flourish lays a table for dinner . . . another unconcernedly carries it off unused. A man struggles desperately with a sweater . . . the sweater has four arms but no hole for the head. One girl is pelting another with itsy-bitsy pebbles; the victim gets tired and throws a bucket of water over her assailant.

The crazy logic of a door sliding on by itself, a man opening it and out stepping a girl, or of their subsequent *pas de deux*, with a boy having a chair strapped to his back so that she sits down while being partnered.[59]

Carolyn Brown, principal dancer with Cunningham's company for almost thirty years, was the "girl" who stepped through the door wearing an antique bridal gown. Cunningham partnered her in an extended duet wearing the chair. At another point in the piece all the dancers suddenly put on sunglasses. These irreverent choreographic choices, with their humor and lavish theatricality, challenged the sacred boundaries between dance movement, pedestrian behavior, and comic gag and inverted the expressive mandate embodied in his solos.

In his third approach to dance making, Cunningham drew upon ballet as well as modern dance vocabularies, as well as his thorough knowledge of musical composition, to elaborate on bodies' positionalities in space and through time.[60] Dances such as *Septet* (1953), *Suite for Five* (1953–1958), and *Summerspace* (1958) displayed intricate step patterns, complex rhythms and changes of weight, and a radical treatment of dancers' dispositions in space. If drawn on paper as a record of the entire dance, paths for bodies traveling through space would form a complicated web of overlapping, crisscrossing trajectories. These dances contained no symmetry and only rare unison. Often the bodies remained erect with the spine occasionally curving forward, side, or back in conjunction with specific shapings of the arms and legs. Movement impulses never traveled sequentially from one region of the body to the next, nor did movements build toward climactic moments in a phrase. Throughout, the dances sustained an

evenness of phrasing and phrase, with leaps or other grand gestures taking on no larger significance than the steps that preceded
them.

Many of these dances applied Cage's theories of chance procedures as generative of new musical possibilities to the creation of
dance movement and the organization of the dance.[61] *Summerspace*, for example, used chance procedures to determine locations of entrances and exits, pathways through space, and the
sequences of movement, ranging from simple to complex, associated with those pathways. Cunningham also used chance to des-
ignate lengths of phrases, number of dancers, and the simultane-
ity of dancers' performances. He taught each of the five dancers
their parts separately and then rehearsed them together.[62] Alternatively, he would invoke chance procedures just before the performance, as in *Rune* (1959) or *Dime a Dance* (1953), asking all
members of the company to appear on stage ready to dance seven
of the thirteen sections of the piece. Yet, "which seven these are
is not known by any of them beforehand, but is determined by
chance means," the program informed the audience.

In contrast to his brooding solos or zany theatrics, these dances
focused especially on the spatial and temporal characteristics of
bodies in motion. This focus eventually prevailed as the epistemological grounding for his entire choreographic vision. Rather
than characters and stories, his dances would present bodies in
motion. Meaning would be located not in the psychological implications of bodily gesture but in the physical characteristics of
movement itself. During the late 1950s and early 1960s Cunningham formulated program notes that conveyed this aesthetic
stance to a bewildered and sometimes resistant audience: "Mr.
Cunningham has said of his choreography that there are not symbols, no stories, no psychological problems. What you see is what
is. Each spectator must determine the meaning of the dance for
himself." And Cage provided this explanation, which the company used repeatedly in its programs and publicity:

> We are not, in these dances and music, saying something. We are
> simpleminded enough to think that if we were saying something we

would use words. We are rather doing something. The meaning of what we do is determined by each one who sees and hears it. . . . I may add there are no stories and no psychological problems. There is simply an activity of movement, sound and light. The costumes are all simple in order that you may see the movement.

The movement is the movement of the body. It is here that Mr. Cunningham focuses his choreographic attention, not on the facial muscles. In daily life people customarily observe faces and hand gestures, translating what they see into psychological terms. Here, however, we are in the presence of a dance which utilizes the entire body, requiring for its enjoyment the use of your faculty of kinesthetic sympathy. It is this faculty we employ when, seeing the flight of birds, we ourselves, by identification, fly up, glide, and soar.[63]

The lift of a leg or a leap might incite momentary exuberance; a gliding trajectory through space, a sense of calm. But these were fleeting associations between motion and emotion that each audience member could experience individually. Where the modern dance of Graham or Doris Humphrey had cultivated the connection between movement and interior psychological states of being in order to move audiences into and through a sustained psychological narrative, Cunningham eschewed the rigors of narrative continuity in favor of a disciplined attentiveness to each moment's motion.

This approach to choreography constructed a radical new identity for the viewer. Rather than encourage all viewers to connect to the universal meaning of the dance, Cunningham's work emphasized the viewer's role as independent agent. The dance offered a field of possibilities into which each viewer entered.[64] Once there they could experience the dance, each in her or his own way. Because the dance rebuffed all efforts to find narrative continuity, it created neither storytellers nor listeners. Adamantly, it said nothing but did something. And its activity and agency were located within the physical possibilities for bodily motion.

Shawn, in his variations on well-known activities, had emphasized the capacity of movement to build upon itself, to generate meaning through reference to its spatial, temporal, and tensile characteristics. Yet his dances always evinced a message—about the glory of work, the power of ritual, or the nobility of world dances—which his dancers as expressive agents conveyed. Cunningham, in contrast, construed his dances as a window onto the indeterminate liveliness of life experience. His dancers, not the zealous messengers of a vital masculine expressivity, attended with concentrated purposefulness to the movement directives that constituted the choreography. In this focus on movement and on the individual response to and interpretation of that movement, Cunningham found protection for his homosexual identity. Shawn's protective closet had disguised the individual sexual orientations of his dancers within the hypermasculinity of their performance personas. Cunningham's closet, in contrast, fractured bodies into parts of equal significance and value so that individuality could only be defined by the activities, all of equal value, in which the dancer was at each moment engaged. Where Shawn had exaggerated his dancers' masculine capabilities, Cunningham neutralized all masculine, feminine, and sexual connotations by focusing on space, time, and motion.[65]

Consider, for example, this glimpse into Cunningham's working process, documented by a German film crew in 1967: A white woman (Sandra Neels) and a black man (Gus Solomons) lie on the floor in close embrace. She lifts her right leg up, circling it around his body and causing them both to roll so that she lies directly on top of him. Her weight does not settle onto his, however, because she continues the leg's gesture by standing on it, rising into a lunge, and finally pushing off the leg to turn and walk away. Approximately six seconds of choreography, Cunningham rehearses it for several minutes. He experiments with different placements of an arm or leg and with the precise calibration of bodies as they roll from side by side to top and underneath. He slows the movement; he lies beside the couple, going through her motions, demonstrating, inquiring, where arms and legs should be placed. Throughout, no one jokes or giggles. Their intimate coupling is treated as one of the infinite number of positions that bodies can inhabit. Cunningham maintains a businesslike and efficient attitude, soliciting through his quiet dedication an absolute and unwavering attention from the dancers.[66]

Later in the film Neels is asked about the meaning of her brief duet with Solomons. She speculates that if she were to question Cunningham about its significance, he would simply eliminate the phrase from the dance not, she seems to suggest, because the question might have drawn to his attention an undesirable referent or effect of the phrase but because the mandate to accept all motions as equivalent had been compromised by her interrogation of this specific phrase. Cunningham's determination to cultivate the body as a neutral field of possibilities prohibited narrative continuity and denied the standard cultural codes for gendered and sexual identities. His approach presumed an absolute equivalence of male and female bodies, and black and white bodies.[67] Living in the kind of world constructed by his dances, homosexual conduct or African American identity would carry valences no different from those of white heterosexual behavior. Both homosexual and heterosexual object choices, black and white aesthetic choices, would hypothetically take place within the same open field of possibilities. Difference, his dances proclaimed, could only be located in the distinctive physical capacities of each individual body's joint flexibility, bone lengths, muscular mass, speed, or dexterity.

Through this determined inquiry into physicality, Cunningham perpetuated the tradition of a nonsexual dancing instigated by the earliest modern choreographers. He also sustained its inherent racism. Solomons, the first black and one of the few nonwhite dancers ever to work with Cunningham, points up the whiteness of Cunningham's approach. The very project of locating identity in a physicality that denied racial difference could only be supported by a tradition that presumed its own universality.[68] The window onto life's indeterminate experience that Cunningham's dances provided did not frame the racial or sexual prejudices operating in that life. Where Cunningham's maleness was destabilized by the profession of dancing, his whiteness remained an unmarked and unchallenged category. His particular version of chasteness thereby deflected any inquiries into his sexual orientation and provided a safe haven for his homosexuality, but it denied the racial inequalities embodied in modern dance and its cultural surround. Focusing on the problematic of race in Cunningham's work thus brings into sharp relief the precise structure of the closet he crafted.

Cunningham's emphasis on behavior rather than interior motivation, and his insistence on the individuality of that behavior, shared much with the research orientation of the leading sexologist of the period, Alfred Charles Kinsey. Just months after Cunningham left Graham's company, Kinsey published his *Sexual Behavior in the Adult Male*. Its extraordinary notoriety and numerous reprintings provided the focus for discussions of homosexuality throughout the entire period that Cunningham was building his career. Kinsey pioneered in mass survey methods, and his study of sexuality involved more than twelve thousand men who were asked hundreds of questions about their sexual preferences and practices. Undoubtedly, the most startling finding of the entire report was that 37 percent of the male population had experienced some kind of homosexual encounter culminating in orgasm.[69] Given the severe social condemnation of homosexuality, he further speculated that a much larger proportion of the population might engage in homosexual relations were they condoned.[70]

The discovery of such a large proportion of homosexual activity caused Kinsey to reformulate the distinction between heterosexual and homosexual. Instead of the inversion model proposed by Ellis and others, he created a seven-point scale along which each individual's behavior might be located.[71] Such a scale shifted scientific inquiry away from the determination of innate and essential features of homosexuality and toward individual behavior:

> It would encourage clearer thinking on these matters if persons were not characterized as heterosexual or homosexual, but as individuals who have had certain amounts of heterosexual experience and certain amounts of homosexual experience. Instead of using these terms as substantives which stand for persons, or even as adjectives to describe persons, they may better be used to describe the nature of the overt sexual relations, or of the stimuli to which an individual erotically responds.[72]

Kinsey's findings obliterated the notion of a clear-cut homosexual type or distinct homosexual body, demonstrating instead an extraordinary range of human sexual practice. Like Cunningham's choreography, they focused on overt action rather than interior identity, and like his aesthetic vision of dance, they construed sexuality as an open field of possibilities.

The extreme debate provoked by Kinsey's studies heightened acceptance but also increased fear and condemnation of homosexuality. In the generally liberal but never reliable arts milieu that they inhabited, Cunningham and Cage could share a bedroom but referred publicly to themselves as "collaborators who shared the same aesthetic principles."[73] Both artists cultivated a conduct that combined precision of action with an openness to interpretive possibilities. Cunningham, in particular, always spoke with great clarity about his goals and objectives but was entirely unwilling to predict what others might think or do. This stance, projected into his choreographic approach, shielded and disguised his homosexuality but also gave it a home.

As much as Cunningham advocated his open field of possibilities, denying the sexual and gendered referents of the dancing body, his dances articulated gender difference, and gestured toward Cunningham's masculine and even homosexual identity. Male and female dancers performed overlapping yet distinctive vocabularies of movement in which men partnered and lifted women. The uprightness and clarity of purpose, the erect and nonorganic movement style, allied his dances with the more masculine ballet tradition than with the feminine modern dance. Even Cunningham's emphasis on the practical material elements of dance composition imbued his approach with a masculine rationality that distinguished it from the chaotic excavations of interiority that his female colleagues conducted.

Within this masculine environment Cunningham circulated as the odd man out. In the early concerts of his works he, like Shawn, offered the only solos that addressed emotional themes. In group works he often remained alone or dancing off to the side, assigning himself the most unusual, preposterous, or quirky tasks. In *Variations V* (1966) he strips a large potted plastic plant of all its leaves, later rides a bicycle, and still later exercises on a blanket, doing sit-ups and a headstand, while three male–female couples perform nearby. Where Shawn constructed a fatherly authority, leading his dancers forward or brooding in their absence, Cunningham fashioned himself as maverick, incidentally isolated and then nonclimactically reintegrated into the group's activities. Like the boys who saw through Shawn's closet, any who would look for it could find Cunningham's difference. But the dancers' and dance's insistence that movement meant movement, their neutral and absorbed execution of each task at hand, effectively obscured his distinctiveness. This strategy, a personal and aesthetic negotiation of white matriarchal modern dance on the one hand and vicious homosexual prejudice on the other, would sustain his work for the next forty years. In one of their last residencies before Cage's death, for example, a gay activist at the University of California, Berkeley, pressed Cunningham and Cage hard to come out of the closet and talk openly about their relationship. Cage responded characteristically by saying, "It's quite simple, really. He does the shopping and I do the cooking."

COMING INTO CONTACT

In 1972 Steve Paxton, a former member of Cunningham's company and a participant in Judson Church experimental concerts in the early 1960s, instigated inquiry into a new approach to improvised partnering. Known as contact improvisation, the form asks dancers to create and focus on a moving point of physical contact between two or more bodies.[74] Privileging momentum and flow over bodily shape, dancers merge their weight, sliding, rolling across and over one another, treating all points on the surface of the body as sequentially connected and as potential next directions along which their point of contact might travel. Dancers are asked to attend to the internal sensations of weight and flow generated by this contact, "letting the dance happen."[75] By maintaining awareness of this contact, rather than of the body's appearance or the dance's organization and coherence, they are able to develop the mutual trust, support, and quick-wittedness necessary to dive into each instant's action and move wherever it takes them.

The practice of contact improvisation became increasingly popular throughout the mid- and late 1970s, spawning local groups
and national networks that organized various occasions for learning and presenting the form. Dancers convened at weekly "jams"
or larger festivals and workshops to practice contact, learning
techniques for falling into or supporting another's body, enhancing their ability to attend to each moment's action. At these jams,
dancers of all degrees of experience generally worked together,
encountering one another's weight, experimenting with qualities
of touch, moving, then watching, and then moving again during
a period of several hours. Performances, hardly distinguishable in
structure or content from the jam sessions, showed the work in
progress. A typical performance, shunning all the formality of a
theater's framing, would implement the same round-robin for-
mat used in workshops: two dancers would begin, joined by a
third or fracturing into solos before reconstituting as new duets,
and continuing until all dancers had taken their turn. Throughout, dancers cultivated the appearance of the pedestrian, smiling,
scratching, rearranging their sweat pants in a thoroughly conscious yet casual way while audience members seated on the floor
surrounded the dancers.

Deftly situated between art, sport, and sociality, contact improvisation functioned throughout the 1970s as both aesthetic
and social initiative. As dance, it contested the boundaries between pedestrian and art movement vocabularies more thoroughly than Cunningham or the Judson experiments, claiming
that its cultivation of agility and spontaneity could make of life a
dance. It promoted egalitarian access to and interaction within
the form, constructing many opportunities for success while
avoiding hierarchies of evaluation. And it offered an intriguing
new experience of subjectivity wherein dancers became defined
by the contact between them. Rather than two separate entities
coming together, they merged with the momentum generated by
both bodies, a momentum that took on a life of its own. Cunningham had asked dancers to immerse themselves in the physical activity of dancing rather than in the psychological or spiritual
associations that movement might generate. Contact improvisa-

tion similarly focused dancers' attention on physical physics, yet the active engagement of bodies, one with another, defied the traditional sense of bodily boundaries, reorganizing the dancers' sense of self as the product of the ongoing interactive process.

As sport, contact improvisation developed a spectacular bodily responsiveness, one that attracted an unusually large number of men into the practice. Dancers passed through or arrived at precarious positionings, defying gravity and charting whole new trajectories for bodies' pathways in space that resulted in breathtaking solutions to momentary physical dilemmas. At the same time contact improvisation shared with sports a workerlike ambiance, devoid of drama or pretense, in which dancers simply focused on the task at hand. They performed with the gusto of athletes and pursued a similar dedication to collaboration yet without the competition that goal-oriented structures encourage. Nor did contact improvisation segregate male from female participants, preferring to approach all bodies as similarly abled. Some of the most sensational moments in contact performances occurred when traditional gender roles in dance were contested or reversed.

As a sociality, a shared sensibility for public interaction, contact provided a focus for group activities, and it served as model for communal living and sharing, group decision making, and the sharing of power. As the number of people practicing contact increased, numerous local and regional organizations sprang up as well as a regularly published national journal, *Contact Quarterly*, that collected impressions and insights into contact as well as announcements for upcoming events. Many practitioners of contact used the form as an organizing force in their lives, traveling from one group of improvisers to another, sharing the dance and their lives. The following letter to *Contact Newsletter*, predecessor of *Contact Quarterly*, shows the way in which contact suffused and almost became a lifestyle for many:

> Entering my contact year number three and living in the midst of what often seems to be the west coast center for contact improv. Number 224 here at the artists' warehouse called Project Artaud is a single large room with loft, kitchen, shower, 14 foot ceiling and large open floor space. . . . John LeFan, his three year old son

Krishna, and I share the space . . . often we share it with others, too. Seamus and Gail from Vancouver have both crashed here at different times ("contact contacts"); Mary from Minneapolis has been here for the past ten days during her SF visit; Storm, Shanti and others from Santa Cruz contacting have spent hours and nights while passing through. Bill Jones from Binghamton stopped in one afternoon to share some incredible dancing during his SF vacation; we look forward to many more guests. . . . This space has become a central meeting ground for business transaction. Mangrove eats and discusses here, is interviewed here, watches videotapes here and parties here. The Bay Area Contact Coalition formed initially for presenting Focus: 9/76 [a teaching workshop] has spent many hours. . . . Last evening Roger Neece from the Boston improvisational company TA YU showed a small gathering a video of his company's performances; Curt showed a video of a Santa Cruz Re-Union performance. It was wonderful to feel the energy and exchange across the continent.[76]

A perpetuation of late 1960s values of spontaneity and communality, groups of contact improvisers lived together, visited other such groups, and mixed dancing with the other activities that comprised their daily lives. Contact's emphasis on sensitivity, spontaneity, and going with the flow of events inspired many dancers, and they worked conscientiously to bring these qualities into their general conduct.

Contact improvisation reflected the communitarian values of the late 1960s, as well as the period's sexual tolerance and feminist concerns, yet it preserved the chasteness of the modern dance tradition. Like Cunningham, contact improvisation gave equal valence to all parts of the body. All sections or joints contained an equivalent potential for moving, even as they moved differently. Cunningham's approach, however, segmented the body and cast its parts into spatially and temporally coordinated locations, whereas contact improvisation charted sequential pathways of touch across the entire body. As a result Cunningham's partnering work took on the appearance of highly unconventional ballet: female dancers, usually erect or cantilevered off the vertical but referring to it, constructed idiosyncratic shapes and maintained these shapes as male dancers, using inventive holds, moved them to a new location, and then all reconfigured as discrete self-propelling entities. Even the duet between Neels and Solomons, the placed quality of both bodies, their vertical carriage even in the horizontal plane, resembled a pas de deux occurring at an odd angle.

In contrast, contact improvisation brought literally every part of the body into moving contact with another's moving body. Bodies passed back and forth across breasts, genitals, and buttocks, and because of the improvisational nature of the practice, it was not at all uncommon for two dancers to come to rest with one's head in the other's crotch. Yet the explicit sexual connotations of this pose were either denied or treated as an irrelevant detail. All parts of the body mattered most as momentum-creating surfaces. Dancers or audience members might chuckle at the physical pairing that fulcrum physics, not desire, had momentarily produced, but dancers' focus and next physical initiatives soon restabilized attention on the ongoing exploration of the kinetic and tactile, but not sexual, potential of the body. The body adventurously mingled with any and all other bodies, yet the logics of sexual desire were never engaged. The democratic distribution of function to all body parts and regions dismantled the necessary hierarchies of erogeneity.

The polymorphous perversity of the contact-improvising body was strikingly evident in the androgynous equality with which women and men partnered each other. Techniques, developed in contact improvisation for guiding momentum and for mutual participation in the perpetuation of that momentum, enabled small, structurally more fragile, bodies to lift and support much larger bodies. Neither size nor sex intervened as a factor that influenced how two bodies might move together. The body's sensual but never sexual promiscuity was also powerfully articulated when dancers of the same sex sustained intimate contact. Opposite-sex duets, common in modern dance and ballet, gestured romance and desire while instantiating limits beyond which bodies might not move toward that desire. Same-sex duets seldom occurred, partially because of the intimations of homoerotic desire they might generate. A radical departure from both ballet and modern conventions, contact improvisation featured both same- and opposite-sex pairs reveling in their proximity and using a single choreographic strategy—a nonerogenized body focusing on the physical experience of weight and momentum—to deflect any presumptions of romantic or sexual attraction.

Nowhere was the arresting allure of this polymorphous body more clearly developed than in performances by Mangrove, an all-male company formed in San Francisco that organized concerts and workshops from 1975 to 1980. Mangrove's life spanned a critical period in the development of contact improvisation, as it consolidated vocabulary and technical skills and generated more proficient and professionally oriented dancers who began to form companies devoted to the presentation of the form or to its use as a primary source for choreographic invention. Founded by four men—John LeFan, Byron Brown, Curt Siddall, and Jim Tyler—each with considerable training and experience in professional theater and dance, Mangrove quickly garnered visibility and professional success, presenting more than 250 performances throughout the United States, Canada, and Europe in the five years of its operation.

Mangrove's success signaled a movement away from the early utopistic vision of dance as a way of life and into the capitalist marketing of dance as a way to make a living. One of its founding members, Brown, wrote the description of life at Project Artaud quoted earlier that captures the community-based ethos of the practice. Yet as Mangrove began to construct itself as a dance company, other San Francisco Bay area members of the contact community resented its insularity and willingness to make money through the form. This reaction reflects the extent to which some contact improvisers saw the form as a way of life and a model for life outside capitalist economic structures. Still, Mangrove perpetuated many of contact improvisation's communal values, replacing the hierarchical organization of the dance company, its choreographer and dancers, with an egalitarian model based on collaborative choreography. And it presented a new vision of masculine identity, far more open, sensitive, and process oriented than other staged versions of typical male behavior.

Mangrove's male bodies collided delicately, careened gracefully, stopped to sense the moment, and then responded wholeheartedly to another's initiatives. Rather than butt into or outmaneuver one another, these bodies mutually constructed an ongoing flow of dance. The dancers did not shape themselves; no pointed feet, extended legs, or curved arms appeared on the dance floor. Such cultivation of the body would have looked artificial and pretentious next to these sweating, deft athletes. Representative of the general male participation in contact improvisation, Mangrove combined astonishing physical daring with a sensuous vulnerability.

Aware of the social and even political ramifications of this vision of manhood, Charles Campbell of Mangrove declared:

> It's clear to me that we are exploring new personal/political/artistic ground for ourselves, as men gently (and aggressively) supporting each other in a non-hierarchical collective improvisational process, and sharing that process in performance, from a position of vulnerability and humor and fear, too. . . . It's all about us as people and as men finding the "people things" which happen in our process of coming into contact.[77]

Not only was the performance a collective display of decision making in process, it also expanded dominant prescriptions for masculine comportment to include new forms of interaction, new ways for men to make contact with one another. Instead of competing, they exuberantly pursued collective goals. Instead of a controlled willful use of the body, they displayed the loss of control and its attendant embarrassments, tediums, and unanticipated triumphs. Instead of bodily insularity and stilted protocols of touch, they showed men in contact with one another's full physicality, treating other bodies playfully, respectfully, and empathically.

Yet nothing in this repertoire of initiatives and responses constructed or alluded to homoerotic desire. Mangrove's mission, like that of contact improvisation generally, focused on establishing realms of physical intimacy other than sexual. Still, Mangrove's rendition of a polymorphous sensuality bore a striking resemblance to the premises on which the French sexual theorist

Guy Hocquenghem based his definition of homosexuality. Pursuing to its most radical conclusions Kinsey's continuum between homosexual and heterosexual identities, Hocquenghem asserts that "homosexual desire, like heterosexual desire, is an arbitrary division of the flux of desire, an 'arbitrarily frozen frame,' in an unbroken and polyvocal flux."[78] According to Hocquenghem, human sexuality generally operates across the same broad spectrum of physical possibilities that Mangrove represented in danced form. Mangrove, however, represented the closeted rendition of that physical spectrum, whereas Hocquenghem articulates the "out" version of the same spectrum, replete with its revolutionary political implications.

Published the same year that Steve Paxton commenced work on contact improvisation, Hocquenghem's manifesto, *Homosexual Desire*, embodied the critical energy generated by Stonewall, the social upheavals, student revolutions and political protests of the late 1960s, and the rise of deconstructionist and other poststructuralist theoretical orientations. Implementing a politics that Kinsey could not have imagined, Hocquenghem charges that homosexuality functioned as a category devised by heterosexual culture to repress its own homosexual desires and to control family and other capitalist economic structures. Using the anus in symbolic opposition to the phallus, Hocquenghem argues that an anal sexuality would obliterate differences between public and private, and social and individual—differences that the phallic organization of sexuality promoted and upheld:

> Ours is a competitive society: competition between males, between phallus bearers. The anus is excluded from the social field, and the individuals created by the rule of the bourgeoisie believe that everything revolves around the possession of the phallus, the seizure of other people's phalluses or the fear of losing one's own. Freud's reconstruction merely translates and internalizes this pitiless rule of the competitive hierarchy. You build between by castrating others; you can only ascend to genitality by trampling over other phallus bearers on the way. You are a phallus bearer only if you are recognized as such by others. Your phallus is constantly threatened: you are in constant fear of losing a phallus which was

difficult to win in the first place. No one ever threatens to take away your anus.[79]

Where the phallic organization of power complements capitalist economic structures in its emphasis on competition, its organization of the family, and its vertical hierarchies of power, an anally based sexuality, a "sexual communism," disperses power horizontally and unreproductively, leading to a playful, nonoppositional communality.[80] Mangrove manifested these playful and noncompetitive homosocial relations, even as it denied a sexual dimension to those relations.

Hocquenghem's antiphallic critique brought into question the very assumptions of progress on which Ellis's conception of homosexuality had been based.[81] The homosexual male, rather than a deviant version of masculinity, now held the promise and power to move society, not forward but into new configurations of pleasure and production. Like Mangrove's dances, made on the spot and for the moment and with no enduring market value, human sexual and societal relations should proliferate promiscuously without ever building toward profit. Like Mangrove's dancing bodies, the sexual body was capable of innumerable revitalizing contacts. Neither the expressive instrument of an autonomous subject as in Shawn's choreography nor a reservoir of physical permutations as in Cunningham's dances, contact improvisation's body, responsive but also generative, proved the endless seminal potential of human interaction.

Seminal but not fecund, the body for Hocquenghem as well as Mangrove, decidedly a male body, nonetheless stood for all human corporeality. The anus, an apt metaphor for theorizing male homosexuality, offered little to the lesbian social body, yet for Hocquenghem it stood as the sign for a revolutionary reexamination of all homosexuality, regardless of gender or race. Likewise contact improvisation, in its pursuit of the androgynous and polymorphous body, denied differences between the sexes while tacitly privileging certain masculine attributes: women were most successful when they showed unusual physical strength, but men were not praised for their softness but for their combinations of strength and daring with grace. Even the pedestrian aesthetic of the practice, while seeming to invite a full range of participants, tacitly asserted a masculine ethos, contrary to the feminine decorousness and pretentiousness of other dance forms. Contact's pedestrian sensibility helped Mangrove's dancers to secure their masculinity, thus guarding against still-prevalent allegations of effeminacy while seeming to represent all men.

Similarly, contact improvisation claimed a universal and natural physicality, even though with very few exceptions its practitioners were white and middle class. Participants did not contemplate any connections to the African American forms of improvisation in music, poetry, or dance that were developing contemporaneously. Black male break dancers, for example, improvised a social critique on pedestrian street corners, collectively presenting individual solutions to crises of gravity, momentum, and anatomical structure and using citation to satirize and triumph over oppressive social figures and forces. Rather than probe the similarities and differences between these distinctive approaches to improvisation, contact improvisers aligned themselves with the white post-Cunningham and -Judson avant-garde and rationalized their choreographic initiatives as an expansion of that tradition. They thereby sustained the whiteness of modern dance even as they began to infuse it with a masculine aesthetic.

Chaste as their performances were in tours across the United States, Mangrove always returned home to San Francisco, a city of unparalleled activism around gay and lesbian rights, with one of the largest gay populations in the country. Here the company's playful physicality could easily be seen to summon up the endless pleasures of pre-AIDS gay sexual culture. Undoubtedly, Mangrove's novelty and popularity, not unlike Shawn's all-male company, derived in part from its intervention into the female-dominated profession of modern dance. Yet, where other than San Francisco could an all-male company enjoy such sustained support?

SWANNING ON STAGE

Matthew Bourne's choreography emerges in the wake of contact improvisation's widespread success in both Europe and the

United States. However, unlike the internationally acclaimed choreographers Bill T. Jones or Lloyd Newson, who draw heavily from contact improvisation's principles for touching and sharing weight, Bourne prefers social dance formats for staging relationships between dancers. All three choreographers have created evening-length pieces that work with narrative elements and build characters, and all three use various strategies for creating critical distance from their choreographed stories. Bourne's work is distinctive in its evocation of nostalgia, constructing the dapper elegance of England's upper crust in the 1930s as in *Town and Country* (1991) or the technicolor glamor of jejune Americans in the 1950s as in *Deadly Serious* (1992). Characters in these dances have no authentic relationship to an expressive self. Pastiched from film, literary, and dance references, they cite multiple movement vocabularies, adopt multiple poses: they are serious one minute, ironic the next, ingenuous, stereotypic, and consummately mobile.

Gay male figures abound in Bourne's work, cast in roles that probe the delights and difficulties of homoerotic relations. In *Town and Country* the covert attraction between two upper-class gay men transforms into the ostentatious flirtation between a young man and woman in a seedy bar served by the two gay men, who now pose as their waiters. The heterosexual couple flaunts their privilege as the gay men closet their attraction. In *Deadly Serious* four men dance out vivid depictions of stereotypic masculine poses and gestures from 1950s movie stars, dissolving boundaries between heterosexual and homosexual masculinities as Peggy Lee sings "Mr. Wonderful." In *Spitfire* (1991) four men dressed in underwear come on to one another with seductive glances and gestures while following the contours of the famous romantic ballet *Pas de quatre*. Yet none of these relationships approaches the amorous involvement, the dedication to one another depicted between Swan and Prince in *Swan Lake*, an attachment remarkable for its intensity and for its extraordinary popularity and acceptance among a mainstream audience. How and why does this evening-length dance achieve its success?

Near the beginning of Bourne's *Swan Lake*, the royal family arrives at the ballet to see a depiction of exactly what his piece is not:

a camp send-up of the generic romantic ballet. Bourne's theater-within-a-theater is replete with magical butterfly creatures that look like male dancers in drag; a vain and conniving sylph; a dorky woodsman who does the sylph's bidding; and surreal monsters whose threatening gestures and eventual demise advance the minimal narrative. They grind through the steps, exaggerating virtuosity, pantomimed passion, and the tedious repetition of phrases. Audience members familiar with the renowned all-male ballet company Ballets Trocadero de Monte Carlo might presume that Bourne's recasting of the swans as male will yield the kind of *Swan Lake* that the Trocadero produced: a satiric, cross-dressed rendition of the original story. Bourne cleverly comments on these expectations by containing them within the miniature theater while developing the main action through meaningful glances between Prince, the Queen, and the Girlfriend.

Who is this Prince? He first appears as a boy, sickly, uninterested in his royal obligations, yet obedient, complying docilely as the large staff bathe and dress him for yet another round of public appearances. He craves his mother's affection, but she coldly rebuffs his pleading gestures. As an adult he comports himself with a regal bearing, yet beneath this decorous veneer his identity crisis rages. Drowning his sorrows at the Swank Bar, lowlife pimps and pushers cruise around him, and his girlfriend parties with other men. Eventually booted from the bar for his boisterous yet ineffectual troublemaking, he witnesses the Prime Minister paying off the Girlfriend but not her rejection of the money. Dejected, deceived, and with no hope of a reciprocated affection, he arrives at the lake ready to end his life.

Act I's choreography constructs this characterization of the Prince through contrasting, action-filled scenes that present a newsreel-like documentation of his life. Within this whirlwind of activities, pantomimed dialogue blends easily with the crisp buoyant regimen of the royals as well as the leering looks of bar customers. Vivid scenery and costumes amplify the effect of abundant realism. The bed in which the young prince lies with his toy swan turns around to become the balcony from which he and his mother wave to their admiring citizens. On one of their jaunts the

Queen commemorates an Andy Warhol portrait of herself and then a new sculpture, a sweating, male nude, which the Prince cannot help but give a second glance.[82] Such tongue-in-cheek excess offsets the sentimentality of the music, revitalizing its ability to convey the Prince's increasingly urgent apprehension that he cannot fit the mold already constructed for him. His final soliloquy, lyrically carving the space with sweeping arcs of arms and legs, expresses the poignancy of his futile search for other values, other meanings in life.

Enter the swans. Like their predecessors, the sprites, nymphs, sylphs, and wilis that populated nineteenth-century ballet stages, these swans exude an uncanny Otherness. Half bird, half man, their head and arm gestures, suggesting a swan's darting beak or curving wing, emerge briefly and then disappear into fulsome leaps, gliding runs, and arcing turns. With languorous sinuosity a wavelike impulse crosses their bodies, only to explode into sharp shifts of posture and weight. At the moment of fullest extension the rib cage will jut out, a leg pull in, unsettling their bodies' vulnerable openness. Then they dart, then gallumph, then balance delicately, and, with intricate precision, swivel into a new pathway, gathering a new momentum. Their costume, with its stiff corsetlike waistband, highlights the musculature of the torso, the softly rippling sequentiality of movement across arms, shoulders, and back. Their shaggy pants, enhancing the dynamism of their weight changes, the height of their jumps, appear comic one moment, noble the next.

This extraordinary synthesis of opposing qualities does not, however, account fully for the swans' Otherness. Their foreignness and charisma grow out of a series of reversals in which they miraculously contravene their aesthetic heritage. First, they are not female, not feminine, and not effeminate. Their bold, strong motions, the size of their jumps, the distances they cover quickly, all pronounce their maleness. Unlike the choreography for the traditional corps de ballet, which erases individual identity, these swans aggressively affirm their individual existence on stage. Each approaches the Prince inquisitively and directly, and each performs the unison phrase with idiosyncratic flare rather than with the faceless anonymity of the female corps. Where the swan maidens of the original *Swan Lake* had endured the magical spell of the evil Von Rothbart, helpless, mute, and unable to extricate themselves from their predicament, these swans live happily in their world apart, needing no rescue. Although their bodies open into positions of exquisite vulnerability, they never collapse into the camp exaggeration of feminine gestures.

Second, these swans do not perform ballet, nor do they execute the well-known choreography of Act II, even though Bourne has created a solo for Swan to the Swan Queen's adagio, a duet for Swan and Prince to the famous pas de deux, and a hilarious quartet to the well-known music of the pas de quatre. The swans' vocabulary contorts classical ballet stipulations for bodily geometry. Hips raise with legs; torsos duck and undulate; legs rotate inward and frequently extend at 45-degree angles to side front or side back. Where the ballet vocabulary constantly presses up and away from gravity, in order to inhabit the aerial, the swans give into gravity, then surge up out of its depths on curving pathways reminiscent of the modern dance choreographer Doris Humphrey's fall and rebound. In their duet Prince and Swan do not observe the traditional gender roles assigned to their parts in ballet. Both carve through space along the same arcs traced out in the Prince's earlier solo, performing increasingly in unison during the course of the duet. Each lifts the other, their faces passionately close to one another. Their only difference, marking swan from human, occurs in the manner of their touch: Swan never grasps the Prince but instead supports and guides him with forearms alone, a gesture reminiscent of wings. Throughout, all the swans sweat profusely, revealing, rather than obscuring, the labor through which their spectacular presence is achieved.

Finally, the swans are not worldly. They dis-resemble all other characters in the piece and in the worlds of ballet and modern dance. Unlike the reserved erectness of the royal entourage in Act I, the swans indulge in the weightiness of their motion. Unlike the swaggering strides and swishing hips of the glitterati at the Prince's ball in Act III, the swans uphold a fiercely Platonic sociality. Like Shawn's male dancers, they seldom touch, yet their athleticism is imbued with a sensual grace that Shawn could not have dared to construct. Menacing and captivating, calculating and alluring, weighty and ethereal, they conjoin the kinds of oppositional attributes ascribed to the nineteenth-century ballerina Marie Taglioni or that may have been achieved in the early works for an all-female cast by Mary Wigman and Martha Graham. Yet those women represented the dark and troubled territory of the psyche, whereas these men dance their way out of a fairytale book, transforming childhood images of magical creatures into a virile and noble reality.

The swans offer up these transcendent possibilities to the Prince, and he leaves their world with a new sense of identity and purpose. However, courtly life and his mother's cold yet wanton ways begin to undermine his new resolve. The arrival at the ball of the leather-clad lady's man who nonetheless bears a striking resemblance to Swan erodes completely his unstable composure. He seizes a gun, his mad confusion creating chaos in the ballroom. A shot rings out. Although it is the Prime Minister who has fired and the Girlfriend who has intercepted the bullet, Prince is carried away, convinced that he is a murderer. Returned to his bed after extensive medical treatment, the swans seep out from under his bed. Rather than the fraternal harmony created in their earlier appearance, they now swirl aggressively around Prince and then turn on Swan, who has dared to desert them for a mortal human. Their vengeful attack on the couple engulfs Swan and leaves Prince dead. His mother rushes in, truly distraught, as Swan cradles the boy Prince, pietà-like, in his arms, hovering in an eternal realm high above the bedroom scene.

Everything about this dance—the Prince's search for a more meaningful identity, the Otherness of the swans, the sensual encounter and then persecution of the couple—points to the homosexuality of the romance between Prince and Swan. And this homosexuality is portrayed sympathetically if tragically. Prince is neither a narcissist nor effeminate, the two models for insufficient evolutionary development implicit in the sexology of Ellis's time.[83] Nor is the distribution of his homosexual and heterosexual tendencies such that he merely prefers the company of men, as

Kinsey's research might suggest. Instead, something deep within him is satisfied and nurtured by his visit to the swans. The daring union across species of Prince and Swan proves the depth of their attachment while it demonstrates the profound prejudice against this kind of coupling. Their homosexual union could thrive only in a world apart. Where the Prince of the original *Swan Lake* failed to register the difference between good and evil and as a result committed both the Swan Queen and himself to their tragic fate, here Prince's resolute faith, although shaken by the vulgar womanizer in black, survives to serve as the vehicle for their final union.

Not only is the union between Swan and Prince rendered with empathy and understanding but their togetherness intimates a utopic resolution of oppositional categories. Prince is both sensitive and dutiful, Swan both cognizant and sexual. Each sutures together the kinds of contradictory attributes on which Prince's world thrives. Rich and poor, governors and governed, male and female—all carefully demarcated, all driving the machinery of the state in Acts I and III—disappear in the swans' enchanted kingdom. In their place the swans offer an egalitarian society that blends labor with pleasure, the rational with the sensual. The swans participate equally in the construction of their world; no hierarchy of skills or placement in space singles out one over another. Swan is not so much their leader—he does not direct or protect them as the Swan Queen in the original *Swan Lake*—as the eccentric who becomes fascinated with a mortal. Together, the swans playfully and masterfully inhabit their world. They cavort, then pause to explore the sensuousness of movement's traversal across the body, then they conquer space, aggressively launching themselves into the air or across the stage. What continually astonishes in this celebration of a sensual identity is that these are male dancers, their masculine musculature and agility imbuing the movement with sufficient rectitude to secure its maleness.

In their synthesis of so many opposing categories, the swans do not take on an androgynous sexual neutrality. Rather, they are sexually charged creatures who occupy simultaneously the positions of desiring subject and desired object. Where formerly a female character was required to focus the objectifying gaze of the masculine viewer, now male figures perform that function. Entering into the swans' world, Prince is introduced to the pleasures of looking and being looked at. Both Swan and Prince enjoy the gazes of one another, surrounded and supported by the reciprocal gazes of the other swans. Their erotics of looking are further enhanced by the fact that the traditional relationship in ballet between the female corps de ballet and the masculine gaze of the viewer has been radically altered by the use of a male corps.

Yet this mutual fueling of the desiring machine never mounts the critique of capitalism that Hocquenghem and contact improvisation had envisioned. Although the swans elaborate an egalitarian vocabulary of motion and gesture, theirs is not a dance that everyone can share. Their exclusive virtuosity never references the pedestrian, never gestures toward a continuum between their spectacular achievements and the movement potential of untrained bodies. Where contact improvisation had assiduously embraced such a continuum, the swans luxuriate in the splendid trappings of a supercharged theatricality. Their bodies glisten not only from the work and pleasure of dancing but also from the theatrical packaging of their achievements. Through their flamboyant style, their audacious gaze, the handsome costumes and dramatic environs, the swans provoke the viewer's desire to possess them at the same time that they merchandise their movement. Their presentation contains no Marxist critique, nor does it ask viewers to participate communally in the making of the dance's meaning. These swans carry no residue of 1970s political aesthetics. They dance out identity in the 1990s.

In the utopian image they construct, the charged yet enigmatic erotics they concoct, these creatures articulate a queer identity. They illustrate an embodied version of queer theory as it developed during the 1990s in dialogue with earlier approaches to sexology. Unlike Ellis or Kinsey, each of whom in a different way attempted to neutralize prejudice against homosexuality through scientific explanations of its unavoidability, queer theory embraces a homosexual orientation both as an enabling reality rather than pitiable inevitability and as a critical place from which to assess the workings of heteronormative cultural values. Like the swans who charge the disrespected categories of male dancer and female corps de ballet with a new charisma, queer theory appropriates the derogatory term for the male homosexual used frequently in the 1950s and 1960s and gives it a new theoretical and political potential. In interventions such as those conducted by Queer Nation in response to the AIDS crisis, the term *queer* has catalyzed the disenfranchisement experienced by homosexuals and directed it toward protest against antihomosexual discrimination and also toward the establishment of new kinds of positive images of gays and lesbians. Queer scholarship has formulated analogous strategies for assessing homophobic prejudice and policy as it has operated in philosophical, social, and literary theories and even in the organization of the academic institution. As Michael Warner in *Fear of a Queer Planet* explains, "The preference for queer represents, among other things, an aggressive impulse of generalization; it rejects a minoritizing logic of toleration or simply political interest-representation in favor of a more thorough resistance to regimes of the normal. For academics, being interested in queer theory is a way to mess up the desexualized spaces of the academy."[84] Drawing on Foucault's scrutiny of the categorization of sexuality and the function of such a category for the perpetuation of state power, queer theory has even interrogated the heterosexual underpinnings of the production of knowledge.

In its brief history as a term affirming homosexuality, *queer* has expanded beyond the representational confines of gay and lesbian identity to embrace the possibility of a coalition among all social constituencies oppressed by the regime of the "normal." Like Bourne's vision of Swan, *queer* has come to signify a coalition politics that transcends race-, gender-, sex-, and class-specific kinds of discrimination. Like the swans, who cite numerous traditions and playfully locate themselves adjacent to but not within the traditional confines of narrative (both inside and out), so too queer theory presumes a fluid and changeable conception of identity that crosses traditional political boundaries between minoritized groups. Scholars who question slippages in the term's usage challenge *queer*'s social agenda in this ambitious yet vague inclusiveness. These scholars' critiques of *queer* elucidate the queer status of the swans and help explain the mainstream popularity and charisma of Bourne's *Swan Lake.*

First, the discipline of queer theory has come under attack as a pseudocoalition, promising inclusion of all minoritized groups yet consistently focused on support of issues and advocacy for white middle-class gay men. The swans embody just such an ambiguous agenda. Their courageous habitation of the denigrated female role universalizes their white male bodies and depicts an imagined community without social discord. Yet no African or Asian bodies integrate their swanery, nor do lexicons of movement that signify ethnic identity weave into their (white) modern dance movement. Thus even as they represent a world beyond prejudice, a world tolerant of difference, the swans constitute a remarkably homogeneous ensemble. Sustaining the traditional performance of whiteness in modern dance, Bourne's choreography uses the absence of racial and ethnic signifiers to moderate the display of sexuality so as to secure his aesthetic goal of a transcendental identity for the swans.

Second, queer theory's championing of a queer "lifestyle" has failed to account for global capitalist economic structures that find in the queer community as currently constituted an ideal market for commodified queer images and products.[85] Although the market's ability to commodify sexual orientation enhances class divides and erodes the public sphere, focusing attention on the individual consumer and reducing opportunities for collective organizing, queer politics has not resisted assimilation into the market, nor do the swans. Insofar as dance can ever construct a marketable product, *Swan Lake* does so. In its carefully crafted integration of pantomime and virtuoso dancing, and in its contrast between the witty precision of the court and the soulful sinuosity of the swans, it reinscribes the aesthetic hierarchies that earlier postmodern choreographers, in the name of a danced politics, had broken down.[86] For $45 per ticket, viewers can feast on the visual and kinesthetic splendor they purvey at the same time that they are moved by the story of an impossible gay male love. Susan

Bordo observes that in advanced capitalism two contradictory impulses compete in the structuring of individual identity:

> On the one hand, as producers of goods and services we must sub-limate, delay, repress desires for immediate gratification; we must cultivate the work ethic. On the other hand, as consumers we must display a boundless capacity to capitulate to desire and indulge in impulse; we must hunger for constant and immediate satisfaction. The regulation of desire thus becomes an ongoing problem, as we find ourselves continually besieged by temptation, while socially condemned for overindulgence.[87]

The swans solve this dilemma magnificently. Virtuoso soloists, the swans are a consumer's delight, yet they also absolve us of our consumer guilt because they are performing the important cultural labor of explaining a gay sensibility.

And for this reassuring yet strange magic they work, we adore them. Their magical charm, however, is achieved at great cost. Not only does *Swan Lake* erase racial and ethnic difference but it erases women almost entirely. Bordo continues: "We would thus expect that when the regulation of desire becomes especially problematic (as it is in advanced consumer cultures), women and their bodies will pay the greatest symbolic and material toll."[88] *Swan Lake* exacts this toll by eliminating the female corps de ballet, the site where female labor was displayed if trivialized, and by retaining only the most stereotypic of female character types: the cold and wanton mother, the bimbo girlfriend, and the sexually promiscuous and ambitious princesses. At the same time it incorporates feminine features into the masculine bodies of the swans, reinvigorating patriarchal authority and endowing the male body with a new seductiveness. Erasing any anxieties that the presence of the female body might have provoked concerning corporeal spontaneity, frailty, fleshiness, or unknowability, the swans cement the bonds of the homosocial world in which white male dominance is ensured. The final image of the dance sums up this new world order: the failed mother weeps over her son's corpse, while the transcendent swan replaces the maternal figure of the pietà, righteously condemning the feminine as he carries the Prince into the global capitalist future.

But, no, this is not fully accurate for, after all, Swan, attacked by his cohorts, has likewise transmigrated from his world to another. He does not represent the queer corporate body of the swans' wedge. But does he, instead, articulate a gay politics? Deviant, like the Prince, he is gay bashed by his own kind. And this is how the closet in Bourne's *Swan Lake* operates. Both the causal relationship between homosexuality and inadequate mothering that the dance depicts and the attack on Swan by his fellow swans issue from a framework of heteronormative assumptions about gay life.[89] Prince's homosexuality, created by the seductive mother's failure to respond to his oversensitive neediness, is represented as a psychic maladjustment that finds resolution only in death. Swan's choice of Prince, which ignites the instinctual fury of the flock, transforms the swans' gay men's society into the hate-filled mob of straight men that has terrorized gay men for centuries. Homosexuality is thus rendered deficient and pathetic on the one hand, unpredictable and bestial on the other.

Where, initially, Bourne's retelling of *Swan Lake* seems to garner sympathy for the gay couple at the female character's expense, placing gay and feminist agendas in opposition, closer examination reveals that the dance conveys neither a gay nor a feminist politics. Both the patriarchy and the closet benefit from its postmodern choreography. Little wonder, then, that Bourne, a gay man, has always claimed that the dance moved beyond the historical specificities of gay politics, and little wonder that *Swan Lake* will tour the world as renowned exemplar of global capitalist cultural achievement. [90] But to imagine the "corps de ballet" that offers a nonracist, nonsexist, nonhomophobic alternative is no easy task. At least Bourne has prompted us to imagine the possibility.

OPENING OPEN CLOSETS

Why choose to discuss Bourne, a British choreographer, over, say, Bill T. Jones or David Rousseve, American choreographers whose work wrestles openly with issues of race and sexuality? I chose the choreographic projects discussed in this essay specifically to track the simultaneous development of whiteness, masculinity, and closeted sexuality in modern dance. A piece such as

Bourne's marks a crucial stage in that development, promising to demolish the closet while shoring up its compromised architecture. Bourne's work also gestures toward the emerging transnational status of modern dance as it, like ballet, begins to circulate globally (with the American Dance Festival opening in Moscow and contact improvisation's vocabulary entering the repertories of countless dance companies worldwide). Within this global economy of modernism, Bourne's is the kind of closet that sustains the history of closeted homosexuality in dance, one of the most remarkably open closets of any profession.

The geneological approach of this essay has worked to uncover epistemological changes in that open closet during the twentieth century. Both Shawn and Ellis, for example, postulate an autonomous bounded self that encloses either a normal or inverted sexuality, whereas Cunningham and Kinsey organize the person as a set of semiautonomous parts whose behavior, sexual and otherwise, takes place along a continuum of possibilities. In Mangrove's and Hocquenghem's protean playful dynamics, individual identity is constantly reconfigured as the product of changing relations with others, while Bourne and queer theory stage identity as series of performances that reference other performances. Each of these theories of identity, in turn, projects a distinctive closeting of homosexuality. Understanding the choreographic strategies through which these closets retain their structural integrity and their openness may help us to place them on stage and to examine their representational operations alongside the dancing they formerly contained.

NOTES

I want to thank Philip Brett, George Haggerty, Jane Desmond, Jacqueline Shea Murphy, and Tirza Latimer for their insightful readings of drafts of the essay.

1. For the first London production, many swans retained torso and armpit hair, although for the video and the Los Angeles production many seem to have shaved.

2. Interview with Matthew Bourne in "An Education Resource for *Adventures in Motion Pictures*," compiled by Elizabeth Marshall (London: Adventures in Motion Pictures, London), 21.

3. Matthew Bourne, interview by Gabriel J. P. Goldberg, *Edge*, April 30, 1997, p. 70.

4. See, for example, Rupert Christiansen, "Lakeside Adventures," *Dance Theatre Journal* 12, no. 4 (spring 1996): 29–31; Donna Krohn, "Moving Upstream," *Dance Now* 5, no. 3 (1996): 22–27; Allen Robertson, "High Voltage," *Dance Now* 4, no. 5 (1995): 2–11; Lewis Segal, "A Swan for the New Ages," *Los Angeles Times*, April 28, 1997, pp. F1 and F10; and Rita Felciano, "Swanderful," *Guardia* 31, no. 36 (May 27–June 3, 1997): 49.

5. Ramsay Burt probes the significance of this observation in *The Male Dancer: Bodies, Spectacle, Sexualities* (London: Routledge, 1995).

6. Admittedly, the comparison of one British choreographer with three American choreographers raises issues that I am not able to address here. For the purposes of this essay, I treat Bourne as part of a Euro-American experimental postmodern tradition that shares certain general choreographic features and draws upon a common choreographic heritage even as it displays distinctive regional and national elements. Bourne, for example, trained at the Laban Center in London with Bonnie Bird, an American dancer and dance educator.

7. For a more thorough presentation of male and female participation in twentieth-century theatrical dance, see Judith Lynne Hanna, *Dance, Sex, and Gender: Signs of Identity, Dominance, Defiance, and Desire* (Chicago: University of Chicago Press, 1988), 143–49.

8. For incisive accounts of physicality in this period, see Robert Allen, *Horrible Prettiness: Burlesque and American Culture* (Chapel Hill: University of North Carolina Press, 1991); Nancy Lee Chalfa Ruyter, *Reformers and Visionaries: The Americanization of the Art of Dance* (New York: Dance Horizons, 1979); Harvey Green, *Fit for America: Health, Fitness, Sport, and American Society* (New York: Pantheon, 1986); and Linda Tomko, *Dancing Class* (Bloomington: Indiana University Press, 1999).

It is beyond the scope of this essay to explicate the multiple influences and sources for Duncan's and St. Denis's artistic initiatives. For an excellent overview of Duncan's work, see Ann Daly, *Done into Dance* (Bloomington: Indiana University Press, 1996), and for a lucid biography of St. Denis, see Suzanne Shelton, *Divine Dancer: The Biography of Ruth St. Denis* (New York: Doubleday, 1981).

9. Duncan, in particular, used class-based evaluations of artistic genres to explain her performances. See Daly's cogent analysis of Duncan's rhetoric in *Done into Dance*. The role of class values in relation to the entire history of modern dance deserves far more serious consideration than I am able to give it here.

10. See Isadora Duncan, *The Art of the Dance* (New York: Theatre Arts, 1928).

11. Although Duncan is reputed to have had at least one lesbian affair—with the famous Loie Fuller—she seems not to have fathomed Whitman's homosexuality.

12. For a probing analysis of gendered and orientalist thematics in St. Denis's famous solo *Radha*, see Jane Desmond, "Dancing Out the Difference: Cultural Imperialism and Ruth St. Denis's 'Radha' of 1906," *Signs: Journal of Women in Culture and Society* 17, no. 1 (1991): 28–49.

13. Shelton, *Divine Dancer*, 55.

14. Phyllis Grosskurth substantiates the popularity of Ellis's book and provides a good overview of its relationship to Ellis's oeuvre in her biography of Ellis. See Grosskurth, *Havelock Ellis: A Biography* (New York: Knopf, 1980), 316. In the foreword to his second edition of *The Dance of Life*, Ellis summarizes Victorian attitudes toward dance as dismissive, acknowledging that during that period dance had been regarded only as "gay and trivial, even tending to immorality" (Ellis, *The Dance of Life* [New York: Modern Library, 1929], ii). As he claims in his introduction to Ted Shawn's *The American Ballet*, Ellis was a longtime dance enthusiast, and he believed that dance deserved new consideration (Ellis, introduction to Ted Shawn, *The American Ballet* [New York: Holt, 1926], x). Influenced by the works of Duncan and St. Denis as well as Diaghilev's Ballets Russes, Ellis launched into *The Dance of Life* decades after his pathbreaking studies of human sexuality as a way to examine life's vicissitudes and to extend his liberal attitudes toward sexual behavior into other aspects of social life. Even though Ellis aspired to ennoble dance, his analysis, synthesizing anthropological literature, histories of bodily comportment, and his own observations, ratifies racist and colonialist cultural presumptions about the intrinsic connection between dance and sex.

15. Ellis cites Edmund Selous (*Zoologist*, December 1901) as the author of this hypothesis (Ellis, *Dance of Life*, 34).

16. Ellis is here quoting Dr. Louis Robinson, who places chimpanzee dances and Pavlova on a single continuum (Ellis, *Dance of Life*, 43).

17. Ibid., 44.

18. Ellis invokes the Darwinian notion of survival of the fittest for his claim that the best dancers are the fittest mates (Ellis, *Dance of Life*, 44–45).

19. Ellis writes: "The dance is the rule of number and of rhythm and of measure and of order, of the controlling influence of form, of the subordination of the parts to the whole" (Ellis, *Dance of Life*, xi).

20. Ibid., 47.

21. "From this point of view we may better understand the immense ardour with which every part of the wonderful human body has been brought into the play of the dance," Ellis writes. "The men and women of races spread all over the world have shown a marvellous skill and patience in imparting rhythm and measure to the most unlikely, the most rebellious regions of the body, all wrought by desire into potent and dazzling images" (Ellis, *Dance of Life*, 46).

22. Havelock Ellis, *The Analysis of the Sexual Impulse*, vol. 1 of *Studies in the Psychology of Sex* (New York: Random House, 1910), 47, 50, 41.

23. Ibid., 43.

24. Ibid., 44.

25. Ibid., 46.

26. I believe that Ellis's recitation of anthropological findings reflects accurately the general assumptions about dancing, the body, and sexuality within the discipline during that period. In some of the cases he cites, however, Ellis presses hard on the connection between dance and sexual desire. The renowned anthropologist Alfred C. Haddon, for example, observed that among the Torres Strait islanders young women formerly looked upon the most accomplished

headhunters as the most desirable husband, and more recently they looked to the most accomplished dancers. But he makes none of the sensationalist connections between cannibalism, sexual arousal, and courtship that are implicit in Ellis's phrasing of the observation. Furthermore, Haddon describes in great detail a number of ceremonial dances in which he makes no mention of sexual arousal whatsoever. See Haddon, *Head-Hunters* (London: Watts, 1932), 88 and throughout.

27. Ellis, *Dance of Life*, 55.

28. Ibid., 46, 55.

29. Ibid., 57.

30. Ibid., 54.

31. Ibid.

32. Ibid., 57.

33. Ibid., 55.

34. Ironically, Ellis's investigation of sexuality emphasized dance's ability to imbue participants and viewers with tumescence in order to challenge theories of sexuality based on "evacuation" and to shift focus to the processes, such as dance, that build up sexual desire. In so doing, he hoped to garner greater attention for female sexuality and its distinctive needs and to create a more open and relaxed environment for the discussion of sexual issues. By embracing sexuality as a vital and vibrant aspect of human life, Ellis implicitly contested the hierarchical valuings of brain and body, and social and species evolution, through which sexuality had been constructed as the most primitive kind of human action. Although Ellis's stance undermines such hierarchies, they continue to circulate around and through his work, and they are dazzlingly evident in the travelogue evidence Ellis quotes concerning the nature of dance.

35. For a succinct overview of how racial and gender stereotypes informed sexology in the late nineteenth and early twentieth centuries, see Sander L. Gilman, *Difference and Pathology: Stereotypes of Sexuality, Race, and Madness* (Ithaca, N.Y.: Cornell University Press, 1985). Also see Carol Groneman, "Nymphomania," and David G. Horn, "The Norm Which Is Not One," both in Jennifer Terry and Jacqueline Urla, eds., *Deviant Bodies* (Bloomington: Indiana University Press, 1995), 219–49 and 109–28, respectively.

36. See Tomko, *Dancing Class*.

37. Shawn arranged several subsequent visits with Ellis and even took his all-male dance company to meet Ellis when they were on tour in London in 1934. See Walter Terry, *Ted Shawn: Father of American Dance* (New York: Dial, 1976) 107, and Ted Shawn and Gray Poole, *One Thousand and One Night Stands* (Garden City, N.Y.: Doubleday, 1960), 263.

38. Terry, *Ted Shawn*, 107.

39. Shawn recollects that in 1916, the University of California Board of Trustees voted to reverse the long-standing policy barring dancers, and in a subsequent motion at the same meeting, approved an invitation to Ruth St. Denis to perform in the Berkeley Greek Theatre. The pageant St. Denis and Shawn created for that amphitheater also played in San Diego and the Shrine Auditorium in Los Angeles. According to Shawn: "Everywhere the hit number was the

Pyrrhic Dance, the first number I ever choreographed for an all-male ensemble. Pyrrhic dances, which date from ancient Greece, originally were part of military training and symbols of victory. My interpretation was not a revival of the Greek classic form but an attempt to capture the spirit of the original.

"Sixteen men dancers, leaping and jumping with power, muscles, and virile strength, created an impact that thrilled the pageant's audiences and won paragraphs of newspaper praise. Many years elapsed before I formed my own group of men dancers, but after the reception of the *Pyrrhic Dance* I always had in the back of my mind plans, choreographies, and dance themes suitable for men dancers" (Shawn and Poole, *One Thousand and One,* 63–66).

40. Ibid., 258.

41. Shawn, *American Ballet,* 21–22

42. Space does not permit a more extensive discussion of Shawn's complex relationship to African American dance and dancers. For example, he taught his *Negro Spirituals* to the African American choreographer Charles Williams, whose company performed them. See John Perpener, "The Seminal Years of Black Concert Dance" (Ph.D. diss., New York University, 1992). At the same time Shawn campaigned stridently against tap dance, which he associated with African American culture.

43. Shawn believed that Negro music as distinct from dance was notable for its spirituality, and he choreographed one of his most popular suites to a set of Negro spirituals. See Shawn, *American Ballet,* 21. For an excellent description and analysis of the workings of race and sexuality in Shawn's *Negro Spirituals,* see Susan Manning, "Danced Spirituals: The Performance of Race, Gender, and Sexuality in American Modern Dance, 1930–1960," in André Lepecki, ed., *Moving Ideologies:Interventions in Dance Theory, History, and Politics* (forthcoming). Manning argues that before World War II, the white dancing body represented all races as part of its aesthetic mission to express universal human concerns, whereas African American dancers were frequently found lacking according to white standards. After the war African American choreographers achieved prominence but only as representatives of specifically African or African American cultural values. White choreographers, by contrast, remained unconstrained by any expectations regarding their subject matter or approach. The argument I am making here complements Manning's analysis.

44. This evening-length work included four solos for Shawn, each depicting the archetypal figure that corresponded to that section's social organization: shaman, poet-philosopher, politician-demagogue, and creative artist.

45. The preponderance of configurations in which the dancers are touching in photos of Shawn's choreography is misleading and probably reflects photographic technology and the aesthetic of the period. Fortunately, Shawn filmed much of his repertory in rehearsal and performance at Jacob's Pillow during this period, and these films survive, providing a good idea of Shawn's choreography and the dancers' style.

46. *Springfield Republican,* 1934, quoted in the company's publicity brochures for several years.

47. These quotations are taken from the documentary film made about the

company entitled *The Men Who Danced*. Filmed at Jacob's Pillow, Lee, Mass., 1985. Producer: Ron Housa. Collection of the New York Public Library at Lincoln Center.

48. For background on Symonds, Carpenter, and Ellis, and for a good overview of the intellectual inquiry into Greek life and homosexuality in Victorian England, see Linda Dowling, *Hellenism and Homosexuality in Victorian Oxford* (Ithaca, N.Y.: Cornell University Press, 1994).

49. Ellis writes: "The congenitally inverted may, I believe, be looked upon as a class of individuals exhibiting nervous characters which, to some extent, approximate them to persons of artistic genius. The dramatic and artistic aptitudes of inverts are, therefore, partly due to the circumstances of the invert's life, which render him necessarily an actor—and in some few cases lead him into a love of deception comparable with that of a hysterical woman—and partly, it is probably, to a congenital nervous predisposition allied to the predisposition to dramatic aptitude" (Ellis, *Sexual Inversion*, vol. 2 of *Studies in the Psychology of Sex*, 296).

50. Ibid., 80.

51. Ibid., 304, 310–11.

52. Ibid., 317–20.

53. Jane Sherman and Barton Mumaw, *Barton Mumaw, Dancer: From Denishawn to Jacob's Pillow and Beyond* (New York: Dance Horizons, 1986), 129.

54. Cunningham presented his first concert of solo works in 1944, accompanied by John Cage playing prepared piano pieces. Solos in that concert included *Root of an Unfocus, Triple Paced, Tossed as It Is Untroubled, The Unavailable Memory Of, Totem Ancestor*, and *Spontaneous Earth*. *Root of an Unfocus* and *Tossed as It Is Untroubled*, described in program notes as "an externalization of a laugh within the mind," remained in his repertory for many years.

55. Clive Barnes, "Movement, Sound, Light," *Dance and Dancers*, September 1964, pp. 17–18.

56. Ibid., 20.

57. Peter Yates, "Merce Cunningham Restores the Dance to Dance," *Impulse*, 1965, p. 16.

58. Cunningham describes *Banjo* thusly in program notes for concerts from this period. As part of this genre, we should also include *The Princess Zondilda and Her Entourage* (1947), and *Story* (1963).

59. Clive Barnes, "Sound, Movement, Light," 20.

60. Cunningham had taught ballet at the American Ballet School during the early 1940s and choreographed two duets for himself and Tanaquil Leclerc entitled *Amores* and *Games*. See Yates, "Merce Cunningham Restores the Dance," 13–17.

61. For an excellent summary of early experiments with chance procedures, see Remy Charlip, "Composing by Chance," *Dance Magazine*, January 1954, pp. 17–19.

62. Cunningham describes the compositional process of using chance procedures in "Summerspace Story: How a Dance Came to Be," *Dance Magazine*, June 1966, pp. 52–54.

63. John Cage, "In This Day," *Dance Observer*, January 1957, p. 10.

64. In an interview for Elliot Caplan for his film *Cage/Cunningham*, Cage comments that he worked hard to create a field within which he could continue to discover new things and to make unanticipated choices. I am arguing that this field similarly protected him as a gay man. See Elliot Caplan, *Cage/Cunningham*, dir. Elliot Caplan, prod. Cunningham Dance Foundation and La Sept, Kultur, 1991, videocassette.

65. In his interviews for Caplan's film Cunningham adopts a resolutely androgynous stance, asking why men's and women's roles in dance shouldn't be exchangeable.

66. The film is entitled *498, 3rd Ave*, prod. Hansjörg Pauli, and is in the collection of the New York Public Library at Lincoln Center.

67. The politics of equality implicit in Cunningham's use of chance were noted by Peter Yates, who observes: "This makes the action by chance only a seeming accidental extension of the freedom of diversity" (Yates, "Merce Cunningham Restores the Dance," 15).

68. For a lucid explication of the problematic of race in Cage's work and its presumption of universality, see George Lewis, "Improvised Music after 1950: Afrological and Eurological Perspectives," *Black Music Research Journal* 16, no. 1 (spring 1996): 91–122. Lewis's analysis helped me to understand how the category of the "experimental" figured in the discourse of whiteness as a justification for the perpetuation of the universalist status of white choreography.

69. Alfred C. Kinsey, Wardell B Pomeroy, and Clyde E. Martin, *Sexual Behavior in the Adult Male* (Philadelphia: Saunders, 1948), 650.

70. Ibid., 662.

71. For an excellent comparison of Ellis's and Kinsey's approaches, see Jennifer Terry, "Anxious Slippages between 'Us' and 'Them': A Brief History of the Scientific Search for Homosexual Bodies," in Terry and Urla, *Deviant Bodies*, 129–69.

72. Kinsey, Pomeroy, and Martin, *Sexual Behavior in the Adult Male*, 617.

73. This is the phrase used to represent the two in Elliott Caplan's film *Cage/Cunningham*.

74. Cynthia Novack's pioneering ethnography of contact improvisation serves as the basis for the analysis that follows. For background on Paxton and a detailed history of the evolution of the form, see Novack, *Sharing the Dance: Contact Improvisation and American Culture* (Madison: University of Wisconsin Press, 1990). My description of contact improvisation passes over important changes in the form as it developed from 1972 into the early 1980s, focusing instead on the form as it had coalesced by the late 1970s. For a detailed discussion of the changes, see Novack.

75. Ibid., 123.

76. *Contact Newsletter* 2 [fall 1976]: 3, quoted in Novack, *Sharing the Dance*, 89.

77. Campbell is quoted in Novack, *Sharing the Dance*, 198.

78. Jeffrey Weeks, preface to the 1978 edition of Guy Hocquenghem, *Homosexual Desire* (Durham, N.C.: Duke University Press, 1993), 35.

79. Hocquenghem, *Homosexual Desire*, 103–4.

80. Ibid., 39–40.

81. In his retheorizing of the concept of homosexuality, Hocquenghem made extensive use of Deleuze and Guattari's deconstruction of Freud's Oedipus complex, showing the connection between Oedipal and capitalist structures and arguing, fabulously, that human society should reconfigure as "desiring machines plugged into the anus" (Hocquenghem, *Homosexual Desire*, 111). Unfortunately, it is beyond the scope of this essay to establish Hocquenghem's argument in full. I refer the reader to Jeffrey Weeks's excellent introduction to *Homosexual Desire* for a lucid account of Hocquenghem's relation to psychoanalytic and Marxist theories.

82. The portrait—a set of multiple, differently tinted likenesses of the queen, reminiscent of Warhol's silk screens—was added for the Los Angeles performances.

83. Richard Dyer identifies the logic of the presumed interconnection between narcissism, the effeminate, and homosexuality as follows: "Gay men fancy people like themselves (men) rather than unlike (women), therefore, their sexuality must be an extension of the their love of themselves. Or—women are naturally more narcissistic than men, and gay men are more feminine than straight men, therefore gay men are narcissistic." Dyer traces this logic to Freud's theory of narcissism wherein the love object of the adult homosexual male reflects not his mother but himself. See Dyer, *Now You See It: Studies on Lesbian and Gay Film* (New York: Routledge, 1990), 67. Although the Prince's mother rejects his affection and need for affection, he is not portrayed as overly self-absorbed, nor does he perform a single effeminate gesture.

84. Michael Warner, *Fear of a Queer Planet: Queer Politics and Social Theory* (Minneapolis: University of Minnesota Press, 1993), xxvi.

85. Noting Queer Nation's emphasis on the individual and on the commodities that enhance a queer lifestyle, Sue-Ellen Case contrasts their interventionist approach with earlier forms of political organizing and protest based on the community: "The site of Queer Nation is not a community, a region, or even a venue . . . instead, it is embedded in ads, shopping strategies, mall demonstrations, and logos. Capitalism, corporate structures, and nationhood are resident in the basic unit of the commodity that functions as its strategy. No alternative to capitalism is imagined—only that its market forces would redirect their address toward the 'Queer'" (Case, *The Domain-Matrix: Performing Lesbian at the End of Print Culture* [Bloomington: Indiana University Press, 1996], 170). For her extensive critique of *queer,* see pp. 150–74.

86. See, for example, Yvonne Rainer's manifestos in *Work, 1961–73* (New York: Press of the Nova Scotia College of Art and Design, 1974) and Sally Banes's comprehensive descriptions of Judson works in *Democracy's Body: Judson Dance Theatre, 1962–1964* (Ann Arbor: UMI, 1983), and her insightful analysis of these performances in the larger artistic milieu of the New York early 1960s avant-garde in *Greenwich Village, 1963* (Durham, N.C.: Duke University Press, 1995).

87. Susan Bordo, *Unbearable Weight: Feminism, Western Culture, and the Body* (Berkeley: University of California Press, 1993), 199.

88. Ibid., 212.

89. Stephen Farber, a film critic and one of the only critics to consider *Swan Lake* as a gay male representation, makes this point in his review of *Swan Lake* from the *Los Angeles Times*, June 1, 1997, Calendar sec., p. 50.

90. At the time this essay was written, 1997, Bourne's *Swan Lake* was on its way to Tokyo and Broadway, with untold other bookings in progress.

6

Dissolving in Pleasure: The Threat of the Queer Male Dancing Body

Ramsay Burt

My aim in this chapter is to discuss some correspondences between postmodern presentations of the queer male dancing body and queer theory based on French poststructuralist philosophy. I am particularly interested in similarities between a poststructuralist critique of the rational unitary subject of the Enlightenment and postmodern performances that disrupt the notion of this subject position, which Kant prescribed as a prerequisite for making aesthetic judgments. Where gender and sexuality are concerned, recent feminist scholarship has made clear that taking a neutral, disinterested position is not possible. My argument is that it is not possible, in a patriarchal and homophobic society, to make disinterested aesthetic judgments about cultural products that challenge normative ideologies of gender and sexuality in order to propose a radically revised imagination of the body's capacity for pleasure.[1] Thus some choreographers, in articulating what I am calling the discourse of the queer male dancing body, reveal the disintegration of this disinterested subject position. Philosophers and psychologists widely reported throughout the twentieth century the disintegration of the rational unitary subject of the Enlightenment, while the viability of the project of the Enlightenment has become a subject of debate between French poststructuralism and German critical theory. While addressing the problem of theorizing sexuality, Roland Barthes and Michel Foucault have written most interestingly about the embodiment of subjectivity. My aim in this chapter is to discuss the ways in which performances of postmodern dance by some gay choreographers position the spectator in relation to the discourse of the queer male dancing body.

I see this discourse as akin to Roland Barthes's *A Lover's Discourse*, which he proposes "is spoken, perhaps, by thousands of subjects (who knows?), but warranted by no one."[2] Barthes conceives of the lover's discourse as a number of figures that constitute the language we use when we are in love to address to ourselves and to the beloved. It is a language of embodied figures. Barthes could almost have been thinking about dance when he writes about wanting to capture "in a much livelier way, the body's gestures caught in action and not contemplated in repose: the body of athletes, orators, statues: what in the straining body can be immobilised: So it is with the lover at grips with his figures."[3] And so it is with the writer analyzing his or her pleasure at watching the dancing body. Of "reverberation" (*retentissement*), Barthes writes: "What echoes in me is what I learn from my body."[4] Whereas Barthes discusses figures in a lover's discourse, this chapter uses the idea of a discourse that is embodied by the dancer and reverberates in the spectator as a way of understanding the social and political context of postmodern choreography by gay artists.

It would, however, be absurd to claim that only gay male dancing bodies performing postmodern choreography by gay male choreographers have the power to reveal the disintegration of the rational unitary subject of the Enlightenment, as clearly such revelations are almost a defining feature of postmodern cultural production as a whole. Nor are postmodern gay male choreographers the only artists involved in redefining the terms of embodied subjectivity and problematizing normative ideas about the body's capacity for sensuous experience—pleasurable or otherwise. Many in the visual and performing arts, including Marina Abramowicz, Ron Athey, Mona Hatoum, Orlan, and Stelarc, are redefining ideas about subjectivity and bodily experience in widely differing ways. What I propose in this chapter is that gay male dancing bodies, because of their positioning within discourses of gender and sexuality, have the potential to subvert notions of disinterestedness and objectivity that are a prerequisite for the rational unitary subject. Within normative thought this subject position is implicitly masculine, because the male body is generally taken as an exemplary, unproblematic, unmarked norm. During the last two and a half centuries, women rather than men have had to prove that they are not distracted by the disturbing, disquieting, and disruptive force of "natural" desires and functions. Gay male dancing bodies signify the possibility that men can dissolve in pleasure within the leaky boundaries not of women but of other men. This blurring of masculine subjects and objects destabilizes notions of male objectivity and rationality that, within Enlightenment thought, guaranteed the disinterestedness of the rational unitary subject.

In keeping with this blurring of subject positions, this chapter presents more than one point of view. When I write about my own response to queer male dancing bodies, I recognize that it is not possible to take a neutral, value-free position. I therefore need to clarify my own investment in this area of research. So whereas Oscar Wilde, passing through customs in New York, famously announced that he had nothing to declare but his genius, I need to confess a more modest, no less valued, but much safer attribute. I must own up to my heterosexuality and, having done so, explain why I am writing about representations of gay masculinity. I first came to this subject through my wish to write about the male dancer in the twentieth century: it is not possible to write much about this without dealing with the issue of dance and homosexuality. This issue is, however, one that has received little attention, so much so that I called my first essay on it "The Dance That Does Not Speak Its Name."[5] In addition to "my" point of view, this chapter explores that of some other critics, including Judith Mackrell's pleasure at the sight of Michael Clark's nude dancing body, and reviews an argument that Bill T. Jones has hypothesized between his own dancing body and white male heterosexual spectators. Poststructuralist approaches to cultural analysis assume that works are open to a multiplicity of readings from differing points of view. Points of view should not be attributed exclusively or monolithically to particular social groups or categories. A gay male point of view need not necessarily be an exclusive one, nor one that is necessarily adopted by all men who have sex with other men. Points of view need to be seen as part of complex and fluid processes of identification and cross-identification, which are themselves part of a coalitional micropolitics through which individuals and marginalized groups oppose normalizing discourses by valorizing "alternative" points of view.

In *The Male Dancer* I argued that structures exist that lead spectators (of whatever gender or sexual orientation) to accept as "natural" a male heterosexual point of view or way of looking at professional male dancers, but I also pointed out that these structures do not always work effectively and are open to subversion.[6] This chapter revisits my concerns in *The Male Dancer*, looking at an area that I now think I may have avoided: the queerness of the male dancing body. I have previously argued against the phallic hypermasculinity of Ted Shawn's and Martha Graham's choreography for male dancers, pointing out that the compulsion to conform to this phallic hypermasculinity is equally oppressive to both heterosexual and homosexual male dancers. While I still go along with my critique of this phallic hypermasculinity, I feel that by stressing commonalities between heterosexual and homosexual masculinity I did not pay sufficient attention to the politics underlying the relationship between sexuality and dance. What I am therefore going to focus on in this chapter are explicitly and unambiguously eroticized male dancing bodies. It therefore proceeds as follows. First, it places the discourse of the queer male dancing body in the context of the historical development of homosexual identities, particularly in relation to the role that cultural expression has played in affirming these identities. It then identifies problems that aesthetic theory has with sexuality in general and homosexuality in particular, pointing to particular areas that are relevant to the work of postmodern gay choreography. I then take these points up in a discussion of works by British and American choreographers that address gay themes or issues, or articulate a gay sensibility.

GENEALOGIES OF THE QUEER MALE DANCING BODY

The discourse of the queer male dancing body has developed during the twentieth century. I argued in *The Male Dancer* that, during the nineteenth century, distaste at professional male dance, which contributed to the virtual disappearance of the male ballet dancer in Western Europe, was not in any way associated with homosexuality. Available evidence suggests that the association between male dance and homosexuality arose only in the early twentieth century with Diaghilev. Michel Foucault controversially proposed that homosexuality as an identity was only created in 1870; before that time homosexuality was defined as a sexual act. Foucault comments:

> There is no question that the appearance in nineteenth-century psychiatry, jurisprudence, and literature of a whole series of discourses on the species and subspecies of homosexuality, inversion, pederasty, and "psychic hermaphroditism" made possible a strong advance of social controls into this area of "perversity"; but it also made possible the formation of a "reverse" discourse: homosexuality began to speak in its own behalf, to demand that its legitimacy or "naturality" be acknowledged, often in the same vocabulary, using the same categories by which it was medically disqualified.[7]

As Foucault is sometimes cited as the originator of the idea of the social construction of homosexuality, it is worth pointing out that he is not saying here that the desire for sexual partners of a particular sex is socially constructed. What he argues is constructed is the idea that homosexuality is an identity that exists deep inside the individual. This conception of homosexual identity as psychological interiority is, for Foucault, a consequence of creating discourses about homosexuality. Interiority is created by compelling homosexuals to think about themselves through the terms of these discourses. The possibility of articulating a "reverse" discourse is thus an unintended by-product of these attempts at social control. For Foucault, attempts to legitimate homosexuality are problematic where they are articulated through the same discourses that are used to disqualify it. Foucault is particularly suspicious of psychoanalysis, and in his work he generally sees the body as an object that is marked and inscribed from outside by normalizing forces that "invest" and penetrate it. Following Nietzsche, Foucault sees embodied subjectivity in terms of surface rather than depth (as does Barthes), and in this chapter I am investigating the performance of the queer male dancing body as a discursive play on and around surfaces and not as an expression of a deep psychological or existential interiority. The threat of punishment for transgression of heterosexual norms (which produces my sense of panic at being thought gay) comes from outside. I find it more productive to think about my pleasure at watching a queer dancing body as something that comes from outside and derives from my response to seductively moving body surfaces, rather than from psychological expression.

Diaghilev was surely aware of Foucault's "reverse" discourse of homosexuality and of the role of culture in articulating it. In the 1890s he met Aubrey Beardsley and went out of his way to take the then broken, impoverished, and ailing Oscar Wilde out to dinner in Dieppe. Later, by presenting Nijinsky in a series of ballets that showcased his talents, Diaghilev not only reintroduced the male dancer to the ballet stages of London, Paris, New York, and other leading Western cities but thereby established a sophisticated gay audience for ballet. By the time of his death in 1929 Diaghilev had made ballet into a forum that in effect created and supported the idea of the artistic homosexual man and defined a homosexual aesthetic sensibility.[8] Since that time ballet has attracted a large metropolitan gay audience, and many gay men have sought careers in the dance world. Richard Dyer suggests that "gay men have been balletomanes for everything from the fact of ballet's extreme escapism from an uncongenial world to its display of the male physique, and to its reputation as an area of employment in which gay men could be open and safe."[9] For most of the twentieth century, particularly in countries where homosexuality was a prosecutable offense, ballet's escapism was the principal means for the expression of gay identities through camp spectacle. Most pre-1960 ballets by choreographers who acknowledged they were gay are rarely explicitly homoerotic but can be seen as double coded—signifying homosexuality to those who know the code but apparently innocent to those who do not (or choose not to recognize it). With the liberalization of the laws concerning homosexuality since the 1970s and the advent of the gay liberation movement, increasing numbers of dance artists have used performance as a means through which to explore and make statements about the changing nature of gay identities. Since the 1960s, unequivocally, queer dance works have asserted sexual dissidence in ways that break with earlier humanistic approaches.

While recognizing that continuities exist between older uses of camp and the parodic and a postmodern use of irony and pastiche that asserts pride in difference, I am concerned in this chapter with the extent to which display of the masculine dancing body is queer; although I will refer to the parodic, I am not concerned here with male dancing bodies that might be considered effeminate. The main object of my theoretical investigation is the pleasures and terrors of watching male dancers who perform masculinity in a manly rather than an effeminate way.[10]

QUEER SUBJECTIVITIES

The "nature" of heterosexuality and homosexuality and the relationship between them is a subject of contestation. The widespread idea that homosexual men are men who only have sex with men (and are therefore entirely different from straight men) is neither true nor useful. In the United States during the 1940s the researcher Alfred Kinsey published findings that 37 percent of men had homosexual experiences to orgasm but less than 4 percent were exclusively homosexual. These statistics have of course been contested, perhaps because they have given support to the idea that only homophobia stops most men from realizing their "true" sexual inclinations.[11]

Some recent commentators, like Jeffrey Weeks, have argued that homosexual identity is something that an individual assumes and does not necessarily relate to sexual activity as such. Michael Warner goes further and asserts that queerness is characterized by a determined resistance to regimes of the normal.[12] Queer theorists have challenged even the idea of social construction. In the passage quoted earlier, Foucault seems to be arguing that it is strategically dangerous to try to legitimate homosexuality by using ways of thinking about it that have been formulated to disqualify it. To speak of homosexuality at all may be to concede that a sexual binary indeed exists that excludes homosexuals from (heterosexual) normality. Where dance is concerned, this is to ghettoize "gay" and "lesbian" dance as somehow different from heterosexual dance. Many choreographers rightly do not wish to have their work categorized in this way and considered to be dealing only with "gay" or "lesbian" concerns and thus in effect excluded from the sorts of broad-ranging critical scrutiny applied to "normal" choreography. It is significant that Michael Warner speaks of queerness rather than "gay" or "lesbian" identities and defines *queer* in an open and inclusive way. At the risk of stating the obvious to someone who has, after all, already chosen to read a book that engages dance theorists and queer theorists, the term *queer* has recently become current within academic discourses as an open term that embraces a wide range of practices and identities that are subversive and oppositional to conventional, normative heterosexual sexuality. For reasons of openness and inclusivity, I am calling the male dancing body that I am discussing *queer* rather than gay and contextualizing it within traditions and conventions of gay cultural formations that should themselves be conceptualized in wide-ranging and inclusive ways.

My aim in discussing figures that are part of a discourse of this queer male dancing body is to identify the ways in which these challenge and destabilize the conventional discourse of heterosexual dance. The latter closes down and limits the ways we can explore gender, sexuality, and other components of identity within dance, setting up rigid barriers between an unmarked, unexceptional normality and a marked Otherness, preserving the fiction of a rational unitary heterosexual subject.[13] By contrast, queer dancing opens up and makes space for new and sometimes subversive pleasures, breaking down or blurring the boundaries of straight discourse and proposing new subject positions. The British dance company DV8's video dance *Never Again* provides a compelling image of this queerness. A straight-identified character (played by Nigel Charnock) falls helplessly and painfully down the half-lit stairs that lead to an underground nineteenth-century men's public lavatory; when he picks himself up, he finds it full of sexually active, queer-identified men and women who doubtless find the idea that this public convenience is for "men only" a meaningless convention. I am therefore not seeking to exclusively define, categorize, and compartmentalize gay dance but to identify the strategies through which some radical dance artists have created new configurations that constitute sites of resistance against the dead weight of conformity to normative heterosexuality. These strategies have the potential to explore a radically revised imagination of the body's capacity for pleasure.

DANCE THEORY INSIDE OUT

In describing my pleasure when watching seductive dancing bodies as something that comes from outside, I am intentionally reversing Doris Humphrey's proposal that modern dance moves from the inside out. This, along with Martha Graham's belief that the body never lies, are in line with a way of conceptualizing the experience of embodiment that is in line with normative heterosexual desire. As Elizabeth Grosz points out, from Plato to Freud and Lacan, desire is predicated upon lack and on a "yearning for what is lost, absent, or impossible" that is projected outside the subject's body onto the body of another whose difference makes him or her Other.[14] Homosexual desire, however, is desire for the same rather than desire for difference. Some queer theorists argue that desire is based not on lack or loss but on recognition and acknowledgment of sameness.[15] Grosz observes that a notion of desire that comes from Spinoza sees desire not as lack but as a form of production, including self-production, a process of making or becoming. This productivist notion of desire can be viewed " 'behaviourally' in terms of its manifest connections and allegiances, its artifice, its bodily impetus."[16] To work with this notion of desire is therefore to reject a notion of identity as something deep inside, which early modern dancers such as Humphrey and Graham believed they could express in their dancing. During the 1930s the American critic John Martin formulated the most developed exposition of the idea that modern dance works from the inside out. We can nevertheless reformulate his ideas and read them against the grain to theorize spectators' pleasure as a reading of surface inscriptions on the body rather than perception of depth.

Martin proposed that when the spectator watches any movement, "instantaneously, through a sympathetic muscular memory you associate the movement with its purpose." He goes on: "Through kinesthetic sympathy you respond to the impulse of the dancer which has expressed itself by means of a series of movements. Movement, then, is the link between the dancer's intention and your perception of it."[17] Believing that, from the dancer's point of view, dance proceeds from the inside out, Martin proposes that this is also the case for spectators, who find within their own bodies their responses to watching movement. He defines this process as "a psychic accompaniment called metakinesis, this correlation growing from the theory that the physical and the psychical are merely two aspects of a single underlying reality."[18] Martin thus has an idealist notion of spectatorship where body speaks to body, conveying "truth" and "reality" in an unmediated way. This notion still has currency: some writers imply that gay artists convey the truth about sexuality by putting on stage the reality of gay experience.[19]

Martin's notions of muscular sympathy and metakinesis describe only a small part of the experience of watching dance and do this somewhat inadequately. If one is speaking of "truths," it is necessary to think of the act of choreographing as the creation of an authentic original.[20] If for one moment we accept that "truths" are indeed disclosed while a dance is being choreographed, they then have to cross many hurdles. The work has to be staged: light and costume design, spacing on the theater stage, rehearsal of steps if the work is an old one—all these can change the original choreography. Then the performance itself may also introduce changes: brilliant dancers may bring out previously unnoticed nuances, while poor ones may not do the choreography justice. Last, spectators could misinterpret what they see. But even if, miraculously, all these hurdles are crossed successfully, taken literally, the idea that a spectator experiences muscular sympathy with the dancer makes little sense. Martin surely does not mean that the spectator watching a vigorous solo ends up fatigued in sympathy with the exhausted dancer. Susanne Langer was surely thinking of Martin when she pointed out that Pavlova does not actually have to feel faint and sick while performing *The Dying Swan* (1907), nor does Mary Wigman require to be told a terrible piece of news a few minutes before performing her tragic *Evening Dances* (1924).[21] Along the same lines Maxine Sheets-Johnstone has argued that in the case of the expression through dance of feelings such as love, neither dancers nor audience members experience actual feeling during the performance.[22]

I take it that Sheets-Johnstone is not saying that audience members cannot be moved by performances but that, although feelings are embodied, the emotional atmosphere that dance performances can sometimes evoke is not the result of a transfer of actual feelings from the dancing body to the spectating body. Emotions are nevertheless embodied, and spectators can undoubtedly have a visceral response to some dance performances. Whereas a traditional model of aesthetic appreciation presupposes a disinterested subject position from which to make aesthetic judgments, visceral responses cause spectators to become involved in the performance and therefore to lose their disinterestedness. Those dances that provoke a visceral response therefore threaten the adoption of this detached critical position. My pleasure when watching seductively moving surfaces of queer male dancing bodies, and another spectator's sense of dis-ease or even homophobic panic at queer dancing bodies, imply a problematic blurring of the distinction between subject and object. Such queer dance, through blurring the distinction between subject and object, signals the fragmentation of the rational unitary subject of the Enlightenment. Martin's notion of muscular sympathy and metakinesis, when purged of the notion of psychological or existential depth, is a useful starting point for conceptualizing the dancer–audience relationship in performances that blur the distinction between subject and object, a condition that, I shall argue shortly, occurs in some queer postmodern dance work.

The visceral response that a spectator may feel while watching dance need not necessarily be an actual instantaneous muscular reaction, as Martin seems to suggest, but can inspire a sense of recognition that draws on the spectator's muscular memory and experience. This imaginative sympathy comes from a recognition of commonality—of what I as an embodied spectator have in common with the dancing body—and it not only draws on my experience but adds to it. To repeat what Barthes said of the experience of reverberation: "What echoes in me is what I learn from my body."[23] An extreme example of visceral response to dancing occurs within a sex show that causes the spectator to become aroused. "Porn is what gives me an erection," W. H. Auden is reputed to have said. "Serious" dance may not illicit quite such a palpable response, and I suspect that no one will admit to ever having stored the memory of a particular way in which a dancer moves and a particular way of looking at the audience while doing so, and later elaborating it within private fantasies.[24] There is, however, the celebrated but surely obscene case of the Russian balletomanes who held a banquet at which the principal course was a dish that included one of Marie Taglioni's used ballet shoes.[25]

To see all dance performance as mere sexual titillation would be reductive, but it is equally mistaken to deny the possibility of any erotic involvement by the spectator watching dance, however much this may go against a Kantian model of aesthetic appreciation. Through our visceral response to performance, dance teaches us about the body, defining and in some cases contesting its socially constructed limits. As Richard Dyer observes, experiential knowledge of the body is generally taken as a given, just experience, rather than socially constructed experiential knowledge.[26] Because the body is gendered, dancing continually redefines and contests the individual's knowledge of the limits of gendered behavior and of sexuality. Discourses enable the transmission of certain kinds of knowledge and information while restricting the communication of other kinds. The discourses of theater dance both enable and restrict the transmission of knowledge and information about sex and bodies. As Elizabeth Grosz observes, "There is an instability at the very heart of sex and bodies, the fact that the body is what it is capable of doing, and what any body is capable of doing is well beyond the tolerance of any given culture."[27] The dancer does not express truths that pass in an unmediated way between body and body but is compelled to repeat figures of a normalizing discourse. As Judith Butler points out, this repetition may not be faithful and the spectator may mis-recognize its import. An uncontrolled supplement always "exceed[s] and confound[s] what appears to be the disciplining intentions" of processes of normalization.[28] The surveillance implicit in spectatorship is one of these processes. Dance performance derives from the European ballet tradition a largely visual way of addressing the audience. As a spectator at a dance performance I *watch* dance—in French a dance performance is called *un spectacle*. While dance performance may induce a bodily response, any such response is mediated through the spectators' eyes and thereby becomes subject to the protocols of the gaze.

The ways in which the male dancer's presence succeeds or fails to reverberate in the spectator's body is clearly central to an understanding of the discourse of the queer male dancing body. Visual cues determine how spectators read dancers' presence. The eyes perceive and mediate what the spectator learns about masculinity and sexuality from watching men dancing and what reverberates in her or his body. Much work on representations of gender and sexuality in cultural forms has made use of the idea, developed initially by Laura Mulvey, of the gendered gaze in film.[29] To summarize this extremely briefly, in response to the spectator's gaze (and the presumption is that it enforces a dominant heterosexual male point of view) men in film look actively and thus avert objectification, while passivity allows women to be turned into an eroticized spectacle. Dance scholars, including me, have used this to develop an account of the ways in which spectators objectify the eroticized body that is the object of their gaze, particularly in relation to the power inherent in the normative male heterosexual point of view.[30] Dancers give some of these cues through the way they present themselves to the audience and in the way they focus their gaze in response to the audience. The interactive visceral aspect of dance performance is a key difference between film or photography and live performance. The fact that dancers are alive in front of us means that we are aware of their presence. As Ann Daly has observed, "Presence is the silent yet screeching excitement of physical vibrancy, of 'being there.' It is one of the thrills of watching dance, to see someone radiate pure energy, whether it is in stillness or in flight."[31] Whereas dancers in a film or photograph may seem to acknowledge the spectator in the way they look into the camera's lens and thus out at the spectator, they are not really there. Live, the possibility of feedback or interaction between performer and spectator exists, and this interaction, I shall argue, can be a figure in the discourse of the queer male dancing body.

To sum up, then, following Grosz, if my pleasure watching the queer male dancing body comes from my desire for the dancing body of the performer, this desire does not come from a psychological or phenomenological interior but develops through a form of interactive production. It is based not on lack or loss but on recognition and acknowledgment of sameness, which manifests itself through making connections on the level of knowledge of the common experience of embodiment. This experiential knowledge needs to be seen as neither neutral nor "natural" but as socially constructed and historically situated. It is something that I learn from the totality of my experience, including appreciation of cultural forms such as dance. The queer male dancing body does not therefore convey truths from deep within the individual dancer to the depth of the spectator about the reality of gay experience. It uses what Daly describes as the screeching excitement of physical vibrancy at the live spectacle of the queer male dancing body to open up, make spaces within, and break down or blur the boundaries of the straight discourse of normative heterosexual sexuality. Attacking the notion of a rational unitary heterosexual subject, it invents new fragmentary and dissolving subject positions from which to experience a radically revised imagination of the body's capacity for pleasure. Having outlined this theoretical structure for conceptualizing spectatorship of queer dancing bodies, I shall now discuss some dance examples that demonstrate how we can use notions of surface and inscription to analyze the staging of queer male dancing bodies in recent choreography.

ELABORATED SURFACES

Mark Morris's *Jealousy* (1985) can be approached as an ironic example of Maxine Sheets-Johnstone's proposition that no actual feelings are experienced by either dancers or audience. The piece is an exercise in manipulating surface signs of feelings about jealousy and about music. Joan Acocella calls it a virtuoso solo, a judgment with which I concur, but the piece is not virtuosic in the usual straightforward sense of performing a spectacularly virtuoso feat of technically difficult bravura steps. The choreography comprises a broad dynamic range of movement material whose difficulties lie in the field of interpretation, particularly in the way the piece articulates and jumps between different layers of meaning.

Many critics have hailed Morris's musicality—his sophisticated understanding of musical structure and his ability to choreograph movement and perform it both with sensitivity toward musical phrasing and in such a way as to reveal subtle nuances within it or to complement it. *Jealousy* is set to a chorus of the same name from *Hercules* (1745), a lesser-known oratorio by Handel. Morris has closely followed Handel's musical structure with his choreography. The music consists of three sections. An opening section in largo tempo sets the words "Jealousy, jealousy, infernal pest, / Tyrant of the human breast! / How from slightest causes bred / Dost thou lift thy hated head!" This slow, rather grand section is followed by a much lighter one in andante tempo; the words "Trifles light as floating air, / Strongest proofs to thee appear" are set in a fugal counterpoint of different voices, each part seeming to gently float around the other like the trifles to which the text refers. This section resolves itself as the voices come together again for a final "Strongest proofs to thee appear" before returning to the opening largo theme and a repeat of the lines "Jealousy, jealousy, infernal pest, / Tyrant of the human breast!"

In *Jealousy* Morris's dancing is associated with the singing parts rather than with the orchestral accompaniment. At times he is a soloist who dominates the singers. For example, at the beginning is a slow orchestral introduction during which Morris, who starts off lying prostrate on the ground, gradually rises up to an extended standing position. But with the last chord of the introduction he turns, spinning 'round twice, and takes up a dramatic stance, reaching this just in time for the first sung word, *jealousy*. Here Morris has taken the lead, but next, as Joan Acocella has pointed out, he represents all four vocal parts as they come in, one after the other: "When Handel's sopranos sing 'Tyrant of the human breast!' in a rising line, on four lurching beats, Morris's leg rises upwards on four lurching beats. Then as the altos repeat the line, his left arm rises in four beats, and when, following that, the tenors take up the line, his right arm rises in the same four beats."[32] Acocella concludes that "the choreography is a physical act of musical understanding" and if here he embodies all four parts, at other moments Morris seems to create for himself a fifth part that harmonizes with the other four, as when he winds and floats along with the musical setting of "Trifles light as floating air."[33]

If Morris might be accused of sometimes mimicking the music in an idiosyncratic and sometimes literal way, this might not be inappropriate to baroque choral music such as Handel's, which sometimes finds similarly idiosyncratic and literal musical interpretations of the meanings of the words it sets: the gently winding fugal setting of "Trifles light as floating air" is an obvious example of this. If Morris often plays with a literal visualization of musical phrases, he can also switch to a literal interpretation of the words. So when jealousy lifts his ugly head, Morris places his crossed arms high on his shoulders and does a neck roll so that his head seems to be raising itself in an almost disembodied way. With the opening words of the piece Morris seems to be the individual who is beset with jealousy, and he touches his bare breast to signify the human breast that is thus oppressed; but the next moment one suspects he may have shifted to become the infernal pest and no longer the person persecuted by it, as he scrunches up his shoulders and shifts his weight heavily from one foot to another, plodding forward like a hideous being in a low-budget horror movie.

Throughout the solo, then, which lasts just under six minutes, Morris assumes a number of different positions in relation to the musical and verbal texts, sometimes working inside or between them, sometimes embodying all the parts at once, and sometimes positioning himself outside them as if they are affecting his vulnerable naked breast. He deftly shifts from one role or position to another with a sophisticated wit and irony. We can only speculate whether Morris's motivation to make this piece was an incident in which he actually experienced jealousy. This is not a Graham-esque dance that speaks the truth about the depths of human feelings but a dazzling articulation of surface signs that continually resist and evade the closure of a definitive interpretation, which might conclude that Morris's *Jealousy* is about something specific. By leaving the spectator unsure whether, or in what ways, Morris might be being serious in this piece, *Jealousy* leaves itself open to interpretation as a queer piece.

Other pieces by Morris are more obviously about queer sexuality than *Jealousy*, such as *jr high* (1982) or *Deck of Cards* (1983). One level on which *Jealousy* is open to a queer reading is through the subject itself. The context of the chorus in Handel's oratorio is that Dejanira, the wife of Hercules, believes her husband has become infatuated with Iöle, a beautiful young princess he captured in a recent war. Dejanira's jealousy is the occasion for the chorus. That Morris is dancing about sexual jealousy, inspired by losing the love of the strongest and most manly hero of ancient Greek mythology, suggests a queer angle on this solo. Jealousy also represents an emotional outburst of a kind more usually associated with women than with men. Jealousy can also be read as queer in the way Morris exposes his naked back and torso. The choreography signifies emotional tensions through contractions in the dancer's chest and arm movements that flex his shoulder blades and the muscles of his upper back. Because Morris's upper body is naked, it reveals the workings of these muscles and thus signifies not only emotional experience but vulnerability to such experience. He sometimes draws attention to his nakedness by almost incidentally touching and caressing his skin as his hands pass across it on the way to take up expressive or sculptural gestures.

Jealousy leaves itself open to interpretation as a queer piece because its multilayered construction often verges on the parodic and therefore the gay tradition of camp cultural expression. Because Morris does not claim to express deep psychological truths about sexual jealousy but articulates instead a complex and unfixable manipulation of surface signs, *Jealousy* aligns itself with a queer sensibility that has origins in a need to present an evasive mask in order to survive in the straight world. Morris thus appeals to a recognition of socially oppressive codes and structures. This shared recognition is of the same kind as the bodily experience that Barthes describes as echoing in him because it is what he learns from his body. Through an emphasis on surface rather than depth, *Jealousy* appeals to those who recognize the ways in which socially oppressive codes and structures are imposed from the outside, inscribing themselves on the body.

EROTICIZED SURFACES

Michael Clark has often drawn attention to eroticized body surfaces in his performances. He has danced "nude except for two giant fur muffs, and I defy anyone not to be moved by seeing that beautiful body, that play of muscles and effortless line close-up."[34] Here Judith Mackrell is describing part of Michael Clark and Stephen Petronio's 1989 performance of *Hetrospective* at the Anthony D'Offay Gallery in London. In a video dance commissioned for London Weekend Television's *South Bank Show* later the same year, both Clark and Petronio dance with fur muffs. Each muff is a long tube of fur material into which the dancer inserts both his arms up to the elbows and that he holds to hide his genitals. The muffs appeared again for a solo by Clark to a Lou Reed song, "Venus in Furs," as part of Clark's *Mmm* (1992). Choreographers occasionally take a prop or device that places a limitation on their freedom of movement and use it as a spur to find new aesthetic possibilities within these limitations—for example, the stretched tube of woolen material in Graham's *Lamentation* (1930) or the cast-iron bath in Susanne Linke's *Im Bade Wanen* (1983). Clark's use of the fur muff is another such exercise. It restricts movement not only because the dancer must conceal his genitals but also because he cannot raise his arms to keep his balance.

When Clark and Petronio dance together in the video, the intention is clearly to make them identical, suggesting that gay desire is desire for the same. Both are naked but for the muffs, both have shaved heads, and in the section immediately following this duet each raises over his head a semitransparent yellow vest imprinted with a photograph of the other's face and covers his own

Michael Clark and Stephen Petronio in a publicity still for *Hetrospective* at the Anthony D'Offay Gallery, London, October 1989 (Photograph by Chris Nash; used with permission)

face with it. This suggests "we are becoming each other." Such emphasis on similarity inevitably accentuates differences. Clark and Petronio have different builds and facial features, in part because the former is a Scot from Aberdeen whereas the latter is an Italian American from New Jersey. When they dance with the restriction of the fur muffs, the differences in their dance backgrounds also become only too evident. Clark began going to ballet classes at an early age and studied it intensively as a teenager at the Royal Ballet School. Petronio says he had no movement training until he was eighteen and discovered contact improvisation at college and was lucky enough to work with Steve Paxton.

The fur muff effectively divides the dancer's body in two, making the pelvis the focal point of any movement; whether the dancer is folding over and sinking back in his pelvis or extending his leg, the spectator's attention is always directed back to the pelvis to see what effect the movement has and whether the penis will inadvertently slip into view. When Clark dances, his movements are initiated in the feet: he points his leg and phrases his movements with beats of his foot. Petronio initiates movement with an impulse in one part of the body—a leg, a shoulder, or the pelvis—and follows it through to other body parts, the momentum of each impulse establishing the duration and phrasing of movements. Through working with Paxton and then with Trisha Brown, Petronio has developed a luscious movement style that is grounded in knowledge of the internal motivation of movement. In retrospect, dancing with Clark may have helped him develop the more architectural approach that characterized his choreography during the 1990s. Similarly, Clark values the lusciousness of internally motivated movement. Critics praise his dancing, not just for his gift for making beautiful shapes with his limbs but for his ability to keep that sense of beauty through the transitions between the shapes so that the transitions become as important as the shapes they disclose.

Clark's ballet training has marked his dancing irrevocably. It has given him a particular knowledge of the body, and, no matter how he may try to get away from this, his classical sense of line (which ultimately distinguishes his dancing from that of Petro-

nio) always asserts itself. Ballet is a discourse of power that subjects the dancing body and inscribes meanings on it. The ballet
vocabulary is not a set of neutral physical postures and movements but a language with a history and traditions. From the
courts of the kings of France it inherits aristocratic and regal conventions of polite bodily presentation, and from the romantic
period it derives its indelible association with heterosexual
courtship. Traditional ballet's inescapable heterosexuality is the
joke behind the Trocadero ballet companies' various camp sub-
versions. Clark's whole career since his highly mythologized act
of dropping out of the Royal Ballet School has been a series of
attempts to escape the fact that his much valued classical sense
of line is that of a prince—and a heterosexual one at that: thus,
throughout the 1980s the dildos, the Nazi salutes, and all the ingenious obscenities that the late Leigh Bowery devised for him.
The fur muff is perhaps the most ingenious of these in the way it
eroticizes the male body in an unmistakably queer manner.

Whether Clark's fur muff was made of real or artificial fur, it
carries with it the association of animality. In popular speech, to
screw like animals is to engage in sex acts for purely physical reasons devoid of emotional attachment or social nicety. Real animal
fur, when warmed by the human body, gives off a musky, sexy
aroma redolent and suggestive of pubic hair, which in this case
the muff both conceals and touches. Clark and Petronio are not
only feeling the luxuriant touch of fur on their penises and testi-
cles but are probably also cupping them in their hands (like Adam
in a Renaissance painting) so as to keep them out of sight as they
move. The fur touches not only their genitals but the sides of
their trunk from their lower ribs to their buttocks and pelvises,
which are visually framed by their fur-clad lower arms. By connecting this expanse of naked skin to the genitals, the muff extends the body's erotogenic surface, suggesting new areas of sensitivity and new points of pleasure. The muff increases the sexual
zone and multiplies the possibilities of physical sensation, drawing attention toward the naked buttocks and anus—forbidden
sites of queer sexual practices.

The fur acts here like tattooing, body piercing, and scarification, all of which were taken up during the 1990s as a way of protesting against and resisting social conformity. Elizabeth Grosz, following Alphonso Lingis, has argued that these forms of self-production constitute an assertion that social and sexual identities are constituted not as psychological depth but literally as surface inscriptions in the form of emblematic markings that are only skin deep.[35] Body building, dieting, and aerobics are all practices that encourage individuals to produce particular types of socially approved bodies—bodies inscribed with sociopolitical meanings. Ballet, Graham technique, and contact improvisation are also practices that produce particular types of socially approved dancing bodies that are similarly inscribed with sociopolitical meanings. When Judith Mackrell defies anyone not to be moved "by seeing that beautiful body, that play of muscles," she is acknowledging the effectiveness of Clark's classical training and attesting to the aesthetic pleasures produced by his exquisite repetition of elements of a highly valued movement vocabulary. But Clark's repetition is nevertheless excessive. It is not just that, by dancing with a fur muff, he transgresses the already destabilized norms of classical ballet but that the seductive assertion of his material sexual dancing body disrupts a conventional appreciation of his balletic line as the articulation of disembodied aesthetic ideals. Through doing so Clark signifies a radically revised notion of the body's potential for pleasure that is almost unmistakably queer.

INSCRIPTIONS

Discussing his response to the gaze of what, during the 1980s, he perceived to be the predominately white audiences for his work, Bill T. Jones observed:

> There is something about the spectators saying, in effect "Perform for us. Show us your body." So it made me extremely aggressive, and maybe that was my desire to impose masculine control—I also assume it was racial. . . . It was a cruel and ironic way that I saw myself. You know: you're a black man—take off your shirt. You're allowed to wiggle your hips in public. You know what they're all thinking, "Oh, I bet you have a dick down to your knees."[36]

Jones brilliantly brings together here in this response, as he frequently also does in his choreography and performance, issues of gender, race, and sexuality. Jones invents this conversation to describe his interaction with the audience. What he uncovers is part of the larger processes of social control through which normative white heterosexual values are imposed on the black male body, closing down possibilities of imagining black gay identities. These processes work through making Jones aware of disapproval of the way he dances and put pressure on him to stop his dancing in a way that is dangerous to normative values. It is clear, however, that in talking confrontationally about this, both here in this interview and elsewhere, Jones's aim has been to confront and resist these pressures. The statement "you're allowed to wiggle your hips in public" can therefore be unpacked in a number of ways to reveal the manner in which meanings are inscribed on the black male dancing body.

Wiggle

Jones reveals the way the black male dancing body is inscribed as racially Other. The cruel way Jones sees himself is as a black dancer who is allowed to dance with a fluid pelvis while other parts of his body move to other rhythms, thus making the hips "wiggle." Brenda Dixon-Gottschild identifies polyrythms as one characteristic of what she calls an Africanist sensibility.[37] They are an element of an African American music and dance tradition that is a retention of the memory of Africa from before the Diaspora. That the white spectator allows black dancers to dance like this reveals the extent to which they are being directed to think of their identity as African Americans through terms dictated by white fear and fascination with difference. Even the penis, which might signify an important common bond between black and white men within patriarchy, is marked as grotesquely oversized, down to the knees and therefore different from an unmarked, unexceptional white normality.

In Public

If the black dancer is allowed to do in public something that by implication "we" only do in private, this is undoubtedly something sexual. As Foucault has argued, the processes of Christian confessional, and then the inspections of modern medicine and psychiatry, have persuaded individual subjects to think about sex and create for themselves a hidden interior space for their sexual identity.[38] Sex has become, Foucault argues, the privileged domain for defining identity. When European explorers and missionaries first came across social dances in West Africa, they judged the way dancers moved their hips to be immodest and depraved because that is the association of pelvic movements within European culture. In the European ballet and folk dance tradition the pelvis and torso move together as one unit. Pelvic movement may in some cases signify sexual meanings in some West African dances, but where participants and onlookers do not consider sexuality, as Westerners do, as something to be hidden, sexuality is nevertheless of central importance to a deeply inscribed sense of self. Where a Western viewer might judge that such social dancing expresses an openness about sexuality, this could be seen as a sign of "primitive" innocence, of being more "natural" than a supposedly superior, advanced, civilized Western counterpart. Therefore, for black subjects to become more advanced and civilized (which white colonial discourse persuades them to want to become), they have to create this Western sense of sexual identity as interiority and thus acknowledge the "obscenity" of such "primitive" dancing.

Hips

The ambivalent white fear of and fascination with the black body leads to another level on which the latter is inscribed as sexually deviant and therefore not properly masculine. The fact that "you" are allowed to wiggle "your" hips in public reveals that "we" are not allowed to do so. Why not? Because "we" are male and "our" gaze challenges "you" to prove that you are too: only girls and gay men wiggle their hips in public. The white male gaze thus threatens to feminize and eroticize the black male dancer, and Jones says he responds by falling back on signs that signify heterosexuality—imposing masculine control and being extremely aggressive.

Cruel

The result is that Jones sees himself in a cruel and ironic way, because he is being forced to look at himself as a black subject from a white point of view. Furthermore he is being directed to think of his identity as a man through normative heterosexual discourses that make him adopt a hard, phallic, hypermasculine style of dancing. The whole cruel process is one in which what is inscribed is an interior recognition that sexuality is private, blackness is inferior, and homosexuality is deviant. The need to be valued as not inferior and not deviant dictates that Jones should be cruel to his dancing body, repressing any possibility of experiencing pleasure, by moving in a hard (and as I argued in *The Male Dancer*) defensive way.

Dick

Jones, as a man who has acknowledged that he is gay, is suggesting that the last thing "we" are supposed to want him to do is to take off his shirt and wiggle his hips and his dick, which in "our" fantasy comes down to his knees. The social mechanisms that inscribe a phallic hypermasculinity on the male dancing body ensure that "we" male spectators are protected from such pleasures. As I have already pointed out, the physical expression of masculinity in dance in the twentieth century has become associated with homosexuality. If the male dancing body is always already queer, this transgression against normative definitions of gendered and sexual behavior carries with it the penalty of punishment. By accepting the inscription of a phallic hypermasculinity on their dancing bodies, black and white male dancers alike defend themselves against the threat of punishment.

By revealing the audience's hidden fears and desires in this way, Jones is pointing out that their relation to the spectacle of his black queer male dancing body is not the detached disinterested disposition that Kant states is the prerequisite for aesthetic judgment. Jones is saying that audiences become involved in an erotic way while watching the spectacle of his dancing body and that underlying this gaze are power relations that enforce normative ideologies of gender and sexuality. By revealing the complex and contradictory nature of the white male gaze and his own responses to it, Jones is seeking to unsettle and disturb the positioning of the audience and individual spectators. He is turning the tables and confronting the audience with the question of whether they really understand what they want out of his performance. Jones is also acknowledging that these are terms that he too must confront and disrupt in order to make some ideological space within discourse for his own complex and contradictory relationship to issues of African American and gay identities, which are the starting point for formulating a black gay identity.

Within his choreography and performance Jones often makes use of framing devices that focus on the erotic and power relations at work in his dance. For example, on a micro level, he often recontextualizes movement material through choreographing steps and movement to the rhythmic patterns of words that often speak of power or sexuality, such as his dialogue with Arnie Zane in *Rotary Action* (1981). On a broader level, in works like *The Last Supper* (1990) and *Still/Here* (1994), the highly charged subject matter of slavery or terminal illnesses such as HIV infection forms a frame that challenges audience members to be aware of the position they already hold in relation to race or sexuality and perhaps reconsider them. Such repositioning involves spectators in what is presented on stage in ways that disrupt the subject position that Kant argued was necessary for making aesthetic judgments. This blurring of the distinction between subject and object does not occur only in Jones's dances but in other queer postmodern dance work as well.

The opening of DV8 Physical Theatre's *Dead Dreams of Monochrome Men* (1988) is a scene informed by an understanding of the power of the gaze similar to that discussed by Jones. It does this by making the audience aware of its own voyeurism through trapping its gaze within a complex structure of desiring and voyeuristic gazes enacted on stage. The setting is a gay disco in which four dancers—Lloyd Newson, Nigel Charnock, Douglas Wright, and Russell Maliphant—lean against a wall and cruise each other with their eyes. Each seems to be seeking a glance that signifies an acceptance and a recognition of similar or compatible desires. It is a vivid demonstration of the power of the male gaze. When Newson attempts to engage Maliphant in erotic play, trapping him against the wall, embracing him and rubbing himself against him, the latter slips away. But it is as if Newson does not notice, because he continues to push himself against a silhouette of a body painted on the wall where Maliphant had been standing, and the rhythm with which he thrusts into this is the rhythm of male genital excitation. On the rebound Maliphant takes up with Wright, who initiates a series of sadomasochistic actions with him. Wright blindfolds him with his t-shirt. Maliphant's wrists are bound and he is undressed and teasingly caressed and then slapped; then he is made to lean against the wall in a vulnerable position and submit to slaps and to being pulled off balance by tugs on the elastic waistband of his underpants. Throughout this scene Maliphant and Wright remain impassive, giving no indication of either enjoyment or distress. Is Maliphant allowing Wright to enjoy being on "top," or is Wright dominating him because Maliphant gets off on being submissive?

While this is going on, Charnock watches from one side. His reactions become so extreme that he gets down on all fours on the floor, like an animal, with his face contorted as if in a silent scream. As his is the only sign of emotion, one possibility is that Wright and Maliphant are merely acting out a scene to cater to Charnock's voyeuristic tastes. However, all three are staging this scene for the spectators' benefit. As the spectators take in Charnock's voyeurism, it unsettles and disturbs their positioning. Charnock's presence challenges and disrupts the possibility of spectators' taking up Kant's disinterested subject position. The interplay of gazes turns the tables and confronts the audience with the question of whether spectators really understand what they want out of this performance. Both Jones and DV8, by blurring the conventional distance between spectator and performance, subject and object, make the male spectator aware of potential pleasures that are outside the norms of white heterosexual masculine sexuality but that the queer male dancing body can do to him or for him.

CONCLUSION

Clark, Jones, Morris, Newson, and Petronio are artistic radicals and gay men who are open about their homosexuality. No causal or necessary connection between artistic and sexual radicalism exists. Some postmodern artists are gay but many more are heterosexual. There are also conservative gay men, lovers of traditional classical ballet or mainstream modern dance, who have no desire to take part in any discussion of the historical or contemporary relationship between theater dance and homosexuality. The publication of this book should do much to open up discussion of this relationship. Where gay radicalism and the radicalism of postmodern choreography, which stages the queer male dancing body, coincide is in their challenge to the notion that aesthetic judgments are made from a disinterested subject position. In this essay I have concentrated on issues concerning the embodiment of subjectivity. One main conclusion that we can draw from these discussions is the extent to which the discourse of queer dance reveals the inadequacy of the notion of the rational unitary subject of the Enlightenment to explain the process of appreciating the spectacle of the queer male dancing body.

At the end of his life Michel Foucault said in answer to an interviewer's question, "I do indeed believe that there is no sovereign founding subject, a universal form of subject to be found everywhere. . . . I believe, on the contrary, that the subject is constituted through practices of subjection, or, in a more autonomous way, through practices of liberation, of liberty, as in Antiquity, on the basis, of course, of a number of rules, styles, interventions to be found in the cultural environment."[39] He identifies here two alternatives: subjection and liberation. Submission to the discourses through which power is applied to the body and inscribes meanings on it results from a lack of understanding about these processes of subjection. More work on what I have called the discourse of the queer male dancing body will aid dancers to liberate themselves and enjoy some autonomy in the way they learn to dance, and it will give them more freedom in the way they choose to position themselves in relation to discourses of social normalization. Instead of being subjected by traditions and conventions of dance techniques and choreography, and methods of staging and performing dance—all of which are penetrated by normative, white, heterosexual ideologies—dancers will then be able to contribute to a social transformation whose difficulties reflect how profoundly it is rooted in the realities of embodiment.

The pieces I have discussed offer me both pleasures and terrors. Pleasures may be derived from looking at eroticized surfaces and at the subtle play of surfaces that cleverly resist the process of subjection. Pleasures may be found in recognition of sameness and in the reverberation within me of what I learn from my body. Terrors lie in the homophobic panic of realizing what these male dancing bodies can do to me and for me, and terrors also lie in having the tables turned on me and being challenged to confront my enjoyment of the voyeurism inherent in my position as a spectator. I also experience the terror of annihilation, of relinquishing the fiction of a neutral unitary subject position and acknowledging my visceral involvement in watching dance that makes me dissolve in pleasure.

NOTES

The theoretical approach that informs this study has developed out of discussions with Christy Adair, Valerie Briginshaw, and Emilyn Claid. I am also grateful to them for their valuable comments on earlier drafts of this chapter.

1. I recognize that *homophobia* is a problematic term, not least if it is used to suggest that the experience of social pressures to conform to heterosexual normality is the same for both men and women. However, I am not developing an argument that depends upon a definition of homophobia. I am merely using it as a convenient label to describe the social pressures to exhibit behavior that conforms with heterosexual normality.

2. Roland Barthes, *A Lover's Discourse: Fragments* (Harmondsworth, U.K.: Penguin, 1990), 1.

3. Ibid., 4.

4. Ibid., 200.

5. Ramsay Burt, "The Dance That Does Not Speak Its Name," *MTD*, no. 4 (1991): 6–11. Oscar Wilde again. In the British context at least, some people in the dance world still do not want the issue of dance and homosexuality discussed at all. Alistair Macaulay, for example, in his essay "Gender, Sexuality, Commu-

nity" argues that Frederick Ashton's homosexuality has little relevance to an understanding of his choreography. This was not publicly acknowledged during his lifetime, but Macaulay argues that now that Julie Kavanagh's 1996 biography of Ashton has discussed his sexuality in detail, the knowledge may actually get in the way of an appreciation of the magic of his choreography. See Alistair Macaulay, "Gender, Sexuality, Community," in Stephanie Jordan and Andrée Grau, eds., *Following Sir Fred's Steps: Ashton's Legacy* (London: Dance Books, 1996), 115–26; Julie Kavanagh, *Secret Muses: The Life of Frederick Ashton* (New York: Pantheon, 1996). I gather that some gay men have found my work on dance, masculinity, and sexuality useful. Others have inferred that it did not say anything they did not know already, whereas a few people have suggested that only gay people can speak about gay experience.

Freud, Havelock Ellis, and other heterosexual-identified sexologists at the turn of the century claimed to explain homosexuality to homosexuals, and I certainly do not aspire to follow them. But if I acknowledge that I may at some time in the past have touched other men's penises and remember what it is like to be touched by another man, I am not trying to make a special case for myself. I am not claiming some knowledge of homosexuality with which to justify my writing about this subject while hiding safely behind the facade of being a "family man." I have no real contact with any gay communities. If I go out in the evenings to see dance performances, I enjoy watching male dancers, but if people are sometimes surprised when I mention my children, I realize that they had thought that, as a man in the dance world, I might be gay. In some situations when this happens nowadays, I am quite pleased to "pass," but when I was younger I found the experience of being thought gay a painfully embarrassing one and a source of panic. What I examine in this chapter is my pleasure in watching male dancers who I know are gay in choreography that is coded as queer, together with my knowledge of the emotional turmoil of homophobic panic. I see these as figures within a larger discourse of the queer male dancing body, and it is as such that I am discussing them.

6. Ramsay Burt, *The Male Dancer: Bodies, Spectacle, Sexualities* (London: Routledge, 1995).

7. Michel Foucault, *An Introduction*, vol. 1 of *History of Sexuality*, (Harmondsworth, U.K.: Penguin, 1981), 101.

8. For further information about Diaghilev, Beardsley, and Wilde, see Richard Buckle, *Diaghilev* (London: Weidenfeld and Nicolson, 1979), 37–38. Emanuel Cooper states that Diaghilev created a sophisticated gay audience for ballet, but the only acknowledgment of this I have found in the extensive literature on the Ballets Russes is Lynn Garafola's discussion of the "dandy" component in the Ballets Russes's English audience (Emmanuel Cooper, *The Sexual Perspective: Homosexuality and Art in the Last Hundred Years in the West* [London: RKP, 1986], 135–36; Lynn Garafola, *Diaghilev's Ballets Russes* [New York: Oxford University Press, 1989], 362–65).

9. Richard Dyer, *Only Entertainment* (London: Routledge, 1992), 43. Peter Brinson, however, wrote a letter to the editor of *Marxism Today*, which first published this essay by Dyer. Brinson argued that the issue of dance and homo-

sexuality was an irrelevant distraction from more important cultural tasks (Brinson, letter to editor, *Marxism Today*, February 1986, p. 29).

10. I am not considering performances by drag kings here but would not exclude those that include dancing from this discussion. Following Judith Butler, I see masculinity as performative and would include the performance work of drag kings in a larger discussion of representations of masculinity in dance.

11. Leo Bersani describes a survey that estimated the gay population in the United States to be approximately 1 percent of the population. "[The] pollsters went to the homes of those interviewed and, while promising confidentiality, asked for each respondent's social security number and name of employer before recording his sexual preference" (Leo Bersani, *Homos* [Cambridge, Mass.: Harvard University Press, 1995], 27). In such circumstances it is not only the statistical result that is dubious but also the underlying motivation of those who commissioned the poll.

In his discussion of the work of the British dance company DV8, Christopher Winter states the opinion that the overriding aim of DV8's work is to expresses the reality about sexuality through a social and psychological realism in the body. This is something I have heard confirmed on many occasions by Lloyd Newson and members of DV8. This company generally devises its work through improvisation based on its members' experiences and responses to the themes and issues with which their work deals. Newson has often said of his works that deal explicitly with metropolitan gay experience, like *Dead Dreams of Monochrome Men* (1988) and *MSM* (1993), that the performers are being honest and are presenting on stage aspects of their experiences as gay men that are in some way "true" for themselves. The underlying subtext of this is the idea that sexuality is either innate or an expression of something interior, and that despite the distorting social pressures to conform to normative heterosexual sexuality, it is nevertheless possible to express the "truth" about sexuality. This view of the expression of sexuality through dance is what I am arguing against. Winter wants to solve a problematic by positing a stable unitary gay identity, whereas I have found DV8's work at its best is a rich and challenging theatrical experience that seeks out and puts pressure on previously unacknowledged points of conflict and contradiction within the social construction of gendered identities and sexualities, demonstrating the fragmentary and provisional nature of subjectivity (Winter, "Love and Language," *Dance Theatre Journal* 7, no. 2 [autumn 1989]: 10–13).

12. Jeffrey Weeks, *Sexuality and Its Discontents* (London: RKP, 1985). Michael Warner writes that "for both academics and activists, 'queer' gets a critical edge by defining itself against the normal rather than the heterosexual, and normal includes normal business in the academy. . . . The insistence on 'queer'— a term initially generated in the context of terror—has the effect of pointing out a wide field of normalization, rather than simple intolerance, as the site of violence" (Warner, ed., *Fear of a Queer Planet: Queer Politics and Social Theory* [Minneapolis: University of Minnesota Press, 1993], xxvi).

13. See Peggy Phelan, *Unmarked: The Politics of Performance* (New York: Routledge, 1993).

14. Elizabeth Grosz, *Volatile Bodies: Toward a Corporeal Feminism* (Bloomington: Indiana University Press, 1994), 222.

15. The attempt to define homosexual desire in ways that are not based on a model of heterosexual normality that desires an Other have been going on since the publication of Guy Hocquenghem's *Homosexual Desire* in 1972, if not earlier. See Guy Hocquenghem, *Homosexual Desire* (Durham: Duke University Press, 1993), including the introduction by Michael Moon and the preface to the 1978 edition by Jeffrey Weeks.

16. Grosz, *Volatile Bodies*, 222.

17. John Martin, *The Modern Dance* (1933; reprint, New York: Dance Horizons, 1965), 12.

18. Ibid., 13.

19. See, for example, Winter, "Love and Language."

20. The idea that choreography is this kind of authentic original seems to me highly problematic, particularly when it comes to evaluating reconstructions and restagings of choreography, or even to understanding how pieces change over a long period in repertory.

21. Susanne Langer, *Feeling and Form* (London: RKP, 1953), 178.

22. Maxine Sheets-Johnstone, *The Phenomenology of Dance* (Madison: University of Wisconsin Press, 1966), 71.

23. Barthes, *A Lover's Discourse*, 200.

24. Eve Kossofsky Sedgwick observes that "some people's sexual orientation is intensively marked by autoerotic pleasures and histories—sometimes more so than by any aspect of alloerotic object choice. For others the autoerotic possibility seems secondary or fragile, if it exists at all" (Sedgwick, *Epistemology of the Closet* [Hemel Hempstead, U.K.: Harvester Wheatsheaf, 1991], 25–26).

25. Barthes says that love's sentimentality is today obscene (Barthes, *A Lover's Discourse*, 175). The balletomanes' love of Taglioni is certainly so sentimental as to seem obscene by late twentieth-century standards.

26. Dyer, *Only Entertainment*, 123.

27. Elizabeth Grosz, *Space, Time, and Perversion* (London: Routledge, 1995), 214.

28. Judith Butler, *Bodies That Matter: On the Discursive Limits of "Sex"* (London: Routledge, 1993), 122.

29. Laura Mulvey, "Visual Pleasure and Narrative Cinema," *Screen* 16, no. 3 (1975): 6–18.

30. See Christy Adair, *Women and Dance: Sylphs and Sirens* (London: Macmillan, 1992); Ann Daly, "The Balanchine Woman: Of Hummingbirds and Channel Swimmers," *TDR* 31, no. 1 (spring 1987): 8–21; Connie Kreemer, "Whose Gaze Is It Anyway?" *Proceedings of the Eighteenth Annual Conference of the Society of Dance History Scholars* (Riverside, Calif.: Society of Dance History Scholars, 1995), 291–99; Susan Manning, "The Female Gaze and the Male Dancer: Feminist Critiques of Early Modern Dance," in Jane Desmond, ed., *Meaning in Motion* (Durham: Duke University Press, 1997), 153–66; Susan Leigh Foster, "The Ballerina's Phallic Pointe," in *Corporealities: Dancing, Knowledge, Culture, and Power* (London: Routledge, 1996), 1–24.

31. Ann Daly, "To Dance Is 'Female,'" *TDR* 34, no. 4 (winter 1989): 25.

32. Joan Acocella, *Mark Morris* (New York: Farrar Straus Giroux, 1993), 162.

33. Ibid.

34. Judith Mackrell, "Michael Clark: *Hetrospective* [at the] Anthony D'Offay Gallery," *Independent*, October 16, 1989, p. 14.

35. See Grosz, *Volatile Bodies*, 138–44.

36. Johanna Boyce, Ann Daly, Bill T. Jones, and Carol Martin, "Movement and Gender: A Roundtable Discussion," *TDR* 32, no. 4 (winter 1988): 89–90.

37. Brenda Dixon-Gottschild, *Digging the Africanist Presence in American Performance: Dance and Other Contexts* (Westport, Conn.: Greenwood, 1996).

38. Foucault first argues this in his *History of Sexuality*, vol. 1.

39. Michel Foucault, *Politics, Philosophy, Culture: Interviews and Other Writings, 1977–84*, ed. Lawrence D. Kritzman (New York: Routledge, 1988), 50–51.

7

What He Called Himself: Issues of Identity in Early Dances by Bill T. Jones

Gay Morris

Bill T. Jones has always put his personal life at the heart of his dances, so it is no surprise that in a 1994 cover story *Time* magazine identified him as a gay, black, HIV-positive choreographer. *Newsweek*, the *New York Times Magazine,* and the *New Yorker* described Jones similarly, and it is probably fair to say that every feature article written about him today speaks of him in these terms. If any element of Jones's persona appears unambiguous, it is his identity. However this was not always the case, and it is worthwhile examining an early defining period in Jones's career when identity was both, as he remarked at the time, "a pivotal idea in everything I do" and a problem to be worked out through his life and dances.[1]

The years are the late 1970s and early 1980s when Jones, still in his twenties, was on the brink of fame. His work was gaining critical attention in New York, where it was seen in important downtown spaces like the Kitchen and Dance Theater Workshop. He was shocking audiences with solos that were explosively emotional and aggressive. At the same time he was creating dances with his partner and lover, Arnie Zane, that explored their relationship within a highly structured postmodern vocabulary. This body of solos and duets pushed Jones to the center of the postmodern stage and on to international celebrity.

The argument I would like to develop here is that Jones's dances demonstrate a struggle for identity centered on questions of power and control manifested through concepts of masculinity. The issues involved fall into three categories, each a form of what I have chosen to call symbolic emasculation. The first is the perception in a dominant white society that a black man is less than a man because he is not fully accorded a white man's power. The second is the notion that a male dancer is less than a man because he occupies the feminized space of the concert stage, and the third the belief (in what Judith Butler refers to as "the epistemic regime of presumptive heterosexuality"[2]) that a gay man is less than a man because he does not sexually reproduce. Jones's response to these emasculating concepts ranged from direct refusal to subversion to apparent acquiescence. In some cases he simply turned his back on what a hegemonic society offered; in others he exploited identity stereotypes, enacting them with charm and force and then turning them against his audiences; in still others he confirmed racial and gender expectations for his own profit, a longstanding tactic of the oppressed. The point I would like to make is that in his art, Jones fought on whatever level he felt necessary to gain control of perceptions of his identity and to empower the "weak" masculinities that his race, profession, and sexual orientation would customarily have forced upon him. The hero of Ralph Ellison's *Invisible Man* notes poignantly, "I have also been called one thing and then another while no one really wished to hear what I called myself."[3] Bill Jones insisted that people hear what he called himself.

Before delving into Jones's identity struggles, it is necessary to describe in more detail the forms of symbolic emasculation that he confronted in his dances. The first centers on race and gender. In *Black Skin, White Masks*, Frantz Fanon's classic study of black identity, Fanon asserts, "It is in his corporeality that the Negro is attacked. . . . It is as an actual being that he is a threat."[4] According to Fanon, this conflation of black corporeality with identity in the white imagination began with skin color and continued on the auction block, where the slave physically represented a unit of labor. It was furthered by the idea of the black man as primitive, less civilized than whites, and consequently the possessor of tremendous sexual powers developed in the freedom of the African jungle. "In relation to the Negro, everything takes place on the genital level," Fanon writes.[5] The Negro is viewed as a penis, as raw sexual instinct, "the incarnation of a genital potency beyond all moralities and prohibitions."[6] In the black male, race and sexuality are united in an eroticized body, and behind the myth of the potent sexualized black male body, forged through slavery and colonialism, looms the specter of the white master. According to the historian Robert Staples, the slave was powerless and as such was denied most of the attributes of white masculinity.[7] Not only was he forbidden any element of control, he had to be controlled. Therefore this uncivilized being who needed to be controlled must be unstable, out of control, and irresponsible. The only masculine attributes allowed the black man were physical strength and sexual prowess; however, these were seen negatively as dangerous and in need of constant surveillance and discipline. Consequently, although the black man may be physically and sexually potent, his masculinity is less than the white man's in its relative powerlessness. Black writers and scholars have referred to this weakness as a form of emasculation, or feminization (in the sense of lack), because in patriarchy strength and weakness are gendered. For example, in an analysis of Booker T. Washington's *Up from Slavery*, Donald Gibson notes that Washington was quick to assure white readers that black men were not interested in possessing the power of white men. In other words, blacks were content with being in the powerless position of women. Gibson writes, "The African American male is feminized in that he is not defined as a man in the terms in which the time defined 'man.' "[8]

The male dancer too is a feminized presence on the concert stage. Tracing the decline of the male dancer in the bourgeois theater of the nineteenth century, Ramsey Burt argues that definitions of masculinity changed with the rise of the middle class.[9] The space for expressing emotion was gradually narrowed for men, as was the possibility of male bodily display—clothing, for example, became more muted than it had been in the eighteenth century. To overtly display emotion or the body was considered effeminate, and the male dancer did both. He also was unable to represent the power and status of men in bourgeois society because he played a subordinate role to women, who ruled the dance stage.

As concepts of manliness narrowed in the nineteenth century, homophobia increased as a means of regulating the behavior of men. "The mechanisms which limit the subversive potential of some representations of masculinity (which include disapproval of male dance) can be seen to serve the purpose of keeping out of sight anything which might disrupt the relations within which men work powerfully together in the interests of men," Burt writes.[10] He argues that although no direct link between homophobia and homosexuality in male dancing existed in the nineteenth century, when gay men conspicuously entered the dance field early in the twentieth century, the apparatus was in place to enforce heterosexual norms on the stage. However, although heterosexuality was compulsory, male dancers were, by their very choice of profession, suspect.

As for the third category of emasculation, the stereotype of the gay man as symbolically castrated (a male who does not sexually reproduce) has been so widely noted that it has achieved general recognition. Judith Butler enlarges on this notion, emphasizing a conflation of heterosexual fear of castration with fear of male homosexuality:

> Castration is the figure for punishment, the fear of castration motivating the assumption of the masculine sex, the fear of not being castrated motivating the assumption of the feminine. Implicit in the figure of castration, which operates differentially to constitute the constraining force of gendered punishment, are at least two inarticulate figures of abject homosexuality, the feminized fag and the phallicized dyke; the Lacanian scheme presumes that the terror over occupying either of these positions is what compels the assumption of a sexed position within language, a sexed position that is sexed by virtue of its heterosexual positioning, and that is assumed through a move that excludes and abjects gay and lesbian possibilities.[11]

Jones himself echoes this fear within the context of race when in his autobiography he relates an incident that occurred at a college gay and lesbian club meeting he attended in the early 1970s. He explained to the group that "it was particularly hard for me to come out because blacks saw being gay as—and I chose my words very carefully—'the ultimate emasculation of the black man.'"[12]

Certainly, such a viewpoint is understandable in terms of black and white power relations. If the black male is already weakened by a lack of power, and what power he has been accorded is based on sexual potency, he is likely to view the loss of that fragment of strength as an "ultimate emasculation."

None of the issues described here were new when Jones began his career; other gay black male dancers had faced them as well, including Alvin Ailey, the country's most influential black choreographer during the 1960s and 1970s. When Ailey started to perform professionally in the 1950s, he had little choice but to support the heterosexual norms imposed on the dance stage.[13] Like most male dancers, he was concerned about potential accusations of effeminacy in his performance, and as a closeted gay man in a virulently homophobic time he may have been especially sensitive. Ailey's solution was to emphasize the stereotype of the potent black male in both his dancing and choreography.[14] He said he was attracted to the work of Gene Kelly because it seemed masculine, by which he implicitly meant heterosexual, and he aimed for a comparable masculinity in his own choreography.[15] In addition to a Lester Horton-based modern dance vocabulary, Ailey stressed West African-derived movements such as pelvis thrusts, hip rotations, and torso articulation, as well as virtuosic jumps, turns, and kicks. His male dancers, often appearing bare chested, created a representation of masculinity that was athletic and sexual and that white critics read as emphatically masculine and therefore heterosexual. P. W. Manchester wrote that in Ailey's dances "the men are men and the women are frankly delighted about it," while Doris Hering giddily compared Ailey's own performing style to "a caged lion full of lashing power."[16] Ailey promoted the stereotype of black heterosexual potency with male virtuosity and sexually charged movement often aimed at the women performers, perhaps accounting in part for Manchester's remark. Hering's reference to Ailey in terms of a wild jungle animal indicates that the notion of the black male as erotic primitive was also part of Ailey's image of masculinity. To some extent Ailey was able to extend the boundaries of permissible representations of black men in works like *Blues Suite* (1958), in which he included elements of anger and despair. However, such pieces did not make up the bulk of his repertory, and the possibilities open to him remained limited if he wished to dance and choreograph on prestigious white stages.

By 1980 Jones had far more options for dealing with racial and gender issues because of the marked social shifts that had taken place over the previous three decades. Born in 1952, Jones was an early beneficiary of the civil rights and gay liberation movements. He grew up with media coverage of the civil rights struggle flashing before him on television and in the daily press. While he was in high school, gay liberation erupted into public consciousness with the Stonewall rebellion of 1969. By the time he reached college, a year after Stonewall, there were not only civil rights organizations on campus but gay ones as well. However, although the times may have been more open to change in the performing arts than they had been for Ailey's generation and those before him, gender issues were only beginning to be addressed.

Typically, Jones's early solos combined movement and words, including song, in a marathon of activity. The words often formed a narrative, but the story was never simply related, it was always woven into and through the movement and given rhythm through repetition and phrasing. The stories Jones told were deeply personal, dealing primarily with his family history and with dreams. The dances for which Jones is best remembered are ones in which he confronted audiences in a highly aggressive manner. One of the earliest of these originally had been part of a larger work entitled *Everybody Works/All Beasts Count* (1975). When he auditioned the solo on its own for the Clark Center Dance Festival at City University of New York Mall, he relates that in a fit of nervousness he injected a clenched fist and an obscene raised finger accompanied by a mouthed curse, then shrugged and smiled. The judges accepted the dance on the condition he eliminate the offending material, which he did.[17] However, in a 1977 video of the dance, recorded at an outdoor performance in New York, Jones alternated sections of ingratiating movement with menacing ones. He seduced the audience with smiles and amusing verbal asides and tore around the stage in virtuosic displays of Ailey-inspired modern dance.[18] Then, suddenly, he switched to walking forward and pointing belligerently at the crowd. At one moment he mouthed a silent "motherfucker" at them. Throughout the dance he was dressed in a business suit; at the end he stripped to his underwear. By 1980, influenced by conceptual artist Vito Acconci's attacks on audiences, Jones had enlarged his own aggressive repertory. In a solo at the American Dance Festival in 1981 he created a dance based on oppositional statements that included, "I love women. I hate women. I love white people. I hate white people. I'd like to kiss you. I'd like to tear your fucking heart out. Why didn't you leave us in Africa? I'm so thankful for the opportunity to be here."[19]

The critical response to these dances was shock. Tobi Tobias, reporting in *New York* magazine, remembered none of the invitation in the *Everybody Works* solo nor any of the dance. She recalled only the violence. "The first time I laid eyes on Bill T. Jones, he was got up like a banker, in a sober business suit, haranguing the baffled summer-festival crowd at the Delacorte, like a soapbox orator. His performance was all words, and pure vitriol; he called it a dance. I couldn't see what it had to do with dancing, but I never forgot him."[20] Her response was not unique. Robert Pierce wrote in the *Soho News*, "I've attended performances in which he brought such an intense aggressiveness to within inches of my chair that I felt physical defense alarms being triggered in my body."[21]

It is important to note that Jones's audiences during these years were overwhelmingly white. He did not court black audiences, he rarely performed in black venues. His scene was the largely white one of the downtown postmodern avant-garde and the special events and festivals at which downtown choreographers were represented. When one looks at the names of the critics who reviewed Jones's performances in the 1970s and early 1980s, the list is a *Who's Who* of white critics writing at the time. The general readership black press seems to have been largely unaware of him, which is not surprising considering where he performed and how little he was known outside the dance community. The single dance magazine that made a point of extensively covering African American performers was *Attitude*, founded in 1982. Two of the four reviews of Jones's work that ran between 1982 and 1984 described him as a "postmodern" choreographer, apparently to set him apart from black dance makers who specialized in Ailey-style choreography or in African or Afro-Caribbean dance forms. Although many black choreographers were producing work during these years, few were doing it in a postmodern mode—Gus Solomons Jr., Donald Byrd, Blondell Cummings, and Bebe Miller were among the handful, and none of these combined movement, language, autobiography, and emotional ferocity in a way similar to Jones's. One of Jones's explanations for his interest in postmodernism was his social background, in which he had long been surrounded by whites. With the exception of his family, Jones's world from the time he reached high school was largely white. He was one of the few blacks in his high school. Soon after reaching college he started his relationship with Zane and many of their friends were white. He has noted that a great deal of the encouragement he received in his early years of performing came from whites—his high school drama teacher, his dance teachers, and colleagues at college and beyond. Zane, of course, was also an influence. When Jones entered the downtown avant-garde, it was with sophisticated white dance audiences in mind.

I want to suggest here that the aggressiveness of Jones's solos was in part calculated to assault these viewers' complacent expectations of the eroticized black male dancer and in the process to transform his identity from passive "feminized" object to active "masculinized" subject. He made his attack on two fronts, that of the black male and that of the male dancer. In a 1984 interview Jones explained, "There is something about the spectators saying, in effect, 'Perform for us. Show us your body.' So it made me extremely aggressive, and maybe that was my desire to impose masculine control—I also assumed it was racial."[22] Feminist theory has long taught that in patriarchy a menacing expression of anger belongs to an active subject and thus is seen as masculine. Jones's aggressive words and gestures toward the audience contested the stereotype of the male dancer as weak and effeminate. Jones actually frightened spectators. What could be less like the befeathered ballet prince or the ineffective poseurs that constituted Martha Graham's gallery of heroes? In his relationship to the audience Jones may have been inspired by the work of Vito Acconci, but for his actual modus operandi he took a page from the book of black nationalism. He was the dangerous black man made familiar by the Black Panthers, Malcolm X, Eldridge Cleaver, and a host of other angry young black men of the 1960s. It was not these men's politics Jones borrowed but their attitude. His dances disrupted stereotypes of the passive obedient black male and in the process took on some of the power of white patriarchy in which anger gains respect. At the same time Jones challenged the prevailing image of the black dancer as an eroticized primitive by abruptly alternating between passive aestheticized object and active pugnacious subject.

However, while Jones's rage dispelled some stereotypes, it reinforced another, that of the uncontrolled black man, violent and dangerous to whites. Robert Staples argues that because black men are denied access to the power available to whites, they challenge this powerlessness through anger, reinforcing the stereotype of being out of control. This gives a false feeling of power, which in fact serves as an excuse for further white oppression.[23] Nevertheless, Jones may have felt that the negative aspects of performing rage were a small price to pay for gaining an active voice. Linked with seduction, anger also became part of a technique of reversal that Jones used in his dances as a tool for disruption and control. This technique was a central element in his early dances and as such needs to be explored in some detail.

One of the important ways in which Jones employed reversal may best be understood through elements of gaze theory. Making a necessary distinction between *look* and *gaze*, Jones sought to control the way in which an audience looked at him, but in doing so he also reached beyond the specific to Lacan's transcendental ideal of the ever-present, all-powerful gaze associated with patriarchy and the phallus.[24] That is to say, Jones challenged not only the specific way in which he was observed as a performer but perceptions of power and weakness embedded in patriarchal society.

Jones was preoccupied with spectatorship and surveillance from the earliest days of his career. "They're watching," he says at the end of *Io*, a 1981 solo. Or they are pointedly not watching, as in the case of a woman who walked out of the same solo and whose exit Jones commented on in an improvised section of the dance. In his autobiography Jones expresses his anxiety at being observed with section titles that read: "They Are Watching Me." "What Are They Thinking about Me?" "What Did They Say?" "What Did They See?"[25] He explains his conflicted feelings at being an object of attention: "I found myself easily seduced by a set of eyes, learned what it is to engage the expectations and needs of spectators. It made me want to please. Or spit."[26]

Conflicts caused by differing ways of being seen can account for Jones's ambivalence. Gaze theory contends that the male is the active bearer of the gaze, not the passive recipient of it, an idea which also pertains to the look. But one of the essential ingredients of the performer's profession is to be looked at. In much of gay male culture too, being the recipient of a look does not hold the stigma it allegedly does among heterosexual males. In addition, black males tend to be the recipient of the white gaze of patriarchal power, which defines them according to generally negative stereotypes and places them in a feminized passive space as patriarchy also does homosexuality and performance. In his dances Jones attempted to gain control of the gaze and in this way to become the active ("masculinized") subject. On the one hand he knowingly seduced audiences with black stereotypes, inviting their look, fulfilling their fantasies. He pulled off his shirt to reveal the beauty of a well-muscled body ("You just know what they're all thinking, 'Oh, I bet you have a dick down to your knees'").[27] He danced a segment in the African jazz style associated with black dance ("You're allowed to wiggle your hips in public").[28] He used his velvet voice to lull the audience with intimacies. Then he turned on them, jolting the crowd with enraged diatribes or mortifying individuals in the audience by singling them out for negative comment. In a 1979 review Marcia B. Siegel conveyed some of the discomfiture that resulted from Jones's whiplash tactics: "You think you're watching him go over the brink of rage or physical control or sanity—and the next minute you could swear he's looking you straight in the eye and telling you the most intimate or loving or shameless things."[29] Deborah Jowitt, dance critic for the *Village Voice,* recalled the first Jones performance she saw in 1977: " 'You want some?' he asked us softly, stroking his body, then cursed us out."[30] With these abrupt shifts Jones attempted to wrest control of the gaze by forcing the audience to abandon preconceived notions of identity and to see him, and through him the black male dancer, in unaccustomed, more "masculine," ways.

Jones also used reversal to look back at the audience, in effect changing places with viewers and thereby gaining control of the look. In his discussion of Isaac Julien's 1989 film, *Looking for Langston,* Kobena Mercer describes a process similar to the one Jones used. "Here the key issue is the motif of the direct look, whereby the black (gay) subject *looks back,* whether as character or as auteur, and thereby turns around the question to ask the audience who or what *they* are looking for." This direct look "draws the viewer into a space that problematizes simplistic conceptions of identity."[31] In his solos Jones often commented on the audience to the audience, for example, speaking directly to the spectators about the woman who had left his performance and of the audience's laughter at her exit, or pointing menacingly at an individual viewer, or, in Jowitt's words, "cursing us out." In these ways he made it clear he was observing the spectators, in short, transforming them from subject to object. This reversal, as Mercer notes, makes simplistic conceptions of identity more difficult to maintain.

Jones used reversal in yet another way to challenge stereotypical assumptions and control the ways in which he was perceived: he alternated extreme tension and emotion, that element of out-of-control maniacal danger, with postmodern cool. Although his anger made the deepest impression on viewers, it was only part of his solos, and often a small part, especially in dances made after 1980. Less commented upon was the detached approach and formal complexity of much of his material. In long sections of solos such as *Sisyphus* (1980) and *Io* (1981) Jones, instead of "working himself into a tizzy" as Arlene Croce dismissively described his more violent moments, focused on complex dance constructions and an unemotional performance style.[32] His smooth masklike face was neutral in expression, as was his voice. He most often spoke as if he were simply thinking out loud. The steps Jones chose eschewed familiar virtuosity as well as the movements centering on hips and pelvis that had come to epitomize black dance. Instead he offered task-oriented abstract movement that made no overt attempt to be read as sexual. He did not invite the look, he stuck to the cool business of postmodernism while reminding viewers through his verbal narratives of the pain of black experience. This aspect of Jones's dances offered a different way of challenging stereotypes by focusing attention on the dancer's conceptualizing abilities and self-discipline rather than his body and emotions. In this sense one might say Jones appropriated white masculine control over the space of rational thought. Not that he was the first to do this—women dancers had long preceded him. First-generation postmoderns such as Yvonne Rainer and Trisha Brown had led the way in the 1960s by rejecting the intuitive emotional position women dancers had traditionally occupied. By 1980 many women choreographers were routinely referred to as brainy and intellectual. However, few black male choreographers had made the leap into formalist postmodernism. By producing these kinds of works, Jones was not only co-opting a white male-dominated space, he was also asserting his right to membership in the predominately white avant-garde. That he was aware of his unusual position at the time is reflected in his frequent, often ironic references to himself as "the black postmodernist."[33]

Jones's performance of gender in his early work at once supported and challenged stereotypes of the emasculated black man and the feminized male dancer. There is no doubt, however, that he explicitly attempted to meet these issues head-on in his work. Jones was less clear about dancing sexual identity during his early career, and it is the confusion we meet in this category that I would now like to address.

Jones has never been a choreographer whose art and life could be separated, and this was especially the case in the late 1970s and early 1980s when his work dealt specifically with events from his past and with his relationships with his family and friends. In 1980 Jones and Arnie Zane had been living together as lovers for nearly a decade, yet Jones rarely mentioned Zane in his solos. When Jones broached the subject of desire, it was almost exclusively in terms of heterosexuality. For instance, in an untitled solo from 1980 Jones began a section with the words, "You glow so beautifully, may I touch it?" while his hand glided over his genitals. He then hid his face with his hand and said, "What about the children?" The dance consisted of accumulations of movement with spoken phrases and bits of song which eventually resolved themselves into suggestions of meaning. There were references to the black body in the song "Jump down, turn around, pick a bale o' cotton; jump down, turn around, pick a bale o' hay. Me and my body going to pick a bale o' cotton." Jones went through a segment of quick semaphoric gestures in which he touched his eyes and circled his genitals. He referred to someone named Adam and a woman, Marie. At another point he said, "Yes, Marie, look out!" He sang "I Believe," he held his hands in prayer. He said, "Yes, Adam."

The dance suggests a situation in which a sweet-talking man tries to win a woman's sexual favors. There's a warning to the woman and there is her belief that heaven will take care of her. Read against the background of Jones's life and the autobiographical nature of his work, the dance builds associations with Jones's mother's devout prayers, her years of pregnancy and the birth of her many children, his sisters' unwanted teenage pregnancies and those of other young girls in the migrant camps the family inhabited. The dance speaks of sex and gender within implicitly racial terms, and the sex is heterosexual. A tale of sexual incest in *Io* also is heterosexual, as is a reference to a girl with whom Jones was involved sexually in high school but did not marry. None of the solos of these years that are recorded on video or that critics speak about or that Jones speaks of in his autobiography or in interviews refer explicitly to same-sex desire.

His duets with Zane reveal the clearest references to homoeroticism, but these are never explicit; they are coded or left open to interpretation.[34] Jones and Zane further suppressed eroticism in their work with a neutral postmodern performance style that Jones called "matter-of-fact" and stage personas that focused on a tough streetwise attitude. However, within a regime of compulsory heterosexuality the simple fact that two men dance on stage in choreography that regularly takes the shape of extended duets is in itself a homoerotic cue, even if the men's gestures and movement do little to indicate desire. Critical response to the two men's dances in the early 1980s indicates that the duets were often read in this way.

Two typical examples of the work Jones and Zane were doing together at the time were *Blauvelt Mountain* (1980) and *Valley Cottage* (1981), the dances that put their partnership on the vanguard map. *Blauvelt Mountain* was divided into two parts.[35] In the first, "A Fiction," Jones and Zane drew on accumulation techniques as well as contact improvisation. The men went through various sequences of accumulated activity, the speed of the movement gradually increasing, while at the same time they improvised word associations. At the end of the section Zane caught Jones in a flying leap followed by a blackout. The second section, "An Interview," began with the two walking around the stage singing a Swiss-German harvest round. Then Zane gradually tore down a wall that stretched across the back of the stage and re-erected it down the center. He wore heavy gloves to change the position of the cinder blocks that made up the wall, walking back and forth at a natural pace, as if doing a job, his shoes making a regular, staccato rhythm. In the meantime Jones, who was barefoot, did a frenetic improvised solo, jumping back and forth over the wall as it grew down the center of the stage. There was no contact between the two during this section. The dance ended when the wall was finished. *Valley Cottage* stressed cooperation and bodily contact more than *Blauvelt Mountain*; for example, one man's hand occasionally rested briefly on the other's shoulder. The dance also included a repeated powerful image of black and white hands forcefully clasped, the rest of the men's bodies made invisible by vertical screens. The pose was like a stop-action frame in a film, reinforced by a halt in the music.

Bill T. Jones and Arnie Zane in *Valley Cottage* duet (Photograph by Lois Greenfield; copyright © 1981 Lois Greenfield; used with permission)

However, if such gestures could be cues for homosexual desire, they could also be ones for racial harmony, a theme Jones often mentioned in conjunction with their work and that tended to deflect the focus from sexuality.

Blauvelt Mountain made oblique references to the two men's life together—they had learned the Swiss song from a friend, they lived briefly in Blauvelt, a town north of Manhattan—but it was not a narrative of their relationship. Neither was *Valley Cottage* (named for the village in which they eventually settled), despite its more intimate atmosphere. However, in a broader sense the dances were about their relationship both in terms of race and gender, and critics appear to have understood this. Like Jones and Zane themselves, critics spoke in coded terms of desire, while referring more directly to the toughness, and by implication the heterosexual masculinity, of the men's stage personas. They used words like *pugnacious* to describe Zane's performance style, and Jones's as having a look of "leashed hostility." Yet they also described the men's relationship on stage in terms of *camaraderie, affection, tenderness,* and *intimacy.* They also invariably mentioned that Zane was white and Jones black, a reference to race in the context of gender that was left unexplored but that must have evoked a host of assumptions, associations, and questions for the reviewers' predominately white readers.

If critics did not refer directly to Zane and Jones's sexual relationship, neither, to judge from interviews, did they, although they lived openly together. In what appears to have been a silent agreement between interviewers and dancers, the subject was not raised. Even Burt Supree, a gay man writing in 1981 for the reputedly radical *Village Voice*, did not report a single comment about how the men's relationship affected their dances. He noted that they shared a house because he interviewed them there, but that was all. Other interviewers were even more circumspect, giving the impression that the two simply worked together. By 1984, however, a sea change had occurred. Gay liberation had made great strides, and increasing numbers of men and women were emerging from the closet. The AIDS epidemic was also receiving a great deal of attention, and political art was now at the heart of the avant-garde. Another interview in the *Voice*, this one by Amanda Smith, entitled "Making the Personal Political," included the choreographers Johanna Boyce, Tom Keegan and Davidson Lloyd (a gay couple), and Jones and Zane. Jones is quoted as saying, "Our work has tried to present us as two loving persons who have been able to love each other above race, class, all of these divisions. That becomes a political statement, that we are saying to any audience that views us, 'This is a viable lifestyle. This is a viable approach to the world.'"[36] Such a statement is a marked change from the early 1980s when Jones and Zane were not actively promoting their sexual relationship as an element of their dance. It was there for those who read between the lines, and many did, but it was rarely stated overtly by them or the press.[37]

In his dancing of sexual identity, Jones appears to have attempted to occupy polar positions at the same time. While delivering coded messages of same-sex desire in his duets with Arnie Zane, Jones was performing violent solos that linked him to the hyperheterosexual attitudes associated with black nationalists.

He also was describing heterosexual liaisons in his solos. Jones speaks at length in his autobiography of his heterosexual relationships in high school. At the same time he hardly mentions same-sex desire while he was growing up. It was, he said, falling in love with Arnie that set the course of his sexuality. Yet here too he stressed that in their relationship he was the one who penetrated—he was, in other words, the one who retained an element of masculine power. This translated into his perception of his dancing as well. "Sometimes when I step onstage," he wrote, "I carry in front of me an invisible phallus. And this phallus is to me what the spear was to the Watusis. It is my virility, my right to be, and the assurance that I will always be. I am in search of the dance in which the phallus is forgiven for being a thing that must penetrate, deflower. This dance will be selfish and self-interested, and yet, fulfilled by filling."[38]

In his interview with Amanda Smith in 1984 Jones spoke of his "obsessions," which also centered on potency and procreation: "I was making dances when I was worried about making babies. I come from a family of twelve. Most people in my family average at least three children. I had none."[39] Contrary to his statement, those obsessions did in fact make their way into his dances in numerous references to potency, pregnancy, and childbirth. And Jones actually did become a father in 1981, after a brief affair with a Detroit woman while he was an artist-in-residence in the Midwest. He and Zane tried to adopt the child but were refused.[40]

To say simply that Jones was bisexual and reflected this orientation in his dance is not an altogether convincing explanation for his opposing representations of sexuality. For instance, it does not account for the directness with which he spoke and danced of heterosexual desire in his work and the absence of direct reference to same-sex desire. One might argue that Jones's insistence on heterosexuality was as much a mask to hide homosexuality as were Ailey's macho representations of the black man—but then how does one account for the duets? These dances may not have been overtly homoerotic, but they were implicitly so and taken as such by a number of viewers. I want to advance another possibility that might explain Jones's simultaneous occupation of polar positions.

That is, that he appropriated some of the power of heterosexual masculinity for the gay black concert dancer. One is reminded of Ellison's Invisible Man stealing electricity from New York's Monopolated Light & Power as a metaphor for co-opting white power to make black identity visible. "Light confirms my reality, gives birth to my form," Ellison's hero says.[41]

Beginning with an element as basic as performance style, Jones adopted a conventionally masculine persona. Compare, for example, his style with that of Mark Morris where feminine cues abound—from gestures such as touching or tossing back the hair to the lush contrapposto he often gives abstract movement. Jones's movement, by comparison, tends to be blunter, less embellished, more squared, and directly forceful, cues in Western patriarchal society that are read as masculine and hence heterosexual. This assumption of heteromasculine posture and body language helped efface perceptions of effeminacy in the male dancer.[42] So did solos that included tales of heterosexual liaisons and attitudes of rage and violence. Even as these elements lessened perceptions of emasculation in the male dancer, they reinforced images of the potent black man, accruing what may be a weak form of power but power nevertheless. Just as some in the black community may be loathe to give up white engendered stereotypes, even though those stereotypes prove to be false positives, the black gay man may be equally loathe to demystify the myths. By co-opting masculine heterosexual power, diminished as it may be for the black man, black gay men still reap whatever benefits are available. When Jones performed before white audiences as an enraged black man, he fulfilled white stereotypes that were racially negative but which were professionally and sexually positive in that they were stereotypes of heterosexual masculinity. The solos thus gained critical attention for Jones in a way they may not have if he had continued to ingratiate himself, reinforcing stereotypes of emasculation. This assumption of heterosexual power spilled over into the duets in which Jones and Zane were viewed as feisty streetwise performers whose movement was tough and matter-of-fact—a far cry from the aestheticized display of modern dance and the sexual baggage that went with it.

In Jones's case fear of the "feminized fag" of castration did not lead to compulsory heterosexuality or masked homosexuality but to a raiding of heterosexual power to counter the emasculating effects of racial and gender stereotypes. In his battle to control the perception of his own identity Jones often manipulated the myths of a dominant society to his advantage. He used his body as a lure, even as he challenged the fantasies that centered upon it. At the same time Jones's refusal to be locked into any prescribed role served to disrupt an abundance of preconceived notions of race and gender. When in the mid-1980s Jones openly avowed the identity we know him by today—a weak identity in the context of emasculating patriarchy—he was able to do so while relinquishing little of the power he had accrued.

NOTES

1. Burt Supree, "Any Two Men on the Planet," *Village Voice*, March 18–24, 1981, p. 73.

2. Judith Butler, *Gender Trouble: Feminism and the Subversion of Identity* (London: Routledge, 1990), x.

3. Ralph Ellison *Invisible Man* (New York: Vintage Books), 573.

4. Frantz Fanon, *Black Skin, White Masks* (New York: Grove, 1967), 163.

5. Ibid., 157.

6. Ibid.

7. Robert Staples, *Black Masculinity: The Black Man's Role in American Society* (San Francisco: Black Scholar Press, 1982).

8. Donald Gibson, "Chapter One of Booker T. Washington's *Up from Slavery* and the Feminization of the African American Male" in Marcellus Blount and George P. Cunningham, eds., *Representing Black Men* (London: Routledge, 1996), 96. See also Stephen Michael Best, "'Stand by Your Man': Richard Wright, Lynch Pedagogy, and Rethinking Black Male Agency," 111–130, in the same volume, and Derrick Bell, "The Race-Charged Relationship of Black Men and Black Women," in Maurice Berger, Brian Wallis, and Simon Watson, eds., *Constructing Masculinity* (London: Routledge, 1995), 193–210.

9. Ramsey Burt, *The Male Dancer: Bodies, Spectacle, Sexualities* (London: Routledge, 1995). See also Lynn Garafola, "The Travesty Dancer in the Nineteenth Century," *Dance Research Journal* 17, no. 2, and 18, no. 1 (1985–86): 35–40.

10. Burt, *Male Dancer*, 23.

11. Judith Butler, *Bodies That Matter: On the Discursive Limits of "Sex"* (London: Routledge, 1993), 96.

12. Bill T. Jones and Peggy Gillespie, *Last Night on Earth* (New York: Pan-

theon, 1995), 82. For an insightful discussion of masculine sexuality and differ-ence within the black community, see Phillip Brian Harper, *Are We Not Men? Masculine Anxiety and the Problem of African American Identity* (New York: Oxford University Press, 1996).

13. For discussions of gender in the life and work of Alvin Ailey, see Jennifer Dunning, *Alvin Ailey: A Life in Dance* (New York: Addison Wesley, 1996), and Thomas DeFrantz, "Simmering Passivity: The Black Male Body in Concert Dance," in Gay Morris, ed., *Moving Words: Rewriting Dance* (London: Rout-ledge, 1996), 107–20; as well as Alvin Ailey and A. P. Bailey, *Revelations: The Autobiography of Alvin Ailey* (New York: Birch Lane, 1995).

14. Ailey was not alone in using this stereotype of black masculinity; it was a common representation on the dance stage. Rather, he choreographically de-veloped it, especially in terms of virtuosic display, and made it a central compo-nent of his work.

15. Dunning, *Alvin Ailey: A Life in Dance*, 26.

16. P. W. Manchester, "The Season in Review," *Dance News*, February 1959, p. 7. Doris Hering, "Alvin Ailey and Ernest Parham," *Dance Magazine*, May 1958, p. 65.

17. Jones and Gillespie, *Last Night on Earth*, 136–37.

18. After taking several classes at the Ailey studio, Jones had rejected Ailey's lush, dazzling technique for postmodernism, an emotionally cool form based in vernacular movement. However, he sometimes used Ailey-style dance as a tool to beguile audiences before turning on them. It served as one way to contrast the old with the new, the ingratiating with the confrontational.

19. Jones, *Last Night on Earth*, 165.

20. Tobi Tobias, "Food for the Eye," *New York*, March 14, 1983, p. 68.

21. Robert Pierce, "The Ingratiating Demon," *Soho News*, April 8, 1981, p. 54.

22. Bill T. Jones, "Movement and Gender: A Roundtable Discussion," *Dance Theatre Journal* 32, no. 4 (1998): 89.

23. Staples, *Black Masculinity*.

24. Gaze theory, which deals with concepts of objectification and power, was developed in conjunction with cinema, where the observed did not look back. I therefore am expanding the use of gaze theory concepts to account for a human agent as the recipient of the gaze and for this agent's attempt to reverse the power of the patriarchal gaze as well as that of the specific look. For a review of gaze theory in relation to queer theory, see Caroline Evans and Lorraine Gamman, "Reviewing Queer Viewing: The Gaze Revisited," in Paul Burston and Colin Richardson, eds., *A Queer Romance: Lesbians, Gay Men and Popular Culture*, (London: Routledge, 1995), 13–56.

25. Jones, *Last Night on Earth*, 149–53.

26. Ibid., 151.

27. Bill T. Jones, "Movement and Gender: A Roundtable Discussion," *Dance Theatre Journal* 32, no. 4 (1998): 90.

28. Ibid.

29. Marcia B. Siegel, *The Tail of the Dragon* (Durham, N.C.: Duke Univer-sity Press, 1991), 65.

30. Deborah Jowitt, "Bill as Bill," *Village Voice*, October 20, 1992, p. 90.

31. Kobena Mercer, *Welcome to the Jungle* (London: Routledge, 1994), 226.

32. Arlene Croce, "Names and Places," *New Yorker*, July 12, 1982, p. 96.

33. See for example, Eric Traub, "Footnotes," *Ballet News*, May 1983, p. 7.

34. Because both Zane and Jones created the duets, it is difficult to say who set the tone of the dances, but since Jones was by far the more experienced choreographer, he may have had a controlling role in the work. At the least, however, the two men agreed on what they would perform and how. Zane had spent most of his early career pursuing photography; it was when Jones persuaded him to study contact improvisation so they could perform together that Zane began to dance professionally. The two formed the Bill T. Jones/Arnie Zane Dance Company in 1982.

35. *Blauvelt Mountain* and *Valley Cottage* were part of a trilogy that had begun in 1979 with *Monkey Run Road*.

36. Amanda Smith, "Making the Personal Political," *Village Voice*, April 24, 1984, p. 75.

37. One notable exception was a group dance Jones choreographed called *Social Intercourse: Pilgrim's Progress* (1981) in which the performers at one point rushed about the stage in gender-blind kissing. In the piece Jones appeared with three other dancers, while Zane acted as administrator. Arlene Croce wrote in a *New Yorker* review that "gay-love" was among the issues dealt with in the work. Croce's remark is one of the few made during the late 1970s and early 1980s that directly mentioned homosexuality in connection with Jones's choreography (Croce, "Names and Places," 96).

38. Jones, *Last Day on Earth*, 131.

39. Smith, "Making the Personal Political," 75.

40. Henry Louis Gates Jr., "Onward and Upward with the Arts," *New Yorker*, November 28, 1994, p. 117.

41. Ralph Ellison, *Invisible Man* (New York: Vintage Books), 6–7.

42. I don't want to imply that Jones consciously assumes this kind of comportment and movement. It is part of what Pierre Bourdieu calls *habitus* and Judith Butler *performativity*, an unconscious but learned set of body techniques rather than a conscious role playing.

Part 2
Social Stagings

8
A Right to Boogie Queerly:
The First Amendment on the Dance Floor

Paul Siegel

The word *dance* does not appear in the U.S. Constitution. Nonetheless, American courts have recognized that some forms of dance under some circumstances do enjoy First Amendment protection. In a 1991 case Supreme Court Justice Byron White explained the relevance of dance to freedom of expression:

> Dance has been defined as the art of moving the body in a rhythmical way, usually to music, to express an emotion or idea, to narrate a story, or simply to take delight in the movement itself. Inherently, it is the communication of emotion or ideas. At the root of all the varied manifestations of dancing lies the common impulse to resort to movement to externalize states which we cannot externalize by rational means.[1]

The main purpose of this essay is to suggest that if Justice White intended these words as a summary of dance's legal status in the United States, he had it only half right. A more correct assessment would point out that dance is only sometimes treated as communicative. Predictably, when dance is seen as communicative—when we take to the dance floor in order to convey a message rather than just to have fun—courts have been most accommodating. As we will also see, lesbians and gays are more likely to be seen as communicating a message through their dance than are heterosexuals. Indeed, precisely because members of the sexual minorities are demonstrably an oppressed people, they may enjoy a greater right to boogie than do others.

Courts that have ruled on the constitutionality of antidance statutes or regulations typically have called upon at least one of two long-standing principles of First Amendment jurisprudence.[2]

First has been the principle that freedom of speech applies not only to linguistically meaningful vibrations of the vocal cords but also to a wide array of behaviors collectively categorized as symbolic conduct. Such nonverbal expressive behaviors as hoisting and saluting a flag (or choosing not to salute one or even to burn one), marching in a parade, or wearing items to express political messages have all been treated as symbolic conduct. Then, too, dance can be a form of social coming together protected by the First Amendment's implicit freedom of association, a right initially restricted only to purely political associations but that has been held applicable to nonpolitical groups.[3] Generally speaking, performative dance has prompted courts to use the symbolic conduct doctrine, whereas social ballroom-type dance not designed to reach an identifiable audience has involved claims to associational freedom.

Gay people have often had to go to court to protect their right to dance in both kinds of circumstances. Here I will explore judicial treatment of dance as symbolic conduct and as associational activity, comparing the fates of straight and gay dancer/litigants.

PERFORMANCE DANCE—DANCING FOR AN AUDIENCE

Dance is, of course, a performing art and, like all art, is intended to impart a message from artist to audience. Perhaps because dance that is *not* specifically gay oriented so clearly enjoys First Amendment protection, such dance events have rarely invited government regulation unless the dancers performed nude or seminude.[4] First Amendment concerns often are intertwined with Twenty-first Amendment issues in these cases—the latter provision both ended Prohibition and gave the states enormous latitude in regulating liquor distribution—in that the dancers typically performed in taverns. One of the earliest cases was *California v. Larue* (1972), which upheld the state's prohibition against topless dancing in venues serving alcohol.[5] The state's fact finding in advance of the litigation had concluded that this form of dance led to a host of secondary effects that the state surely could prohibit:

Customers were found engaging in oral copulation with women entertainers; customers engaged in public masturbation; and customers placed rolled currency either directly into the vagina of a female entertainer, or on the bar in order that she might pick it up herself. Numerous other forms of contact between the mouths of male customers and the vaginal areas of female performers were reported to have occurred.[6]

The Supreme Court's holding in *Larue* makes no sense in the absence of Twenty-first Amendment considerations. We would not fathom the government's prohibition of movies like *The Warriors* or of gangster rap music on the ground that some viewers or listeners will be led to act out in violent or otherwise antisocial ways. As Justice John Paul Stevens put it, in dissenting from a later decision that upheld New York State's prohibition of nude dancing in establishments that serve liquor, "it would be most difficult to sustain a law prohibiting political discussions in places where alcohol is sold by the drink, even though the record may show, conclusively, that political discussions in bars often lead to disorderly behavior, assaults and even homicide."[7] A few years later, when the Court upheld a similar provision in Kentucky, Justice Stevens's dissent questioned the Court's practice of permitting Twenty-first Amendment jurisprudence to overshadow the First Amendment. "It is surely strange," he chided the Court's majority, "to suggest that a dramatic production like *Hair* would lose its First Amendment protection because alcoholic beverages might be served in the lobby during intermission."[8]

In its two most recent decisions concerning nude or seminude dancing, the Court has been unable to produce majority doctrine. The first, *Barnes v. Glen Theatre* (1991), resulted in a highly fractured 5–4 decision upholding Indiana's public indecency statute as applied to nude dancing, even in establishments that did not serve liquor.[9] Three justices in the majority felt that the state's interest in "fostering morality" was sufficient to outweigh whatever First Amendment protection nude dancers may enjoy. Justice Antonin Scalia alone held that nude dance is completely beyond the scope of First Amendment consideration. Justice David Souter, also voting with the majority, felt that the state could prevail only because of its desire to prevent such secondary evils as prostitution. He emphasized, however, that nude dancing is not entirely devoid of First Amendment protection. "Dancing as a performance directed to an actual or hypothetical audience," he wrote, "gives expression at least to generalized emotion or feeling, and where the dancer is nude or nearly so the feeling expressed, in the absence of some contrary clue, is eroticism, carrying an endorsement of erotic experience."[10] The four dissenting justices expressed puzzlement at the majority's importing of a public indecency rationale to the area of dance performance:

> The purpose of forbidding people from appearing nude in parks, beaches, hot dog stands, and like public places is to protect others from offense. But that could not possibly be the purpose of preventing nude dancing in theaters and barrooms since the viewers are exclusively consenting adults who pay money to see these dances. The purpose of the proscription in these contexts is to protect the viewers from what the State believes is the harmful message that nude dancing communicates.[11]

More recently, the Court upheld an Erie, Pennsylvania, ordinance that, while on its face covered virtually all categories of public nudity, was clearly enacted in response to public outrage about the goings-on at night clubs featuring nude dancers.[12] The Court again failed to produce a majority opinion. However, the conjunction of the four-justice plurality opinion and Justice Souter's separate concurrence makes clear that a majority of the Court now is willing to use a relaxed form of First Amendment scrutiny whenever the state seeks to control the secondary effects of nude dancing, such as prostitution and an increase in related criminal activity.

Promoters of dance and musical events involving gay performers and/or likely to attract gay audiences have also needed to go to court to win the right to take to the stage. In the 1980s organizers of the Miss Gay America pageant, an annual event for female impersonators that began in 1972, made an oral contract to stage the competition in Oklahoma City's municipally operated Myriad Auditorium and began the costly preparations and publicity necessary to stage such a spectacle.[13] Apparently, a higher-level administrator at the Myriad, when alerted to the nature of the proposed event, refused to approve the contract, because he believed the event, as "an open expression of homosexuality," would violate prevailing community standards.[14]

The promoters prevailed when they sued in federal district court but on the relatively narrow ground that the city had placed too much unfettered power in the hands of this particular bureaucrat, thus virtually ensuring that unconstitutionally arbitrary decisions would emerge. But the court went out of its way to express its opinion of the nature of the exhibition:

> [The pageant] includes a talent competition with singing and dance, expression which is protected by the First Amendment. . . . Defendants merely argue that the exposure of a male in female attire is immoral, [but] there are no state laws prohibiting a man dressing as a woman. . . . [The city] contends that a blatant showing of men parading in women's apparel is not artistic. Such a judgment is subjective. While this Court may agree that such a "pageant" may not rise to the level of artistic endeavor that "Hair" or "La Cage aux Folles" represent, it is still expression. . . . The First Amendment is not an art critic.[15]

The city had also expressed concern that the pageant would glorify homosexuality on stage and that most if not all the performers would surely be homosexuals. Not content to simply remind Oklahoma City that "homosexual expression is protected" by the First Amendment, the court added this bit of commentary on popular culture: "Whether the pageant is an open expression of homosexuality is irrelevant. In view of acclaimed performances by Dustin Hoffman, Julie Andrews, Flip Wilson, Harvey Korman, Tony Curtis and Milton Berle in the roles of female impersonators, such impersonations may not be necessarily equated with homosexuality."[16]

The far more sexually charged genre of dance involved in the Supreme Court's decision, discussed earlier, to uphold the application of Indiana's public indecency statute to nude or seminude dancing may explain how an opposite ruling resulted in this Oklahoma case. Still, both cases dealt at least in part with government officials' fear of "secondary effects"—prostitution and organized crime in Indiana, presumably an increase in homosexual activity in Oklahoma. Such feared secondary effects were sufficient to justify upholding the Indiana statute. The federal court in Oklahoma, interestingly, felt obliged to remind us that cross-dressing and homosexuality are not the same. Yet the event at issue was not billed as the "Female Impersonators of America" pageant, it was called the "Miss *Gay* America" pageant. By downplaying the event's links to overt homosexual conduct, the court avoided the more difficult question—how much should the law *care* about the number of audience members who might have same-sex relations at home after seeing homosexuality "glorified" on stage?[17]

A much more spontaneous dance performance than those in question in the Miss Gay America pageant was at issue in a case from the 1980s against a Minneapolis health club that had ejected one of its gay members. The Minnesota Court of Appeals reports the circumstances surrounding Philip Blanding's dance: "On March 17, 1983, there were only a few people at the Club. Blanding and two others were working out on a piece of equipment. When a certain tune was played over the sound system, they discussed whether it was an Irish jig for St. Patrick's Day or something else. One of them said it was a schottische, and Blanding said he would show them how it was done. He did four or five quick steps."[18]

A club manager described the incident as disruptive and was overheard to tell another member of the club that he was "not going to put up with this gay stuff anymore." Blanding successfully fought the club's decision to ban him, in that the local civil rights ordinance included references to sexual orientation discrimination in public accommodations.

The *Blanding* case is interesting in part because of what it does not say. Nowhere does the court address the club owner's equation in his mind of dancing in the company of same-sex companions with same-sex sexual orientation. Is the underlying assumption that men who dance with—or for—other men are gay? Or, given that Blanding could have been teaching his buddies how to make more of an impression on their next date with their girlfriends, is the assumption instead that men who *dance* are gay? Then, too, consider that the local ordinance protected Blanding precisely because the club management equated his behavior with a homosexual "acting out." When a gay patron dances—even the schottische (as opposed to whatever disco or country western or other steps are in fashion at the time in gay bars)—is he "acting gay"?

Shifting our focus from Minnesota to the West Coast, fears that too many audience members who might be inspired to dance in the aisles at performances by such artists as Todd Rundgren and Patti Smith would be gay led the Burbank, California, city council to refuse to rent out its Starlight Bowl to these artists' promoters. (The council also nixed a Jackson Browne concert because some council members objected to his political activism in opposition to nuclear power.) A federal appellate court had no trouble deciding that such arbitrary uses of government authority were violations of the First Amendment.[19] Because the decision flowed so naturally from well-established judicial precedent, the court did not need to address the more interesting sociocultural questions the dispute posed. For example, if a group of heterosexuals dances in the aisles at a Rolling Stones concert, does this action serve an identity-affirming symbolic function any more or less than gay patrons dancing at a Patti Smith concert?

This brief review of the performance dance case law has certainly provided a window to the judiciary's handling of First Amendment issues raised by artists' argued right to communicate symbolically with their audiences. Yet most First Amendment litigation involving dancers has concerned more social nontheatrical events. We next turn to a review of that body of case law.

SOCIAL DANCE—DANCING FOR ONESELF

Long before the number of queer political associations flourished, each with its own 501.c (3) tax-exempt foundation, almost the only public place where gays congregated with regularity was at bars.[20] Thus the earliest freedom of association cases spurred by the nascent gay rights movement in this country involved the revocation of liquor licenses. A complete review of this body of case law is beyond the scope of this essay, which focuses only on cases in which the issue of patrons dancing together played a key role.[21]

Much of the early case law—circa the 1950s—comes from California, because the bars there were very profitable and the state courts were rather progressive at the time.[22] As early as 1951 the California Supreme Court held that "members of the public of lawful age," whether gay or straight, "have a right to patronize a public restaurant and bar so long as they are not committing illegal or immoral acts."[23] In response the state legislature passed a statute explicitly forbidding the gathering of "sexual perverts" in establishments serving liquor. Although the court struck down the law in 1959, it emphasized that "conduct which may fall short of aggressive and uninhibited participation in fulfilling the sexual urges of homosexuals . . . may nonetheless offend good morals and decency."[24] Of special relevance for us is the court's suggestion that had the investigating officers encountered such behaviors as "women dancing with other women," its ruling might have been different.[25]

Thus it is no surprise that a state appellate court, in upholding the revocation of a liquor license from Hazel Nickola's San Mateo–area tavern, paid special attention to the patrons' enjoyment of same-sex dancing.[26] This 1958 case is best understood by examining excerpts from the testimony offered at trial by sheriff's department and undercover agents from the Division of Alcoholic Beverage Control:

> There were between 100 and 250 patrons in the establishment, over 90 per cent male. . . . There was almost continuous dancing taking place during these visits. The vast majority of dancers were men dancing with other men in close and affectionate embrace. Many of the men had their arms wrapped around each other's waists, or shoulders, or buttocks. Many men were observed kissing or fondling or biting each other, or holding hands, and other men were seen sitting on the laps of their male companions and kissing and fondling each other. The few female patrons were dressed in mannish attire, and most of them danced with each other. Some of the male dancers, while dancing, wrapped their arms around the buttocks of their companions and vigorously rotated their pelvic

areas, to the evident enjoyment of other patrons. Men were seen powdering their faces, talking in effeminate voices, and generally acting like over-affectionate females. Two of the agents were solicited to dance by a male patron who was called Ramona. . . . Other evidence could be referred to, but the above summary is illustrative of the type of activity observed in the tavern over a rather lengthy period.[27]

A few years later New York's highest court, while upholding a liquor license revocation, at least said that not all same-sex dancing by patrons would subject tavern owners to this particular sanction.[28] Again, testimony of an undercover police officer was dispositive. Here, the officer said that he saw "approximately 14 males dancing in the rear portion of the premises," that they were "dancing to a slow record," and they were "embracing one another and gyrating and moving."[29] If the justices' words are to be taken at face value, this alone would have been permissible—the court said it would not punish bar owners for allowing their patrons, heterosexual or homosexual, to engage in such activities. But the police also testified that the patrons of this particular bar "[felt] each other's private parts and posteriors" while dancing, behavior that the court concluded crossed the line. "Fondling of the primary sexual organs in licensed premises on a public dance floor," the court tells us, "clearly constitutes disorder whether between heterosexuals or homosexuals."[30]

The more contemporary practice of truly treating same-sex and opposite-sex dancing in bars as constitutional equivalents resulted from neither a landmark Supreme Court decision nor any federal legislation. Rather, the change was a more evolutionary one, beginning in some courts' willingness to attribute elements of freedom of association to same-sex gatherings in general.[31]

Broadening the focus now to social dance in venues other than bars, let me note at the outset that the U.S. Supreme Court has held that social dancing not designed to impart a message to an identifiable audience merits no First Amendment protection, either as symbolic conduct or as freedom of association. Yet the case law has involved situations in which the state has had on its side the additional interest of protecting minors. Thus generalizing from the Court's holdings to situations involving adult dancers, gay or otherwise, should be done with caution.

The leading case is *City of Dallas v. Stanglin* (1989). The operator of a skating rink that also boasted a dance floor sought unsuccessfully to overturn a city ordinance requiring that "juice bars" catering to underage customers must admit *only* those aged fourteen to eighteen. The argued state interest was to ensure that adults who might be predisposed to take advantage of minors not be given such a convenient opportunity to socialize with teens. In upholding the rulings of the Texas courts, a unanimous U.S. Supreme Court said that the Constitution does not recognize "a generalized right of 'social association' that includes chance encounters in dance halls."[32] Interestingly, the statute at issue did permit minors and adults both to patronize the skating rink proper, though not the dance hall. The Court saw no logical contradiction here, reasoning that "skating involves less physical contact than dancing," and while "the differences between the two activities may not be striking," they were sufficient to pass constitutional muster.[33] One wonders what the Court might have done with a venue boasting intergenerational wrestling instead of skating. Is skating a uniquely innocent activity, or is dancing an activity uniquely likely to lead to the kinds of genital-groping behavior observed by undercover police in the tavern cases discussed earlier?

In a 1985 case from rural Arkansas the U.S. Court of Appeals for the Eighth Circuit upheld a school district's refusal to rent its gymnasium to a group of parents that wanted to hold a dance for (presumably heterosexual) teenaged children, apparently "because some members of the board, or some people in the community, believe that dancing which involves physical contact between the sexes is immoral or irreligious."[34] The court found that the parents' claims did not even raise First Amendment issues:

> The plaintiffs simply want their children to have the opportunity to dance for social or recreational purposes, for their own edification, and not for the enjoyment of an audience. The dancing here is not claimed to involve any political or ideological expression. It is not intended to convey any kind of message, unless it be the mes-

sage that the plaintiffs do not believe that dancing is wrong. In these circumstances, it is our view that conduct as opposed to speech is involved.[35]

To reach this conclusion the court felt the need to distinguish the situation in Arkansas from the facts of an earlier decision from another federal circuit involving the Gay Student Organization at the University of New Hampshire.[36] Since the 1970s gay student groups have had to go to court literally dozens of times to win formal campus recognition and access to such tangible benefits as student activity-fee funding, or both. The New Hampshire case is unusual in that the university was perfectly willing to recognize and fund the group but only for educational as opposed to social purposes.[37] Same-sex dances were especially to be avoided, because media coverage of a gay dance had prompted the governor to pressure the school's board of trustees to forbid any further use of funds for same-sex social events. The federal appellate court that found for the students began by suggesting that the line between social events and the kinds of political events that the state knew it had no authority to restrict is not always a clear one:

> Even a lecture or discussion, which appear to be the only types of meetings which the [university] would allow the GSO to hold, becomes a social event if beer is served beforehand or coffee afterward. Teas, coffees and dinners form the backbone of many a political candidate's campaign, and yet these activities would seemingly be subject to prohibition. While a university may have some latitude in regulating organizations such as fraternities or sororities which can be purely social, its efforts to restrict the activities of a cause-oriented group like the GSO stand on a different footing. Considering the important role that social events can play in individuals' efforts to associate to further their common beliefs, the prohibition of all social events must be taken to be a substantial abridgment of associational rights, even if assumed to be an indirect one.[38]

The court further suggested that even purely social dances, when convened by openly queer organizations, cannot help but have an element of performance to them. Such events necessarily convey a message to all who care to notice, the court tells us. The message is "that homosexuals exist, that they feel repressed by existing laws and attitudes, that they wish to emerge from their isolation, and that public understanding of their attitudes and problems is desirable for society." (One wonders what percentage of gay dance bar patrons are aware of the political sophistication they are demonstrating by their choice of leisure activity.) Given the context of the dance at issue in the *Bonner* case from New Hampshire, the appellate court felt comfortable concluding that dance "is itself a form of expression protected by the First Amendment."[39]

In the Arkansas skating-rink case the court found that the Gay Student Organization dances described in *Bonner* were "efforts to organize the homosexual minority and educate the public as to its plight," thus "convey[ing] an ideological message." By contrast, "the social dancing involved here [Arkansas]," the court opined, "is quite different, because it is not designed to convey any particular idea."[40] Might the decision have been different if the parent-plaintiffs were all members of the local PFLAG [Parents and Friends of Lesbians and Gays] chapter seeking to create an amiable and *safe* space for their children to socialize?

More recently, gay students at the University of South Alabama canceled a planned dance out of fear that media coverage of the event would incur the wrath of the state government.[41] Their fears were well founded. It seems that the student government at Auburn University, also in Alabama, had voted not to recognize the campus's gay group, an action promptly reversed by the school's administration. As a result, the state legislature passed a law prohibiting any expenditure of state money for campus groups that "promote" or "foster" a lifestyle inconsistent with Alabama's sodomy statute—although it permitted funding of groups that oppose such a lifestyle. While a case seeking to overturn that law was pending—it has since been found to be a blatant violation of the First Amendment—the dean of students at the University of South Alabama suggested to that campus's gay group that it cancel the dance planned to celebrate its first anniversary as an officially recognized campus organization.

The precedent involving the University of New Hampshire's

Gay Student Organization proved invaluable to a young man from Cumberland, Rhode Island, who wished to take another young man to his high school prom. Here is how U.S. District Judge Raymond J. Pettine described Aaron Fricke's predicament:

> Most of the time, a young man's choice of a date for the senior prom is of no great interest to anyone other than the student, his companion, and, perhaps, a few of their classmates. But in Aaron Fricke's case, the school authorities actively disapprove of his choice, the other students are upset, the community is abuzz, and out-of-state newspapers consider the matter newsworthy. All this fuss arises because Aaron Fricke's intended escort is another young man. Claiming that the school's refusal to allow him to bring a male escort violates his first and fourteenth amendment rights, Fricke seeks a preliminary injunction ordering the school officials to allow him to attend with a male escort.[42]

The high school prom dispute also stands on the border between dance as performance and dance as social event. We do not normally think of social dance as conveying a message to a larger audience, but Aaron Fricke's choice of a prom date surely was designed to be expressive. Fricke testified that "his attendance would have a certain political element," and Judge Pettine concluded that "his message will take a form uniquely consonant with the setting he wishes to attend and participate in like everyone else."[43] So it was that Judge Pettine insisted that Fricke be permitted to take a same-sex date to the prom.

An unpublished 1984 case from California resulted ultimately in Disneyland's rescinding its policy against same-sex dancing.[44] Teens Andrew Exler and Shawn Elliott were ejected from the park after they had danced together during a "Date Night" in the autumn of 1980. Plaintiffs' attorney Ron Talmo shared with the court what he took to be a fundamental irony of the case:

> At the same time that my clients were dancing at Disneyland I'm home watching *Fiddler on the Roof*, and if the Court is familiar with *Fiddler on the Roof*, there's a dramatic scene in there where the radical male crosses the line at a wedding and asks a female to dance with him, and all the males are upset because males only dance with

other males. . . . It's custom all over the world that males dance with males, females dance with females.[45]

In contrast, Disneyland's attorneys argued that "if these two gentlemen are permitted to dance together, then the next step is they will be permitted to ask others that they don't know to dance."[46] Interestingly, they did not feel the need to paint the scenario any more elaborately, to carry the narrative to the next step. To be asked to engage in same-sex dancing, they thus argue, is an obvious affront to community morals.

While Exler did not succeed in 1980 in having a preliminary injunction issued against Disneyland, four years later another Orange County judge, ruling in the same case, found that the park had violated the teens' rights under the state's Unruh Civil Rights Act.

CONCLUSION

Queer people in America certainly do not enjoy the full measure of constitutional rights granted to heterosexuals. One need look no further than the Supreme Court's 5–4 ruling in *Bowers v. Hardwick* (1986), which upheld the constitutionality of sodomy statutes as applied to consensual same-sex conduct.[47] That gays alone are advised to not "tell" if they are to be retained in the military is further evidence of this blatant inequality.[48]

The lesson of the case law discussed here, however, stands in counterpoint to the generally true assertion that gays are a legally oppressed minority in this country. Plainly put, queer people seem to have been granted in recent years at least the same and likely more rights to boogie than have heterosexuals. This is especially true with respect to social dancing. Whereas the Supreme Court has told us that no constitutional right to engage in such activity exists, lower federal courts have on several occasions suggested that same-sex dance *always* carries communicative elements and thus merits First Amendment protection.

This perhaps counterintuitive status of the law should not really be surprising, given that gay litigants are generally more likely to prevail when they are able to make plausible First Amendment claims to freedom of expression, rather than depend upon Fourteenth Amendment arguments asserting a right to equal protection of law or to a right of privacy.[49] Although we tell ourselves that we are an "invisible" minority, the gay rights movement is, at its core, a free speech movement. Implicit in this characterization is the unlikelihood of our suffering antigay discrimination in the absence of some kind of communicative action that ends the invisibility. How we choose to become visible might be by coming out to a potential employer, participating in political associations likely to attract media attention, or even by taking to the dance floor.

NOTES

1. *Barnes v. Glen Theatre*, 501 U.S. 560, 586 (1991) (White, J., dissenting).

2. In other situations beyond the scope of this essay the nature of queer dancing was part of a legal dispute. One hospital orderly's having insisted that a same-sex coworker dance with him, for example, was a portion of a sexual harassment claim. See *Morgan v. Massachusetts General Hospital*, 901 F.2d 186 (1st Cir. 1990). Then, too, a federal district court in New York ruled in a Lanham Act (unfair business practices) case that a nightclub could call itself the Tunnel (a name also used by the plaintiff organization to describe its gay-friendly Sunday dances) in that the former was marketed more narrowly to a leather audience. See *Lobo Enterprises v. The Tunnel*, 693 F. Supp. 71 (S.D.N.Y. 1988).

3. U.S. Supreme Court cases that speak to symbolic conduct include *Stromberg v. California*, 283 U.S. 359 (1931); *West Virginia Board of Education v. Barnette*, 319 U.S. 624 (1943); *Texas v. Johnson*, 491 U.S. 397 (1989); *U.S. v. Eichman*, 496 U.S. 310 (1990); *Hurley v. Irish American Gay, Lesbian, and Bisexual Group of Boston*, 515 U.S. 557 (1995); and *Tinker v. Des Moines School District*, 393 U.S. 503 (1969). Pertinent First Amendment cases include *NAACP v. Alabama*, 357 U.S. 449 (1958), and *Griswold v. Connecticut*, 381 U.S. 479 (1965).

4. See, for example, *Southeastern Promotions v. Conrad*, 420 U.S. 546 (1975), in which the U.S. Supreme Court held that live theatric and dance events enjoy the same degree of First Amendment protection as motion pictures do against prior restraint by government interference.

5. *California v. Larue*, 409 U.S. 109 (1972).

6. 409 U.S. at 111.

7. *New York State Liquor Authority v. Bellanca*, 452 U.S. 714, 719 n.3 (1981) (Stevens, J., dissenting).

8. *City of Newport, Kentucky v. Iacobucci*, 479 U.S. 92, 101–2 (1986) (Stevens, J., dissenting).

9. *Barnes v. Glen Theatre*, 501 U.S. 560 (1991).

10. 501 U.S. at 581 (Souter, D., concurring).

11. 501 U.S. at 590–91 (White, B., Marshall, T., Blackmun, H., and Stevens, J., dissenting).

12. *City of Erie v. Pap's A.M.*, 120 S. Ct. 1382 (2000).

13. *Kristie v. City of Oklahoma City*, 572 F. Supp. 88 (W.D.Okla. 1983).

14. 572 F. Supp. at 90.

15. 572 F. Supp. at 91.

16. 572 F. Supp. at 91.

17. This is the same strategy that a number of federal courts have used in holding it unconstitutional for state university administrators to withhold official campus recognition from organized groups of gay and lesbian students. In response to the administrative claim that sanctioning these groups will lead to an increase in sodomy violations, the judicial response has not been "so what?" but, rather, "no, we don't think it will, actually." See, for example, *Gay Alliance of Students v. Matthews*, 544 F.2d 162 (4th Cir. 1976).

18. *Blanding v. Sports and Health Club*, 373 N.W.2d 784, 787 (Minn. Ct. App. 1985).

19. *Cinevision Corporation v. City of Burbank*, 745 F.2d 560 (9th Cir. 1984).

20. Paul Siegel, "Lesbian and Gay Rights as a Free Speech Issue: A Review of Relevant Case Law," in Michelle A. Wolf and Alfred P. Kielwasser, eds., *Gay People, Sex, and the Media* (New York: Harrington Park, 1991), 221.

21. A more complete review of the case law is available in Rhonda Rivera, "Our Straight-Laced Judges: The Legal Positions of Homosexual Persons in the United States," *Hastings Law Journal* 30 (April 1979): 913–24.

22. William N. Eskridge Jr., "Challenging the Apartheid of the Closet," *Hofstra Law Review* 25 (spring 1997): 867.

23. *Stoumen v. Reilly*, 234 P.2d 969, 971 (Cal. 1951).

24. *Vallerga v. Department of Alcoholic Beverage Control*, 347 P.2d 909 (Cal. 1959).

25. 347 P.2d at 912.

26. *Nickola v. Munro*, 328 P.2d 271 (Cal. Dist. Ct. App. 1958).

27. 328 P.2d at 272–73.

28. *Becker v. New York State Liquor Authority*, 234 N.E.2d 443 (N.Y. 1967).

29. 234 N.E.2d at 443.

30. 234 N.E.2d at 444.

31. Eskridge, "Challenging the Apartheid," 869–70.

32. *City of Dallas v. Stanglin*, 490 U.S. 19, 25 (1989).

33. 490 U.S. at 27–28.

34. *Jarman v. Williams*, 753 F.2d 76, 78 n.3 (8th Cir. 1985).

35. 753 F.2d at 78.

36. *Gay Student Organization v. Bonner*, 367 F. Supp. 1088 (N.H. 1973), *aff'd* on other grounds, 509 F.2d 652 (1st Cir. 1974).

37. At the University of Georgia the gay student group had been denied permission to host a conference that would have included a dance. But the right to dance was not a central theme of the case. See *Wood v. Davison*, 351 F. Supp. 543 (N.D.Ga. 1972).

38. *Bonner,* 509 F.2d at 659–60.

39. 509 F.2d at 661.

40. *Jarman,* 753 F.2d 76, 78.

41. *Gay Lesbian Bisexual Alliance v. Sessions,* 917 F. Supp. 1548 (M.D.Ala. 1996), *aff'd sub nom. Gay Lesbian Bisexual Alliance v. Pryor,* 110 F.3d 1543 (11th Cir. 1997).

42. *Fricke v. Lynch,* 491 F. Supp. 381, 382 (R.I. 1980).

43. 491 F. Supp. at 383–84.

44. *Exler v. Disneyland,* #342021 (Super. Ct. Orange County, Cal., 1984). The case was first filed in 1980 and decided four years later. Apparently, the park management maintained for a few years thereafter that the injunction issued against it applied narrowly only to the immediate plaintiffs and that it thus had the right to continue to enforce the same-sex dancing ban against any other patrons. Under threat of further litigation involving new plaintiffs, the park changed its policy in 1989 (Mary Lou Felton, "Disneyland Pledges No Sex Bias: Three Gay Men Drop Suit over Dancing," *Los Angeles Times,* September 30, 1989, p. 23).

Nowadays, of course, the Disney company is very gay affirming; it embraces annual "Gay Days" at Disneyland and Disney World and has incurred the wrath of fundamentalist groups for some of its programming, notably the ABC-TV series *Ellen.*

45. *Exler v. Disneyland,* trial transcript, p. 14. The transcript was provided by attorney Ron Talmo.

46. *Exler* transcript, 17.

47. *Bowers v. Hardwick,* 478 U.S. 186 (1986).

48. Paul Siegel, "Second-Hand Prejudice, Racial Analogies, and Shared Showers: Why 'Don't Ask, Don't Tell' Won't Sell," *Notre Dame Journal of Law, Ethics, and Public Policy* 9, no. 1 (1985): 185–213.

49. David Cole and William N. Eskridge Jr., "From Hand-Holding to Sodomy: First Amendment Protection of Homosexual (Expressive) Conduct," *Harvard Civil Rights Civil Liberties Law Review* 29, no. 1 (1993): 319–86. Gays are not uniquely able to call upon their minority status to claim what may seem to some a special measure of First Amendment protection. That rap music performs a special political and artistic function within the African American community, for example, went a long way toward ensuring that the obscenity prosecution in Florida against Luther Campbell and 2 Live Crew would ultimately be unsuccessful. See *Luke Records v. Navarro,* 960 F.2d 134, 136 (11th Cir. 1992). Contrast this, however, with *Golden v. McCaughtry,* 937 F. Supp. 818 (E.D.Wis. 1996), and *Betts v. McCaughtry,* 827 F. Supp. 1400 (W.D. Wis. 1993), upholding prison policies of withholding from prison inmates any CDs ordered by them bearing the distributor's "parental advisory" label regarding song lyrics, despite both courts' recognition that rap music might disproportionately be so labeled.

9

Queer Kinesthesia:
Performativity on the Dance Floor

Jonathan Bollen

> I want to consider queer as movement.
> —*Elspeth Probyn*, Outside Belongings

What would it take to consider queer as movement? What resources would such an undertaking require? And what kind of analysis could it generate? In this chapter I take Elspeth Probyn's proposal literally. Drawing on Judith Butler's performative theory of gender, I investigate the social dancing performed at gay and lesbian dance parties in Sydney, Australia. I ask what really matters about dance-floor practice and pursue an analysis of the kinesthesia of queer identifications and the choreography of queer desiring.

GETTING HOME, OR WHAT COUNTS AS REAL

> The problem with the Ball is how to get home afterwards. . . . Anyone who acquiesces to the beat of the Ball at Mardi Gras acknowledges an alien rule: that the signs of sex are free from the burden of representing anything, they are set loose for promiscuous play. . . . But once outside the alien zone of understanding, once outside the orbit of the beat, the bashers lurk in the shadows, ready to attack the gap between sign and body.
> —*Mackenzie Wark*, "A Queer Peace Came over Me"

It may seem odd to begin a chapter exploring the specificities of lesbian and gay dance-floor practice by invoking the dilemmas of getting home. Whether it involves running the gauntlet of queer bashers lurking in the shadows, dodging the odd straight press photographer desperate for that morning-after shot, or sliding into the relative safety of a taxi ("So, had a good night, fellas?"), the dilemmas of getting home are far from the pleasures of the dance floor. Indeed, such is the significance of the post-party process that it even has a name, or two: "recovery" is what you do on the day after, "coming down" is what you go through. It may be eased by the delights of good company, the odd vodka and lime, and the promise of sex, or it may be deferred by a quick shower, a fresh change of clothes, and then out for more partying, but there is something inevitably resolute about getting home—*in the end.*

I begin with that inevitably obvious trope of escape-return that structures the narratives of many a dance-party experience, because it can present a challenge for an analysis of dance-floor practice that seeks to investigate what is happening on the dance floor when lesbians and gay men dance. What is the relation between the dance floor and the everyday? What is the nature of the boundary that separates the two? And how might that boundary serve to circumscribe not only an analysis, but also the very possibilities of the dance floor itself?

The dance floors I am investigating come into existence for discrete periods of time, usually between ten and twelve hours, within the bounded, access-controlled site of what was once Sydney's Royal Agricultural Society Showground (now Fox Movie Studios). These dance floors are central, both structurally and experientially, to the large dance parties that have been held as fundraising events for Sydney lesbian and gay community organizations since the early 1980s. The largest of these dance parties, attracting up to twenty thousand participants in recent years, are produced by Sydney Gay and Lesbian Mardi Gras to finance the organization's annual month-long cultural festival that culminates in a spectacular nighttime street parade at the end of February. Yet from a party goer's perspective, this fund-raising function is often secondary. The significance of the Mardi Gras Party, held after the parade, and the Sleaze Ball, held in early October, is their status as large-scale community events, as experiential touchstones of lesbian and gay community. During the 1990s, these dance parties became central to an ongoing debate articulating relations between lesbians/gays and straights in terms of community, discrimination, and cultural respect.

The "straights-at-the-parties" debate has been long-winded, exasperating, and intractable. It has generated letters to the community press, public meetings and consultations, regulations on membership and ticket purchases, and incitements of communitarian responsibility. And yet, as any piece of "straights-at-the-parties" rhetoric makes clear, it is the dance floor that is at the heart of the matter. The relative ease with which the dance floor is imagined as an "alien zone of promiscuous play," a safe place free from the violence of a homophobic world, has demanded the exertion of an elaborate set of policing mechanisms to ensure that the dance floor lives up to its promise. This is a utopian promise that literalizes a metaphor: the dance floor as ecstatic vision and grounded experience of gay and lesbian community.

Yet to demarcate the queer *communitas* inside a dance party from a hetero-normative everyday outside the event is to circumscribe the dance floor as a domain of subversive play, isolated from the demands of the everyday to which dance-floor escapades are bound to return. Such an analysis triggers a domino effect of mutually exclusive distinctions, that adhere rigidly to *either* the dance floor *or* the everyday: safety/violence, fantasy/reality, freedom/constraint, liberation/oppression, subversive/hegemonic, queer/banal, homo/hetero. This is precisely the analysis that informs Mackenzie Wark's dramatization of the dilemmas of getting home. Indeed, the only assault to date on the common-sense resilience of such an analysis has been Walter Hughes's brilliant proposal "that disco is less a decadent indulgence than a disciplinary, regulatory discourse."[1]

In his essay, "In the Empire of the Beat: Discipline and Disco," Hughes analyzes gay disco as a disciplinary practice whereby "the power of constructing homosexuality . . . and the pleasure attendant on this exercise of power" are seized from the everyday and redeployed on the dance floor as gay men's erotic submission to disco's "insistent, disciplinary beat."[2] Nevertheless, an analysis based on queer reversal remains contingent upon the determinants it contests. As Gregory W. Bredbeck has argued, Hughes "totalizes a relationship between hegemony [the everyday] and subculture [the dance floor], assuming, first, that power emanates only from dominant discourses, and second, that resistance happens only against hegemony."[3] Bredbeck outlines an alternative analysis of gay disco that would examine

> both how identity is embedded within the material processes of specific social rituals and in specific social spaces, and the extent to which such spaces and practices suggest a need to look at gay identification in its own specific social manifestations, not simply in relation to the categorizations of hegemonic ideology.[4]

Following Bredbeck, the approach taken here withholds large-scale characterizations of the relation between the dance floor and the everyday in order to detach that array of distinctions from their rigid adherence to one or the other. It pursues an analysis from a position, as it were, on the dance floor, not as a space set free from the demands of the everyday, but as a space where precisely those demands, as Hughes would suggest, are redeployed in effective ways. In doing this, it engages Judith Butler's theorization of performativity to articulate corporeal practices and disciplinary regulation to the processes of identification and desiring. It also contests what counts as real.

One of the more disabling effects of a rigid separation of the dance floor from the everyday is that whatever happens on the dance floor is thereby rendered vulnerable to dismissal with such disarming exclamations as "It's only a dance party! What difference does it make in the real world?" Yet, if Brian Currid is correct, "the complicated play of identifications that circulate around the dance floor reveal that all identity and community performances are contingent on *how real they feel*, not how real they are."[5]

DANCING AMONG OTHERS

There is a third term forgotten in this haste to liberate ourselves from the law. Identity is ambiguous because body performance is never singular. And body performance is never singular because between the body and the law is the other. I have already suggested that it is the other who causes the dance. I want to also argue that, as we dance with the other, identity is not only ambiguous and open to change but limited in its potential.
—*Rosalyn Diprose, "Performing Body-Identity"*

In *Gender Trouble*, feminist philosopher Judith Butler proposes a performative theory of gender identity that presents a challenging yet appealing analytical apparatus for a project investigating the specificities of lesbian and gay dance-floor practice. The challenge is that "gender ought not to be construed as a stable identity or locus of agency from which various acts follow; rather, gender is an identity tenuously constituted in time, instituted in an exterior space through a *stylized repetition of acts*."[6] Its appeal for an analysis of dance-floor practice is that this stylization "must be understood as the mundane way in which bodily gestures, movements, and styles of various kinds constitute the illusion of an abiding gendered self."[7] In such an analysis, the dance floor would become the site for an investigation of those stylized acts, those ways of moving, or movement practices by which gendered and otherwise sexualized identities are sustained. A performative analysis of gay and lesbian social dancing would be able to link the specificities of dance-floor practice to larger questions about experiential manifestations of the sexual identities "lesbian" and "gay."

The risk, however, in mobilizing a *performative* theory of identity to analyze dance-floor *performances* is that the dance floor might be construed, in opposition to the everyday, as simply a site for "proliferating gender configurations *outside* the restricting frames of masculinist domination and compulsory heterosexuality."[8] This is the kind of (mis)application of performative theory that Butler redresses in subsequent work. It is one that celebrates the political promise of performative theory—that gender enactment be repeated with difference—while forgetting that it is precisely through repetition that the enactment of gender is secured. But, as Rosalyn Diprose suggests, Butler's theory lends itself to such (mis)applications because "for the most part, there are only two terms in her account: the performing body and the law."[9]

In *Bodies That Matter*, Butler substantially reworks the performative theory of gender in an articulation of the processes by which bodies come to matter, "where 'to matter' means at once 'to materialize' and 'to mean.'"[10] According to Butler, a performative interpellation ("It's a girl!" or "It's a boy!") initiates and sustains a process of ongoing "citation" of regulatory norms that materialize the body as gendered. Materialization is thus both the process through which bodily matter takes shape and the process through which bodies become significant, become signifying bodies.[11] Conceiving performativity as a citational process ensures that the materialization of gender is always a "re-citation" of regulatory norms. And because the body is materialized over time as a "sedimentation" of citational acts, its capacity to reinvent itself remains contingent upon the ongoing "re-citation" of regulatory norms.

> The paradox of subjectivation (*assujetissement*) is precisely that the subject who would resist such norms is itself enabled, if not produced, by such norms. Although this constitutive constraint does not foreclose the possibility of agency, it does locate agency as a reiterative or rearticulatory practice, immanent to power, and not a relation of external opposition to power.[12]

Butler's reworking of the theory of performative identification considerably strengthens it against analyses that would propose that dance-floor practices could secure performative effects beyond the operation of regulatory norms. Here, it is important to note that however tightly Butler binds the subject's relation to the law, a notion of repetition with difference remains central to "the possibility of agency." Regulatory norms are never simply reproduced because "reiterations are never simply replicas of the same."[13] Rather, performativity is a citational process that implies degrees of "approximation" and "failure," partly because regulatory norms acquire their authority across the history of their reiterative citation, but also because regulatory norms never govern in advance the differing social contexts of their future deployment.[14] Yet the contribution of social context in enabling the production of difference remains largely underdeveloped in Butler's theorization of performativity as citationality in *Bodies That Matter*.[15]

In her essay, "Performing Body-Identity," Rosalyn Diprose reworks Butler's performative theory of gender by building a notion of social context into the account. Whereas Butler has recourse to "the paradox of subjectivation" and the logic of repetition with difference to account for the limitations and possibilities of "performing body-identity," Diprose articulates that circumscription and potential in social terms: "as we dance with the other, identity is not only ambiguous and open to change but limited in its potential."[16] There is also a more particular reason to take up Diprose's work. Butler's reworking of performativity entailed a rhetorical shift away from the *enactment* of gender as a *kinesthetic* stylization toward the *materialization* of gender as a *morphological* process. Casting the theory of performativity in terms of the materiality of bodies raises questions about practices, like dancing, which may not secure their performative effects within a material register. Diprose, on the other hand, expands the choreographic rhetoric of Butler's earlier work.

Diprose reconfigures the relation between the "performing-body" and "the law" by inserting between them the constitutive role of the other. Following the phenomenology of Maurice Merleau-Ponty, she argues that "the emergence of a body we can call our own . . . occurs through the organisation of the body in reciprocal relation to others."[17] Here, the other performs a mediating role between the performing-body and the law: "The law works through the other with whom you dwell."[18] In tracing the role of the other in constituting the self, Diprose outlines "a system of indistinction . . . between my own body as it feels to me, its visual or objectified image and the body of the other."[19] Notably, Diprose describes this "system" of "syncretic sociability" in kinesthetic terms: "the transfer of movements and gestures between dispersed bodies."[20]

This is an appealing point of departure for an analysis of the dance floor as social context. A dance floor is a space in which the presence of others is crucial. In other words, a dance floor really only happens, *as a dance floor*, when there are other people dancing on it. Indeed, touring a dance floor before or after its use only serves to elicit that sense of excited anticipation or ghostly potential that is characteristic of the empty or abandoned theater. Thus one of the defining features of the dance-floor experience is an involving engagement in relations with others. Understanding how relations with others are negotiated is central to understanding the possibilities and limitations of the dance floor as social context. I shall draw two insights from Diprose's rearticulation of the performative proposal to structure an analysis of sociality on the dance floor at gay and lesbian dance parties in Sydney.

"Dwelling-with-Others": Closeness and Openness

As bodies are constituted and live as an interworld of potentiality opened onto others, we have no means of "knowing" or becoming a body other than through a familiar dwelling-with-others in the world.
—*Rosalyn Diprose, "Performing Body-Identity"*

How are dancers "opened onto others" on the dance floor? How is a dance floor "dwelling-with-others" negotiated and experienced? And what social demands does the dance floor make of those who are dancing there? These questions invite consideration of dance-floor relations in terms of proximity (distance between bodies), orientation (where one is facing), and the negotiation of social relations.

To step onto the dance floor at a gay and lesbian dance party is to step into a dense mass of moving bodies. The first task is finding somewhere to dance. Moving through the dance floor entails moving through networks of ongoing social relations. Finding somewhere to dance entails inserting one's self into these networks. For a group of party goers, finding somewhere to dance may entail a linear weaving through the dance floor, in and among others, until a space presents itself in which the group can collect together to dance with each other. For an individual party goer, this process may entail seeking out others, already on the

dance floor, with whom to dance. But whether it is done individually or with a group, the process of finding somewhere to dance
is an experience of taking on the social structure of the dance
floor, negotiated with "respect" for the networks of social relations one is moving among, and acceded to in being taken into
those networks once somewhere to dance is found. "I come
across groups of people or couples and there's space around them
that I can move through. And I'm conscious of that. I mean, I
wouldn't go and start dancing right in the middle of a group of
people. But I do find that there are spaces around those groups
or couples and occasionally individuals for me to use to dance in"
(Olivia, Hand in Hand 1995).[21]

Once you have found somewhere to dance, relations on the
dance floor are experienced as an ongoing "opening onto others."
Dancing on a dance floor means negotiating the demands of proximity and faciality. By proximity, I mean not only the spatial distance between bodies, but also how that spatial distance becomes
an experience of social distance, how dancing with someone is to
be "close" to that person. By faciality I mean bodily orientation,
but in its interactional sense: eye contact and facial expressions, but
also uses of the front of the body, front-to-front interactions,
changes in frontal orientation, and how exposing your "face" is to
be open to social interaction. Whom you are dancing near, where
you are facing, and to whom you address your dancing: this is how
social relations are ventured, negotiated, and sustained on the
dance floor. It is also how social relations are enacted as party goers
manipulate relations by making orientational shifts, by extending
or retracting facial engagements, and by pursuing subtle locomotional trajectories, useful for their lack of apparent intentionality, to
move away from someone without disturbing him or her or to
make a move on someone without alarming that person.

On a dance floor, party goers are exposed to a constantly unfolding and always involving profusion of social relations. Attending to these relations, to their implications and potentials, is
one of the pleasures of the dance floor, a pleasure that can sustain
interest for hours. It is also one of the demands that the dance
floor makes. One party goer I interviewed spoke of a "hierarchy"

of social engagement on the dance floor whereby he would engage in proximal relations of faciality—what he termed "dancing around" someone—"more often with my boyfriend, less often with people that I know, and not at all with strangers, unless, you know, I might smile at them, or whatever" (Jack, Mardi Gras Party 1995). Other party goers drew distinctions between dancing with a partner or friends and dancing "alone" with strangers.

Dancing with friends entails a clustering of social relations on the dance floor, or what one party goer described as "who's there and what configurations are forming and breaking down and reforming" (Jason, Sleaze Ball 1993). During the first few hours at a dance party, when the dance floor is relatively uncrowded, it is easy to observe how party goers dance facing each other, in couples or small clusters of three or more. It is here that an array of everyday socializing actions—greetings, waves, smiles, glances, pointings, kisses, hugs, laughter, chats—is incorporated into more dancerly actions, all of which serve to demarcate who is dancing with whom. "And you might go and dance with one individual friend for a while or turn around and dance with the group in a little circle and whatever. And you'll even talk to people, to friends, and they'll say where's so and so, and you'll say just over there, and you point, and someone's wandered off for ten meters or so and then [they] come back" (Jason, Sleaze Ball 1993).

As the dance party proceeds and as the density of bodies on the dance floor increases, these small clusters come to interpenetrate each other and a network of interconnected social relations is woven across the dance floor. This happens when party goers alternate between dancing with a partner or friends and dancing with others around them, by making changes in orientation, extensions of faciality, and adjustments in proximity. "Well usually I'm sort of dancing and I'm looking around and I have a tendency to turn around at the same time, not just dance in the one direction, and because I'm smiling a person might smile back at me and you sort of move closer to each other and then you just sort of adopt a similar dance style, not so much the style, probably the rhythm, and probably dance with them for a while, and then one of you will turn back to the other partner or whoever you were with" (Ricardo, Mardi Gras Party 1995).

In my experience, an active exposure to and engagement in dance-floor relations, with friends and with others dancing around me, is associated with the earlier hours of a dance party, and with a mode of dance-floor sociality party goers call "having fun." Here there is an interest in what is happening around you and in attending to your involvement in dance floor relations. There may be an interest in initiating these relations, but perhaps not an investment in their ongoingness. In other words, as Ricardo explains, after turning around and dancing for a while with someone else, you turn back to whomever you were dancing with previously.

Party goers contrast "having fun" on the dance floor with a more "serious" mode of dance-floor sociality that I associate with the later hours of a dance party. While both modes operate through manipulations of proximity and faciality, the more "serious" mode may be marked by a stronger investment in the ongoingness of dance-floor relations, by an interest not only in their initiation but also in their sustainment. Hence, the transitory relations of "having fun" transform into the more "serious" relations of "cruising" when the directionality of attention is maintained, when facial engagements are sustained, and when ongoing proximity demands ongoing engagement. "But how do I recognize the fact that someone is taking attention? Well, I suppose the eye contact is very—has a lot to do with it. But also whether the person is actually in the vicinity, close to you. I feel that that's obviously got a lot of indication of how they're reacting towards you. If they turn their back and start sort of going off somewhere, well obviously they're not dancing with you or to you or wanting to engage with you. But it's not for very long. It depends. For some people it's a fleeting glance. It's like sampling. They'll go through and sample a lot of people just to see what their reactions are. It's—it can be something like a few minutes to only a few seconds to a lot longer, to many minutes or hours even" (Mitchell, Hand in Hand 1995).

The dance floor demands an engagement in social relations, sustained through a negotiation of closeness (proximity) and openness (faciality). But there are also ways in which dancers moderate and, in some cases, resist those relations. For example, you can refuse to be cruised by looking, turning, or moving away, and partners can disengage from others around them by maintaining close proximity and ongoing facial engagement. More generally, party goers distinguish between a kind of dancing that involves being open to interaction with those around, perhaps through flexible orientational shifting and exploratory locomotional trajectories, and another kind of dancing, usually achieved by closing the eyes, that affords a temporary respite from interaction, but still demands a degree of awareness of other dancers. "Sometimes I'm just totally involved in myself, especially if I am really into it. . . . I just don't notice anyone. I just dance with my eyes closed. I just love that. And even if you have your eyes closed you're still aware of people around you and the lights still affect you. Otherwise, when I dance with my eyes open, I guess you just vaguely scan through the crowd, check out people" (Rebekah, Hand in Hand 1995).

But if opening or closing their eyes readily allows party goers to moderate temporarily their engagement in faciality, moderating proximal distance from other dancers usually involves finding somewhere else to dance. Here a distinction is often made between a more densely packed center of the dance floor and the edges, where there is more room to move, or between dance floors that are more crowded, usually with men, and others, like women-only dance venues, that are less crowded. "Well the RHI would always be much more crowded so you don't have to be aware of what you're doing. You don't even have to do anything almost because there's no room to do it. Yeah, no one's going to notice and you can't really do what you want to do. So that's more of a sort of vaguely move and that's it. But like the women's space will be like more—yeah it depends on how much room there is and that women's space at Mardi Gras you've got more room to dance so you've got more room to move and do what you want to do, so I guess it's more expressive and you're more aware of all your movements. So it depends on whether it's crowded or whether you've got room" (Rebekah, Hand in Hand 1995).

The relation between the amount of space and the movement potential is the extent to which dancers define each other's kinespheric reach: the less space you have, the more restricted and more uniform the movement becomes; the more space you have, the more open the movement possibilities are to variation, to innovation and irregularity. As the negotiation of kinespheric reach comes to literalize distinctions in terms of similarity-repetition and difference-variation, body density on the dance floor exerts one of the dance floor's most forceful demands.

"An Invasion of Gestures": Synchronicity and Imitation

The lived body, which is the self, is socially constituted: it is built from the invasion of the self by the gestures of others who, by referring to other others, are already social beings.

—*Rosalyn Diprose, "Performing Body-Identity"*

How might the dance floor provide occasion for an "invasion of the self by the gestures of others?" How might dancers come to incorporate each other's movements? And how might this invasion and incorporation operate to constitute the dance floor as a space of shared kinesthesia? These questions invite consideration of dance-floor relations in terms of synchronicity (temporal cohesion), imitation (kinesthetic exchange), and the dance floor's consistency as a choreographic ensemble.

For Walter Hughes, the beat is disco's most insistent disciplinary force: "the beat brooks no denial, but moves us, controls us, deprives us of our will," such that "dancing becomes a form of submission to this overmastering beat."[22] But if, as Diprose suggests, "the law works through the other with whom you dwell," the beat may register its disciplinary effects not through direct infliction, but through the way in which others dancing to the beat rhythmically textures the choreographic ensemble in which you dance.[23] The synchronicity of the dance floor, the dancing together in time, is secured through a system of reciprocal indistinction: dancing to the beat of the music is dancing to the beat of the other. "And it's just fantastic if you're on the dance floor and you're just having a good time and you're following the rhythm of the music and you're kind of feeling sensual about it all and someone around you is like—I know some people who use words like 'feeding off you'—they're like feeding off your rhythm and your excitement and they're looking at you and they're in that rhythm with you . . . and you're having fun together" (Benjamin, Mardi Gras Party 1995).

Here it is important to understand that the dance floor is not only a site for the performance of dance practice, it is also a site for training and rehearsal, and a site where distinctions between these modalities of practice are blurred. To the extent that party goers report experiences of learning to dance, this learning is most often located on dance floors. Dancing like others on the dance floor may be part of a conscious project, a kind of "becoming-other" through dancing the other's moves: "if there's somebody who I really admire and there's something about their dance I can't describe what but I just think that dance looks really groovy then I'll try to incorporate that into what I do" (Rebekah, Hand in Hand 1995). Or it may be a more incidental effect of "falling in step" with other dancers: "when I see someone else doing something that I do at times then I might fall into that step at the same time, but it's not something that I wouldn't normally do" (Ricardo, Mardi Gras Party 1995).

One party goer I interviewed regarded this imitative sharing of dance moves as a kind of generative motor for his dance practice, an ongoing appropriation and incorporation of other dancers' moves. "I'll be looking at others who are around me, generally at the distance rather than in the foreground, closer to me. If there's something that I see that looks good, I will try to move into that other move. I don't dance in a stock standard type of dancing like a few people tend to do. . . . I like to be a little more diverse. (Can you think of an example of a move that you saw?) . . . Well it happens all the time. It's something that's not once or twice throughout the night. It's something that's constantly changing. I'm sort of eclectic as I say. I'm kind of picking from the crowd what I like and trying to adapt it into the way I'm moving" (Mitchell, Hand in Hand 1995).

But whether the sharing of kinesthetic resources occurs in the present moment—"picking from the crowd"—or whether it is the result of an accumulation and re-performance of past dance-floor experiences—"a stock standard type of dancing"—the pleasures of dancing on a crowded dance floor are often the pleasures of slotting into a choreographic ensemble, where "moving in a way that fits together" means "connecting" with other dancers. "So it's a place where I can be real confident, and I get really nice vibes back from people, and you connect with people who come up and dance with you. . . . (What sorts of things tell you you've connected with someone?) That's an interesting question. Well, eye contact and smiling on a very obvious level. But just fitting in with their dancing and feeling like 'Ok, we've clicked,' and we're moving in a way that fits together" (Karen, Hand in Hand 1995).

This sense of fitting into a choreographic ensemble can extend from individual interactions, to groups of party goers dancing together, and across the entire dance floor. But it is at moments when the ensemble is disrupted that the significance of dancing in a way that "fits together" is most clearly revealed. If there is explicit agreement on dance-floor etiquette, it concerns the issue of party goers accidentally bumping into each other. Almost all the party goers I spoke to made reference either to incidents where others on the dance floor had bumped into them or to the care they take not to bump into others. Usually, the concern is framed in terms of spatial accommodation, such that accidental bumping occurs when party goers take up a lot of space on the dance floor, without adjusting their kinesphere and accommodating their actions to the available space. "And I hate it when people move into a space and then they just decide they're going to stay there and they're elbowing you every second beat, you know. So I'll be very aware of them, and I'll just basically get them with my body and get them out of the way. And I'll do that for other people, too, if it's happening to somebody else" (Karen, Hand in Hand 1995).

Of course, the density of bodies on a dance floor varies, and while redressive measures are sometimes necessary, more often the experience is one of dancing within the spaces between others, adjusting one's movements to the space available, and interactively negotiating the available space with others. But given that space on the dance floor is constantly moving and that its negotiation entails anticipating how others are moving, I would propose that the capacity to dance in a way that "fits together" is what enables party goers to dance without bumping into each other. Hence, one party goer explained how he liked dancing with a group who are "all dancing much the same" since, in addition to enjoying a sense of "togetherness," it was unlikely that they would bump into each other because their dancing would "kind of fit together" (Ken, Hand in Hand 1995). Another party goer recognized getting bumped as something that tended to happen during the first few hours of the party. "Usually at the beginning of the night and people always bump into you and stuff. Especially men, they're quite bigger bulk, so they don't realize. If they just half bump into you, they knock you five meters away. It's like arrgh! But then that disappears magically" (Rebekah, Hand in Hand 1995).

In the "magical disappearance" of getting bumped, I would recognize the emergence, over time and across a dance floor, of a kinesthetic consistency, grounded in the imitative synchronicity of dancing in a way that "fits together" and collectively sustained in the negotiation of dance-floor space, the accommodation of other dancers, and the avoidance of bumping into each other. Thus, if there is a "law of the dance floor," it operates not through some overarching interpellation (The beat says: "Dance!") but within the interstices between dancing selves and dancing others.

Quoting Merleau-Ponty, Diprose suggests that "our 'freedom'. . . is not limited by others taking over control of our body, but by 'the lessening of the tolerance allowed by the bodily and institutional data of our lives.'"[24] If the dance floor increases "our tolerance to embodied projects,"[25] it may do so because it demands, in the openness and closeness of relations to others, an exchange and alternation of kinesthetic experience through which we become, in a sense, less like ourselves and more like each other. This is not to come under an overarching and uniform disciplinary regime. Rather it is to be exposed to a multiplicity of disciplinary possibilities, an opening onto the possibilities of other ways of moving, ways of becoming-other through movement.

QUEER KINESTHESIA AND THE MORPHOLOGICAL IMPERATIVE

Somehow, inscription and bodily matter combine. Somehow the subject is not merely made but also remakes herself. There are limits to that remaking, both cultural and physical, though it is no easy matter to specify what are these limits, and what are the limits to these limits. My current view is that it is within movement that subjectivity is made and remade, that we are moving subjects.
  —*Philipa Rothfield, "A Conversation between Bodies"*

To claim that "we are moving subjects" is, at one level, stating the obvious. Yet resources for a kinesthetic theory of subjectivity are surprisingly thin on the ground. Grappling with the materiality of the body, feminist theories of embodied subjectivity, drawing on the poststructuralist legacy, have construed the body as an inscribed surface, a sculptured form, a cartographic terrain. These accounts have favored exteriorized models of corporeality, a view from the outside where social, cultural, and historical forces can be observed at work, inscribing and incising a bodily surface: the law is written on the body. Here, action is external to the subject, and there is little sense of an interior agency willing the body to move, directing and controlling its actions.[26]

Yet what if a body's capacity for action were considered not as evidence of an autonomous, independent agency, but as evidence of a body's enculturation, its training and participation in socialized and cultured ways of moving? This I take to be the promise of a performative theory of identity, yet it is a promise that is compromised when what matters about a body is only registered in terms of its shape, its morphology, its contoured materiality. What would it take to register what matters about a body in terms of the body's experience of moving, its capacity for action, its choreographic repertoire? The emphasis on materiality has been important in addressing feminist questions of sexual difference, in registering gender as the materialization of sexed morphology. Theorizing sexualities, especially queer sexualities, makes other demands. I will begin, however, by exploring the limits of Butler's morphological account of queer sexualities before moving on to analyzing some of the performative effects of gay and lesbian dance-floor practice.

Imaginary Morphologies: The "Feminized Fag" and the "Phallicized Dyke"

In calling for a re-articulation of theorizations of gender to theorizations of sexuality, Butler observes that:

> homophobia often operates through the attribution of a damaged, failed, or otherwise abject gender to homosexuals, that is, calling gay men "feminine" or calling lesbians "masculine," and . . . the homophobic terror over performing homosexual acts, where it exists, is often also a terror over losing proper gender ("no longer being a real or proper man" or "no longer being a real and proper woman").[27]

Here, Butler explicitly maps social manifestations of homophobia onto her reading of the psychoanalytic "threat" by which subjects assume heterosexed positions. Indeed, a working knowledge of social homophobia is quite helpful in understanding Butler's rendering of penis envy and the threat of castration as psychoanalytic figures of homosexual abjection. Earlier, Butler considers an excluded domain of relations which confounds the phallic organization of normatively sexed positions.[28] What this domain yields are the "inverted versions of heterosexualized masculinity and femininity": masculine feminization and feminine phallicization. Deftly redescribed in the vernacular of American homophobia, these become Butler's figures of abject homosexuality: the "feminized fag" and the "phallicized dyke."[29]

While their dyke-iness and fag-iness are far from self-evident, it is hardly deniable that these figures might possibly signify homosexual abjection. As unintelligible repudiations, they are certainly shadowy figures in the psychoanalytic account. But is it possible to give them some form, to explore their morphology and make them matter? If so, and shifting to a more local vernacular, it might go something like this: the interpellation that is effected by the terms "lezzo!" and "poofter!" initiates and sustains a process, a "lezzo-ing" or a "poofter-ing," which is the forcible production of abject homosexuality, a materialization of those specters which haunt the assumption to heterosexed positions. What we are ostensibly faced with here is the law's spectacular failure to fully gender its subjects: a failed gender performativity which is not merely that mundane failure which compels the ongoing citation of gender norms, but also the very figure of the law's punishment made flesh. That this materialization might not be suffered as punishment, or rather, that this punishment might be the occasion of erotic investment should be obvious. But the extent to which these imaginary morphologies are intelligible surely remains open to question.

For clearly, somehow and sometimes, the phallicized dyke and the feminized fag *are* intelligible morphologies. But might not these morphologies (to the extent that they remain unintelligible) be better described as figures of an abject transgendering? Perhaps the intelligibility of gay and lesbian identities, where their gender remains intact, is actually secured through the abjection of medically transgendered bodies: the castrated male and "penisized" female whose fag-iness or dyke-iness, where it appears, is rendered unintelligible as a "homosexual" identity by either a history or future of "heterosexual" relations. And so in performative processes of homosexualization, the questions become strangely skewed: to what extent do lesbians and gay men approximate the imaginary morphologies of "phallicized dykes" and "feminized fags"? That is, to what extent is there an assumption to those abject morphologies relegated by the hegemonics of compulsory heterosexuality? And to what extent does that assumption fail? Indeed to what extent is failure guaranteed, given that those imaginary morphologies, redescribed as figures of an abject transgendering, serve to mark a heterosexual latency or potential?

This approximation and failure, which confounds heterosexed positions, this ambivalently oscillating movement, is perhaps better characterized not as an imaginary morphology but as a queer kinesthesia, as queer styles of moving as a sexualized body among other sexualized bodies. For if sexed morphologies are merely effects forcibly secured in the naturalized "matter-ing" of bodies, then performative processes of homosexualization, with their ambivalent resistance to the morphological imperative (by which I mean the compulsion to heterosexed positions), may register their effects kinesthetically, in a kinesthetic disruption of naturalized, gender-appropriate action. If this were the case, the performance of queer kinesthesia would open a rift—the rift that the naturalizing forces of heteronormative subject formation attempt to foreclose—between bodily matter and bodily action, between morphology and kinesthesia, between what a body is and what a body does.

Queer Kinesthesias: "Girly Poofter" and "Cool Dyke"

Recognizing the potential of a gendered analysis of dance-floor practice was something of a breakthrough in the research; although once recognized, it acquired a stability of its own. As a category of kinesthetic style, "girly" does lay claim to a certain ethnographic validity, but it is not intended that it define a fixed repertoire of moves. Rather, it serves as a prism which refracts a coalescence of moves and gendered effects. Other style categories would divide up a dance-floor constituency in different ways, refracting a different repertoire of moves and inviting analyses which operate along other axes of other-identification: age in terms of grown-up sexualized seriousness versus childlike playful fun, ethnicity in terms of the corporeal restraint of Anglo dance inhibition versus the corporeal involvement of African American dance traditions, and class in terms of the banal uniformity of communal participation versus the extravagant excesses of glamour, stardom, and fame.

Dance-floor styles that are characterized as "girly"—as "girly disco," "girly drag show," or "girly poofter"—are perhaps most readily defined as that which a heteromasculine kinesthetic disenables: up and over-the-top arm gestures, hands that "flap around," lightly articulated support shifts, and, most distinctively, a swishing lateral pelvic action with fluid torso inclusion that is sometimes known as "sashay." "Flamboyant" and "extrovert," "girly" is most readily performed to those genres of dance music that in dance-party terms are similarly described: "girly disco," "girly handbag," "girly house," and "girly pop." As such, its performance draws extensively on the "show girl" choreography of gay-male drag shows as party goers lip-sync along to the diva's lyrics, mime the sentiments of overwrought emotions, dramatize narratives of histrionic proportions, and otherwise "camp it up" by posing and pouting, and "creating a drama with your hands."

Of course, a "girly" kinesthetic is hardly ubiquitous among gay men on a dance floor; nor is it their exclusive preserve. I have observed it more often performed by younger gay men, and their straight female friends, as a way of "having fun" on a dance floor and as a vehicle for displaying pop-cultural skills. For other gay men, "girly" may be an option, resourced on occasions as an alternative to a more "serious" kinesthetic style. One party goer I spoke to explained that he had two styles of dancing, corresponding to two styles of music: "girly drag show" for dancing to "girly music" at the beginning of a party, and a more "groovy, filthy, sexy" style for dancing to the "slower, heavier" music that is played "after the party has peaked" (Ken, Hand in Hand 1995).

For those gay men who relish its performance, "girly" dancing may be an occasion of disidentification from a dance-floor background of communal participation: "I can actually get into quite a primal thing, but that actually takes a while to come through. . . . I think I'm a bit more of a showgirl" (Walter, Sleaze Ball 1995). Then there are gay men for whom "girly" is a style against which to define their dancing; and those that do have said they prefer a style which is, not surprisingly, more "masculine" or "a bit more macho" (Michael, video discussion 1995).[30] And here it is important to note that "girly" tends *not* to be a style of dancing performed when gay men are cruising or sustaining themselves on the dance floor in a cruisable state. "Sometimes I'll be on the dance floor and you see all these butch guys dancing and you'd be doing a sort of Diana Ross sort of [style] and you'd feel like, really, how tragic. But that's in the context of picking up men, and image on the dance floor, and stuff like that. But you know, I tend to have a better time when that's not in the vicinity" (Walter, Sleaze Ball 1995).

Just as a "girly" kinesthetic is resourced in various ways, and on various dance-floor occasions, there are numerous kinesthetic styles which, by contrast, it throws into relief. A more "masculine" kinesthetic may also be variously resourced: in the strength of pulled-down pectorals, flexed arms, and clenched fists, as gym queens pump their athleticism; in the weight of a pelvis slung low, shoulders rolled forward, and support on the heels, as leather men "get down and dirty"; or in stomping feet and punching fists as others get into "that tribal pumping feel" and generate "that male energy kind of stuff" (Benjamin, Mardi Gras Party 1995). But for my purposes, the kinesthetic called "girly" found its most asymmetrical counterpart, when I was told how "there's definitely the cool way for dykes to dance" (Karen, Hand in Hand 1995).

When I asked Karen to explain what she meant, she said, "it's similar to the boys, I think that's where it comes from." I have recognized "the cool way for dykes to dance" as a kinesthetic style which is inflected—as are the more "masculine" dance styles performed by gay men—with a "toughness" that accrues around weight. In contrast to the lightness of "girly," the kinesthetic of "cool" is less "up and out" and more "down and into it." It is distinguished by a restrained range of arm gestures, either held contracted low or swung around the torso, and by a torso "hunkering down," or tilting, twisting, and shifting, but without the isolation of lateral pelvic action. It has a low sense of gravity, weight held back on the heels, and support shifts, when they occur, tend to be heavy.

Again, such a description hardly exhausts the repertoire of lesbian dance-floor styles. Nevertheless, it would seem that resourcing a "girly" kinesthetic is less of an option for lesbians. One party goer described how before she came out she used to dance and lip-sync like a drag queen, but since coming out, her dancing has changed. She said she would not be comfortable doing "girly movements" any more. In that discussion the phrase "maybe it's a lesbian thing" served to mark how her identification as lesbian entailed something like a dance-floor disidentification with "femininity." "Well it's not conscious, I don't think. But I just know that my dancing is not the same now as it used to be. And I would not—like I know it's fun to dance like Samuel dances. I know that's really fun. But I just would not do it. I don't find myself dancing in that way. . . . So I danced like a drag queen and I was comfortable doing that when I was straight. . . . And I used to love singing along. But I would never do that now" (Emma, video discussion 1995).

As kinesthetic styles, "girly poofter" and "cool dyke" afford experiences of moving as a sexualized body that offset the demand for consistently gendered performance and expand a body's capacity for movement beyond the constraints of the morphological imperative. As dance-floor enactments, "girly poofter" and "cool dyke" detach the performance of gender from its morphological moorings and invigorate the resulting *frisson* between morphology and kinesthesia with homoerotic potential. As instances of "becoming-other" through movement, enactments of queer kinesthesia would suggest that those shaming injunctions that would otherwise compel a consistently gendered performance are somehow suspended on the dance floor. Certainly, there is some sense of play. "I like to keep my feet as firmly on the ground as I can and then swing my hips. I like to bump and grind so there's a bit of sexual stuff going on. And I was also in drag so it's playing up that feminine–masculine thing. So one minute I'm thrusting my pelvis and the next I might be just a real femme sex kitten" (Gerald, Sleaze Ball 1995).

But to play around with gender is not to escape its determinants. Rather, the agency of "playing up that feminine–masculine thing" would be, as Butler suggests, "a reiterative or rearticulatory practice," a resourcing of the kinesthetic styles of gendered performance.[31] For dance-floor performances of queer kinesthesia are not undertaken in isolation. Rather, as Walter discovered when he caught himself "doing a sort of Diana Ross" among "all these butch guys," or as Emma explained in describing how she would not perform "girly moves" any more because they are "for somebody else to do," such performances are enacted in relation to other dance-floor performances articulating other relations to gender. Indeed, just as lesbians negotiate variations on the kinesthetic of "cool dyke," "girly poofter" remains open to an unexpectedly "straight" form of policing whereby its performance can sanction men as un-cruisable, as failing to perform their gender with stability. Feeling the force of such a sanction, one party goer described an attempt to divest himself of the kinesthetic habits of "girly." "I noticed this year at this party I danced differently to how I have previously and I think it's a comment I got from a boy I was going out with. . . . I've never actually danced with him [but] he made a comment saying he didn't like blokes who danced in a girly sort of way and waved their arms around a lot. Now, I don't think I dance in a girly sort of way but I was conscious that I do wave my arms around a lot. So I was more conscious of where my arms were in relation to my body and instead of putting them up in the air, I put them up in front and out to the side sort of thing which was really weird, and I concentrated a bit more on moving my chest and my upper body separately to my lower body" (Ricardo, Mardi Gras Party 1995).

Although dance floors at gay and lesbian dance parties provide opportunities for performing gender with difference, they are clearly not sites of unbridled gender fluidity. There is no simple escape from the regulation of gender, just different ways of moving it around. If dance floors enable the resourcing of queer kinesthesias, they do so only to the extent that the performance of "girly poofter" and "cool dyke" are tolerated by other dancers and, indeed, by the dancers themselves. That such queer kinesthesias are not merely tolerated, but pleasurably indulged and even demanded, is obviously not evidence of some temporary escape from the everyday regulation of gender. Rather, it demonstrates the performative labor with which lesbian and gay dance-floor practices rearticulate the regulation of gender by denaturing the link between morphology and kinesthesia and queerly engendering a body's capacity to move.

WHAT REALLY MATTERS: CHOREOGRAPHIES OF QUEER DESIRING

We know nothing about a body until we know what it can do.
—*Gilles Deleuze and Felix Guattari*, A Thousand Plateaus

A performative theory of identity conceptualizes identity as a "work-in-progress," an ongoing outcome in a process of ongoing production. For Butler, this ongoing production is the process of "morphogenesis," the "materialization" of a specific morphology, the intelligibility of which is the entitlement of "bodies that matter." In this formulation, there is a sense in which to analyze a process of identification is to seek material evidence of performative effect. In other words, the emphasis on materiality has a tendency to shift analytical focus from performative process to material product, to what is materialized through performative acts. But clearly the materiality of morphological difference is not the only way to register the intelligibility of bodies. What other kinds of bodily intelligibility, what other ways of differentiating bodies, could be brought to bear?

As I have analyzed them, gay and lesbian dance-floor practices do not so much "materialize" the morphology of bodies, as "choreograph" their kinesthetic capacities. And this "choreography" demands an analysis—a reality-registering apparatus—that cannot so much "see" kinesthetic habituation as "feel" it. For kinesthesia cannot be read off the surface of the body in terms of matter, shape, or form. It must be read as movement, in the ongoingness of movement, and in how that movement feels. This is where the resources of movement analysis, a different kind of bodily intelligibility, have a contribution to make to a performative analysis of identities conceptualized and experienced as "a stylized repetition of acts."

Registering kinesthetic difference is key to registering the reality of the dance floor's performative effects. The notion of queer kinesthesia is an attempt to describe how the regulation of gender may be negotiated through movement, through a marshalling of kinesthetic resources that disarticulate ways of moving from the demand for consistently gendered performance. To the extent that the regulation of gender is complicit in the regulation of sexuality, an interest and investment in the performance of queer kinesthesia may be characterized as an enacted critique, in some cases a kind of parody, of a heterosexual model of desire that operates on the logic of morphological difference. In kinesthetically queering the performance of gender, gay men and lesbians experience ways of moving and ways of desiring that are sometimes ambivalent, sometimes hyperreflexive, about the morphological moorings of gender. Indeed, queer kinesthesia would invite an analysis of desire that is predicated not on the logic of morphological difference but on a choreography of kinesthetic engagement.

In "Sexualities without Genders and Other Queer Utopias," Biddy Martin argues how "antifoundationalist celebrations of queerness rely on their own projections of fixity, constraint, or subjection onto a fixed ground . . . in relation to which queer sexualities become figural, performative, playful, and fun."[32] According to Martin, the risk is that queer sexuality is cast as a "mobile and fluid" kinesthetic figure against the ground of a "stagnant and ensnaring" morphological gender.[33] This is precisely the risk I have taken in attempting to register how dance-floor performances of queer kinesthesias acquire performative purchase on a heterosexual model of desire predicated on the logic of morphological difference. For even if queer theories have invested in metaphors of kinesthetic mobility—and, in so doing, have projected a morphological rigidity onto feminist theories of gender— they have rarely furnished resources adequate to a kinesthetic analysis of sexuality; nor, for that matter, of gender. Rather, it has been the question of desire that has mobilized queer theory.

Of concern to Martin are (dis)articulations of gender and sexuality as they are sustained across relations between feminism and queer theory. But I would suggest that her characterization of these relations in terms of morphological stagnation and kinesthetic mobility is indicative of a rift between psychoanalytic and Deleuzian models of desire. It is the psychoanalytic model of "desire as a lack, an absence that strives to be filled through the attainment of an impossible object" that is predicated on morphological difference,[34] and it is a psychoanalytic feminism that Martin invokes. More important, it was within such a framework that Butler re-theorized performativity as the materialization of sexed morphology, and thereby offset the kinesthetic mobility inherent in the earlier formulation of performativity as "a stylized repetition of acts."[35]

In contrast, the Deleuzian model of desire eschews the "hylomorphic" (matter-form) model of embodied subjectivity that has been central to feminism's critical inheritance of the psychoanalytic legacy.[36] Rather, as Elizabeth Grosz explains, the Deleuzian model figures desire as movement.

> Instead of aligning desire with fantasy and opposing it to the real, instead of seeing it as a yearning, desire is an actualization, a series of practices, bringing things together or separating them, making machines, making reality. Desire does not take for itself a particular object whose attainment it requires; rather it aims at nothing above its own proliferation or self-expansion. It assembles things out of singularities and breaks things, assemblages, down into their singularities. It moves; it does.[37]

Here, desire and movement are inseparable, indistinguishable, and immediately tangible. As Elspeth Probyn elaborates, movement for Deleuze is mobilized by desire, and "bodies, and desire, are only of interest inasmuch as they engage with others."[38] Indeed Probyn's explanation of how movement-desire might work in everyday practice offers a succinct and vivid mechanism, distinctly embedded in lived sociality and without the rhetoric of evasive fluidity, that would seem tailor-made for articulating how dance-floor performances at gay and lesbian dance parties are mobilized and sustained as experiences of choreographing desire: "Simply put, a body, moved by desire, propels itself into networks and milieux of bodies and things. In turn the milieu must be conceived of as a dynamic arena of social action."[39]

To take up this approach would be to conceptualize the dance floor as choreographed by desire, the dance practice as desire enacted. Here the dance floor demands of "dwelling-with-others" in closeness and openness become an engagement in desiring relations; the danced potential of "becoming-other" through "an invasion of the self by the gestures of others" becomes an enactment of desiring capacity; and these demands and potentials, relations and capacities, would be propelled and retracted, ventured and resisted, by the desires of those dancing among others. In this way, the limits of queer kinesthesia would come to reside less in the performative force of regulatory norms and more in an exposure to the perils of becoming-other. "It's really weird. I sort of have a contradictory view of straights at dance parties. I don't have a major problem with them, but usually when I'm having fun and feel really uninhibited, you . . . pick something up from the way they dance or whatever. . . . Yeah, and I quite like the way gay people dance around you. . . . It's more fun and you seem to fit in better. You don't feel as self-conscious as when there's straight people around" (Ricardo, Mardi Gras Party 1995).

To "pick something up from the way they dance" is to be alerted to a different mode of dance-floor practice premised on a different nexus of movement and pleasure. But it might also be to take on their style, to begin dancing like them, to risk, in a sense, "becoming-straight." This is a limit imposed from within a dance practice that monitors its kinesthetic pleasures as queer identification and choreographs its becoming-other as queer desiring.

What then, *in the end*, might gay and lesbian party goers take home from the party? Memories, of course, but memories of moving in ways that feel real; memories of moving that remember the pleasures of performing with difference the demands of the everyday; memories of moving that provide ongoing resources for ongoing performances. Here is another way to get home: "That is a really good feeling, just walking through the grass and it's morning and it's really clear and there's all these people, like a few cars driving past, and they look at you but you don't care because you've still got a few other strangers, who you don't know [and] who've been at the same place, walking around you. So you feel safe. Yeah, that's really nice" (Emma, Sleaze Ball 1993).

NOTES

1. Walter Hughes, "In the Empire of the Beat: Discipline and Disco," in Andrew Ross and Tricia Rose, eds., *Microphone Fiends: Youth Music and Youth Culture* (New York: Routledge, 1994), 148.

2. Ibid.

3. Gregory W. Bredbeck, "Troping the Light Fantastic: Representing Disco Then and Now," *GLQ* 3 (1996): 94–95.

4. Ibid., 103.

5. Brian Currid, " 'We Are Family': House Music and Queer Performativity," in Sue-Ellen Case, Philip Brett, and Susan Leigh Foster, eds., *Cruising the Performative: Interventions into the Representation of Ethnicity, Nationality, and Sexuality,* (Bloomington: Indiana University Press, 1995), 192, emphasis added.

6. Judith Butler, *Gender Trouble: Feminism and the Subversion of Identity* (New York: Routledge, 1990), 140.

7. Ibid.

8. Ibid., 141, emphasis added.

9. Rosalyn Diprose, "Performing Body-Identity," *Writings on Dance* 11–12 (1994): 13.

10. Judith Butler, *Bodies That Matter: On the Discursive Limits of "Sex"* (New York: Routledge, 1993), 32.

11. Ibid., 4–12, 230–33.

12. Ibid., 15.

13. Ibid., 226.

14. Ibid., 12–16, 107–11, 226–30.

15. In her subsequent work, *Excitable Speech: A Politics of the Performative* (New York: Routledge, 1997), Butler does address the question of "context," drawing on both "social" (Bourdieu) and "linguistic" (Derrida) senses of the term (141–59).

16. Diprose, "Performing Body-Identity," 13.

17. Ibid.

18. Ibid., 15.

19. Ibid., 13.

20. Ibid.

21. Interview material is drawn from ethnographic research I undertook at and around gay and lesbian dance parties and dance clubs in Sydney from late 1993 to the end of 1996. Quotations from interviews are identified by pseudonyms and by the events after which the interviews were conducted. Parentheses within a quotation enclose my questions or comments during the interview. The interviews quoted here refer to the following dance parties: Sleaze Ball 1993 (October 2, 1993), Mardi Gras Party 1995 (March 4, 1995), and Sleaze Ball 1995 (September 30, 1995) produced by the Sydney Gay and Lesbian Mardi Gras organization; Hand in Hand 1995 (June 10, 1995) produced by the AIDS Council of New South Wales. All four events were staged in pavilions at the former Royal Agricultural Society Showground, Sydney.

22. Hughes, "In the Empire of the Beat," 149.

23. Diprose, "Performing Body-Identity," 15.

24. Ibid.

25. Ibid.

26. See, for example, Elizabeth Grosz, *Volatile Bodies: Toward a Corporeal Feminism* (Bloomington: Indiana University Press, 1994).

27. Butler, *Bodies That Matter*, 238.

28. Ibid., 103.

29. Ibid., 103–4.

30. In September 1994, I staged a video documentary of a gay dance club in Darlinghurst, Sydney. The following year, I invited two groups of participants in that production to view the documentary and discuss their reactions.

31. Butler, *Bodies That Matter*, 15.

32. Biddy Martin, "Sexualities without Genders and Other Queer Utopias," *Diacritics* 24 (1994): 104.

33. Biddy Martin, "Extraordinary Homosexuals and the Fear of Being Ordinary," *Differences* 6 (1994): 101.

34. Grosz, *Volatile Bodies*, 165.

35. Butler, *Gender Trouble*, 140.

36. Gilles Deleuze and Félix Guattari, *A Thousand Plateaus: Capitalism and Schizophrenia*, tans. Brian Massumi (Minneapolis: University of Minnesota Press, 1987), 408.

37. Grosz, *Volatile Bodies*, 165.

38. Elspeth Probyn, *Outside Belongings* (New York: Routledge, 1996), 49.

39. Ibid.

10

White Boots and Combat Boots:
My Life as a Lesbian Go-Go Dancer

Ann Cvetkovich

One of my peak experiences as a go-go dancer was performing with Girls in the Nose (GITN), Austin's now-defunct lezzie rock band, at the official rally for the 1993 March on Washington for Lesbian and Gay Rights. Although my moments in the limelight of this national public spectacle were brief—barely five minutes— they were of high intensity. On stage in front of at least a half-million queers on the Mall, with the Capitol behind me and the Washington Monument looming large in the distance, I put my shaking booty on display and used the power of dance to "make lesbianism as attractive as possible."[1]

My presence on stage was an impromptu surprise, the fulfill-ment of that classic American fantasy in which the understudy gets to perform for the big show. Kathy Smith, one half of Lez Nez, Girls in the Nose's go-go dancing duo, pulled out of the trip to Washington at the last minute, and I got word the day before the march that my services were needed. I hastily pulled together a borrowed costume consisting of a black lace body stocking, a pink velour minidress that I unbuttoned to the navel, a long black "Cher" wig that Allison Faust, the other half of Lez Nez, had gra-ciously donated from her large collection, and my very own mo-torcycle boots. (Even when they're not classic white vinyl, a les-bian go-go dancer's boots are one of her most important fashion statements.) Committed to the utopian principle that go-go dancing is a democratic form accessible to anyone who frequents the disco floor, I considered my lack of rehearsal time no imped-iment to my power to entertain the vast crowd. Allison quickly taught me the choreography that she and Kathy have incorporated into some of the songs, but she also reassured me that it wouldn't matter if I forgot the moves.

Our performance was a blur. Slotted close to the end of the mammoth six-hour rally, our allotted seven minutes were cut back to five, which meant dropping one of the three songs from the medley the band had prepared. But we did get to perform excerpts from two classic GITN songs: "Breast Exam," a public service message that attests not only to the urgent necessity of the monthly ritual but to its sexual powers as well, and "Sodomy," which rewrites the multiple prohibitions of Texas law into multiple possibilities for pleasure. ("Oh my god yes that's me / Doing all kinds of sodomy / I've got holes count 'em three / Some for you and some for me . . . Behind closed doors I invite you / to take the pleasure of me raw / In chambers dark I invite you / No judgment, no penalty, no law.")[2] As Joanna, the band's percussionist, led us in the choreography she designed for GITN's version of a breast exam—"Take the tops of these three fingers, go around, go around let 'em linger"—I exposed my breasts, bare under the black lace, to the nation's gaze. Allison and I then turned "Sodomy" into a frenzied free-for-all, as we graphically underscored the song's invocation to the sexualized body: "Anal, oral, vaginal too, and oh so rational when I love you." At one strategic moment I lifted my skirt to reveal my hidden accessories—a leather harness and a black latex dildo—and I mock butt-fucked Allison. Complementing GITN's humor, open sexuality, and in-your-face outness, we seized go-go dancing's tradition of sexiness and spectacle and made it our own.

Most of the audience was probably too far away actually to see our performance unless they were watching one of the huge video monitors posted at regular intervals down the length of the Mall. Earlier that day I had watched RuPaul's televised image and marveled at how brilliantly she used this medium to establish herself as a visual icon. Dressed in a majorette-inspired outfit of stars, stripes, and sequins, she combined national symbols and a drag queen aesthetic to provide serious competition for gays in the military as the public face and body of the queer nation.[3] I can only hope we projected a fraction of her visual power. From our immediate vantage point on a stage that towered high above even the closest members of the audience, though, it was hard to tell. Rather than feeling larger than life, I felt dwarfed by the size of the stage and the crowd. Broadcast around the world on C-SPAN and recorded by Austin's *Let the People Speak!* for later broadcast on local access cable, our performance, especially the dancing, may have had a greater impact on television than it did live. The camera's close-ups offer a more intimate perspective on the performance, capturing the nuances of gesture and costume. The challenges of performing for two different kinds of visual scale, of appearing both live and mediated, and the disorientation and even disembodiment that it produced reflect the double-edged nature of the march itself. Was its audience other queers, a way of displaying ourselves to one another in the public space of the nation's capital? Or was it an event staged for the rest of the nation, a bid for mainstream power and visibility? The material difficulties of transporting a performance designed for the intimate space of the club to the stage of the Washington rally reflect the challenges that have faced gay and lesbian politics in the 1990s and the pitfalls of the politics of visibility and assimilation.

There are, then, larger issues at stake in making lesbianism visible through the specific medium of dance at the March on Washington. Along with the singers, musicians, comedians, and politicians who took the stage, we used the power of bodily movement to rally the crowd and to create a focal point for this gathering of the people as a literal body. Like that of many participants, our presence was symbolic, participating in a liberal politics of inclusion that gave a moment of representation to as many segments of the gay and lesbian public as possible.[4] The particular presence of GITN signaled the possibility that a form of lezzie rock existing mostly in subcultural contexts could gain access to a larger public—I'm quite certain that many people in the audience, queers included, had never seen anything like Girls in the Nose, and whether they liked it or not, they had to acknowledge us as part of the national cultural public sphere.[5] Our role as dancers was additionally distinctive because it added the visual spectacle of movement and costume to an event that largely privileged oral modes such as political speeches and songs, which can be easily amplified and presented to a large audience.[6] Although without the power of televisual technology it would have been literally invisible to most of the audience, dancing draws attention to the performative nature of political events such as rallies and marches, which always involve a choreography of bodies. Television has changed the face of both politics and music, enabling new forms of visual spectacle that complement oral forms of communication and reach vast live audiences. GITN's performances show the influence of MTV and music videos, which redefined the role of the visual in the marketing of music; two of the most popular performers of MTV's first decade—Michael Jackson and Madonna—owe a considerable measure of the success of their videos to their skill as dancers. Moreover, both have ties to queer culture through the ambiguous sexuality of their presentation and the popularity of their music in dance clubs. GITN's use of visual spectacle, accentuated by its inclusion of go-go dancers, also reflects another development of the 1980s, a move away from the tendency within the women's music associated with lesbian feminist culture to reject the fashions of mainstream culture. (Another important Austin lesbian band, Two Nice Girls, broke new ground in lesbian dress codes by wearing sequined dresses at the 1991 Michigan Womyn's Music Festival.) Highlighting the band's theatricality, the dancers use the sexual codes already present in popular dance to render lesbian sexuality visible, thus providing an important complement to the band's musical message.

As a go-go dancer on the Mall, I embodied a form of what Lauren Berlant has called "diva citizenship" through which a fantasy of access to state power is enacted by a literal visit to Washington.[7] The dancer is a microcosm of the forms of embodiment central to all large demonstrations, especially those in Washington, which put a mass of bodies publicly, and specifically visually, on display in order to make demands and create political power. At such events the dynamics of a politics of visibility are most evident; bodily visibility makes its strongest bid for equivalence with political power even as the catachrestic nature of this equation is also most apparent. A march puts large numbers of people on display with a minimal degree of choreographic planning. The rally that is frequently its endpoint is an occasion to keep the crowds together over time; important as the content of the speeches and performances might be, they are also a means for producing the spectacle of the audience offstage. The televisual broadcast of demonstrations can be something of a distortion because of the overemphasis on the stage, although in the case of the one-hour video marketed by the march organizers and the six-hour cable-access broadcast, the staged events do provide a microcosm of gay culture through the inclusion of a diverse range of performers and speakers.

Every march on Washington exists in the historical shadow of the 1963 march mythologized as central to the civil rights movement. Moreover, Martin Luther King's "I Have a Dream" speech fosters the fantasy that a singular oral performance can move both the crowd and the nation. In seeking to match that power, a march on Washington for gay and lesbian rights inevitably raises questions about the connections between civil rights and gay and lesbian rights and their corresponding political styles. The 1963 march owed some of its power to the critical mass generated by many other, much more violent, protests and marches in more local and regional contexts, especially in the South. Similarly, the 1993 march built on a history of AIDS activism and queer activism in the immediately preceding years. The results of the demands brought to the national arena were ultimately ambiguous, far more so than in the 1963 case, which can be viewed at the very least as a catalyst for the Civil Rights Act of 1964. The 1993 march took place against the backdrop of the issue of gays in the military, which proved to be the death of any real support for gay activism from President Bill Clinton. Instead of an equivalent to the Civil Rights Act, we have had the possibility of a Defense of Marriages Act and an assimilationist gay politics that has subsumed other forms of queer politics that would demand social transformation rather than inclusion in the existing national order. Yet in both cases the measurement of political gains is difficult, and the more obviously mixed success of the 1993 march underscores the need to evaluate such national spectacles as symbolic performances whose effects, even as they take place in the literal space of the state, are in fact broadly cultural.

I'm interested in how the politics of this moment might be evaluated through dance and movement, including not just my go-go dancing on stage but the spectacle of the crowd. Each group and issue has its own visual and movement style; gay and lesbian public marches have been noted for their incorporation of theatrical spectacle, including drag, dance, and disco. Indeed, the look of the marches is an important locus of political controversy, and 1993 raised anew the ongoing questions of whether we should be memorialized as drag queens and leather dykes or as gays in the military (another kind of drag) and families that belong to Parents and Friends of Lesbians and Gays (PFLAG). Such images are deployed in a variety of contexts both homophobic and antihomophobic. (Perhaps most notable is the recontextualizing of footage from gay and lesbian marches in right-wing videos such as *Gay Rights, Special Rights* so that what is intended as an expression of pride is offered as incontrovertible visual evidence of perversity.[8]) One of the most famous slogans of recent queer politics has been "We're here, we're queer—get used to it." But a significant variation (and variation is central to political chants) includes not just words, and the particular rhythms of the chant, but movement: "We're here"—raise the left arm overhead; "We're queer"—raise the right arm overhead; "We're faaaabulous"—spread the arms wide in full diva posture, embellish with head movements and a forward thrust of the chest; "Get used to it"—pause or, if desired, punctuate by clenching a fist. Queer politics has found particular ways of combining style and militancy that point to the power of dance and movement in the political arena. Along with other ephemera such as banners, speeches, slogans, chants, and meeting minutes, the archives of activism should include the styles of movement through which political positions and goals are made manifest.

My investigation of lesbian go-go dancing, then, is a way to stake out, through a specific example, the more general field of a cultural politics of movement and its relevance to other fields such as queer theory. The specificity of dance and the moving, not just speaking, body in the production of public power demands attention. Accentuating the power of physical presence, dance is a crucial medium for putting the body on display and for being able to arrest attention in a way that promotes visibility. One can also do so in the register of the visual through, for example, the use of a costume, certainly a key part of GITN's performances. But a costume must be put into motion, and the simple accessible steps of disco and popular dance not only attract attention to an outfit but underscore the role of gesture and the body in the politics of visibility. I want to look more closely at some other moments from the archives of go-go dancing in order to suggest the value of such inquiry to understanding the cultural politics of dance and the role of movement in the public sphere.

DOCUMENT OF A SUBCULTURE

I present my anecdotal evidence from Washington as an example of the forms of documentation and testimony that are crucial for studying the intersections of queer theory and dance.[9] As Peggy Phelan has eloquently suggested, the documentation of performance can be an exercise in belatedness, leaving a record only of the loss or absence of the body.[10] Especially in the case of social and popular dance, which is less systematically documented even than theatrical dance, personal testimony may be an important way to create an archive of the dancing body. Moreover, in using my own experience as a dancer as a resource for dance criticism, I seek to trouble the boundary between practice and criticism that has affected dance studies in particular, because conceptions of dance ground, and are grounded in, distinctions between mind and body.[11] My experiences as a dancer have given me unprecedented access to key moments and spaces in lesbian culture that scholarly research would have trouble investigating.

One of my goals here is thus to create an archive, to preserve the story of GITN's accomplishments from my perspective as a go-go dancer. That moment on stage in 1993 looks very different now in the wake of the flood of stories about "lesbian chic" that appeared in the mainstream media in the months following the March on Washington.[12] Since then the constantly shifting relations between lesbian subcultures and mass culture, and between alternative and mainstream publics, have been dominated by the story of the mainstream media's interest in lesbians and lesbian culture. One recent media event was the double story of Ellen Morgan and Ellen DeGeneres's coming out and, more recently still, the cancellation of *Ellen*. In danger of being lost in accounts of lesbian visibility within and to mainstream culture is its accompanying prehistory, the story of how lesbian subcultures, such as that which surrounded GITN in Austin in the late 1980s, embraced and appropriated mainstream culture.

GITN had a long history before its appearance in Washington. Founded in 1985 by Gretchen Phillips, a musician with roots in Austin's punk rock scene, and Kay Turner, a folklorist with an interest in women's spirituality, GITN was as much a performance concept as a band. As a band in which girls played loud guitars, it provided a very early and prescient version of what Gretchen Phillips calls "lezzie rock." By now girl bands of all musical and sexual persuasions are ubiquitous, but I would argue that GITN remains distinctive for having been influenced by both lesbian feminism and mass culture, domains often seen as mutually exclusive. Other significant influences include ideas from folklore studies about ritual and collectivity (inspiring performances that aim for carnivalesque humor and inversion) and Motown and other forms of black popular music.[13] GITN songs are both polemical and irreverent, politically correct and politically incorrect, covering topics such as the need for menstrual huts, the problems of having not just two girlfriends but two altars, and feminist theory ("I want my Jesus to be / Gender confused and downwardly mobile / Just like me").[14] Especially central to the GITN mission is the celebration of women's sexual pleasure; in addition to the previously mentioned songs about breast exams and sodomy are such tunes as "Hips," "Bite Me," "Honorary Heterosexual Lesbian," "Medusa" (in homage to Hélène Cixous), and "Meat" ("Big chunks of meat slowly burning / In my pit"). Oriented toward spectacle, costume, and theater, GITN had a range of different go-go dancers on an occasional basis, but by 1988 Kathy Smith and Allison Faust had become a regular fixture. I became a huge GITN

The many moods of Lez Nez. *Left*, Lez Nez (*left*, Kathy Smith; *right*, Allison Faust) dressed for a Girls in the Nose show at Chances, Austin, Texas, 1993; *right*, Lez Nez at the last Girls in the Nose show in Austin, Hole in the Wall, 1994. (Photograph at left courtesy of L. E. McMorris; used with permission)

fan in large measure because its go-go dancers were a locus of identification for my fantasies of stardom, more compelling to me than the musicians because I had more experience with dance than with music.[15] Reliving my childhood fantasies of white boots and miniskirts and the jerk, I was able to see how the spectacle of femininity could be lesbian and feminist.

Lez Nez and GITN broke new conceptual barriers at a time when prosex feminism, Madonna studies, and queer theory, especially ideas about drag, performativity, butch-femme, and popular fandom were still in the developing stages. The sensibility represented by the band was completely absorbed by and normalized within lesbian and academic cultures during the 1990s, spawning hybrids of mainstream and alternative cultures that were previously unimaginable.[16] But more visible and well-documented phenomena such as Madonna fandom and theories of performativity were meaningful because they spoke to already existing experiences, providing a legitimating conceptual apparatus that articulated the links between what might otherwise seem disparate or random experiences and cultural forms.[17] Adding GITN's contributions to the record adds depth to an archive that can be deceptive because theoretical essays and MTV videos are more accessible than memories of nights in clubs.[18]

Creating a GITN archive is a challenge because the band's significance lies not just in its songs or its live performances but in the public cultures it was able to foster. The archive needs to include spaces like Chances, the lesbian club that was open for more than ten years in Austin before it closed in 1993 (not, surprisingly enough, for financial reasons but because the owner wanted to move on to other projects). A space for a range of activities—political benefits, pool playing, music, volleyball, and socializing— Chances was a bar that also functioned as a community center and that was especially notable for catering to a mixed crowd while still remaining lesbian centered. Within such a venue a lesbian band is more than just a form of musical entertainment; it becomes a vehicle for the production of public culture.[19] GITN capitalized on this potential by sponsoring a variety of formats, including "hoot nights" in which a bunch of bands play covers related to a theme, such as songs by Madonna or Cher or women's music. Chances was also a home base for activist groups such as ACT UP, Women's Action Coalition, and the Lesbian Avengers, and GITN played a variety of benefits for these groups and others. Such local scenes vary from one town to another, and Austin's status as a music town (as well as a college town) means that the dyke scene overlaps with the music scene, creating mixed audiences for GITN and Two Nice Girls. Regional alternative scenes have now become a nationally recognized phenomenon, perhaps most notably in the case of the success of Nirvana and the Seattle grunge scene but also visible in the attention Austin has received through the film *Slacker* (and, more recently, the television series *King of the Hill* and MTV's *Austin Stories*). Yet these national narratives are famous for their inaccuracies, homogenizing the diversity and specificity of local cultures in their rush to market them. Within gay and lesbian public culture, New York and San Francisco often dominate accounts of the queer national zeitgeist, in a process through which what are actually forms of local culture stand in for a national one. In addition to regional variations, differences of class, race, and age suggest the problems with such generalizations and the need for specific stories. As part of that process, the local nuances of Austin's development and GITN's history need to be told because they are in danger of being overshadowed by overly narrow attention to the lesbian chic phenomena of the 1990s. Earlier developments did not so much produce lesbian chic (as if it were the big event waiting to happen) as constitute the density of historical circumstances of which lesbian chic is just one part. Events such as the coming out of Ellen and *Ellen* have been enabled by other public and counterpublic cultures, such as Chances, in which straight people have had access to lesbian culture.

Within the context of public culture broadly conceived, the go-go dancer has an important role to play in producing a visual spectacle. She participates in many different forms of live public culture: bar culture, which has played a crucial role in making space for gay and lesbian publics to develop; disco culture, a more recent form of bar culture and a more openly out form of gay bar culture; and music clubs, where live performance adds a theatrical dimension to drinking and socializing.[20] While GITN was incorporating go-go dancers as part of its performances, many clubs in other cities were beginning to include dancers. Examples include San Francisco's Club Q, founded by Page Hodel and featuring a choreographed floor show with dancers who also dance individually on scaffolding raised above the audience, and New York's Clit Club, founded in 1991 by Julie Tolentino and Jocelyn Taylor in a tiny club in which a couple of dancers at a time perform on risers.[21] Every town has its own style. (I remember one visit to L.A.'s Club Skirt, which featured go-go dancers who looked exactly like what they were rumored to be—straight girls on loan from a topless bar.) Lez Nez's distinction, in addition to being part of a live musical performance rather than dancing to the recorded music of a disco, lies in its degree of humor and camp, which is very different from the more serious eroticism of both Club Q and the Clit Club.

Lez Nez's camp approach is especially evident in its costumes, which combine thrift store chic, femme power, and lesbian sexuality. For example, although the Lez Nez dancers make liberal use of lingerie, they often camp it up with versions of form-fitting bras and girdles from the 1950s and 1960s. Their wigs alone—promoted by GITN as the lesbian sex toy for the 1990s—could be the subject of an entire paper. Just as much a prosthetic device as the dildo, the wig similarly mimes and exaggerates a gendered signifier—the hair—and provides the protection of a disguise and the creative freedom of an altered identity. Another crucial accessory is combat boots, which can give a dyke, and even butch, spin to other more feminine items of clothing. Lez Nez raids an archive of femininity, signified by different articles of clothing, in order to perform it with a difference. The aim is not just the display of the dancing body but through the dancing body the display of a femininity that can be sexy and fun, rather than oppressive. Lez Nez moves right past the impasses of feminist critiques of fashion to present a range of possibilities that defy any simple binarism of antifashion and profashion.

Lez Nez performs lesbian femme drag, a concept that can be overlooked if drag is assumed to mean cross-gender dressing. The recent craze for drag kings within lesbian cultures has certainly opened up a wide range of possibilities in this latter category, but equally rich is the world of the lesbian drag queen. Although related to gay male drag, Lez Nez's lesbian femme drag ultimately differs from it by being less serious about the details, introducing a necessary freedom from rigid demands about makeup and beauty that many women continue to find oppressive. (GITN, for example, has a song about pantyhose: "Let nylons be bygones / Got to get air to the zone.") But by suggesting that the work is parodic, I do not mean that it is not invested in the cultural forms that it appropriates. In the process of detaching itself from compulsory fashion protocols, Lez Nez's sense of style also conveys a love of femme fashion options. An especially powerful device for Lez Nez is the change of costume. Often, the dancers strip down during the course of the show, beginning with a costume that may not allow much mobility but that transmits a powerful visual message. They can exploit the erotic drama of disrobing to something more revealing (and easier to dance in), as well as the disjunctive power of moving from one style to another. Costumes and concepts have mingled indiscriminately to produce roles such as the girls of Lambda Lambda Lambda, the only lesbian sorority at the University of Texas; women of the land since ancient times, complete with animal skin costumes and plastic dog bones in the hair; 1970s-style feminists with Birkenstocks and wire-rimmed glasses (at a performance for the National Women's Studies Association conference); Ludmilla and Sorga, go-go dancers who have defected from Kunt, Homoslovakia (see photograph on page 328 for examples). Thrift store shopping is a crucial part of Lez Nez's fashion aesthetic, and Allison Faust's memories of particular costumes often include stories about serendipitous visits to locations such as the Korean Presbyterian thrift store in which she found matching homemade square-dancing outfits. Costumes for another performance came from two garbage bags of polyester that a friend found in an alley; at one-minute intervals during the show, Lez Nez donned a different item from these grab bags.[22]

Lez Nez's costumes are matched by the dancing, which combines eroticism and humor in mutually complementary ways. Although the dancers' open eroticism conveys an important part of GITN's prosex sensibility, the humor takes the edge off, allowing them to redefine eroticism so as to remove the hazards of being a sex object in an unwanted way. The result is not merely ironic distance, however; the Lez Nez dancers display a dyke sexiness that generates its own forms of fascination and fandom. In addition to choreographing gestures that mime the words of a song, Kathy and Allison mix and match different styles and sensibilities within one song, letting their facial expressions, for example, counter their bodily movements. As with their clothing, their dance styles mine a popular archive, conjuring the go-go girls of the early 1960s or interpretive dance modes of the later part of the decade or the hustle of the 1970s. It's easy enough to overlook their actual dancing in favor of their look and costumes, but I would argue that the two are closely related and that their costumes provide a material register of the archive of styles also present in the dance.

Lez Nez performs "Breast Exam" with Joanna Labow, Girls in the Nose show at Chances, 1993. In the background, members of the Girls in the Nose are dressed in Lez Nez costumes from previous shows. *From left to right,* Lisa Wickware, Kay Turner, Darby Smotherman (on Drums) Gretchen Phillips, and Julie. (Courtesy of L. E. McMorris; used with permission)

Especially in retrospect, I am struck by how the pleasures afforded by Lez Nez exceed what theories of performativity might say about them. My own experience has been crucial to arriving at a point where I don't think any theory can fully account for the actual complexity of how space, audience, costumes, movement styles, and subcultural formations contribute to specific instances of performance. I would now be reluctant to answer the question of whether go-go dancing (or pornography, or fashion, or any number of other cultural forms coded as feminine) can be a lesbian or a feminist mode of expression in the abstract, because until I actually saw Lez Nez perform in the flesh, I had not really understood the performative possibilities of go-go dancing. Performance, and specifically dance performance, is an embodied form of queer theory and exceeds theory in its capacity to make abstractions material. Although we have now learned a great deal about gender performativity from Judith Butler, in retrospect it might be important to think of these modes of performance as having invented her rather than the other way around. (Indeed, given Butler's desire to dissociate performativity from literal theatrical performance, especially drag, it might be a good time to think performance without theories of performativity.[23]) Academic attention to queer culture may, of course, seem a relatively marginal trend compared to mainstream media attention. But both developments raise questions about the significance of a subculture's history once it achieves mainstream visibility. The trajectory from GITN to *Ellen* is not necessarily a direct one, and an emphasis on what the mainstream can do with lesbians occludes what lesbians have been doing with the mainstream by responding to its versions of femininity. If *Ellen* or celebrity lesbianism become the benchmarks of lesbian visibility, we miss out on Lez Nez's weird and wacky spectacle of a sexually explicit, sexually perverse love affair with popular culture. In the catalogue of styles and gestures that goes into just one of Lez Nez's performances can be found a wide range of lesbian performances of femininity that cannot be subsumed under a single or monolithic theoretical category.

GO-GO GIRLS FOR THE LESBIAN COUNTERNATION: ON THE LAND AND IN THE CLUBS

While my experience at the March on Washington remains unprecedented, it was definitely matched by my appearances at one of the capitals of lesbian feminism, the Michigan Womyn's Music Festival, where GITN performed in 1994 and 1995.[24] An annual event since 1976, the festival is one of the longest-running and largest of the cultural festivals that emerged in the 1970s as a locus for lesbian culture. The festivals, which turn their back on urban centers of patriarchy and politics such as Washington, and even emerging gay metropolitan centers such as New York and San Francisco, have sought out space that can be women owned and operated in order to establish the alternative nation of "women's land." The rural location of many festivals has also

Girls in the Nose at 1995 Michigan Womyn's Music Festival. Ann Cvetkovich (*left*) and Kiersten Connolly (*right*), substitutes for Lez Nez, perform "Breast Exam" with Joanna Labow (*center*).

been influenced by a 1970s back-to-the-land sensibility and by economics. The Michigan festival's stability and autonomy are the result of the organizers' owning the land in a relatively affordable region of rural Michigan. Every August, women, most of them lesbians, convert the land into a small city that they build and run. By literally building a community from the ground up and building community from the labor of working on the land, the women of the Michigan festival use the power of both land and culture to create an alternative cultural capital to Washington and, if not a lesbian nation, then a lesbian counternation.

In the course of sustaining itself for more than twenty years, the festival has evolved along with lesbian feminism, becoming a place where even lesbian separatism is up for intense debate, along with issues such as sadomasochism, transgenderism, lesbian parenting, and racism. GITN's invitation to perform signaled an important shift in the festival's sensibility and its embrace of a new generation of lesbian culture. Tribe 8 also appeared for the first time in 1994, a performance that has become legendary for bringing punk rock, mosh pits, and stage diving to the land and for inspiring heated discussions about not only those topics but violence against women, sadomasochism, and intergenerational relations.[25] Rather than confirming the existence of generational differences between 1970s lesbian feminists and 1990s queer punk dykes, the appearance of new styles on the land has ultimately served as a way of acknowledging the continuity of radical spirit between these two generations. (Furthermore, an overemphasis on intergenerational differences privileges conflicts between two styles of white lesbianism. Michigan provides a forum for a range of performances by women of color and thus challenges any binaristic account of the generational styles to be found at the festival. The racial politics of the festival's prominent inclusion of women of color in the program is complex because it both evidences the desire of white women to include cultural difference and provides a vehicle for women of color, especially African American women, to convene.) Like GITN's appearance in Washington, the band's performance at Michigan signaled the possibility of national exposure for the local lesbian subculture in Austin. Each location, and its accompanying notion of public culture, represents a different approach to creating a national culture. In Washington the goal is to displace the nation by queering it and reaching straight audiences; in Michigan the nation is displaced by turning away from engagement with nonlesbian culture and creating an alternative to it. (Michigan is also more explicitly international and transnational, drawing workers and audiences from a number of nations other than the United States, although primarily from Canada and Western Europe.) Both kinds of events—marches and festivals—create national public cultures and communities, and Michigan thus raises the same questions for the go-go dancer as does Washington—what forms of cultural politics does a dance performance produce?

As an event on a national scale, the Michigan festival has some of the literal largeness of the March on Washington—three outdoor stages accommodate much larger audiences than most clubs. But GITN's performance there was also dramatically different from its March on Washington appearance because the one-hour time slot provided an opportunity to show the band's range and build rapport with the audience. Moreover, Michigan performances draw on an unprecedented intimacy between performers and audience. For reasons that begin with, but exceed, its policy of women-only space, the festival creates a distinctive form of public culture. Performance is only one highlight of a festival experience in which the audience is engaged in many other kinds of activities than watching shows, including working, meeting people, shopping, going to workshops, and camping in safe space. Rather than being marked off from other parts of daily life, performance at Michigan is part of a continuum that breaks down the distinction between performance and other kinds of activity, including labor, all of which are reconstructed as arenas of pleasure and creativity in the utopia of Michigan. Indeed, the performers are considered the last "work crew" to arrive on the land, and the festival's cultural events are also a vehicle for the creation of an intentional community of workers and then festival goers, in which the goal is to explore the meaning of community. The performances are a crucial vehicle, but not the only one, for the creation of a public, and the relation between audience and performers is more active than in contexts where an audience is joined only through the shared act of attending a performance. For example, many audience members are part of the workers' community that spends a month building the space for the week-long festival, and even festival attendees have to work two shifts in order to make an active contribution as producers of the festival, not just consumers. (Along with performing for GITN, both Gretchen Phillips and I worked at the festival, erasing even further the traditional boundaries between performers, production staff, and audience.) Thus a Michigan audience already possesses a tremendous amount of cohesion as a community before it comes to a show; performances are not the only mechanism for creating solidarity.

For us as go-go dancers, these factors facilitated a greater degree of sexual openness in our performances, which could draw on the festival's atmosphere of collective eroticism. In 1994 I performed with Allison Faust again, and in 1995 I performed with Kiersten Connolly, who in the intervening year had become a partner with me in regular performances in Austin with the Gretchen Phillips Xperience (GPX). With a full-length show we could plan a series of costume changes, and in both years we ended the show with matching outfits to capitalize on the visual power of being doubles for one another. The first year, Allison and I wore pink polka-dot stretch jumpsuits with chiffon bell bottoms. The next year Kiersten and I wore gold stretch full-length sheath dresses. We fully exploited the homoeroticism of identical twins, and we were greeted with enthusiasm by a crowd primed for the spectacle of a fashion statement. The Michigan crowds of the 1990s were ready not only for dildos and harnesses on stage but were eager for wigs and costumes.

Performing at Michigan made me conscious of the careful boundaries I maintain, even in lesbian clubs, in order to distinguish between a sexual performance oriented toward lesbians and a sexualized performance that caters to men. In a mixed crowd, queering the performance can be important, to signal its lesbianism and/or its difference from other kinds of erotic dance. I have most frequently opted for wackiness rather than sexiness to make this clear (or to confuse audiences) because overt lesbian sexuality on stage still runs the risk of being construed as entertainment for men. (One friend reports that two straight men in the audience for a recent show during Austin's SWSW (South by Southwest) music festival, at a very straight club, spent a good part of the performance trying to figure out what gender we were.) In the "safe space" of Michigan the necessity of allowing for mixed audiences is gone, and the freedom to explore both humor and sexuality in the glow of an endlessly appreciative dyke audience is truly exciting. GITN's Michigan performances were extraordinary shows for me, some of the best ever in terms of the actual dancing, because the crowd inspired a level of physical exertion that propelled me onward. At its best, dancing on stage extends the powers of a night at the disco to create an ecstatic loss of control.

Go-go dancing's power to intensify the readily available pleasures of the disco is one reason that during the past few years I have welcomed the opportunity to dance regularly with the Gretchen Phillips Xperience in Austin. Local performance is a more intimate experience than dancing in Michigan or Washington; the venues are small clubs often equipped with stages designed for bands but not dancers. I think of my work with GPX as serial dancing, a chance for go-go dancing to be a regular part of my life and an outlet from the seriousness of academia, which I often experience as an arena of disembodiment. Go-go dancing offers an immediate gratification that contrasts with writing's protracted temporality, a freedom from professional responsibility that contrasts with the obligations of teaching, and a lesbocentric community that contrasts with academic institutions. Compared to other kinds of dance performance, it requires a relatively low investment of time and materials, because it does not require a big stage, rehearsals, or expensive costumes. Rather than constituting a pure escape into leisure culture from professional culture, though, my go-go dancing is very much in dialogue with other forms of labor and creativity in my life, informing those other activities by providing alternative versions of them.

My key principles in planning both costumes and dances are improvisation and flexibility. I rarely consult with my dance partners before the day of the show, but we're still able to come up with different unifying costume themes—dressing in one color, cross-dressing as boys, or wearing a particular item of clothing, such as bathing suits, pajamas, or polyester caftans. Regular visits to thrift stores make it easy to acquire and maintain an extensive wardrobe because no item is too wild for the stage. Go-go dancing thus constitutes a form of lesbian drag culture. Even though I rarely wear the white go-go boots that I coveted as a child, preferring Lez Nez's tactic of wearing dyke boots for comfort and contrast, I can play out a multitude of costume fantasies. (I do have a pair, but because the vinyl does not breathe at all and the cut is very narrow, they are virtually impossible to dance in.)

My constant accessories are a wig and sunglasses, which provide a comfortable disguise and enable a certain distance from the audience. In addition to giving me the freedom to look without being observed, these accessories provide an instant face, eliminating the need for elaborate makeup or hairstyling. (In fact, wigs have introduced me to a big-hair world whose pleasures I simply had no notion of after a lifetime of resistance to femininity.) As a sexual icon, the go-go dancer has been a figure of suspicion because she so closely resembles the erotic dancer. Yet lesbian contexts have found ways of refiguring the forms of sexualization that dancing produces. For example, the go-go dancer can control the power of the audience's gaze in the same way that a femme top can use her seductiveness to maintain control of a sexual encounter. Subtle variations on skimpy clothing distinguish us from heterosexual erotic dancers. I often wear an old-fashioned bra that turns my breasts into cartoonish cones, and one of my favorite outfits features a pair of men's boxer shorts beneath a garter belt and stockings.

Particularly with a lesbian audience that may recognize a degree of irony in our performance of sexuality, I have always found being the center of visual attention to be a form of power rather than objectification. Having a partner is also a form of protection because we can interact in a way that shuts out the audience. We can dance together in a sexually explicit way and make it clear that we are not addressing ourselves to a heterosexual male audience, by choosing forms of sexual explicitness that signal a lesbianism without men, such as wearing dildos and harnesses and using fingers to mime digital penetration. In these details lies a world of variation that dramatically transforms abstract questions about the performance of femininity; its lesbian possibilities are varied and differ significantly from heterosexual codes. Ultimately, though, context is crucial, and the same performance and gestures may have a different meaning when the audience is predominantly lesbian or when men are excluded from the audience.

With GPX I have worked with a variety of different dancers, often two others, but my most consistent partner has been my friend Kiersten Connolly. Working on a regular basis allows us a chance to build a dance rhythm together even if we improvise all our moves. Working with a partner can make us more comfortable and more fearless, allowing us to focus on one another rather than the audience, and we respond to one another as we move among dance styles. With a degree of predictability that is part of its attraction, I can count on each show to bring a moment when I will be totally absorbed by the music, inside my body rather than my head. I lose myself in social dance as I have never done in choreographed theatrical dance, and the combination of costume, partners, and audience heightens the experience.

WHAT IS GO-GO DANCING?

I've talked about go-go dancing as the occasion for public culture and as a vehicle for the display of fashion. But what about the actual dancing itself? How does motion serve as the specific medium for the production of spectacles and publics?

As part of the still largely unchronicled history of social dance forms, go-go dancing is linked to the rise in the early 1960s of the discotheque, an institution that plays a central role in gay public culture, not least because of the opportunity it affords for cruising.[26] Disco is in turn related to the popularization of rock music in the 1950s, which enabled new forms of popular dance that separated the couple and allowed the individual dancer to display her skill. According to D. Duane Braun, the go-go dancing craze was imported from Paris in the early 1960s and stimulated a wave of dance trends, such as the frug, the hullaballoo, and the jerk, that built on the popularity of the twist, which was introduced in 1961.[27] Placed in cages or on platforms, go-go dancers substituted for the presence of a live band and demonstrated the new dances for the public. Eventually, dancing became so free form that there were no steps or gestures that required instruction, but in the early 1960s the go-go dancer helped bridge the transition from the choreographed steps of ballroom to the less demanding conventions of disco. In the process she also became a generational icon, like the flapper of the 1920s, combining fashion, sexuality, and movement to become an embodiment of cultural trends.

Like so much of American popular culture, go-go dancing exists at a locus of cross-racial cultural exchange and the long history of white appropriations of African American forms. The twist was popularized by the success of such Chubby Checker hits as "The Twist" and "Let's Twist Again," but it received special attention in the national media in 1961 and 1962 when prominent white people started frequenting the Peppermint Lounge in Manhattan.[28] In a 1965 story about discotheques the *Saturday Evening Post* tracked the success of the dance teacher Killer Joe Piro, who got his start as the first white man to win a jitterbugging contest in the late 1940s.[29] Also part of the dance craze of the early 1960s were the samba, the bossa nova, and other Latin-inspired forms. Thus behind the figure of the white girl dancing on stage is a complex racial history.

A full history of social dance from a cultural studies perspective would include not only an account of its status as a vehicle for race relations but also a discussion of its role as an arena for public sexuality and counterpublic spheres. The styles of the disco combine the visual and the physical, setting the sexualized body on display in a sanctioned public way. In the 1970s, when disco and rock music had separate audiences, disco flourished among specific audiences, including white working-class cultures, people of color, and gay men. (Think of how John Travolta immortalized disco as an Italian American form in *Saturday Night Fever* and taught us how to "do the hustle," the 1970s dance craze that briefly reintroduced the need for lessons.) Dance culture, even more so than live music culture, offers an inexpensive and accessible form of counterpublic culture, requiring only a turntable (or two), a room, and a DJ to create entertainment.[30]

The dance fads of the 1960s inaugurated an era of social dancing as individual and thus "queered" the heterosexual couple that is the foundation for ballroom and other styles of social dance. Commenting on the popularity of the new dance styles among women, Killer Joe Piro said, "The girls really love these dances. The girl is free to do what she wants to. She couldn't let herself go before the Twist. They must have been swearing under their breath for years—led around, pushed around, held down. Now they can be as wild as they feel. Watch any discotheque and you'll see it's the girls who go. On the dance floor they've got no inhibitions."[31] My own memories of go-go dancing, derived from magazines and television, not from time in the clubs, are part of the archive that structures my adult performances. As a child, I responded to the go-go dancer of the 1960s as the popular culture variant of dance fantasies that were also inspired by the ballet classes I was taking at the same time. The go-go dancer's white boots and miniskirt created a spectacle of iconic femininity that matched the image of the ballerina in her tutu and toe shoes. She was the poster girl for a new style of femininity that was sexual, free, and open. The steps of go-go dancing, just as much as the steps of ballet, offered an instructional medium for achievement.[32] More needs to be written, and from a queer perspective, about how young girls construct and use these femme fantasies. In my case, for example, dance allowed me to be the girl my mother would not let me be in her insistence on a no-nonsense, no-frills style. Just as butch styles and gay male femininity can be forms of resistance to compulsory gender identities, so too can femme lesbianism be a way to reclaim stigmatized identities and failed identifications too often overlooked if we assume that gender nonconformity has to consist in (the most obvious forms of) cross-gender identification or if constantly mutating forms of misogyny lead to the dismissal of all forms of femininity.[33] In the contrast between the ballerina and the go-go dancer a complex racial imaginary is at work, because the former signifies not just the proper femininity but the whiteness of elite culture, whereas the latter has associations with a range of styles that are coded as non–Euro-American.[34]

Although popular dance might seem to be a form of training for heterosexuality, the solo dancer is afforded a power that has nothing to do with boys or men. The teaching and transmission of popular dance styles often fosters a homosocial world of girls practicing dances that tend to be of little interest to boys. (Indeed, social dancing became a less attractive experience for me when it involved dancing with boys who danced grudgingly, and dance clubs were an important catalyst for my coming out because they were populated by other women and gay men who loved to dance.) One 1960s commentator for *Life* echoed this sentiment when he said, "The critical point in listening comes when a girl becomes old enough to feel a serious interest in a boy. When she is pinned, when her big interest goes from the group to just one boy, then she starts losing interest in rock'n'roll. She wants to stop dancing by herself, and start dancing with this one boy—in his arms—and to regular dance music."[35] Go-go dancing provides a forum for putting one's skill as a dancer on display, constituting itself as a performance worthy of an audience. Although it may require less training than theatrical dance techniques, it is potentially more accessible and can be performed more informally. For young girls, the dance class itself can be a scene of performance and femme power that should be considered an important context for social dance.[36]

Furthermore, the popular culture consumed by young girls in the 1950s and 1960s, including images of countercultures from mass culture sources such as the *Time* and *Life* articles about go-go dancing or TV shows such as Dick Clark's *American Bandstand*, form the basis for adult lesbian culture of the 1990s. Recovering these earlier histories, through memory and nostalgia, and across the land mines of feminist cultural politics, is work that I do through the act of dancing, not just through my academic research. Sixties-style go-go dancing and its fashions remain a point of reference in my current dancing, a way of conjuring that era of history and my childhood experience of it. Lesbian camp makes a tradition of such appropriations, taking the styles of a prefeminist femininity and making them its own, divesting historical images of these styles' oppressive power and returning to them with the pleasure of nostalgia. The dances of the 1960s— the swim, the jerk, and the twist—are part of my go-go dancing repertoire, which occupies a fluid space between improvised and fixed movements. Lesbian go-go dancing is irreverent enough to include many kinds of quotation, and I have thrown in steps learned in ballet and modern classes as well as popular styles. Being able to perform movements that are recognizable as learned steps becomes a sign of skill, taking the free form of the disco and codifying it. At the same time the improvisational openness offers flexibility, because it is possible to revert to a free form or change steps at will.

Especially important is go-go as a rhythm-based form of dance grounded in repetition and variation. Although it may seem mo-

notorious when compared to theatrical dance, anybody who is truly dedicated to popular dance probably understands the pleasures of subtle variations on a basic rhythmic pattern. (Any classically trained dancer who performs the same steps in one class after another also appreciates the powers of repetition.) Tuned to the beats of the song, the disco dancer and the go-go dancer are the moving equivalents of the song's drum and bass lines. The go-go dancer is like the musician in a jazz or swing band who plays certain set patterns and then takes a solo. But the pleasure is as much in playing with the ensemble as in the solos. Doing the same thing never gets boring, especially because repetition is not sameness; in any dance club part of the voyeuristic pleasure resides in watching every single person's unique style, the characteristic body language that reveals personality. (Discos are such important cruising grounds because they let the body rather than speech become a vehicle of self-revelation.)

Improvisation is crucial to go-go dancing in which a movement vocabulary provides an underlying structure of learned steps that is infinitely adaptable to any music. Being able to perform without excessive planning is an essential part of the pleasure it provides. As a form of dance that can take place in spaces usually reserved for musical performance, go-go dancing is more flexible than theatrical dance and can draw on the more informal and popular audiences that go to clubs rather than to theaters. (In fact, sometimes the stage has been so small that we have had to stay in one spot throughout the entire show, a constraint that produces its own forms of innovation when the movements are confined entirely to the hips and arms.) Compared with other forms of live performance, go-go dancing has many attractions, especially because of its accessibility.

Ultimately, go-go dancing has triumphed over theatrical dance in my experience. Having practiced both, I would say I have gotten far more pleasure out of my nights in clubs than from all the diligent hours spent in classes, rehearsals, and performances. Theatrical performance, with its ambitions to impress an audience with technical skill or make meaning out of the steps, might be unnecessary when the simple pleasure of the body in motion is enough. Even very simple movements can produce the ecstasy that the intensity of performance also provides. In the dance fads of the 1960s and in lesbian appropriations lie a wealth of possibilities for reclaiming the power of femininity and the power of dance for creating and sustaining publics.

Attention to this phenomenon also opens up important directions for a queer dance studies to investigate dance as an arena of female bonding, femme creativity, and lesbian camp. Lesbian go-go dancing joins such spectacles of femme performativity as Annie Sprinkle's Post-Porn Modernist show, Lois Weaver's dance performances with Peggy Shaw in Split Britches theater, and lesbian sex work, including the many genres of erotic dancing.[37] Indeed, one dividend of increased attention to dance in cultural studies would be an enhanced appreciation for performances that have been devalued through the combined dismissal of femininity and dance. Just as the recent flurry of interest in drag kings has shown the many styles of masculinity that lesbians can adopt, including female masculinities, so too do these displays open up room for the performance of femininity as a powerful and creative resource.[38] My life as a lesbian go-go dancer is part of this important tradition. For that reason I have wanted to write about it, although not without some ambivalence because doing so challenges my creation of dance culture as an alternative to intellectual culture (even if that separation is based on a suspicious split between mind and body). Yet they do, of course, converge in my own body and identity. My conviction that dance offers something that theory does not has been confirmed by Sandy Stone's account of why performance has become a preferred mode of presentation for her ideas:

> It's [performance is] the way I do my theory. . . . When I am in front of an audience, a live audience, doing whatever it is that I'm doing, my theory arises in that moment, in the interaction, and it arises only because I think about what I am thinking in response to what the audience is thinking in that moment. . . . It's as if the audience collectively had an idea that they wanted me to manifest, and my job was to figure out what that thing was and then to manifest it. Frequently, I don't know what happened until I go back

and look at the documentation, and then if I think about it for a while, I can maybe write it down, but more and more I am discovering that I can't write it down at this time. But I can reperform it, and so I build it into the next performance.[39]

I share Stone's sense of performance and interaction with an audience as a occasion when something, including theory, that is not available in words can be made manifest. Stone offers a theory of performativity that departs from Judith Butler and other queer theorists by stressing performativity's connections to new languages of communication enabled by the body. According to Stone, "Rather than simply being a passage point for always-already socially understood symbols, the body is a source of new symbols which are taken up by social networks and incorporated into a larger cultural language which includes words and gestures but is not limited to them."[40] Thus my attraction to those moments, which I have described inadequately here, when dancing allows me a kind of ecstasy, a moment when one is not only transcending the body but also supremely in it, in a state where thinking is in the service of movement. Dance teaches me a new cultural language, contributing to my academic life because it challenges the accustomed labor and hierarchy of thinking that has made dance and movement a mode of expression that is inferior to verbal modes. Go-go dancing any time, any place, not just in times and places saturated with public significance such as Michigan and Washington, gives me that knowledge and that pleasure.

NOTES

This writing would not have been possible without the opportunity to perform, and I thank Kay Turner and Gretchen Phillips for envisioning go-go dancers as integral to Girls in the Nose and the Gretchen Phillips Xperience, as well as for many hours of delicious conversation. With Fausto Fernos, Patty Lou, and especially Allison Faust and Kiersten Connolly, I have experienced the very special bond of dance partnering. I also owe thanks to Jane Desmond for the inspiration of this project and her other dance scholarship, which made writing about dance finally seem desirable; her response to drafts has made this a wonderful collaboration. I also want to acknowledge the many people who have shared the open secret of my life as a dancer, especially the friends I made during six years of ballet classes at Cornell University's Helen Newman gym: Peter Saul, an extraordinary dance teacher; Patrick Riordan, my first queer dance partner, both on stage and at the Common Ground; and Zofia Burr, who has been my partner in ballet classes and lesbianism equally.

1. Gretchen Phillips, cofounder of Girls in the Nose, declared this to be the mission of Two Nice Girls, one of the other lesbian bands she started in Austin in 1985. See her liner notes for *Lesbian Favorites: Women Like Us* (Rhino Records, 1997).

2. Both songs are available on *Origin of the World* (1992). GITN also has two earlier releases, *Chant to the Full Moon, Oh Ye Sisters* (1988), and *Girls in the Nose* (1990). A 1994 music video, *Breast Exam*, features a live performance of the song at Austin's now closed lezzie club, Chances, and interviews with women talking about breasts. In addition to great footage of Lez Nez, the video has some brief shots of my performance as a back-up dancer. Tapes, CDs, and videos are available from Girls in the Nose, P.O. Box 49828, Austin, Texas 78765.

3. RuPaul was drawing on a tradition of flag drag that includes Madonna's *Rock the Vote* segment for MTV in 1992, in which she was draped in the flag and flanked by two flaming go-go boys in white t-shirts, denim shorts, and combat boots, and Sandra Bernhard's performance of "Little Red Corvette" in *Without You I'm Nothing* (1991), in which she wears a cloak made of the flag and strips to a G-string and pasties adorned with stars and stripes. For a reading of these performances see Lauren Berlant and Elizabeth Freeman, "Queer Nationality," in Lauren Berlant, *The Queen of America Goes to Washington City* (Durham, N.C.: Duke University Press, 1997). For more on Sandra Bernhard, see Ann Pellegrini, *Performance Anxieties: Staging Psychoanalysis, Staging Race* (New York: Routledge, 1997).

4. For an important discussion of the politics of equal representation, see Eric Clarke, *Virtuous Vice: Homoeroticism and the Public Sphere* (Durham, N.C.: Duke University Press, 2000).

5. Recent work on the public sphere has been influenced by Jurgen Habermas, *The Structural Transformation of the Public Sphere* (Cambridge, Mass.: MIT Press, 1989). Other work that explores its implications includes Craig Calhoun, ed., *Habermas and the Public Sphere* (Cambridge, Mass.: MIT Press, 1992), and Bruce Robbins, ed., *The Phantom Public Sphere* (Minneapolis: University of Minnesota Press, 1993). Especially important for my purposes is Michael Warner's essay "The Mass Public and the Mass Subject" (included in both anthologies), which explores visual display of the public celebrity, especially the visibility of bodies and faces, as a mode of access to the public sphere and as a means of political, not just cultural, representation.

6. Jane Desmond has commented on how dance occupies a lower position in the hierarchy of aesthetic genres because of the privileging of the written document. Another version of this hierarchy prevailed at the march, where most artists were musicians and comedians and writers; visual artists, actors, or dancers were scarce. Dance has allowed me to ride on the coattails of the success of lesbian musicians as celebrities and therefore to participate in far more prominent public cul-

tures than those in which my academic writing circulates. See Jane Desmond, ed., introduction and "Embodying Difference: Issues in Dance and Cultural Studies," both in *Meaning in Motion: New Cultural Studies of Dance* (Durham, N.C.: Duke University Press, 1997), 1–25 and 29–54, respectively.

7. See Berlant, *Queen of America*, esp. chap. 2, "The Theory of Infantile Citizenship," and chap. 6, "The Queen of America Goes to Washington City: Notes on Diva Citizenship," 25–53 and 221–46, respectively.

8. See Ioannis Mookas, "Faukt Tines: Homophobic Innovation in *Gay Rights, Special Rights*," in Grant Kester, ed., *Art, Activism, and Oppositionality: Essays from Afterimage* (Durham, N.C.: Duke University Press, 1998), 287–304. The essay includes extensive discussion of how the video juxtaposes the 1963 and 1993 marches on Washington. For the video see Jeremiah Films (producer), *Gay Rights, Special Rights*, 1993.

9. Each product released by Girls in the Nose bears the inscription "Document of a Subculture." With two of its original members trained as professional folklorists, GITN shows a high degree of self-consciousness about preserving those popular forms that might not be visible within the dominant culture. Like folk culture, dance has often been lost to scrutiny or marginalized by aesthetic hierarchies. Dance's lowly position in the hierarchy of art forms is also related to the mutually constitutive distinctions between high culture and folk culture, especially because dance has been a powerful mode of popular expression.

10. See Peggy Phelan, *Unmarked: The Politics of Performance* (New York: Routledge, 1993).

11. See Desmond's introduction to *Meaning in Motion*.

12. Examples include the following cover stories: Eloise Salholz, "The Power and the Pride," *Newsweek*, June 21, 1993, pp. 54–60; Jeanie Russell Kasindorf, "Lesbian Chic," *New York*, May 10, 1993, pp. 30–37; Leslie Bennetts, "k.d. lang Cuts It Close," *Vanity Fair*, August 1993, pp. 94–99. The last includes Herb Ritts's photos of k.d. lang posing in butch-femme drag with Cindy Crawford.

13. Kay Turner, personal communication, February 1998. Turner mentioned the influence of not only her doctoral training in folklore but her childhood in Detroit in the 1950s and 1960s. For an overview of the band's history and mission written by Kay Turner, see Lee Fleming, ed., *Hot Licks: Lesbian Musicians of Note* (Charlottetown, P.E.I., Can.: Gynergy Books, 1996), 44–49. Also indicative of Turner's hybrid sensibility in which mass culture, folk culture, and subcultures coexist are her publications, including *Lady Unique Inclination of the Night*, a journal of feminist spirituality; *I Dream of Madonna: Women's Dreams of the Goddess of Pop* (San Francisco: Collins, 1993); and *Between Us: Lesbian Love Letters* (San Francisco: Chronicle Books, 1996). Both books and journals are illustrated with collages that are visual emblems of Turner's hybrid aesthetics.

14. Lyrics are from the song "Incongruity," *Origin of the World*.

15. Allison Faust describes the struggle to be taken seriously as a member of the band and the need to battle the assumption that Lez Nez was a dispensable accessory. The challenges included making sure there would be room on stage for the dancers and getting funded for travel to out-of-town performances.

16. See Arlene Stein, "Sisters and Queers: The Decentering of Lesbian Feminism," *Socialist Review* 22, no. 1 (January–March 1992): 33–55, and Stein, "Androgyny Goes Pop: But Is It Lesbian Music?" in Arlene Stein, ed., *Sisters, Sexperts, Queers: Beyond the Lesbian Nation* (New York: Plume, 1993), 96–109. The now-defunct publications *Outlook* and *Outweek* provide a valuable archive of the late 1980s and early 1990s.

17. The relevant bibliography is vast, but examples of Madonna studies would include Cathy Schwichtenberg, ed., *The Madonna Connection* (Boulder, Colo.: Westview, 1993); Lisa Frank and Paul Smith, eds., *Madonnarama* (Pittsburgh, Pa.: Cleis, 1993); and Ann Cvetkovich, "The Powers of Seeing and Being Seen: *Truth or Dare* and *Paris Is Burning*," in Ava Collins, Jim Collins, and Hilary Radner, eds., *Film Theory Goes to the Movies* (New York: Routledge, 1993), 155–69. On theories of performativity, see Judith Butler, *Gender Trouble: Feminism and the Subversion of Identity* (New York: Routledge, 1990); Butler, *Bodies That Matter: On the Discursive Limits of "Sex"* (New York: Routledge, 1993); and Andrew Parker and Eve Kosofsky Sedgwick, eds., *Performativity and Performance* (New York: Routledge, 1995).

18. On queer archives and evidence, including the role of memory in documenting the history of subcultures, see José Estéban Muñoz, "Ephemera as Evidence: Introductory Notes to Queer Acts," *Women and Performance* 16 (1996): 5–19.

19. See the materials on the public sphere cited in note 5 for more on the concept of public culture. The concept of public has displaced the notion of subculture in its reference not just to a group of people but to a specific institutional space through which identity and community—or a public—can be constituted. Also significant is the notion of a counterpublic, a concept developed by Miriam Hansen in her foreword to Oskar Negt and Alexander Kluge, *Public Sphere and Experience: Toward an Analysis of the Bourgeois and Proletarian Public Sphere* (Minneapolis: University of Minnesota Press, 1993).

20. For more on bar culture and its relation to gay and lesbian history, see Madeline Davis and Elizabeth Lapovsky Kennedy, *Boots of Leather, Slippers of Gold: The History of a Lesbian Community* (New York: Routledge, 1993); Esther Newton, *Mother Camp* (Chicago: University of Chicago Press, 1972), and *Cherry Grove* (Boston: Beacon, 1993); and George Chauncey, *Gay New York: Gender, Urban Culture, and the Making of the Gay Male World, 1890–1940* (New York: Basic, 1994).

21. See Deborah P. Amory, "Club Q: Dancing with (a) Difference," in Ellen Lewin, ed., *Inventing Lesbian Cultures in America* (Boston: Beacon, 1996), 145–60.

22. These details are culled from personal communications with Allison Faust and Kathy Smith, July 1998. For a wonderful account of the thrift store sensibility shared by Lez Nez, see the 'zine *Thrift SCORE*, which Faust first recommended to me (available from Al Hoff, P.O. Box 90282, Pittsburgh, Pa. 15224). Al Hoff has also published a trade book based on the 'zine, *Thrift SCORE* (New York: HarperPerennial, 1997).

23. See the revised account of Butler's theories of performativity in *Bodies*

That Matter. Equally significant for queer theories of performativity is the work of Eve Kosofsky Sedgwick, but her work has been less caught up with dichotomies between subversion and containment, and she has sought to critique this impasse. See Sedgwick, "Queer Performativity: Henry James's *The Art of the Novel*," *GLQ* 1, no. 1 (1993): 1–16. For incisive accounts of both Sedgwick and Butler, see Biddy Martin, "Extraordinary Homosexuals and the Fear of Being Ordinary" and "Sexuality Without Genders and Other Queer Utopias," in Martin, *Femininity Played Straight: The Significance of Being Lesbian* (New York: Routledge, 1996), 45–70 and 71–94, respectively.

24. My very first chance to perform with GITN was at another women's music festival, Rhythmfest, in Cloudland, Georgia, in September 1992. That performance was captured on camera as part of a segment about Rhythmfest in Ellen Spiro's documentary *Greetings from Out Here: A Queer's Eye View of a Strangely Straight (or So We Thought) Southern Universe* (1993). Available from Video Databank, 37 S. Wabash, Chicago, Ill. 60603.

25. See Gretchen Phillips, "I Moshed at Mich," in Evelyn McDonnell and Ann Powers, eds., *Rock She Wrote* (New York: Delta, 1995), 80–86; and Ann Cvetkovich, "Sexual Trauma/Queer Memory: Lesbianism, Incest, and Therapeutic Culture," *GLQ* 2, no. 4 (1995): 351–77.

26. Scholarship that combines dance studies and cultural studies has yet to pay extended attention to social dance as opposed to theatrical dance. And within gay and lesbian studies, disco remains to be fully analyzed. One important beginning is Richard Dyer's "In Defense of Disco," in Corey K. Creekmur and Alexander Doty, eds., *Out in Culture: Gay, Lesbian, and Queer Essays on Popular Culture* (Durham, N.C.: Duke University Press, 1995), 407–15.

27. See D. Duane Braun, *Toward a Theory of Popular Culture: The Sociology and History of American Music and Dance* (Ann Arbor: Ann Arbor Publishers, 1969). Braun's sources are primarily popular magazines such as *Life*, *Time*, and *Newsweek*, which suggests the difficulty of constructing an archive for studying this phenomenon. Yet limited as these popular media might be, they were also my primary source for information about go-go dancing in the 1960s.

28. For accounts of the twisting rage, see "And Now Everybody Is Doing It: The Twist," *Life*, November 24, 1961, pp. 74–80; "The Twist," *New Yorker*, October 21, 1961, pp. 46–47; "Instant Fad," *Time*, October 20, 1961, pp. 54, 56. I am indebted to Braun's book for these sources. Also very informative is the Canadian film *Twist* (1992, D: Ron Mann), which gives attention to African American dance clubs in which the twist was popular, as well as to Hank Ballard, whose band first released a recording of "The Twist," which was later covered to much greater acclaim by Chubby Checker.

29. "Discotheque," *Saturday Evening Post*, March 27, 1965, pp. 21–27.

30. There is growing body of scholarship in cultural studies on popular music, including African American forms such as rap and hip-hop. Still to be fully explored is the complex relation between music and dance in these cultural trends. See, for example, Andrew Ross and Tricia Rose, eds., *Microphone Fiends: Youth Music and Youth Culture* (New York: Routledge, 1994); Tricia Rose, *Black Noise: Rap Music and Black Culture in Contemporary America* (Hanover,

N.H.: Wesleyan University Press, 1994); Michele Wallace and Gina Dent, *Black Popular Culture* (Seattle: Bay Press, 1992); and Andrew Ross's essay on Jamaican dance hall culture, "Mr. Reggae DJ, Meet the International Monetary Fund," in Ross, *Real Love: In Pursuit of Cultural Justice* (New York: New York University Press, 1998).

31. "Discotheque," 23.

32. Angela McRobbie discusses how films such as *Fame* and *Flashdance* construct fantasy narratives about dance as a means of female achievement. See McRobbie, *Feminism and Youth Culture: From "Jackie" to "Just Seventeen"* (Boston: Unwin Hyman, 1991), 189–219.

33. Examples of gay male explorations of childhood fandom include Wayne Koestenbaum, *The Queen's Throat: Opera, Homosexuality, and the Mystery of Desire* (New York: Poseidon, 1993), and Kevin Kopelson, *Beethoven's Kiss: Pianism, Perversion, and the Mastery of Desire* (Stanford, Calif.: Stanford University Press, 1994), both of which could be construed as the notes of a sissy boyhood in which queer gender and sexual identity are formed through cultural experience. Constance Penley's *NASA/Trek: Popular Science and Sex in America* (London: Verso, 1997) points to the importance of taking seriously the fantasies of little girls, in this case fantasies about the space program and becoming an astronaut.

34. The beginnings of an investigation of how dance serves as the specific vehicle for the cross-racial fantasies of young white girls can be glimpsed in accounts of Madonna's fascination with Latino and African American cultures. See Stein, "Sisters and Queers," Stein, "Androgyny Goes Pop," and esp. the essays by Laurie Schulze, Anne Barton White, and Jane D. Brown, Thomas K. Nakayama and Lisa N. Penaloza, Ronald B. Scott, and Cindy Patton in Schwichtenberg, *The Madonna Connection*, the essays by thomas allen harris, Andrew Ross, and bell hooks in Frank and Smith, *Madonnarama*, and my essay in Collins, Collins, and Radner, *Film Theory*. Patton's essay, "Embodying Subaltern Memory: Kinesthesia and the Problematics of Gender and Race," 81–105, is especially valuable for its account of how dance can be a vehicle for the transmission and manifestation of cultural memory and for its sophisticated approach to the complexities of appropriation and cross-identification.

35. "Hear That Big Sound," *Life*, May 21, 1965, p. 94.

36. In her essay "Dancing Bodies," Susan Leigh Foster analyzes the forms of bodily discipline produced by different techniques of dance training, suggesting that these dance forms are also worthy of attention. For many amateur dancers, dance classes are a form of social dance, providing pleasures that are independent of preparation for performances on stage. See Desmond, *Meaning in Motion*, 235–57.

37. See "Annie Sprinkle," in Andrea Juno and V. Vale, eds., *Angry Women* (San Francisco: Re/Search Publications, 1991), 23–40; Sue-Ellen Case, ed., *Split Britches* (New York: Routledge, 1997); *Policing Public Sex: Queer Politics and the Future of AIDS Activism*, ed. Dangerous Bedfellows (Boston: South End, 1996).

38. See Judith Halberstam, "Mackdaddy, Superfly, Rapper: Gender, Race,

and Masculinity in the Drag King Scene," *SocialText* 52–53 (1997): 104–32, and Halberstam, *Female Masculinity* (Durham, N.C.: Duke University Press, 1998).

39. Bryan Fruth and Frances Guilfoyle, "This Laboratory, My Body: A Conversation with Allucquere Rosanne (Sandy) Stone," *Velvet Light Trap* 41 (spring 1998): 39.

40. Quoted from "transgender" page of Sandy Stone's web site, <www.sandystone.com>. Accessed Oct. 2, 2000.

11

29 Effeminate Gestures: Choreographer Joe Goode and the Heroism of Effeminacy

David Gere

A gangly man in his late thirties stands at the head of the room, preparing to deliver a lecture. He is wearing black—black cashmere sweater, black linen pants, black leather belt, black Italian shoes— the ostentatious colorlessness of the outfit serving to emphasize both his pallor and the formality of the occasion. The man's head inclines forward and his hands fidget in his pockets as he inspects his notes, which rest on a simple music stand. A video monitor at his side displays its static blue screen. After a pause he adjusts his lanky frame, swallows noticeably, and commences to speak in a soft, deceptively caressive voice.

I want to speak today about effeminate gestures. This is a subject about which I am, uh, something of an expert. Any boy in America could tell you, if he dared talk about it at all, what he has learned concerning the ways in which a man or man-child ought to move his arms and hands—and, more important, how he oughtn't. On a recent trip to visit my parents, who live in a sleepy village in central New York State, I learned this lesson firsthand. (*He begins now to gesture—elbows akimbo, fingers flaring, shoulders hunched forward—moderately at first but with increasing amplitude.*) While attending a neighborhood Christmas party, I found some childhood friends and was talking to them—with animation—when the host walked up beside me and said in all seriousness, "Can you talk without waving your hands?" (*The last line is delivered in a gruff offhand manner, which causes the speaker's body to become visibly constrained.*)

My host was not just talking about waving, of course, nor just about hands. He was talking about the particular way in which I

Joe Goode in his *29 Effeminate Gestures*, 1987 (Photograph by Bill Pack; courtesy Joe Goode Performance Group; used with permission)

manipulated my body and hands together. After this encounter I tried to analyze exactly what I was doing and what he was seeing. (*Demonstrating, now, with mock enthusiasm:*) Perhaps, I thought, it is the way the hands dart and punctuate the air, like moths flying around a light. Perhaps it is the volume, the arc, the looping, the "excess" of gesture. More likely, I thought, and secretly feared, it is something telltale about my use of the wrist. (*He abruptly flings his wrist forward, leaving the hand to dangle midair.*) My host had caught me red-handed, if you will, smack in the middle of an outburst of proscribed gesture, an outburst he no doubt found effeminate.

(*Recouping himself, now professorial:*) What exactly, then, are the physical codes that signify effeminacy? And what are the unspoken rules that dictate against effeminate gestural behavior? At the outset it is essential to recognize that such codes and rules will vary as a function of culture, race, and socioeconomic status. The disciplinary regime I am going to discuss today applies specifically to a boy who was brought up in the 1960s and 1970s in a lower-to middle-class white community in a suburban East Coast setting.[1] Let's start with the basics (*demonstrating now with quasi-military precision*):

1. The arms are to be held down at all times. To raise them, to widen beyond an acceptable range, is to invite censure and isolation. Straight arms may be raised as if to signal, but curves are to be avoided at all costs. To curve is to be expressive, and to be physically expressive is forbidden.
2. Fingers are to be held inward, toward the body, concealed. Ever had someone fool you into looking at your fingers, only to find yourself fumbling from the preferred female (fingers extended) to the male position (fingers curled into fists), or vice versa? This is a classic schoolboy's trick. In the 1960s and 1970s any boy who turned his hands out instead of in risked the label of effeminacy.
3. Legs must be crossed broadly, one ankle placed firmly on the other knee, not both knees together. Moreover, all loose appendages must be kept under strict control. Arms may be tied in a protective knot. Fists—not the open hands, mind you—may be planted on the hips, like the ultramasculine Mr. Clean. (Never mind that he wears an earring.) Or hands may be clasped behind the back, preferably while puffing out the chest.

This rudimentary list of rules governing the language of the body could go on and on, encompassing such crucial subcategories as how to raise one's hand in class; how to hold one's books; how to applaud; how to walk; how to throw a ball. (*Between each "how to" the speaker mimes alternately the designated masculine and effeminate versions.*) Given that effeminacy is such an extremely rigid and controlling concept in American society, I often wonder how much more interesting the topography of everyday gestural language would be if men did not feel overly constrained by these strictures, if they did not fear the effeminacy label. Imagine straight Wall Street brokers in their suits and ties, caressing the air with rounded palms while discussing the rise and fall of the NASDAQ index. Picture baseball players waving to fans with fluttering fingers. (*Embodying the broker, then the baseball player, the speaker visibly relishes the sensuous curve of the palms and the playful twiddling of fingers.*) Conjure a world in which arms and hands would dance freely.

(*Sarcastically:*) "But if you talk too much. If you feel too much. If you enjoy the aesthetic of too much . . ."[2]

In 1987 San Francisco choreographer Joe Goode created a brief and compelling solo that reveals and confronts these unspoken gestural sanctions, rendering them conscious and thereby—I would argue—assuaging their sting. The piece is called *29 Effeminate Gestures,* the number twenty-nine reflecting the quantity of discrete movements Goode strings together to create his basic phrase. I am going to describe this work as part of an investigation of the manner in which Goode's choreography isolates and comments upon gender-specific behavior, theorizing the efficacy of effeminacy in the process. I do this by way of extending Goode's commentary into verbal discourse, thereby giving it life in a new medium.[3]

(*Videotape rolls.*) The piece begins in semidarkness with the sound of what could be a foghorn; in actuality, it is Goode's voice bellowing, "He's a good guy." This is the vocal component of Goode's swarthy caricature of American manhood, a vision of what a young man like Goode, who was born in a small town in Maine and brought up in blue-collar Virginia, might be taught to consider acceptable physical behavior.[4] Dressed in coveralls and heavy boots, Goode embodies the swagger of the automotive mechanic even as he spins the guffaw of the "good guy" into a dozen inventive rhythmic variations. (*The speaker intones in a deep voice:*) "*He's* a good *guy* . . . he's a *good* guy . . . he's a *good good good good good good* guy." As the bellowing patter continues, Goode whips out a working power chainsaw and brutally destroys a wooden chair—the perhaps too-obvious implication being that those men commonly referred to as good guys are actually violent and crude.

(*The voice rises an octave.*) Then Goode effects a magical transformation. The coveralls are peeled down. Shoes and socks come off to reveal soft vulnerable bare feet. And as the buzz saw continues to whir noisily—an irritant; a reminder of the bellowing "good guy"—Goode commences his catalogue of gestures. These, then, are the movements that comprise Goode's iconography of effeminacy.

WRITING THE TWENTY-NINE GESTURES

He lowers his gaze and places his hands dramatically on the chest, as if to feel the shape of the breasts.

Goode embarks on his catalogue of effeminate gesture with a pointed reference to the secondary sexual characteristics, the biological differences between the male and female of the species that feminist theorists distinguish from gender—that is, those aspects of male and female roles that are culturally constructed.[5] Fleeting though it is, this image proves oddly disturbing: Goode seems to be suggesting, as some branches of feminist theory have done, that even the biological differences between male and female are culturally constructed.[6] Look at him: a man drawing breasts on his body, inscribing femaleness there.

(*As if telling a secret:*) A personal observation: I do not have breasts. I barely have pectorals. But I vividly recall trying to develop these mysterious curves in my body as a teenager, when I would furtively practice push-ups in the privacy of my closet-sized room. My father found me at this once—wasn't this the kind of manly exercise a young boy was *supposed* to be performing in his bedroom?—yet he admonished me, "What do you want, breasts or something?" As a boy who was already all too conscious of being different from other boys, I thought I heard my kindly father saying: You don't want to develop breasts, do you? You don't want to be a woman.

I didn't want to be a woman. It was already clear to me, from my mother's tenuous fulfillment as a housewife and from the struggles of my three sisters for sexual equality, that it was easier, *luckier*, in the United States to be male than female, in the same way that it was already obvious to me that, in this heterosexist society, it would be easier to be straight than gay. But I cannot deny that I was compelled by the roundness of pectorals and wanted a pair of my very own. In fact, it was disturbing to me that this particular muscularity was not developing on my body. Other boys had pecs. The Greeks had pecs. So did the hunky men in the magazine advertisements with which I was, frankly, fascinated to the point of obsession. But what are muscular pecs if not breast substitutes? Shields perhaps but breasts too.

(*Matter-of-factly:*) American men in general, and urban gay men in particular, enjoy a highly charged and extremely ambivalent relationship to their pectoral muscles. A photo-finishing shop in San Francisco's Castro District is famous for its window decoration: row upon row of color snapshots of shirtless boys, all proudly displaying their pecs. I note a clear bias in these shop window photos for the well-developed pec, the rounded dome, the smooth nipple rising to a firm peak. (My own flat-chested body type is nowhere to be found.) It is said that some gay men develop particularly large nipples by making them the object of erotic play: pulling, tweaking, biting, "raunching." These nipples are being sucked, configured as sites of erotic nurturance, the mere thought of which conjures images of my father commenting sternly in the background: "What do you want, breasts or something?"

And so it is that, at the outset of his piece, Goode theorizes the breast, that is, the pec, as central to the physical language of effeminacy, demonstrating the radical possibilities for reshaping and regendering the body that result from the conscious performance of gender. Breasts are soft tissue, pecs decidedly firm and muscular, but breasts and pecs are more alike than they are different, especially at their climax in the nipple. It is possible, then, that the bodily choreography commonly coded as effeminate inspires fear and loathing to the degree that it blurs the distinction between breasts and pecs, the biological female and the biological male.

The hands sweep up in a flicking gesture to frame the face, which is tilted toward the light, a Renaissance virgin captured at the instant of the annunciation: rapture.

Posing in such a way as to receive light is to submit one's self to God's ray (that is, God's manhood), to the heteropatriarchal gaze, to the domination of one who conceives of himself as "top." That is, to pose in the light is to be a "bottom," the receiver, the weak, the submissive. This is a central aspect of Goode's understanding of effeminacy.

Interestingly, this form of submission carries with it unmistakable resonances of enlightenment, of the spiritual if not the sexual variety. Christian doctrine is brimming over with references to the necessity of the believer's submitting to God's will, of letting God have his way with him: certain things are beyond one's control and must be given over to God. In his essay "A Preface to Transgression," first published in 1963, Michel Foucault notes that the full flowering of sexuality as a "natural" expression coincides not with the twentieth century but rather with the dawning of Christian mysticism, with its obsessive focus on "fallen bodies and of sin": "The proof is its whole tradition of mysticism and spirituality which was incapable of dividing the continuous forms of desire, of rapture, of penetration, of ecstasy, of that outpouring which leaves us spent: all of these experiences seemed to lead without interruption or limit, right to the heart of a divine love of which they were both the outpouring and the source returning upon itself."[7] Spiritual transcendence, then, can be seen as essentially contiguous with sexual ecstasy, with the result that spirituality may be read into many gestures coded as effeminate. Not coincidentally, this gesture is closely related to a pose struck by Judy Garland, James Mason at her side, in the 1954 version of *A Star Is Born*. As duplicated in publicity stills and advertisements, the image resonates with spiritual transcendence—at least for Garland fans.

The body is drawn up to its full height, the right hand shooting upward (the left pulling away and low, behind) as if to catch someone's attention at the other end of a train platform; the body lurches forward two steps.

Getting attention. Whether effeminate gestures are specifically calculated to gain attention, or if they simply perform that work as a side-effect (in a culture that finds such physicalizations abhorrent) is subject to debate. No doubt, the answer depends on the personality and intention of the individual gestural performer. In Goode's case, however, the intention is obvious: the effeminate gesture is purposefully overlarge, a garish maneuver extended to an

Judy Garland gesturing with James Mason in *A Star Is Born*, 1954 (Courtesy of the Academy of Motion Picture Arts and Sciences; copyright © Warner Bros. Pictures, Inc.; all rights reserved; used with permission)

amplitude of 200 percent when a mere 20 would suffice. This effect is brought into particular relief when effeminacy is performed on Goode's large-scale frame. (He stands well over six feet tall and weighs, I would guess, close to two hundred pounds.) When he lurches forward, the air in the room seems to shift to adjust to the movement of such a large volume. Enthusiasm comes unbridled. The gestures are effulgent, rich, creamy, *excessive*.

In their book, *The Politics and Poetics of Transgression*, Peter Stallybrass and Allon White shed light on the efficacy of excess by illuminating the Russian theorist Mikhail Bakhtin's notion of "grotesque realism," the idea that the excessive body (displayed in carnivalesque manner) functions as a critique of official culture.[8] Likewise in *29 Effeminate Gestures*, in which Goode's excessive effeminacy could easily be interpreted as the symbolic realization of an extroverted strategy of resistance. The message: Take your gestural socialization off my body. I will "choreograph" myself as I please. Excess is enabled when the chains constraining one's corporeality break and shatter to the floor. Exaggeration, then, is Goode's dramatic demand for gestural freedom.

The head tips back slightly, lips smiling coyly; the arm previously thrust in the air is now broken at the wrist, fingers fluttering in a perky 1940s wave.

This gesture marks the first appearance of the broken wrist, a movement largely coded in the West to mean gay. Every boy knows that the broken wrist implies weakness—the angled arm serving as a visual metaphor, perhaps, for a broken weapon.[9] But consider the other, subtler aspects of this gesture. Feel it in your own body. (*The speaker cajoles his audience to participate.*) Imagine you are meeting a friend at the airport. You see your friend down the corridor and you want him to see you. You thrust your arm up, straight as an arrow and as high as it will go, and quickly too, so as to attract maximum attention, the fingers and palm spread wide. This is the masculine version of the gesture. Now modify the movement slightly to render it effeminate: twist your head back and away from the arm that is thrust in the air, creating a corkscrew curve in the torso; raise your eyebrows overenthusiastically; drop your hand at the wrist; flutter your fingers. What do you feel like now? *Who* do you feel like now?

When I perform this gesture, I picture myself as Tallulah Bankhead, to whom Susan Sontag refers in her important (seminal?) "Notes on 'Camp'" as one of "the great stylists of temperament and mannerism." Indeed, this move is supremely redolent of the attitude and atmosphere of the United States before, during, and after World War II. Rooted in the 1940s, it is strongly gendered as female in an era when female/male gendering was much more clearly differentiated than it was at the end of the century. (Interestingly, the 1940s was also a period of massive gender confusion, with women taking on work roles that had previously been the sole province of men.) However, of all the component parts of this gesture, the mannerism of the fluttering fingers is the most subversive. Masculine fingers never flutter; they are open, flat, unarticulated. Masculine fingers are stiff. The mobile fingers, then, serve as a gesture of resistance, as powerful as the middle finger when held erect. In their own blithe way these fingers silently speak the words *fuck you*.

The body inclines at a forward angle, chest thrust forward; the head tilts back, eyes closed, mouth dropping open: ecstasy.

Again, this is the ecstasy of the submissive "bottom"—the vulnerability of the open mouth ready to be kissed or to be spat into. The open mouth and the closed eyes might also indicate preparation for that ultimate effeminate performance, man-on-man fellatio, for to submit to male power is to become *effeminated*.

I use this term advisedly, having consulted that great bible of English dictionaries, the *Oxford*, in search of the verb form of the word *effeminate*. The transitive form, *effeminate* (rhymes with *differentiate*)—meaning 'to make into a woman; to represent as a woman' or, in the intransitive form, 'to make womanish or unmanly; to enervate'—can be traced four centuries to 1551.[10] From that earliest citation the notion of woman is conflated with weakness. This is one root of the lingering misogyny in the West, explored to great effect by such scholars as Londa Schiebinger and Thomas Laqueur.[11] To be like a woman, then, is to become enervated, to have one's strength drained away. There is, of course, no indication in this usage that the state of womanhood is culturally determined. The differences between the sexes are, rather, presented as biological fact. The manifestations are physical, even if the causes are related to licentious living, as indicated in *Oxford*'s citation from Thomas Shadwell's Restoration comedy *Libertine* (1676): "Luxurious living . . . effeminates fools in body." When a boy in modern-day America is accused of being effeminate, he too is being thought of as womanish, as enervated, as one of those "fools in body."

It is crucial to note here that the adjective *effeminate* cannot be attached to *woman*, only to *man*. The notion of an effeminate woman is an impossibility, a paradox, on account of the implication of perversity embedded in the term: a woman made womanish is not perverse but rather normal. Effeminacy is never, then, a reference to the feminine. It is an epithet flung exclusively at aberrations of masculinity. It is never equivalent to the female but is reserved, rather, for the male rendered "not-male."

The body twists forward, right hand crisscrossing the torso to rest on the left breast; the head twists in the opposite direction, mouth drawn into a smirk: distaste.

Here Goode reveals the first taste of effeminacy refracted as bitterness. Up to this moment his gestures have explored a territory of wonder and ecstasy marked by innocence. He has reinscribed the body, broken the gender rules. Effeminacy has emerged as a bold strategy to resist arbitrary societal restrictions, as a "not-male" category that serves to critique standard notions of masculinity. But the entry of distaste evokes an image of a new and different sort, of the hard-bitten woman, the "bitch," whose cynical humor has come to be associated with gay camp. Why the bitchiness? Is this, as some commentators on camp have suggested, a naked manifestation of misogyny? (Do gay men really think women are like that?) Or does it represent the reclaiming—from a position deemed weak by society at large—of the power and efficacy of red-hot anger? These questions have been debated during the course of more than thirty years of theorizing on camp, a body of theory so voluminous it resists summarizing. But a quick review, beginning with Susan Sontag's foundational 1964 "Notes on 'Camp,'" may help to contextualize current perspectives.[12]

Throughout her famous essay Sontag identifies exaggeration as a key element of camp. "Camp is a vision of the world in terms of style—but a particular kind of style," she writes. "It is the love of the exaggerated, the 'off,' of things-being-what-they-are-not."[13] But what exactly is being exaggerated, what is it that is off? Sontag precisely identifies the point of distortion as localized at the site of the rigid conventions legislating gender roles. The displacement of these roles results in the creation of what Sontag calls the image of the "androgyne," a smooth blend of male and female choreographed in the gestures and postures of the body:

> Camp taste draws on a mostly unacknowledged truth of taste: the most refined form of sexual attractiveness (as well as the most refined form of sexual pleasure) consists in going against the grain of one's own sex. What is most beautiful in virile men is something feminine; what is most beautiful in feminine women is something masculine. . . . Allied to the Camp taste for the androgynous is

something that seems quite different but isn't: a relish for the exaggeration of sexual characteristics and personality mannerisms.[14]

In Sontag's conception, then, the attraction of camp lies in its
ability to subvert standard notions of gender and amplify elements of the individual personality, as opposed to facilitating
quiet acquiescence to gender roles, rigid roles that inhibit personal expression. Beauty lies in going against the grain, a concept
that can easily be translated into choreographic terms when so-
called feminine gestures are performed on a male body. (Indeed,
the dynamic embodiment of gender, the set of physicalizations
we perform every day of our lives, is a constant ongoing choreography: the dance through which we define ourselves and society defines us.)

At its most provocative, then, Sontag's essay clarifies the degree
to which gender is a performance, a concept Goode would almost
certainly embrace. Sontag writes: "Camp sees everything in quotation marks. It's not a lamp, but a 'lamp'; not a woman, but a
'woman.' To perceive Camp in objects and persons is to understand Being-as-Playing-a-Role. It is the farthest extension, in sensibility, of the metaphor of life as theater."[15] Perhaps unwittingly,
then, Sontag provides support for the central notion of modern
feminism: that gender is a cultural performance, that it is not natural but that it is constructed.

*The arm unfurls forward as if picking a piece of lint off an angora
sweater.*

But almost in the same instant Sontag denies a central tenet of
feminism: that consciousness of gender construction is fundamentally political. Sontag suggests repeatedly in her essay that
camp is only about style, with the result that she unconscionably
downplays content—especially *political* content. For Sontag, "It
goes without saying that the Camp sensibility is disengaged, de-
politicized—or at least apolitical."[16] But what could be more political than a man, dressed like a man, gesturing like a woman
picking a piece of lint off her bosom? With such an action a man
says, I am fully aware of the arbitrary nature of these codes, and I
resist their hold on my body. This is not about style but about

challenging societal restrictions. It is about transgression, which Foucault, in a stunning metaphor, likens to a flash of lightning illuminating the limits of darkness—"its role is to measure the excessive distance that it opens at the heart of the limit and to trace the flashing line that causes the limit to arise."[17] The task of camp, then, is to take the measure of societal limitations on gender and sexuality, to shine a light on the space beyond the horizon line of acceptability.

Thumb and fingers rub together, squirming like tentacles, to release the errant particle.

In the last thirty years countless writers have roundly criticized Sontag for removing camp from its necessary, integral relationship to the political subversiveness that is part of the gay sensibility. D. A. Miller, in a 1989 essay titled "Sontag's Urbanity," disses her "Notes on 'Camp'" as thoroughly as if she were nothing more than a piece of lint and he were discarding it/her.[18] According to Miller's analysis, Sontag establishes camp as "a primordially gay phenomenon, emerging within the formation of a specifically gay subculture, at the interface of that subculture with the homophobic culture at large."[19] So far so good. "But when once Sontag has evoked the gay lineage of Camp, she proceeds to deny it any necessity." Miller quotes Sontag: "Camp taste is much more than homosexual taste. . . . One feels that if homosexuals hadn't more or less invented Camp, someone else would." Miller again: "That unblinking embrace of counterfactuality can only be understood as not just expressing, but also fulfilling, a wish for a Camp theoretically detachable—and therefore already detached—from gay men."[20] In other words, when Sontag argues against the gayness of gay camp, she is not only dishonoring but disempowering gay men.

More recently, the cultural critic Moe Meyer has echoed Miller's criticisms.[21] In the introduction to his 1994 edited volume, titled *The Politics and Poetics of Camp*, Meyer suggests that Sontag's version of camp, "with its homosexual connotations downplayed, sanitized, and made safe for public consumption," serves to remove discussions of camp (as sign) from homosexuality (as referent).[22] Meyer argues that, on account of Sontag's de-

taching camp from homosexuality, "the discourse began to unravel as Camp became confused and conflated with rhetorical and
performative strategies such as irony, satire, burlesque, and travesty; and with cultural movements such as Pop."[23] To unravel the
discourse, he explains, is to drain away its power, to neutralize it.

Like Miller, Meyer takes the view that Sontag's discussion of
camp as style or sensibility has served to depoliticize what is in-
herently political. Seeking to undo Sontag's move, to roll it back,
Meyer focuses on the use of camp as a "political and critical" strategy in the work of ACT UP and Queer Nation, two political
groups that remind us of the "oppositional critique embodied in
the signifying practices that processually constitute queer identities."[24] Through their work—primarily to provide access to AIDS
funding and care but also to unmask homophobia in the culture
at large—these organizations seek to demonstrate that being
queer is, by its very nature, a critique of heteronormativity. Which
leads Meyer, at the outset, to constitute a new camp manifesto:
"Camp is political; Camp is solely a queer (and/or sometimes gay
and lesbian) discourse; and Camp embodies a specifically queer
cultural critique."[25] The implications for Sontag's definition of
camp are devastating: "un-queer" uses of camp such as those proposed by Sontag are now reconceived as mere appropriations and
"no longer qualify as Camp."[26] In Meyer's view, which I support,
Sontag's camp is no camp at all.

Which brings us back to the place where this particular discussion began. Why are images of the bitch integral to Goode's depiction of effeminacy? What function do they serve? I would argue
that, rather than being baldly misogynistic—as it would appear—
appropriations of the bitch assist in establishing a coalition between women and homosexual men as oppressed classes. Bitchiness, dismissiveness, imperiousness are among the few strategies to
which Western women were allowed unencumbered access in the
last century, let alone earlier centuries. Through the performance
of effeminacy these strategies become available to disempowered
men as well. A central aspect of effeminacy, then, is the political
identification of gay men with the contemporary icon of the bitchy
woman.

The hand pulls back to cover the mouth, which is distended now in an attitude of mock horror, the body and head dropped forward in fear and revulsion.

Classically, effeminacy has been conflated with fear, and images from popular culture only serve to magnify this conflation. Consider the scene in *The Rock* (1996), a thriller starring Nicholas Cage and Sean Connery, in which Connery, who plays a dangerous and physically unkempt convict, is having his locks shorn by a fey and unabashedly effeminate stylist. Suddenly, Connery makes a bolt for freedom, nearly murdering a man by throwing him off the balcony in the process, and rushes to the elevator—where he finds himself confined with (who else?) the effeminate stylist. The ultramasculine Connery remains coolly impassive as the elevator glides to the ground floor, barely glancing in the other man's direction. (Effeminacy may be flamboyant but from a masculine perspective, it is tantamount to disappearance.) Finally, though, the filmmakers focus on the stylist, visibly shaking and cowering as he crouches in the corner of the elevator. Turning to Connery the stylist moans, "OK, I don't want to know nothing. I never saw you throw that gentleman off the balcony. All I care about is, are you happy with your haircut?" As he intones these lines, the stylist clasps his hands to his chest, as if he were the soul of sincerity. The audience laughs on cue, and effeminacy is put in its traditional place, as a sign for frivolity. This is how effeminacy is viewed from the masculinist Hollywood perspective: as invisibility, as weakness, as an open opportunity for homophobic humor.

The entire body turns away to hide the eyes, palms of both hands thrust forward like shields.

Weakness is similarly reencoded here, where the gestural performer cannot look, cannot see, is *afraid* to see. Think of all the cartoons depicting a woman standing on a chair, horrified, while a tiny mouse scurries around the kitchen floor. Or the insidious notion that all women faint at the sight of blood. (Women faint at the sight of life?) Effeminacy is refracted as hypersensitivity, which is then exaggerated into gripping, morbid fear. The effeminate man—like the cartoon woman—is depicted from the masculinist perspective as lacking bravery.

The back of the right hand, extended away from the body, gesticulates as if to dismiss an offending visitor.

But look what happens as Goode's gestures of fear escalate in intensity, transformed now into fearless haughtiness. As mentioned earlier, imperiousness (with its cognate, haughtiness) has been one of the few power strategies available to women and, by identification, to effeminate men. The juxtaposition of this gesture with companion gestures of unbridled fear demonstrates the way in which effeminacy resembles weakness but, in fact, epitomizes power, a seeming conundrum. The connecting linkage is rage. A quote from Goode himself provides a telling analysis:

> There's a lot of anger I feel about the role of women in this patriarchal society. And, as a gay man, I'm often treated more like a woman than like a man. So I can really sympathize with what they are going through. We give a lot of lip service to liberation in this era, but what I really see is that the world *still* isn't ready for people to be people. We are *still* dominated by this traditional male psychology that says that what is really important here is me. Not women, not fags, not niggers, but white old *me*. That's what really dominates. We all buy into it. How could we not?[27]

Thus anger is transformed into political action, which provides gay men and lesbian/straight women with a common bond. Yet straight men often seek to dismiss such action as harsh or laughable. In this equation—as Goode says—gay men are treated more like women than like men. And, of course, it is in the best interest of patriarchal society to view insurgencies by women or effeminate men with deflating disdain.

Now the head turns back to the front, mouth covered with the palm of the right hand, elbow jutting forward, heel of the left hand pressing against the left hip as if to say, "Really?!"

A new question arises: If effeminacy serves as a conscious strategy of defiance for gay men, or for men in general who do not want to conform to rigid notions of masculinity, how does it function for young boys who are not capable of adult-level conscious reflection? While working through the issues in this essay, I have often found myself recalling examples of boyhood gestural socialization, of moments when, out of fear, I forced myself to

Joe Goode gestures as if to say, "Really?" after which he turns, ending with a finger-fluttering wave over the shoulder. (Photographs by Bill Pack; courtesy Joe Goode Performance Group; used with permission)

change the way I crossed my legs, or held my arms, or adjusted the tilt of my head. Most times, these messages were internalized: nothing was said aloud, but of course mere words would have been unnecessary. I had absorbed the rules and regulations of gestural behavior through constant example. This internalization of gestural proscriptions is, no doubt, shared in some form by every boy and girl, regardless of sexual orientation.

But oftentimes gestural socialization is more aggressive, more intrusive, more excruciatingly bald than that. Parents, grandparents, siblings, classmates, their parents, teachers—any or all of these are capable of playing the role of gestural commissar. Here is a telling example from an autobiographical story by Alan Erenberg, contained in the collection *From a Burning House* (1996) by the AIDS Project Los Angeles Writers Workshop:

> When I think back over my life, I remember that as a boy it was very hard to be just me. There I was, just ten years old, happily minding my own business, and I immediately knew that my father disapproved of me, of something "queer acting" about me. I knew because of his "humming."
>
> "I'm going to have a signal with you, Alan," my dad once told me. "Whenever you act too much like a girl, I'm going to hum 'Hum hum hum.'"[28]

Imagine: the next time you break a gestural injunction, a person in authority will point out your infraction. It is a secret code between you, a tune you will hear from across the room. You are standing talking to a friend with a hand pressed against one hip, for example, and you hear it, "Hum hum hum." You have broken the rule of symmetricality. (No body curves allowed.) You open your eyes too wide, and you hear it again, "Hum hum hum." (No large facial expressions.)

The previous gesture—"Really?"—is rotated into a skulking turn, left palm now pressed up against the lower back.

You swivel turn, and you hear it, "Hum hum hum." And suddenly—when you are old enough to recognize the tune—you realize that the humming duplicates the first three notes of that melody made famous by Burt Parks: "There she is, Miss America."

The turn ends with a finger-fluttering wave over the right shoulder, accompanied by a furtive glance.

Many boys would ignore the hummed correction. A few would respond with a comeback even more boldly effeminate than the original bodily infraction: a pin-up pose and a coy wave accompanied by a Betty Grable incline of the head. For an adolescent, such a response would constitute the epitome of defiance. Effeminacy is a fundamentally defiant activity.

Eve Kosofsky Sedgwick has written compellingly of the political situation of effeminate children in a 1993 essay titled "How to Bring Your Kids Up Gay: The War on Effeminate Boys," and my argument consciously extends from that text.[29] To chilling effect Sedgwick reveals that when the DSM-III—the diagnostic bible of the psychological profession—was published in 1980, the entry designating homosexuality as a pathology had been excised, but few seemed to notice that the adult pathology had been replaced by a new and equally execrable entry pathologizing children:

302.60. Gender Identity Disorder of Childhood.

While the decision to remove "homosexuality" from DSM-III was a highly polemicized and public one, accomplished only under intense pressure from gay activists outside the profession, the addition to DSM-III of "Gender Identity Disorder of Childhood" appears to have attracted no outside attention at all—nor even to have been perceived as part of the same conceptual shift.[30] Sedgwick is aghast at this replacement and, equally so, that it has gone largely unremarked by the gay movement—even though, as she notes, effeminacy is the cause of such rampant prejudice among schoolage children that gay youngsters are two to three times as likely to attempt or commit suicide than their straight peers. She attributes the lack of attention to "effeminophobia," the generalized fear of effeminacy that reflects the "marginal or stigmatized position to which even adult men who are effeminate have often been relegated in the [gay] movement."[31]

But then Sedgwick goes a step further, providing an even more devastating theory for the lack of political work on behalf of effeminate boys: that the gay movement has spent so much of its political energy striving to destroy the stereotype that men who love men are feminine, effeminate, womanish, enervated, weak, that the effeminate boy must be erased. The gay movement cannot represent, let alone embrace, him lest he provide support for the notion that adult gay men are effeminate too. The effeminate child is therefore shunned or at the very least ignored. This blindness is painfully ironic considering that—as reported in a study by A. P. Bell, M. S. Weinberg, and S. K. Hammersmith, quoted by Sedgwick—"Childhood Gender Nonconformity turned out to be more strongly connected to adult homosexuality than was any other variable in the study."[32] The effects, as pointed out by Sedgwick, are deplorable: "In this case the eclipse of the effeminate boy from adult gay discourse would represent more than a damaging theoretical gap; it would represent a node of annihilating homophobic, gynephobic, and pedophobic hatred internalized and made central to gay-affirmative analysis. The effeminate boy would come to function as the discrediting open secret of many politicized adult gay men."[33]

Taking up where Sedgwick leaves off, nowhere is this internalized effeminophobia more insidious than in the phenomenon of gay personal ads, in which anonymous writers are free to describe themselves and their fantasy mates in revealing detail. For example, a recent edition of the Boston *Phoenix* (chosen at random) carries 161 advertisements for "men seeking men," of which 67 identify the ad writer—or the dream man whom he is seeking—as "masculine" or "straight-acting."[34] A simple ratio shows that more than 40 percent implicitly state that they do not want to be perceived as—nor do they want a boyfriend or sex partner to be perceived as—effeminate or gay. Here are two classic examples:

> Real man, solid, good-looking, active, very masculine, straight-acting, 28yo GWM seeks similar muscular GWM with same qualities, 25-34yo.

> GWM, 24, blk/grn, 5'5", 140 lbs, non-smoker, clean-cut & shaven, thin with muscular build, extremely straight-acting & appearing—"wouldn't know!"

Occasionally, these denials of homosexuality, replete with references to masculinity and the appearance of heterosexuality, are ac-

companied by related code words, such as *normal* or, more am-
biguously, *clean-cut*. Meanwhile, only one ad in this edition of
the *Phoenix* identifies the writer as "fem" (short for "feminine"
or "effeminate").

> FEM SKS GWM: Blond with beautiful eyes, enjoys having fun
> with friends, dancing, shopping, clubbing, spending time with
> someone I can relate to. I'm really funny and always making the
> best of the worst.

It is a singularly brave man who advertises his "beautiful eyes," an
appetite for seemingly frivolous feminine pursuits, humor. Meanwhile, three neighboring personals in the same issue are even
more explicit in their distaste for effeminacy, all of them incorporating some version of the stock phrase: "No fats or fems."
Though far from scientific, the patterns that emerge from this
single issue of the *Phoenix* could be duplicated—with regional
variations, of course—in any city in the United States. If these attitudes were expressed openly in the straight press, the gay community would be up in arms.

The level of hatred toward men who perform their genders effeminately is extraordinary, all the more so because it has been so
effectively internalized. It is worth taking a lesson here from
those who write on the subject of colonialism, particularly as it is
manifested in the realm of dance. In her 1995 book on Argen-
tine tango, Marta Savigliano suggests that the circle of colonialism is not complete until the colonized subject begins to "colo-
nize" himself or herself.[35] In other words, the colonial paradigm
is not just a struggle between colonizer and colonized, locked in
a perpetual cycle of dominance and submission. Rather, it is a dynamic process in which the colonized subject eventually comes
to function as her own colonizer, her own personal oppressor.
Likewise, I would suggest, with gay men and their attitudes toward effeminacy. Having internalized the prejudice in American
culture at large against effeminate boys and adult men, gay
men—the very men who might be expected to embrace the
coded meanings of effeminacy, the identification with oppressed
women, the struggle to gain power—instead practice open abhorrence of any trace of their own effeminacy. Thus the perfor-

mance of effeminacy requires even more bravery within the gay community than outside it.

Now the face and hands are drawn taut together, mouth puckered, thumbs and forefingers pressing together, pinkie fingers unabashedly sticking out.

Here, at last, is the single gesture that rivals the broken wrist as the distinguishing icon of effeminacy: the raised pinkie. A masculine man firmly grasps his beer bottle in the palm of his hand, dwarfing the bottle, surrounding it, controlling it. An effeminate man delicately balances his (porcelain) teacup between his thumb and forefinger, allowing the other fingers to pull back in a rounded shape and the little finger to thrust upward in a fluted question mark. A readily available depiction of this phenomenon appears in a scene from the film *The Birdcage* (1996), the remake of the French comedy *La Cage aux folles*, in which the character played by Robin Williams, who is gay but coded as masculine, attempts to teach his effeminate lover, played by Nathan Lane, how to pass for straight. The octave of the voice descends, conversation turns to football, and the telltale question-mark pinkie is tamed downward. This is arguably the most hilarious scene in the entire film, featured in the film's trailer as a key selling point. It is especially funny, I would suggest, because Lane's pinkie, the embodiment of his effeminacy, keeps popping back up, a sign of his resistance to retraining.

So what is it about the decorative pinkie that inspires such a frenzy of societal fascination and discomfort? It is nothing but a digit, one in ten, curling back when its assistance in grasping an object is not strictly necessary. Why shouldn't the owner of that finger take the opportunity to supersede function with style? That little pinkie doesn't hurt anyone, now does it? And yet its curve is taken by many as a calamitous affront, as a sign for the degradation of culture, for the downfall of the Western world. It is almost as if the little pinkie were a Stealth weapon, a diminutive cultural question mark capable of unsettling the established order. Think of it: How is it that three inches of bone and flesh are capable of such dramatic commentary? Perhaps the effeminate man with his arsenal of mere gestures is a more powerful actor than one would think.

*"Who, me?" The expression speaks silently as the head draws side-
ways, mouth in a wide pout, hands draped nonchalantly over the
chest.*

Indeed, just as the apparent weakness of effeminacy is constantly
superseded by its underlying strength, this gesture of false innocence neatly masks its underlying subversiveness: the little girl who
has pulled her sister's hair and immediately, instinctively, turns angelic. This is also a classic gesture of the femme fatale, the dark and
dangerous woman who appears, on the surface, to be weak and in-
sipid but who in fact packs enormous backstage power. This is
weakness standing in for manipulative control. In gay parlance the
exercise of power from a place of supposed weakness has a special
name: it is called "topping from the bottom."

*The left hand sweeps up the face to capture a tendril of curly hair,
teasing the hair upward; lips are parted: seduction.*

Seduction, a power that oppressed women have long harnessed
for their own means, is perhaps even more intriguing when performed by a man for an audience both male and female. Look at
me. See my beauty. Kiss my lips. These are the messages spewing
from nearly every fashion magazine cover. But what if the cover
shot depicts an effeminate man? Such an image seduces the on-
looker, distracting him from his ordered life and drawing the attention to something strangely beguiling: the surface allure of
gender performance. Effeminate seduction grabs hold of the
forces of attraction that undergird the patriarchal order and radically unsteadies them.

*Both hands tip back at the wrist, framing the upturned face in a
final sultry pose.*

The effeminate pose is a symbol of that unsteadiness. For to
pose effeminately is to perform against the grain. And to perform
against the grain is to exist in a state of radical self-consciousness.
And to exist in a state of radical self-consciousness is to resist the
determinism of gender naturalism. And to resist the determinism
of gender naturalism is to realize that there is not one set of imperatives governing the woman and yet another the man. And to
realize that no one set of imperatives governs the woman and yet
another the man is to know that gender is culturally determined.

And to know that gender is culturally determined is to be freed from the slavery of gender. Thus the effeminate man doubles as a cultural abolitionist whose goal is nothing less than to set us free from the tyranny of gender.

AFTER THE GESTURES

The entire string of twenty-nine gestures takes but a minute to perform; it flies by in what seems a mere instant. But Goode chooses to elongate the moment, bringing the phrase back five times, each embellishment featuring a slightly different twist.[36] On the second repetition Goode layers a textual track over the poses. This section of the piece might be called "effeminacy defined," with the choreographer intoning a series of dependent clauses—"if you talk too much; if you feel too much; if you gesticulate too much"—that fail to resolve. In the third round Goode borrows a postmodern strategy from the choreographer Trisha Brown, accumulating and layering the gestures, cutting against them with the sounds quickly recognized as deriving from those boy games known as war. Miraculously, the coy brush of the buttocks coincides with bombs bursting, or the twirling of fingers coincides with the rat-a-tat-tat of artillery fire. Implicitly, the juxtaposition poses a question: Which behaviors—the effeminate come-ons or the military posturing—are the socially acceptable ones? Fourth round: Goode peels off his t-shirt and ties it around his head like a sheet of blond hair. He opens the gestures up, widens them, until they become what we recognize as dance vocabulary. The accompaniment evokes Polynesian slit drums, a veiled reference to cultures in which the effeminate man, the *mahu*, holds a respected role in society as teacher and surrogate mother. Soon the drumming is layered with electronically synthesized sounds that seem, almost painfully, to force a relationship between Polynesian societies, even if a romanticized version of those societies, and the contemporary United States. The music reminds us that the effeminate man has a place in Polynesia. But does he in Topeka?

In the fifth and final round Goode continues repeating the sequence of gestures while blaring gender-modified lyrics to a tune from *Fiddler on the Roof*: "Is this the little *boy* I carried?" As he invokes the father, the very model of appropriate gender-specific behavior, an electric drill—the second power tool of this performance, following upon the earlier chainsaw—descends as if from the stage sky. At first Goode points it like a gun. He wields it cruelly, angrily. He turns it on himself.

But then, in a shocking shift, he places the vibrating drill against his cheek, caressing it, transforming the dangerous weapon into the object of his attraction. He nuzzles it, turning loaded gun into caressing phallus, as sound and light fade away to nothing.

HEROIC EFFEMINACY

The relationship between this dance, performed on a stage to the obvious delight of its audiences, and the revelations that may be wrought from it is an inextricable one: here is a case where performance literally coincides with theory. Yet Goode does not think of himself as a theorist. He told me that he has never read Sontag or Miller or Meyer, let alone Sedgwick. Likewise, he has never felt moved to look up the definition of *effeminate* in the *Oxford English Dictionary*. Still, when I shared this text with him—an exercise in dialogic editing inspired in part by the ethnographer Steven Feld—Goode told me that he recognized the power of his gestures when they were translated into theoretical terms.[37] Though his own initial response to the gestures had been one of abhorrence (he had struggled to surmount his own discomfort in making this piece, he said), he soon developed an awareness that the gestures were laden with inordinate potential, with untapped strength. In fact, in reviewing the gestures with me, he counseled against interpreting any of them as the mere reaffirmation of a cliché or stereotype. "I think there is an element of comment—which is the power of camp—that exists in *all* of the gestures," he said. "It was a huge thing for me, making the piece. I realized I was uncomfortable being with really effeminate people, as if I would be found out by association. Now I adore effeminate people and fancy the company of drag queens."[38]

The configuration of the effeminate man as object of adoration finds its basis in a classic formulation: that he is powerful, efficacious, a warrior, a hero—all of which can be discerned from an analysis of Goode's gestures. Identified and defined by corporeal qualities as subtle as the incline of his head or the angle of his wrist, the effeminate man places himself in the eye of the storm, in the center of the terror caused by society's ambiguous differentiation of the breast from the pectoral muscle. He makes brave incursions into the realm of the spirit, discovering the valor in vulnerability. Through his movements of excess, he demands— and wins—freedom from bodily restrictions. His mobile fingers boldly affront the false protectors of gender norms. He identifies with women and artfully appropriates the high practices of haughtiness, bitchiness, and imperiousness—not as female impersonation but as tools in the performance of the "not-male." He subverts depictions of himself as fearful by activating the efficacy of raw anger. He fights against the disgrace of his erasure not only within normative heterosexuality but within normative homosexuality as well. He curls his pinkie as a sign against the "naturalness" of masculinity. And he savagely disorders a culture that values testosterone gone amok, as manifested in the games of war.

The philosopher and queer theorist Judith Butler provides further support for the heroism of the effeminate in her essay "Critically Queer," an extraordinary piece of writing that empowers gender warriors, AIDS activists, and drag queens all at the same time.[39] In this concluding section I want, first, to consider the ways in which Butler's argument intersects with effeminacy, even though her essay, strictly speaking, concerns itself with queerness more generally. And then I seek to show how, through Butler's essay, we can mine the inextricable relationship between queerness and effeminacy.

In a passage titled "Gender Performativity and Drag," Butler critiques and extends a notion to which she had alluded imprecisely in her earlier *Gender Trouble*.[40] In that text she had presented the idea that drag is performative—that it constitutes, in her words, "statements that, in the uttering, also perform a certain action and exercise a binding power."[41] Butler was referring here to the performative as defined in the work of J. L. Austin, exemplified in the marriage ceremony where the words *I pronounce*

you husband and wife dramatically alter a legal and familial relationship. According to Austin's theory, such proclamations are
paradigmatic performative acts. Some readers of *Gender Trouble*,
however, had taken Butler's discussion of this formulation in relation to drag to mean that all performative acts, particularly
those associated with gender, are a kind of drag, "that gender was
like clothes" to be changed at will.[42] In "Critically Queer" Butler
takes the opportunity to correct herself: "The practice by which
gendering occurs, the embodying of norms, is a compulsory
practice, a forcible production, but not for that reason fully de-
termining. To the extent that gender is an assignment, it is an
assignment which is never quite carried out according to expectation, whose addressee never quite inhabits the ideal s/he is
compelled to approximate."[43]

Taking this clarification a step further, then, I would suggest
that the effeminate boy or man is one who, metaphorically speaking, receives his gender assignment in the mail yet refuses to pay
the postage due. The envelope is addressed to him and it bears the
imprimatur of official correspondence. But he rejects it. Furthermore, there are many kinds of effeminacy, a whole spectrum of ef-
feminacies, if you will. Each includes certain elements of the assigned gender along with pointed aspects of refusal, concatenated
in ways that are completely unique to the individual—what's
more, to the individual at a given moment, for the balance of acceptance and refusal of the gender assignment may change over
time. What Butler helps us to understand, then, is that gender is
not only constructed but that it is fluid and malleable and that,
even though femininity and masculinity are presented as pro-
scriptive ideals, they are never fully realized as such.

Butler also argues that drag, as demonstrated by the arguably
assimilationist documentary film *Paris Is Burning*, "is not unproblematically subversive" and that it can serve to reinscribe heterosexist norms even as it ironizes them.[44] But this is where it becomes clear that effeminacy differs from drag in a crucial way:
effeminacy is primarily corporeal, which is to say that it is choreographed on the body, whereas drag is determined by a choreography of fashion. The effeminate man does not "cross-dress" but

rather "cross-gestures," displaying upon his bodily frame a range of movements lifted not from his assigned column A but rather from the strictly off-limits column B. Thus in the absence of the material paraphernalia of drag it is nearly impossible to imagine a scenario in which denaturalized heterosexual norms would be "reidealized" by effeminacy, to use Butler's word. The bodily practices of effeminacy, I would argue, are more directly and consistently subversive—and more dangerous—than drag and are therefore less likely to be co-opted by popular culture.

Moreover, as Butler points out, a term that has been used to "abject" a population—she is speaking of the term *queer*, but I might replace it with *effeminacy*—"can become the site of resistance, the possibility of an enabling social and political resignification."[45] Thus, whereas the insult of *effeminacy* is clearly capable of injuring its addressee, it can also become a bulwark of resistance, an insult absorbed and reconfigured as a badge of honor. The very word itself can be resituated to signify strength and heroism, as I am seeking to do in this essay, and as I believe Goode aspires to in his dance. Butler is, in effect, suggesting a radical union of two modes of performativity here: the discursive or citational performativity theorized by Austin and the theatrical performativity that is the parlance of scholarship on performance. Indeed, the imposition of gender norms, which is at the heart of this matter, has the effect of a quasi-juridical citation, a decree that must be adhered to, and which—from the perspective of heroic effeminacy—must be opposed. Butler writes: "This kind of citation will emerge as *theatrical* to the extent that it *mimes and renders hyperbolic* the discursive convention that it also *reverses*. The hyperbolic gesture is crucial to the exposure of the homophobic 'law' that can no longer control the terms of its own abjecting strategies" (the italics are Butler's).[46] Thus Goode's exaggerative mode of theatricality "mimes and renders hyperbolic" a set of citations, or societal instructions regarding the particularity of gender, that are, by virtue of their performance on the biologically male body, an act of resistance, a reversal of conventions, a refusal to obey the law. But the performance of effeminacy exposes more than the conventions of gender. It also uncovers the gross matter, the ugly root, of homophobia itself, rendering it visible and thereby vulnerable to subversive attack. This configures effeminacy as a most potent weapon, as phallic power channeled in undiluted form through a limp wrist.

Recently, I was forced to undergo that phallic rite of passage known in academia as "the job talk." This is the moment when, having survived the open call for applications, a potential faculty member is asked to spend one or two days with the prospective employer—a visit designed to climax in a public lecture at which one demonstrates one's academic prowess, one's scholarship.

In this high-pressure situation did I dare deliver the talk I had been developing on Joe Goode's *29 Effeminate Gestures*? The academic lecture is a decidedly manly forum, academia being dominated by the ideals of masculinity: certitude, verbosity, strength, vigor. What would it mean to my chances of employment if I were to present myself as an expert in, uh, effeminacy? What would it mean to throw a limp wrist in the direction of my listeners? To flutter my fingers in greeting? To be (effeminately) seductive? In fact, as I had designed the talk, I would be required not only to screen Goode's piece on videotape but to enact many of the gestures myself and, in one case, to ask members of the audience to enact them with me. A test session with scholar friends before the actual public session proved a dismal failure. In such circumstances I found myself too shy to perform the gestures full force. My limp wrist was halfhearted, my eyes more furtive than coy. I was sweating. Somehow the academic situation seemed to intensify the citational force of masculinist gestural injunctions, and I was supremely aware of their gender-normative weight bearing down upon me.

But then, on the day of the talk, anger rose in me like a clean-burning flame. When I stood up in that formal meeting room to begin my job talk, I was filled with fury, and I consciously channeled that pent-up fury into the gestures. My limp wrist became unpredictably tricky, an icon of flamboyance, a disorienting beacon. A swivel turn became a whirl of energetic subversion, devilishly unapologetic. While enumerating a list of basic bodily injunctions, I began to interpolate impromptu commentary on the manner in which members of the audience were sitting in their chairs. With particular relish I teased a prominent member of the selection committee about the way he was crossing his legs. When it came time to request audience participation, I spared no one. I was on fire.

Shockingly, I got the job. How could this be? What had happened? This momentary and unplanned fusion of theory and performance, of dance and scholarship, of the aesthetic and the political, served to underline for me the extraordinary efficacy of effeminacy, of exaggeration, of performance (in the theatrical sense), and resistance to performative citationality (in the Austinian sense). Afterward someone reminded me of the question that had started it all: Had I yet learned to talk without waving my hands? No, I answered (*with a self-conscious gestural flourish*). Never.

NOTES

This is an expanded version of a paper first presented at "Engendering Dance, Engendering Knowledge: Dance, Gender, and Interdisciplinary Dialogues in the Arts," a conference of the Congress on Research in Dance at Texas Women's University in Denton, November 3–6, 1994. I would like to thank Susan Leigh Foster, Marta Savigliano, and Jeff Tobin for their insights and suggestions. Nevertheless, the final form of this essay and any inadequacies of it are solely my own.

1. These rules of masculine gestural behavior ought to be seen as part of a genealogy of subjugation, as per the terms of Foucault's analysis in "Docile Bodies" (in *Discipline and Punish: The Birth of the Prison*, trans. Alan Sheridan [New York: Vintage, 1979], 135–69). Foucault dates the acceleration and the increasingly meticulous detail of bodily subjugation to the classical period in Western Europe, when was formed "a policy of coercions that act upon the body, a calculated manipulation of its elements, its gestures, its behaviour. The human body was entering a machinery of power that explores it, breaks it down and rearranges it. . . . Thus discipline produces subjected and practised bodies, 'docile' bodies" (138). Foucault invokes the military arts as an example of the subjugation of docile bodies, alongside the detailed apparatuses of Christian practice. I would argue that the laws of masculine physicality in the 1960s and 1970s in the United States are an analogous twentieth-century practice.

2. This quote and the descriptions that follow are based on two films of Joe Goode's *29 Effeminate Gestures*: a single-camera videotape created as documentation of Goode's February 22, 1992, performance at Theater Artaud, and

a glossier 1989 version created expressly for *Alive from Off Center*, part of a half-hour program titled "From San Francisco: Dancing on the Edge" (prod. Linda Schaller, videotaped at KQED, San Francisco, for Twin Cities Public Television). The latter, directed by Tim Boxell, was substantially adapted from the original, with the interpolation of new group-dance material at the beginning of the piece and a shortened sequence of gestures. Whenever differences appear, the theatrical performance has been considered axiomatic.

3. Readers may recognize here a version of the tactic used by Roland Barthes in *S/Z* (trans. Richard Miller [New York: Hill and Wang, 1974]), in which Barthes appropriates Balzac's short story *Sarrasine* and, to use his own word, manhandles it. That is, he cuts Balzac's text into 561 fragments and categorizes each one within a scheme of five codes: hermeneutic, semantic, proairetic, cultural, or symbolic. In Goode's case the analysis of discrete gestures does not require manhandling insofar as Goode's title explicitly informs the viewer that the piece is a catalogue, albeit an unnumbered one. Thus the spirit of this analysis may be closer to Goode's than Barthes's was to Balzac's, if only because I am performing a poststructuralist operation on a postmodern choreography.

4. In a profile of Goode in *Dance Magazine*, Janice Ross reports that Goode was born in Presque Isle, Maine, and that he moved with his parents and two sisters at the age of seven to "what he acidly describes as 'dinner mint green' army project housing in Hampton, Virginia" (Ross, "San Francisco's Joe Goode: Working Hard to Be the Bad Boy of Modern Dance," January 1989, p. 48). Goode's was not, however, a military family. His father ran a printing press and his mother worked as a secretary (personal communication, December 9, 1997). After finishing high school Goode remained in Virginia and eventually enrolled at Virginia Commonwealth University, earning a bachelor of fine arts in drama there in 1973. He then moved to New York where he studied dance for five years, eventually landing in San Francisco in 1979. He quickly joined Margaret Jenkins's dance company and began making his own dance-performance works in the early 1980s.

5. This discussion does not cover the entire set of twenty-nine gestures, if only to save the reader from becoming mired in detail. The gestures I feature in this essay do, however, follow in chronological order and are all contained in the more readily available *Alive TV* version of the piece.

6. Perhaps the foundational document here is Gayle Rubin's "The Traffic in Women: Notes on the 'Political Economy' of Sex," in Rayna R. Reiter, ed., *Toward an Anthropology of Women* (New York: Monthly Review Press, 1975), 157–210.

7. Michel Foucault, *Language, Counter-Memory, Practice: Selected Essays and Interviews by Michel Foucault*, ed. Donald F. Bouchard (Ithaca, N.Y.: Cornell University Press, 1977), 29.

8. Peter Stallybrass and Allon White, *The Politics and Poetics of Transgression* (Ithaca, N.Y.: Cornell University Press, 1986), 9.

9. In her essay "The Renaissance Elbow," Joaneath Spicer argues that the firmly angled elbow conveys associations with "boldness and control," especially in European portrait painting from 1500 to 1650. She offers a photograph of Mick Jagger in a parallel pose as evidence of the enduring nature of this sig-

nification, but I must disagree with her on this point: I read Jagger's elbow as effeminate. In fact, in many socioeconomic classes in the modern West angled wrists, elbows, and fingers strongly denote effeminacy or, at the very least, androgyny (Spicer's essay appears in Jan Bremmer and Herman Roodenburg, eds., *A Cultural History of Gesture* [Ithaca, N.Y.: Cornell University Press, 1991], 84–128).

10. The full *OED* citation for this early reference reads thus: "1551–6 ROBINSON tr. *More's Utop.* (Arb.) 40 It is not to be feared lest they shoulde be effeminated, if thei were brought up in good craftes."

11. For further discussion of historical change in notions of biological sex, see Londa Schiebinger, "Skeletons in the Closet: The First Illustrations of the Female Skeleton in Eighteenth-Century Anatomy," in Catherine Gallagher and Thomas Laqueur, eds., *The Making of the Modern Body: Sexuality and Society in the Nineteenth Century* (Berkeley: University of California Press, 1987), 42–82; and Thomas Laqueur, *Making Sex: Body and Gender from the Greeks to Freud* (Cambridge, Mass.: Harvard University Press, 1990). On this point, Laqueur writes of Patrick Geddes, a late nineteenth-century biology professor, who "used cellular physiology to explain the 'fact' that women were 'more passive, conservative, sluggish and stable' than men, while men were 'more active, energetic, eager, passionate, and variable'" (6).

12. Susan Sontag, "Notes on 'Camp,'" in *Against Interpretation and Other Essays* (New York: Dell, 1966), 275–92.

13. Ibid., 279.

14. Ibid.

15. Ibid., 280.

16. Ibid., 277.

17. Foucault, "A Preface to Transgression," in *Language, Counter-Memory, Practice*, 35.

18. D. A. Miller, "Sontag's Urbanity," in Henry Abelove, Michèle Aina Barale, and David M. Halperin, eds., *The Lesbian and Gay Studies Reader* (New York: Routledge, 1993), 212–20.

19. Ibid., 213.

20. Ibid.

21. Moe Meyer, introduction to *The Politics and Poetics of Camp* (London: Routledge, 1994), 1–22.

22. Ibid., 7.

23. Ibid.

24. Ibid., 1.

25. Ibid.

26. Ibid.

27. Ross, "San Francisco's Joe Goode," 50.

28. Alan Erenberg, "The Humming Story," in Irene Borger, ed., *From a Burning House: The AIDS Project Los Angeles Writers Workshop Collection* (New York: Washington Square Press, 1996), 17.

29. Eve Kosofsky Sedgwick, "How to Bring Your Kids Up Gay: The War on Effeminate Boys," in *Tendencies* (Durham, N.C.: Duke University Press, 1993), 154–64.

30. Ibid., 157.

31. Ibid.

32. Ibid., 158. This assertion is contained in Alan P. Bell, Martin S. Weinberg, and Sue Kiefer Hammersmith, *Sexual Preference: Its Development in Men and Women* (Bloomington: Indiana University Press, 1981), 80.

33. Sedgwick, "How to Bring Your Kids Up Gay," 158. Though the title of the Bell/Weinberg/Hammersmith study refers to both men and women, boys and girls, it is significant that Sedgwick's essay treats men/boys almost exclusively. Indeed, according to the American Psychological Association, the diagnosis of "gender identity disorder of childhood" means something quite different for effeminate boys than it does for masculine girls, the former based primarily on the exhibition of behavioral codes associated with stereotypical female activities, the latter solely on a girl's belief that she has or will acquire a penis. Sedgwick points out the asymmetry of these diagnoses (see pp. 156–57) before launching into her larger argument.

34. *(Boston) Phoenix*, June 21, 1996.

35. Marta E. Savigliano, *Tango and the Political Economy of Passion* (Boulder, Colo.: Westview, 1995), 23–26.

36. Note that in the Tim Boxell video for *Alive TV*, the embellishments are truncated.

37. Steven Feld, "Postscript, 1989," in *Sound and Sentiment: Birds, Weeping, Poetics, and Song in Kaluli Expression*, 2d ed. (Philadelphia: University of Pennsylvania Press, 1990), 239–68.

38. Personal communication, December 11, 1997.

39. Judith Butler, "Critically Queer," in *Bodies That Matter: On the Discursive Limits of "Sex"* (New York: Routledge, 1993), 223–42.

40. Judith Butler, *Gender Trouble: Feminism and the Subversion of Identity* (New York: Routledge, 1990).

41. Butler, *Bodies That Matter*, 225.

42. Ibid., 231.

43. Ibid.

44. Ibid.

45. Ibid.

46. Ibid., 232.

Part 3
Reflections and Extensions

12
A Mistress Never a Master?

Jane Feuer

This will be a most oblique response to Kevin Kopelson's essay, "Nijinsky's Golden Slave." Oblique because I know little about Nijinsky, because most queer theory is male homosexual theory in disguise, because I am not a dance critic but rather a shamefully addicted fan of ballet in general and Balanchine in particular, and because, as a lesbian, I must be experiencing lesbian erotics when I look at the dancing body, *n'est-ce pas?*

The last assertion is probably the most disputable—after all, object cathexis is not the same as sexual identity. So let me phrase it differently outside the framework of erotic identity politics where one can always dispute matters of taste: why should ballet—which we can at least hypothesize has largely been about imaginary and/or phallic-footed *females*—be so culturally identified with a gay male fan culture?[1] Why hasn't classical/neoclassical ballet been the focus of a lesbian erotics, subculturally speaking?[2] Furthermore, why did the binaries of modern dance and feminism and ballet and sexism become so firmly entrenched in the cultural imaginary of the dance public?

And what does any of this have to do with Nijinsky? I find the analysis of Nijinsky salutary because it describes an erotics around ballet that is the exception rather than the typical case of the homosexual balletomane-ballerina diva pairing. Arguably, mainstream ballet criticism has long been about gay men's fantasy attachments to ballerinas (or to male choreographers via ballerinas)—even when those gay male critics are named Arlene Croce. So the emphasis on homoerotics is a corrective but still about gay men. It fails to question an assumed hierarchy of taste cultures whereby homosexuals are supposed to drool over dancing girl

385

swans (or desire to *be* swans, as in the case of drag ballet), whereas lesbians are supposed to fixate on women professional golfers. I'm writing against a widespread assumption that as a feminist and a lesbian, I'm supposed to prefer modern/postmodern dance as the art of female choreographers on relatively undistorted female bodies. Is my preference for ballet and Balanchine, then, the expression of an old queen's sensibility trapped in the body of a dyke? Is there at least a theoretical potential for a lesbian erotics around ballet?

In 1974 Arlene Croce made the observation that "it is partly because a ballerina isn't a woman but an abstraction of one that ballet attracts homosexuals in such large numbers." She goes on to say that homosexuals and feminists both overvalue the sexuality of ballet, although from different ends of the spectrum: homosexuals celebrate ballet because it distorts women, while feminists condemn it for the same reason. Croce counters that "the arabesque is real, the leg is not."[3] From a political perspective this is of course antifeminist and homophobic, but it makes sense if one is arguing for the autonomy of ballet as an aesthetic practice from a neo-Kantian perspective.

From a "queer theory" perspective, of course, she has it all wrong: the *leg* is real, but the arabesque is not. And Croce's own critical practice often belied this emphasis on form and abstraction, as when she scolded ballerinas for not being feminine enough. Thus her preference for Suzanne Farrell over Merrill Ashley. I take Ashley as a prototype because she was the most "butch" of all Balanchine's dancers, and this is exactly what Croce disliked about her. In fact, she once wrote a *New Yorker* review in which she addressed Ashley directly, chiding her for not looking at her partner when they danced together:

> By calling on Ashley's nondancing resources as a ballerina, Balanchine may have issued her the most critical challenge of her career [in *Ballade*, made on Ashley in 1980]. Ashley's partner in this ballet is Ib Andersen, the new soloist from the Royal Danish Ballet. . . . He doesn't leave a vivid impression, largely because Ashley doesn't make much of him. . . . He comes on and she freezes, like a deer at bay. . . . When she dances alone, she doesn't appear to be

thinking of him, or even thinking of love . . . no matter how strongly Andersen dances. . . . He must dance in a vacuum until Ashley recognizes him as her lover. Then his solo will not be just a solo, and the little girls behind him will become projections of Ashley, or of her desire, not just an ensemble."[4]

One can imagine a queer/lesbian reading of this ballet that would make a very different interpretation of this moment. From a "leg is real" perspective—in other words, *over*interpreting the sexuality of the ballet—one might ask, why should a lesbian ballerina act out her love for a gay male partner?

Even Croce describes Andersen as "a Laurie to her Jo," emphasizing the curiously *asexual* component to the pairing.[5] So why couldn't *Ballade* be about the independence or even sexual indifference of a ballerina to her partner, an interpretation Croce herself makes of Suzanne Farrell's performance of *Diamonds*?[6] Perhaps Croce finds Farrell to be feminine enough that her independence is not a threat to the heterosexuality of the pas de deux as a formal component of classical ballet. But Merrill Ashley in her sheer technical proficiency was a threat to the feminine image of the ballerina. If she can't dance with the women she loves (because the codes of her art form prohibit it), why not emphasize this by stressing the nonheterosexual aspects of partnering in ballet, an art form in which the ballerina is assumed to be the visual focus and the danseur is assumed to be effeminate? Thus it seems to me that both queer theory and Croce in practice do acknowledge the sexuality of ballet, although to very different ends.

A lesbian perspective might uncover new meanings in the tropes of classical ballet, for example, in the frequent intertwining of members of the corps in Balanchine ballets (not to mention the hand-holding of the cygnets).[7] In order to do so, however, lesbians would have to read against the grain of the choreographer's presumed intentions as—no doubt—many of us are already doing. Feminist film criticism long has advocated the idea of reading against the grain as a way of combating the inherent male control of the look in classical cinema. And of course all "queer readings" are against some grain or other, because queer theory depends on the idea that gays and lesbians have been excluded from representation and thus must be read out of texts in which their presence is in some way closeted.

And yet—in revisionist attempts to redefine classical ballet the idea of male–male partnering has proved far more common as a subversive choreographic technique than has any similar attempt at female–female partnering and not always for the most politically correct reasons. Revisionist ballet choreographers often happen to be gay men (just as mainstream ballet choreographers tend to be). Even a conservative queer choreographer like Jerome Robbins played with the idea of the male pas de deux.

There are perhaps aesthetic reasons why female–female partnering is not more common in contemporary ballet. As the Ballets Trocadero de Monte Carlo's all male *Swan Lake* en pointe shows us, the idea of a ballerina lifting another ballerina (even if in drag) is funny to contemporary ballet audiences. Arlene Croce has written that "drag ballet provides one answer to the question of why men impersonating women are funny, while women impersonating men are not; it has to do with gravity. (A heavy thing trying to become light is automatically funnier than a light thing trying to become heavy.)"[8] Yes, but humor is culturally determined; the more we see something, the more we get used to it, and men dancing with men now seems almost normal. The entire tradition of the ballerina en pointe sets up an ideal of femininity that is hard to shake and that renders any contemporary attempt at female partnering ludicrous rather than revisionist.

Our boldest attempts at new visions of gender in ballet have been those in which classical ballet is rethought from a homoerotic perspective. In this regard no production has been more influential than Matthew Bourne's *Swan Lake* (see chapter 5).[9] The most controversial aspect of this production was the rewriting of the swans as powerful but effeminate males in tacky feathered pantaloons. Although there *is* a parody ballet—a nineteenth-century butterfly entertainment with a tiny ballerina and amazonian corps de ballet—in *this* production of *Swan Lake*, critics have greeted the production as a whole as more than just a satire of an old warhorse. Yet technically speaking, Bourne avoids simply sending up *Swan Lake* by adjusting the choreography so that men do not dance en pointe as they do in true parodies of *Swan Lake*. The White Swan sequence, which takes place in a park, features familiar birdlike poses and arabesques, but they are done by men, not by drag queens in toe shoes. The supported arabesques of the Prince and the Swan Queen are played for equality, and the lifts are performed by the powerfully muscled naked swan who easily supports the more effeminate and fully clothed prince. The choreography is made for a swan danseur, not for a male ballerina. This becomes obvious when the four male cygnets pound their way onto the stage, and we realize that their foot-stomping is a parody of pointe-work. Now we can laugh. Everything before this can be read as a demonstration of masculine beauty.

The drag ballet companies did all the traditional steps, but this more authentically artistic version avoids them. Indeed, the Black Swan pas de deux is more Twyla Tharp than Petipa, as the Prince dances a sinister tango with the leather bad-boy Swan. The ensemble dances are more like vogueing than classical ballet.

Reviews of the London, Los Angeles, and New York productions of Bourne's *Swan Lake* disagree as to whether this production is a musical, a theater piece, a dance melange, or a true ballet (with Tchaikovsky's score intact). Regardless, it is an interpretation of one of the cornerstones of the ballet repertoire and its homosexualization seems in retrospect inevitable.

Even during a period when female dancers frequently played both male and female roles, there was not a travesty *Swan Lake*.[10] For now, the lesbian reading of this ballet exists mainly in the resisting minds of individual audience members. We await the great feminist choreographer who will realize this vision. Or will it always be the case that a ballet master can be homosexual but a ballet mistress can never be a master?

NOTES

1. See Susan Leigh Foster, "The Ballerina's Phallic Pointe," in *Corporealities: Dancing, Knowledge, Culture, and Power* (London: Routledge, 1996), 1–24.

2. Foster writes, "Whereas the opera also boasts a strong lesbian following, the ballet holds little if any interest for the lesbian viewer" (Foster, "Ballet's Phallic Pointe," 19, n.).

3. Arlene Croce, "The Two Trocaderos" in *Afterimages* (New York: Vintage, 1979), 80.

4. Arlene Croce, "Ashley, Balanchine, and 'Ballade,' " in *Going to the Dance* (New York: Knopf, 1982), 276–77.

5. Ibid., 277.

6. Arlene Croce, "Free and More Than Equal," *Afterimages* (New York: Vintage, 1979), 125–29.

7. This would be, of course, to do violence to the emerging historical study of dance. In her work on the travesty dancer, for instance, Susan Leigh Foster theorizes that even when a woman assumed the male role, the spectator positioning is still masculine. She argues this on the basis of historical audiences for ballet but also from a Lacanian perspective, which my argument is rejecting and which Foster in part wishes to reject too—at least for future ballet dancers (Foster, "Ballet's Phallic Pointe," 10ff.).

8. Croce, "Two Trocaderos," 80.

9. I am basing my analysis on a BBC videotape of the London production.

10. I base this on Foster's comment in "Ballet's Phallic Pointe" that travesty dancing did not extend to tragic ballets (10). No doubt there has been some kind of lesbian *Swan Lake* somewhere but none that has come to international attention the way that Bourne's production has.

13
Opening Sequences

Jennifer DeVere Brody

There's joy in repetition.
—*The artist formerly known as Prince*

This is my memory.
My memory is not my enemy . . .
My memory is my enemy.
What time is it?
—*Bill T. Jones*, Last Night on Earth

MAKING TIME QUEER

In the *Oxford English Dictionary*, the word *sequel* precedes *sequence*; as a consequence, we can see that one organizational principle, alphabetizing, suggests another equally arbitrary or rather strategic organization: time and space. Although both sequel and sequence address spatiotemporal dimensions, the former is usually seen to be more temporal than the latter, which is regarded as relatively more spatial. In an effort to rethink these categories, the title of this essay, "Opening Sequences," refers not only to temporal openings but also to spatial beginnings.

As the anthropologist Jonathan Boyarin reminds us,

> The very notion of "progress," of stepping forward in time, exemplifies how the metaphorical structures of our language betray that bifurcation [between time and space], displaying in particular a tendency to borrow terms connoting spatial relations in our references to change over time. We have a notion of "progress" that metaphorically discusses temporal sequence in terms of spatial distancing and vice versa: we speak of distant times, we think of long-ago places, if not in so many words.[1]

The time–space binary that Boyarin tries to dissolve is reproduced with each performance of Bill T. Jones's danced memoir, *21*. Jones first danced the piece in the late 1970s (time), in his bedroom (space) for a sleeping audience of one (Jones's lover, Arnie Zane). *21* is danced, written, and spoken.

More specifically, *21* works through a series of citations of canonical icons such as Michelangelo's *David*, Muhammad Ali, and pantomime postures such as "eek a mouse nineteenth-century melodrama." Bracketing with bravado, Jones's performance epitomizes the term *equivocal*. His performance highlights (non)-referentiality, making every moment of movement into a bodily pun. The first public performance of *21* took place in Waterloo, Iowa, in 1984 (re-created for video with Tom Bowles). Jones dances, apparently seamlessly, and then breaks down his moves into specific gestures that are labeled (by spoken text) numerically, in sequence, from one through twenty-one. Next, he repeats the series of gestures, giving each a cultural tag (rather than a number) such as Apollo Belvedere, Adam, pregnant woman, art deco, and so on. That several tags refer to styles (as in historical art styles) and are performed chronologically is important because the technique underscores Jones's understanding that time itself is a cultural artifact.

Once the audience is familiar with the gestures, Jones defamiliarizes them. That is to say, Jones forces the audience to read his gestures in a new way. Rather like learning language, the audience must learn to recognize (re-cognize) the letter *A* as the same as but different from the letter/mark *a*. The dance makes clear that meaning is more than one thing at the same time. For example, his pose "male beefcake, tits to the sky," when repeated in his spoken narrative also refers to his jailed brother's girlfriend's "tits." Such titillating juxtapositions and repetitions of defiant differences complicate questions of signifier and signified.[2] (These juxtapositions and repositions recall Gere's discussion in chapter 11 of the forced binary opposition between pectorals and breasts.)

Interestingly, in his autobiography Jones recounts how he learned the alphabet. He remembers learning his ABC's and then suddenly halfway through the recitation, "ABCDE . . . WHACK!"

he felt the wallop of a strap wielded by his mother, Estella. Jones "tried to do the ABC's on [his] own, [but never] got much further than F or G. [He] never picked up with the lesson again"— he never finished the sequence.[3] This may be one way of understanding Jones's interest in unfinished sequences as well as a way of thinking about the mortality of the body (viva interruptus).

By turns pedagogical and presumptuous, referential and reverential, as well as self-reflexive and unconscious, *21* is a dance in which, paradoxically, the rigid structure leads to the most fluid gestures. Jones claims that in *21* "levels of memory slip in and out of [his] control . . . [and that] the whole is a matrix under which the fluid, most unconscious dancing should happen—that's the problem, by solving a problem that is what dance is." He used a similar strategy in *Still/Here* (time/space) in which he "set up a field of movement material and juxtaposed it to a text, thereby challenging viewers to process what they are seeing and hearing simultaneously. My assumption is that the result is greater than the sum of its parts. However, *Still/Here* succeeds in using movements at various levels of abstraction, to channel and amplify specific spoken information."[4] In short, Jones's works often choreograph memory, movement, and identity in complicated and compelling ways. Jones's performance seeks to queer time by dancing through remembered spaces and poses. Indeed, ideas about the queer space/time of Jones's danced memoir are the (vanishing) point of this opening sequence.

Fast Forward.

TAKE 21

The opening sequence to a 1996 performance of the dance (which I participated in, watched, and reviewed on videotape), began with repetitions of a word, *memory*, that were almost like an incantation. The word is spoken as the dancer, clad in loose drawstring-tied white pants and facing the audience at center stage, swipes his abdomen with one hand, walks forward and then stage right, comes to rest on a piano, folds his hands, crosses his legs, looks left and then right—and then at audience. He repeats the word *memory* and walks back to the starting point to begin the sequence again. Only this repetition, as with each successive one, will be slightly different—added steps punctuate other parts of the sequence. The audience laughs when he leaves out one major segment of what has become a dance sequence. Jones smirks, shrugs, and with a "throwaway hand gesture" decides not to go through the motions the audience now anticipates and expects. The audience remembers the movement that was (not) there. In the last go-round of the opening sequence, Jones leaves out (or does he?) a segment, assured the moves now reside in the audience's memory. What this opening sequence suggests is that memory is shared—that it is made and to a certain extent collective. Jones pauses at the piano. Rest/Stop/Caesura.

Jones then speaks in the third person about his first sexual experience with a man. He begins doing poses from an earlier sequence, mixing up their original order, and says:

> 1971 Bill T. Jones has sex [*pause*] with a young man for the first time. As he performs a series of quick gestures with his body, he speaks the following words:
> Pele
> male beefcake
> sex like never before
> to the groin
> [*Jones, speaking as his mother:*] "You ain't a man yet—you gotta get your education."
> Oh my God
> and after
> [*Jones, speaking as Arnie Zane:*] "I give you my word, Missus Jones."
> One two three oh my God Amsterdam.

These quoted phrases (danced and spoken) are simultaneously remembered and enacted impersonations of Jones and others. His narrative performance questions the truth of his body. His is a dance of dissemblance and resemblance as well as reassemblage. The piece itself is never fixed or stable because Jones has been improvising/revising the crucial story of his "coming out" every time he's performed it in twenty-one years; as we know, coming out, like housework, is never done. The piece emphasizes that one is always in the process of becoming . . . out. It also might be said to demonstrate that queerness is always already about disrupting the reproduction of a "lily white is right" canon and static notions of the subject.

But in reading the performance itself, where does one "mark" queerness *exactly*? When Jones discusses the first time he slept with a man, Arnie Zane? When he narrates the story of his brother's being "turned out" (raped) in prison? It may be important to remember as well the Arlene Croce approach to "queering" Jones's work. This tactic of queering the canon requires that one *not* view Jones's work (in a reversal of Supreme Court Justice Potter Stewart's statement about pornography—that he knew it when he saw it); for Croce, we know queer art when we must *not* see it. Because Jones's identity precedes him, that is, his status as black, gay, and HIV positive is known, his art, which is autobiographical, must be queer. Croce's epistemology of queerness is faulty and one I would suggest we not practice.

The supposed telltale signs of difference, marked in many ways, appear in the eyes of the spectator, who may always read perversely, queerly, as does Jones himself. Queer is not stable—it resides in multiple registers; indeed, this may be its value, generally speaking. I believe that Jones's ability to play with the practice of referentiality, to make his gestures refer to other things, is an example of queering. Jones's sly alterations, iterations, and reiterations of the sequence do, I think, queer what might have been canonical references. His shifting additions, subtractions, and supplements queer the signifiers deployed in this performance. In this sense we can understand the performance theorist Joe Roach's claim that "repetition is an art of re-creation as well as restoration. Texts may obscure what performance tends to reveal."[5] It is significant too that Roach's formulation applies specifically to what he terms "circum-Atlantic" culture with its obscured black traces, which he deems "forgotten but not gone." Roach's comment also emphasizes that "text" that is not performed (activated) is static. Such ideas have implications for writing-dance-narratives.

Jump cut.

Albert "Cubby" Broccoli, who directed numerous James Bond

films, established the opening sequence of the series in *Dr. No*
(1962). The stylized beginning, now a convention, serves as a recurrent opening sequence of every film in the series. The opening
sequence (the first of usually three openings—the most famous is
the second opening, which juxtaposes female nudes and guns,
and changes significantly with each new theme song and individual film) displays a playful, ironic use of film conventions, much
in the way Bill T. Jones's performances of *21* signify on the conventional arrested images/shots/stills he uses as elements with
which to form other stories. In their textbook on film David Bordwell and Kristin Thompson claim that "the first step in analyzing
any film, is to segment into sequences . . . [which, like theatrical
scenes,] refer to distinct phrases of action occurring within a relatively unified space and time."[6] However, the cultural critics
Tony Bennett and Janet Woollacott argue:

> It is not possible to analyse a cultural phenomenon constituted in
> this way merely by studying the various "texts of Bond" one by one
> and *sequentially*. To seek thus to stabilise them as objects of analy-
> sis would be to abstract them from the shifting orders of inter-tex-
> tuality through which their actual functioning has been organised
> and reorganised. This would be to close off in advance the possi-
> bility of understanding the concrete history of their functioning in
> diverse social and ideological relations of reading.[7]

The specific patterns and sequences only appear to have been set
and congealed in a strictly formalist reading of the "Bondian for-
mula." Nevertheless, the formulaic opening of the Bond series
contrasts with the improvisational opening of Bill T. Jones's dance
(or any live performance). *Unlike* filmic sequences, or even video
tape, which, once printed, can be rearranged only through mechanical manipulations such as the literal cutting of the film or
printed matter—recall Roland Barthes's de/re/construction of
Balzac's story in *S/Z*—live performances are "one-time only"
events—always somewhat out of reach, they can only be recalled,
remembered. The sequence gathers meaning through its spatiotemporal context. As Peggy Phelan remarks, "The ontology of
performance maps a gateway [opening] across another order of
production and reproduction."[8] By messing with sequences in his

improvised performances, Jones queers the imagined stability and natural logic of sequence, allowing his audiences to participate in seeing arbitrarily arranged, evanescent scenes of/from his life.

After the performance Jones explains that he was "very interested in sequential movement. . . . In *21* I tell that story. I try to keep coming back into sequence, remembering where you [*sic*] left off . . . letting the accidents happen."[9] This eloquent description resonates with Roach's contention that "under the seductive linearity of its influence, memory operates as an alternation between retrospection and anticipation that is itself . . . a work of art."[10] Indeed, each author I have mentioned is interested in questions of autobiography, "biomythography," or the "chronobiological basis of narrative."[11] If, as Stuart Hall following Benedict Anderson argues, identities "are not to be distinguished by their falsity/genuineness, but by the style in which they are imagined," then the style performed is crucial. We can read (have read?) about style and identity in essays by David Gere and Gay Morris, collected here (before).[12]

David Gere's essay, "*29 Effeminate Gestures*" (chapter 11), argues for the efficacy of what he terms "heroic effeminacy." In so doing, Gere's piece translates or "extends" Joe Goode's danced performance of *29 Effeminate Gestures* into "verbal discourse [written or captured on the page], thereby giving it life in a new medium." Gere's attention to his own gendered performances and to the processes through which movement is translated and transmitted, both on the page and on various stages, works well with the issues of queerness, space, time, and performativity discussed here. Gere's emphasis on the congealing effects of repeated gestures—of danced/lived/embodied experience—reminds us of the significance of the mode of transmission as a mediator of meaning and how one reads retrospectively.

If the resignification and indeed valorization of effeminate gay males is the focus of Gere's piece, Gay Morris's study of the early dances of Bill T. Jones (chapter 7) complements Gere's by focusing on Jones's embattled, heroic performances of masculinity. Morris argues that Jones's "symbolic emasculation" is situated in three aspects of the dancer's identity: namely, his race, profession, and sexuality. In short, Morris claims that as a "gay black concert dancer," Jones, who "wanted to control the perception of his own identity," performed masculinity in a aggressive, ultimately subversive and empowering way. An aspect of these works, including Jones's, that I wish to applaud is the attention paid to masculinity and femininity as performative modes/codes/roads. Jones has commented on his own sense of movements as gendered. For example, he asserts, "There is an emotional feeling I get when my arms are liquid and moving through space that feels soft, supple, inviting, giving—all terms that I apply to women. Slashing and striking is something I attribute to men."[13] Jones's discourse here assigns and reproduces gendered actions that can be performed by different bodies, regardless of "sex." In a discussion of "feminine movement," the feminist Susan Brownmiller says, "I perform now without props and from memory."[14] Similarly, Jones performs various masculinities and femininities without props and from memory.

Gay Morris explicates Jones's masculinity as something produced in dialogue with femininity and race. Morris reopens the early archives of Bill T. Jones's work in order to set the stage for later developments in Jones's life, concluding her piece by claiming: "When in the mid-1980s Jones openly avowed the identity we know him by today . . . he was able to do so while relinquishing little of the power he had accrued." Morris's "emplotment"—reading backward to find clues to the Jones "we" know "today" (and I would add by which we may not know him tomorrow)—is a choice with certain ideological implications. In reading retroactively, Morris has (re)produced a somewhat linear narrative of Jones's development. This is not a criticism but rather a reminder of Hayden White's work on the emplotment of history. White reminds us, "The important point is that most historical narratives can be emplotted in a number of ways." Therefore we must pay attention to the narratives we choreograph on the page. What is proper order? What does it mean to be out of sequence? In what order do we narrativize text?—and to what end? I would answer toward a perpetually open . . .

Rewind.

QUEERING MARKED TIME

We're almost out of time. Are we out of time?
            —*Bill T. Jones*

Jones's query, "are we out of time" again exemplifies the confusion of space/time.[15] The gestures he performs are made poignant because he (like you and I as well as the terminally ill patients with whom he works) is running out of/into time. Jones has spoken and written about how time changes when one is aware that death is imminent. One's perception of the semantic distinction between living and dying bodies changes under certain conditions. When Jones worked with terminally ill people for his aptly titled piece *Still/Here*, he incorporated excerpts from *21*. He directed each of the Survival Workshop members to create "a gesture portrait of themselves." As a form of both pedagogy and performance, Jones asked the group to explicate and supplement the gesture with spoken words. He asked them: "What does that mean? Could you perform the gesture and tell us something about what you've learned? Could you perform the gesture and tell us something you've never told anybody else before? . . . Could you conceive of your life as one smooth line? Where does it begin? And where does it end?"[16] In other words, how is one's life represented?

Again, Boyarin helps us to think about this problem when he notes:

> We move "through time" as much as we move "through space," and this motion is not separated into spatial sequences on one hand and temporal sequences on the other. However, this does not mean that the distinction between time and space is entirely arbitrary. . . . We can call the body a "rubric" in which spatiality and temporality coexist indissolubly, in which their necessary unity is most clearly shown. When you die in time you dissolve in space.[17]

Exceptions to Boyarin's thesis are found not only in technologies of preservation such as embalming but also in painting, print, and film, each a technology that fixes narrative forms.

Jones is aware that to blur the boundaries between life and

death—to see them as part of a continuum—upsets canonical notions of the absolute difference between these states. Indeed, in his ongoing work with other terminally ill people, he uses as an aid a technique borrowed in part from the improvisational *21*. He writes: "My own process involved the intuitive combining of the survivors' gestures to make phrases, plumbing my own body's imagination, or borrowing from existing forms—capoeira and karate among them—to create expressive dance sequences."[18] Thus even the process of making dance is revealed to be highly collaborative—blurred, shared, borrowed.

The emphasis on translation, juxtaposing dancing/words, telling stories of the body, embodying telling stories, adds weight/wait to Toni Morrison's claim: "We die. That may be the meaning of life. But we *do* language. That may be the measure of our lives."[19] Moreover, like musical measures, dance sequences can be reinterpreted, repeated, and replayed.[20] Here/now/still we yearn for the impossible "joy of repetition"—we desire opening sequences.

. . . *Now I'll explain what I am trying to do.* I repeat the gestures that opened the dance.

Time Out

Cut!

Credits

NOTES

1. The Artist also formed a Minneapolis band called, appropriately for this essay, "The Time," led by singer Morris Day.

2. Jonathan Boyarin, "Space, Time, and the Politics of Memory," in *Remapping Memory: The Politics of Timespace* (Minneapolis: University of Minnesota Press, 1994), 7.

3. Bill T. Jones and Peggy Gillespie, *Last Night on Earth* (New York: Pantheon, 1995), 25–26.

4. Ibid., 262–63.

5. Joseph Roach, *Cities of the Dead: Circum-Atlantic Performance* (New York: Columbia University Press, 1996), 286.

6. David Bordwell and Kristin Thompson, *Film Art: An Introduction* (New York: McGraw-Hill, 1994).

7. Tony Bennett and Janet Woollacott, *Bond and Beyond: The Political Career of a Popular Hero* (New York: Methuen, 1987), 59, emphasis added.

8. See Peggy Phelan, *Unmarked: The Politics of Performance* (New York: Routledge, 1993), 178.

9. Quoted in discussion after Riverside Performance of *21*.

10. Roach, *Cities of the Dead*, 32.

11. "Biomythography" is Audré Lorde's neologism. See Lorde, *Zami, A New Spelling of My Name: A Biomythography by Audré Lorde* (Freedom, Calif.: Crossing Press, 1982). "Chronobiological basis of narrative" is from Michael Holquist's article, "From Body-Talk to Biography: The Chronobiological Bases of Narrative," *Yale Journal of Criticism* 3, no. 1 (1989): 1–35.

12. See Stuart Hall, "Cultural Identity and Diaspora," in P. Williams and L. Chrisman, eds., *Colonial Discourse and Post-Colonial Theory: A Reader* (London: Harvester Wheatsheaf, 1994), 237.

13. Jones is quoted in Johanna Boyce, Ann Daly, Bill T. Jones, and Carol Martin, "Movement and Gender: A Roundtable Discussion," *The Drama Review* 32, no. 4 (1988): 98.

14. Susan Brownmiller, *Femininity* (New York: Fawcett Columbine, 1984), 172.

15. It is beyond the scope of this essay to provide a full reading of this brilliant and complex text. All "translations" of both spoken and embodied words are my own and are based on my observation/participation in the live event as well as subsequent reviews of a tape of the performance. I note the discrepancies to underscore that every reading is partial. A video version of *21* is listed as "recreated for video with Tom Bowles, 1984" in *Last Night on Earth*, 280. Jones's improvisation is augmented and often site (cite?) specific. For example, in the Riverside, California, performance I discuss here, he captions—as concert performers from rock musicians to comedians often do—one of the gestures as "Pregnant *Riverside* Housewife" (verbal emphasis during the performance).

16. Jones and Gillespie, *Last Night on Earth*, 253.

17. Boyarin, *Remapping Memory*, 21.

18. Jones and Gillespie, *Last Night on Earth*, 258.

19. Toni Morrison, *The Nobel Lecture in Literature* (New York: Knopf, 1993), 22, emphasis in the original.

20. According to the composer Ethan Nasreddin-Longo, in music a sequence, "is a figure that is heard once and is then repeated at another pitch level, or in another harmony, not just once but usually several times. The term thus captures the serial nature of the phenomenon. Sequences themselves are not usually the musical 'point,' as it were: they are a kind of musical connective tissue, leading from one place to another. Frequently, at least in tonal music, they lead from one key to another. In tonal music the order of iteration is important [because] some harmonies must follow others." Conversation with the composer. Riverside, Calif., 1996.

14
Looking from a Different Place: Gay Spectatorship of American Modern Dance

Susan Manning

Is it possible to historicize and theorize gay and lesbian spectatorship of American modern dance? That is, do gay and lesbian viewers experience modern dance in distinctly different ways from straight viewers? If so, how do we go about recovering the difference, given that most published reviews record responses as perceived from dominant social locations and omit responses as perceived from alternate social locations? If we manage to recover differences between queer and straight spectatorship, can we avoid essentializing gay and lesbian subjects? Do the dynamics of lesbian spectatorship parallel or diverge from the dynamics of gay spectatorship? And what are the implications of theorizing "queer spectatorship" as opposed to "gay and lesbian spectatorship"? Most important, why does the inquiry matter?

These are questions that preoccupy me; Susan Foster's "Closets Full of Dances" (chapter 5) and Julia Foulkes's "Dance Is for American Men" (chapter 4) help me think through this complex of issues. Read together, the two essays illuminate gay spectatorship of Ted Shawn's dances and raise provocative questions about the possibilities for gay (queer?) spectatorship of modern dance from 1930 to the present. Here I will probe the implications of Foster's and Foulkes's essays for a discussion of gay spectatorship. Although this essay cannot answer all the questions I enumerated earlier, perhaps I can offer starting points for inquiry.

Although neither Foster nor Foulkes focuses on spectatorship, both provide evidence for a difference between gay and straight spectatorship of performances by Shawn and His Men Dancers. Whereas most newspaper reviews interpreted the dances in the heterosexist terms promulgated by Shawn, published memoirs and unpublished letters demonstrate that some gay viewers interpreted the dances in homophile terms. Foster quotes Barton Mumaw's memoir, which recalls "a more subtle response to our work by young men . . . pretending a fascination with our streamlined DeSoto in an attempt to disguise their real interest." Thus, she notes, "some audience members saw straight past Shawn's manly ideal to the possibility of male homosexual love celebrated and honored in the noble forms of the dance." Both Foster and Foulkes rightly connect this idealization of homosexual love to the writings of Havelock Ellis that so influenced Shawn.

From today's perspective, it is clear that the anonymous young men Mumaw describes, as well as Shawn's supporters (Lucien Price, Walter Terry, John Lindquist), whom Foulkes describes, recognized a homoerotic subtext in his choreography. In fact, the subtext appears so clear to our vision—whether looking at photographs, watching old films, or seeing revivals of the work in performance—that we wonder how anyone in the 1930s could have missed it. Yet Foster and Foulkes convince us that, in the historical context of the depression and the approach of world war, Shawn's choreographic imagery carried multiple levels of meaning—in Julia Foulkes's words—"as an example of America's potency, as a sign of essential differences between men and women, and as an ideal of homosexual love between men." In other words, Foster's and Foulkes's essays suggest that some gay spectators saw Shawn's Men Dancers differently than did many straight spectators.

Note the qualifying terms *some* and *many*. I am not positing that all gay spectators interpreted Shawn's choreography in one way, all straight spectators in another way. On the contrary: I am assuming that all levels of meaning were available to all spectators in the 1930s and that individual spectators perceived some levels as more resonant than others, depending on a myriad of influences, most of which are beyond the reach of historical research. It is certainly likely that many gay spectators recognized the homophobic frame as well as the homoerotic subtext in the choreography. It is equally plausible that at least some straight spectators recognized the subtext as well as the frame. I am developing a model of spectatorship that posits performance as an arena within which spectators may consider perspectives other than those conditioned by their social identities outside the theater, as a cultural space where spectators negotiate their simultaneous habitation of multiple and overlapping social formations.

For gay spectators of American modern dance, this means straddling the boundaries between gay subculture, ethnic/racial/immigrant subcultures, and/or class formations. Indeed, the project of American modern dance involves an interplay of diverse subcultures, dominant cultures, and the dissident middle class, the class fraction within which modern dancers stage their opposition not only to middle-class norms but also to upper-class privilege. My terminology comes from Raymond Williams via Alan Sinfield. Understanding artistic production and reception as a set of social relations, Williams and Sinfield analyze twentieth-century culture in terms of dominant cultures in the plural (established elites, mass media, middle-class norms), dissident middle-class cultures (catalyst for many developments conventionally designated "high art"), and subcultures (social formations premised on collective experiences of systematic discrimination, common life choices, and/or shared tactics for maneuvering within dominant cultures).[1]

It goes without saying that a comprehensive history of spectatorship is impossible. Nevertheless, one can generalize from fragmentary evidence documenting the responses of individual spectators and argue for the probability of divergent spectatorial responses from divergent social locations, social locations defined in terms of dominant and dissident cultures and subcultures. Thus juxtaposing evidence of spectatorial response gleaned from Mumaw's memoir, Lucien Price's unpublished letters, John Lindquist's photographs, and the reviews pasted in Shawn's scrapbooks demonstrates a divergence in views of Shawn's Men Dancers from the social location of gay subculture and from the social location of dominant culture.[2]

In one sense the "changing epistemology" of the closet that Foster traces so elegantly through modern dance accords with changing relations between gay subculture, dissident middle-class culture, and dominant cultures. As these relations change over time, so gay spectatorship of American modern dance changes over time. Here I am reading Foster's essay against itself. Although Foster acknowledges that closeting did not preclude gay spectatorship, her argument emphasizes parallels between choreographic strategies for closeting sexuality and written discourses on homosexuality (Shawn and Havelock Ellis, Merce Cunningham and the Kinsey Report, Mangrove and Guy Hocquenghem, Matthew Bourne and queer theory). Foregrounding what she backgrounds, I would argue that the "changing epistemology" of the closet resulted in changing forms of gay spectatorship.

My reversal of emphasis reflects a somewhat different conceptualization of the closet from Foster's. Although Foster does not specifically cite Eve Kosofsky Sedgwick's important *Epistemology of the Closet*, Foster's contention that "modern dance has staged with consummate clarity the embodied version of the closet's changing epistemology" clearly alludes to Sedgwick's work. Sedgwick challenges progress narratives of gay and lesbian history and asserts that "the reign of the telling secret was scarcely overturned with Stonewall."[3] On the contrary, Sedgwick believes and Foster reaffirms, "the epistemology of the closet has given an overarching consistency to gay culture and identity throughout this century."[4] Although I do not dispute the validity of this claim, I want to pay more attention than do Sedgwick and Foster to "consequential change" over time "around and outside the closet."[5] In so doing, I am following the lead of George Chauncey, who scrutinizes when and how the term *closet* came to characterize gay lives (not until the 1960s) and argues that earlier constructions of gay life reveal patterns that are distorted by post-Stonewall understandings.

Chauncey's *Gay New York* illuminates the shifting relations between gay subculture and other social formations during the 1930s, when Shawn's Men Dancers were crisscrossing the United States. In Chauncey's periodization, the 1930s was a decade of transition, when the gay world that had flourished in the public sphere since the 1890s gave way to the era of the closet, when state legislation pushed homosexuality out of the public sphere. In other words, the boundaries between gay subculture and dominant and dissident cultures were more permeable before the 1930s than after. Shawn's Men Dancers both embodied the assumptions of the gay world and participated in the transition from the gay world to the closet.[6]

As Chauncey argues, from the 1890s through the 1930s the gay world understood male sexuality in terms of gendered personae, distinguishing "fairies"—overtly effeminate men who were assumed to solicit male sexual partners—from "normal men"—men who abided by social norms of masculinity irrespective of whether their sexual partners were male or female. This conceptualization of sexuality makes sense of most reviews of Shawn's Men Dancers, as exemplified by the passage that both Foster and Foulkes quote: "vigor limned by restraint . . . a hale and rugged lyricism . . . which of these qualities apparent in Shawn's work can be called effeminate?" Before and into the 1930s, if a gesture did not read as effeminate, it read as manly.

Not until the 1930s, Chauncey argues, did state legislation construct a closet around gay subculture. This legislation, prompted partly by the social crisis brought about by the depression, accompanied a shift from understanding sexuality in terms of gendered personae to understanding sexuality in terms of sexual object choice, the conceptualization that continues into the present. As Foulkes suggests, performances by the Men Dancers participated in the transition from Chauncey's gay world to the era of the closet: Shawn's "manly men may have conformed to heterosexual norms, but they were challenging common homosexual images of sissies. And, in this way, Shawn helped change the definition of homosexuality from gender inversion to same-sex object choice, through visual display of the male body itself." Beginning in the 1930s and thereafter, gayness did not depend on the performance of gesture but on the choice of a sexual partner.

As Chauncey and other historians have shown, relations between gay subculture and other social formations changed significantly after 1940. During World War II the U.S. military for the first time declared homosexuality ground for discharge, yet officers made exceptions for innumerable soldiers considered essential to the war effort. Thus many gay soldiers experienced what

Allan Bérubé has characterized in his oral history as "coming out under fire." Yet as soon as the war was won, the military enforced the official policy and dismissed many gay soldiers. After the war many dishonorably discharged gay (and lesbian) veterans settled in San Francisco, where they founded the first gay rights organizations. At the same time state harassment of gay men intensified, as the dominant culture conflated "communists and queers" as interrelated threats to the "American way of life."[7]

These changes in turn occasioned changes in gay spectatorship of American modern dance, which Foster illuminates through her discussion of Merce Cunningham. As her essay makes clear, Cunningham's formalist aesthetic both closeted *and* signaled his homosexuality. On the one hand, "Cunningham neutralized all masculine, feminine, and sexual connotations by focusing on space, time, and motion." Yet within his dances Cunningham "circulated as the odd man out," allowing "any who would look for it [to] find Cunningham's difference." At the same time Cunningham's choreography staged whiteness as "an unmarked and unchallenged category," thus extending the racism that also informed Shawn's dancing, as both Foulkes and Foster acknowledge.

In many ways Mangrove, an all-male collective of contact improvisers, encountered radically different conditions for production and reception than did Cunningham. Based in San Francisco from 1975 to 1980, Mangrove staged a new image for the male dancer—combining "astonishing physical daring with a sensuous vulnerability"—in the years between the emergence of the Gay Liberation Front and the onset of the AIDS crisis. Foster reads Mangrove's performances as a variation of the racial and sexual politics of Shawn and Cunningham, for the company presented the "nonerogenized body" within the frame of whiteness, a nonerogenized body that exuded an overall sensuality. The group's "polymorphous sensuality," Foster believes, staged a closeted version of Guy Hocquenghem's 1972 manifesto, *Homosexual Desire*, which celebrated anal sexuality and critiqued phallic sexuality.

Foster does not include evidence of alternate spectatorship of Mangrove, as she does in her discussions of Shawn and Cunningham. Because I have no information about the group other than what she provides, I cannot argue decisively for gay spectatorship of the group's work. Nonetheless, I wonder whether evidence does exist for spectatorship from subcultural social locations (reviews in the gay press?) and whether gay spectators might have read the imagery of the male–male duets performed by Mangrove in the revolutionary terms proposed by Hocquenghem. In other words, as with Shawn and Cunningham, might choreographic strategies that Foster reads as attempts at closeting homosexuality also be read as attempts at addressing gay spectators?

Foster opens and closes her essay with a discussion of Matthew Bourne's *Swan Lake*. In the end, she concludes, the work reveals "heteronormative assumptions about gay life" and "conveys neither a gay nor a feminist politics." Thus, she believes, Bourne's *Swan Lake* exemplifies the problematic social agenda that Sue-Ellen Case, among others, has identified with queer theory. Although I am swayed, I am not convinced by Foster's argument. Granted, the mainstream press omitted mention of the work's gay thematics. (But the mainstream press never acknowledged the homoeroticism of Shawn's choreography, either.) Granted, the narrative frame does include elements of heteronormativity. (But so did the choreographic frames for Shawn's choreography.) Once again I would ask whether divergent readings are possible from the social locations of dominant culture and of gay subculture. Foster's analysis cannily accounts for the mainstream success of Bourne's work, but does her analysis also account for the passionate response accorded the work by gay spectators of my acquaintance?

That I am not fully persuaded by Foster's reading of Bourne's *Swan Lake* perhaps reflects a difference in our views of queer theory. Foster is suspicious of the "pseudocoalition" that queer theory promises and that Bourne's swans embody, for although both promise "inclusion of all minoritized groups," both become advocates for "white middle-class gay men." Moreover, both queer theory and Bourne's swans remain uncritical of their commodification by global capitalism. These insights are beyond dispute, as Foster acutely pinpoints limitations in contemporary dance politics and cultural politics. Yet, however much I respect (and in many ways share) Foster's perspective, I have found queer theory useful for quite different reasons.

Skeptics might say that queer theory's "defining itself against the normal rather than the heterosexual" allows me and many other straight academics to work in gay and lesbian studies.[8] Although it is true that queer theory's "resistance to regimes of the normal" has enabled me to ask questions I did not feel qualified to ask before, it is also true that queer theory has prompted me to interrogate my own sexuality in a way that I had not before.[9] Moreover, queer theory contributes to the model of spectatorship I am developing, for it reminds me how complex is the interplay between subjectivities and social identities.

My model of spectatorship derives from my own theater going as well as from my historical research. Although my life experience generally conforms to the norms of dominant culture, these norms do not fully circumscribe my experience in the theater. On the contrary, I go to modern dance in part to encounter perspectives other than those conditioned by my social identity outside the theater. Seeing Mark Morris Dance Group or Bill T. Jones/Arnie Zane Dance Company or Urban Bush Women, I glimpse what the world might look like from the perspectives of gay subculture and/or African American subculture. This kind of spectatorship surely reflects my privilege in the social order, for I perceive myself as enlarged rather than as erased by the choreographic imagination of modern dance. Many other viewers may well have the opposite experience—feeling excluded by the elitism of the form or its persistent binary of whiteness and blackness or its sexual and gender politics. Perhaps it is only from a position of privilege that I may posit that spectators read across the diverse social locations they inhabit.

In *Gay and After* Alan Sinfield speculates on the effect of post-Stonewall gay and lesbian subcultures on social and sexual practices at large:

> What has occurred, I suspect, is that while many people who once would have been married and/or covert are now leading an openly gay or lesbian life, a further cohort that would once have scarcely allowed themselves fantasies is now having covert same-sex experi-

ence. And, beyond that, almost certainly, there are people who are thinking about it, but as yet hardly doing anything. The relative legitimation that the lesbian and gay movement has achieved has allowed everyone to move one space over.[10]

Participating in post-Stonewall dance culture, reading in gay and lesbian studies and queer theory, and researching multiple spectators of American modern dance have allowed me to move one space over. When I first became serious about dance viewing twenty-five years ago, I lived in a world of compulsory heterosexuality. Being straight did not seem like a choice but like a given, both the ideal and the default option. Now I can look back and recognize my heterosexuality as a choice and discern other desires not pursued.

Recently, while watching a female duet at a concert sponsored by a university dance department, I experienced a startling shift in perception. It was the sort of duet I had seen innumerable times before: two young female dancers exploring a range of movement qualities and spatial relations. Earlier I might have read their interaction as suggestive of close friends, but that level of meaning would have seemed less important than the formal structure of the choreography. Now, all of a sudden, I read the two young women as lovers and their movements as suggestive of same-sex intimacy and erotic desire.

Why did this duet look so different to me now? Had this alternate level of meaning been present before, but had I simply overlooked it? If so, what had revealed this meaning to me now? The hours I had spent during the previous few months recovering the passionate responses of lesbian viewers to the dancing of Isadora Duncan? (The concert took place at an annual meeting of the Society of Dance History Scholars, where I was presenting a paper on lesbian spectatorship of American modern dance.) Had my historical research made me see differently than I had before, as if in sympathy with the lesbian spectators of Isadora Duncan? Or had introspection—memories and fantasies stirred by my research—made me see differently? Was I catching a glimpse of a response from a social location distant from my own? Or on a continuum with my own? Was I experiencing what might be termed "queer spectatorship," a response contrary to "regimes of the normal"?

Given the complications of any individual act of spectatorship, it perhaps seems foolhardy to historicize and theorize the process. Yet the lived complexity of spectatorship compels my attempt to fathom what modern dance might have meant to other watchers in other times and other places.

NOTES

I would like to thank John O. Perpener III for an invitation to deliver the 1995 Lorado Taft Lecture at the University of Illinois at Urbana-Champaign, where I first ventured to speak about gay spectatorship. Most especially, I would like to thank Alan Sinfield, 1997 Avalon Distinguished Visiting Professor of Humanities at Northwestern University, who emboldened me to retrieve the lecture manuscript from my drawer two years later. An earlier version of this argument appeared under the title "Coding the Message" in *Dance Theatre Journal* 14, no. 1 (1998): 34–37. An elaborated version, including material on lesbian spectatorship, will appear in a subsequent book on the performance of race, gender, and sexuality in American modern dance.

1. Raymond Williams, *The Sociology of Culture* (New York: Schocken, 1981); Alan Sinfield, *Faultlines: Cultural Materialism and the Politics of Dissident Reading* (Berkeley: University of California Press, 1992); Alan Sinfield, *Cultural Politics—Queer Reading* (Philadelphia: University of Pennsylvania Press, 1994).

2. The method and theory underlying this model of spectatorship applies equally well to historicizing, for example, the difference between black and white spectatorship of American modern dance. See my article, "Black Voices, White Bodies: The Performance of Race and Gender in *How Long Brethren*," *American Quarterly* 50, no. 1 (March 1998): 24–46, for an application that focuses on divergent views of 1930s modern dance from the perspectives of Euro-American dominant culture and African American subculture.

3. Eve Kosofsky Sedgwick, *Epistemology of the Closet* (Berkeley: University of California Press, 1990), 67.

4. Ibid., 68.

5. Ibid.

6. Although Chauncey writes that "the state built a closet in the 1930s and forced gay people to hide in it," he carefully notes that this use of the term *closet* is anachronistic. See George Chauncey, *Gay New York: Gender, Urban Culture, and the Making of the Gay Male World, 1890–1940* (New York: Basic, 1994), 9.

7. Allan Bérubé, *Coming Out under Fire: The History of Gay Men and Women in World War II* (New York: Free Press, 1990); John D'Emilio, *Sexual Politics, Sexual Communities: The Making of a Homosexual Minority in the United States,*

1940–1970 (Chicago: University of Chicago Press, 1983); David Savran, *Communists, Cowboys, and Queers: The Politics of Masculinity in the Work of Arthur Miller and Tennessee Williams* (Minneapolis: University of Minnesota Press, 1992); Robert J. Corber, *Homosexuality in Cold War America: Resistance and the Crisis of Masculinity* (Durham, N.C.: Duke University Press, 1997).

8. Michael Warner, introduction to *Fear of a Queer Planet: Queer Politics and Social Theory* (Minneapolis: University of Minnesota Press, 1993), xxvi.

9. Ibid., xxvi.

10. Alan Sinfield, *Gay and After* (London: Serpent's Tail, 1998), 13.

15

"I Never See You as You Are": Invitations and Displacements in Dance Writing

Peggy Phelan

What can we say with certainty about the relationship between dance and sexuality? Most of us notice that movement performance is sexy both in the doing and in the watching. The mathematical rigor of waltz, the sweaty exuberance of square dancing, the percussive pulse of samba, the glittering, blinking eyes that punctuate Balinese dance, the precise calligraphy of Chinese opera, the spinning ballet of great basketball players, the thrusting surge of soccer stars all whistle the body into heightened focus in the same way sex does. But such a huge observation does not tell us much about how, exactly, sexuality and movement performance are related. Too often this challenging question is displaced onto an apparently enthralling, albeit distracting, interest in the question of the sexual (mis)adventures of particular movers. The relationship between dance and sexuality is far more intriguing than the gossip-driven standard, "Is she or isn't she?" These days such a question is hardly a magnet for most inquiring minds. Usually, of course, she is. But the more difficult analysis of how her lesbianism comes to inform her dancing (and/or her writing about dancing) is left undone.

This may not necessarily be a tragedy. But it is useful to mark the displacements that occur between an analysis of specific dances and speculations about the sexuality of dancers. The vast majority of these displacements are licensed by an earlier displacement within movement performance itself; these displacements may constitute the intellectual equivalent of kinesthetic empathy. In these movements we begin to feel some of the intellectual eroticism inspired by the question: What is the relationship between movement performance and sexuality?

Loie Fuller reminds us that the woman who dances is always partnered. A resolutely solo performer, Fuller's dances nonetheless stage an intricate pas de deux with technology on the one hand and with the gaze and desire of her spectator (both contemporary and historical) on the other. In order to stage this dance Fuller displaced her body from the center of the spectacle. She did this by eliminating the categories that had hitherto defined dance as both an aesthetic and physical performance. Julie Townsend (in chapter 2) cites Crawford Flicht's concise summary: "[Fuller's] serpentine dance has no steps, gestures or poses." The movement central to Fuller's performance is, rather, a matter of light, optics, patented fabrics, and accouterments. It is, in short, a dance of supplements that renders the dancer's body itself supplemental. Thus Fuller stages a dance that is not one. As Luce Irigaray has brilliantly shown, the woman, and perhaps most especially the lesbian, embodies "the sex which is not one."[1]

But what is the function here, in the bleary eyes of our much stimulated gaze, of that slenderly vague but so potent article, *the*? The woman, the lesbian, the dancer. Haven't we had enough of such impossible consolidations? Has it not been demonstrated, tout court, that these singular terms are themselves symptoms of a desire for coherence that this world (always too much with us) refuses to provide? (This world which is not one?) And what are the implications of the assault on the fictive consolidations of *the* for those of us who love the dance (et la danse)?

Displacing the spectator's gaze from her body to her manipulation of mechanical spectacle, Fuller underlines the eroticizing of the technological, a useful thing to track in these dawning days of the new technologies. But what, exactly, is the erotic core of our technological fetishism? Surely, it must be related to the putative assurances of the mechanistic, the allure of the impersonal, rather than the unreliable vagaries of the individual and specific technician. To love the technological is in some sense to love that which is outside the failures and the freedoms of the nonmechanistic human. It is, perhaps, to prefer formal mechanisms to personal manias.

Townsend suggests that Fuller's experimental early dances might be profitably read as a "searching for, or re-searching of, an artistic identity that had implications for sexual identity." I like Townsend's generative vagueness here: "implications for." Yes. Perhaps the article *the* might search for a similarly vague implication: the lesbian who dances in Paris at the Folies-Bergère might have "implications for" a lesbian dancing in Michigan at the Womyn's Music Festival, whose story Ann Cvetkovich documents in chapter 10. But if this vagueness is to be generative rather than the symptomatic desire of contemporary queer theory for historical continuity, we must consider a little more precisely how the impersonal sustains passionate erotic theaters.

Lovers often recite the story of how and why and when they fell in love. The symptomatic assertion of historical continuity in erotic autobiography expresses itself primarily as an oft-repeated story of a moment—*the* moment, indeed—of the original stirrings of eroticism. But this original moment frequently occurs well after the first meeting. In Fuller's case it took her two years before she began to suspect that Gabrielle Sorère was "fond of" her. The repetition of the story attempts to interpret what motivated that mutative transformation. Fuller repeats the story because the change is in some deep way inexplicable, resistant to coherent rationalization. The story tries to capture psychic movement, a transformation in erotic, narrative, and autobiographical possibilities. Such a movement is what we might tentatively describe as a positive trauma (at least for the first few moments, weeks, months, years, decades . . .), and like all traumas it has the feature of latency.[2] That is, it cannot be comprehended fully by the conscious mind when it is being experienced. Thus Fuller's need and desire to recite, and thereby to return to, that first moment. The repetition of the story renders the moment familiar and bearable, even while it underlines the need for a story, an explanation, another version of the interpretation of the force of that moment.

In their fascination with this common erotic performance, Loie

Fuller and Gabrielle Sorère were exemplary. Sorère's deft retelling of "the moment"—"I never see you as you are but as you appeared to me that day"—has something of the almost mystical about it. But, perhaps more interestingly, it also has something liberatingly impersonal about it. To say "I never see you as you are" is both a high compliment to someone who spends her life performing and creating elaborate stage illusions and a declaration of allegiance to an unusual erotic ethic. Such a declaration might well be received as an aggressive denial of Fuller's specific presence in the present tense of their erotic theater—but only if one subscribes to the fairly conventional idea that erotic love is somehow motivated by the beloved's personality or physical attributes. Fuller and Sorère seemed to have felt that erotic love is indeed theatrical, an exchange that involves, above all, a heightened sensitivity to form and structure, rather than to the personality of one's lover. Fuller glosses Sorère's comment about the impression of that first appearance, when she suggests the possibility that Sorère's love for her is "intimately mingled with the love of form, of colour and of light, which I interpreted synthetically before her eyes when I appeared before her for the first time." This appearance is, of course, a performance, one that takes on faith a nonpossessive and impersonal love. She refers to "the love of form" rather than to "her love" or "my love." The mutuality of their love for form, color, and light grounds their interpretation of the first moment. (It is impossible to tell in this retrospective account exactly what Fuller means by "the first time," having already noted that it was two years before she recognized Sorère's interest in her.) Fuller's narrative also describes her sense of the force of her performance on her ideal spectator. For if this appearance summoned Sorère's love of form, color, and light, it also surely summoned Fuller's "intimately mingled" narrative of her own eroticized relationship to her performing self. What intrigues me about their narratives is their apparently shared assumption that a love of form, color, and light can serve as an interpretation of what sustained their erotic bond for so long. Sorère attempted to love Fuller both privately and publicly—as her singular love object and as an independent artist much beloved by her fans. Writing about Fuller's fire dance, Sorère expresses the force that this movement, from the singular to the collective (and back again), had on her: "The flames die into a single flame, which grows to immensity. You might think that human thought were rending itself in the darkness."

The performance of *the* sexual combines both the fantasy of an original consolidation and the force of that consolidation's disappearance. "I never see you as you are" is not, for either Fuller or Sorère, the occasion for lamentation. It is rather the reason to keep looking—historically, erotically, imaginatively, spiritually.

Fuller's and Sorère's attempts to explain and recite what drew them to each other rehearses that same moment in which dance critics and scholars fall in love with dancing. That love leads some to spend their lives writing about dance, some to keep dancing, some to "intimately mingle" writing and dancing, some to watch far too many videotapes, and some to join go-go groups. While such love finds particular emphasis and focus in the performances of specific movers, most dance writers' love of dancing exceeds their love for a particular dance/r. Attempting to articulate this "excess," the writer is moved to record her fascination with something that both precedes and succeeds the particular dance that inspires her writing.

"I never see you as you are" might be a good axiom for the dance critic because it acknowledges that the dance opens up an inquiry that passes through the dance in search of something else. This "passing through" cannot be accomplished without the dance as its ground and focus. Thus in this sense the writer continues the dancer's movement, albeit on another stage—the stage of the page. The dance inspires the writer to mark the movement the writer herself makes between her observations as viewer and her leaps as writer, between her active spectatorship and her rhetorical performance. These moves in turn put into motion and circulation words and thoughts that would not have otherwise come into being. Translating the swirling images and thoughts inspired by the dance into written language, the writer is returned to the unbridgeable alterity of the language of dance and the language of writing. Jeté. Comma. Pointe. Para. Plié. Period.

Fuller and Sorère understood that the erotic love they inspired in each other was rooted in the physicality of their bodies, even while it exceeded the particularity of each other. They understood, in short, the difference between "having a female lover" as we might say in our acquisitive, capitalist way, and "being a lesbian." The difference between being and having is among the most contested in psychoanalytic thought, for in the movement between being and having the individual subject forms a social identity. Dance and the writing it engenders are participants in this social process: here, the notion of response is necessarily bilingual; replies might be tapped or typed.

Fuller and Sorère seemed to manage to be, at once, in love with each other and in love with their own capacity to be in love. This is the duality that I hope a dance theory alert to sexuality of movement might remain alive to.

Ann Cvetkovich's witty essay, "White Boots and Combat Boots," is no less a performance than her dancing on a tight stage in a wig and boots. But just as the latter performance includes serious advice about breast exams and pointed protests against incest and rape, the former performance is concerned primarily with documenting the historical record of a group of bands, performers, venues, and producers that have made possible the staged embodiment of explicitly lesbian dance.

One implication of Cvetkovich's work is that dance historians and lesbians are both acutely aware of the dangers of failing to document histories. And her own performance as a lesbian dance historian here alerts us to the doubling of that enterprise. The effort not to let an important chapter in queer culture go unrecorded is much the same effort the dance historian feels in regard to recovering the notations and scores for performances created by the Cambodian classical court theater. Both acts must follow an explicitly political, historical, and aesthetic trajectory. The tendency to treat "reconstruction" as a politically neutral activity is spurious. For whether the text is *The Rite of Spring* or "Sodomy," the motivations for the reconstruction always touch the ideological.

Cvetkovich's essay moves back and forth between the particularities of her autobiographical journey, documenting her role in various go-go performances, to a recovery of the more general context of lesbian movement performance in the United States. That is, she moves from her own performances to the performative iteration of lesbian bodies moving on and off elusive and impermanent stages. Cvetkovich is interested in the history, pleasures and constraints of her own body as well as the history and pleasure of the collective body politic as figured and made possible by lesbian dance, however fleetingly.

Taken together, the work of Townsend and Cvetkovich asks how writing itself might partner a dance history that is always in the process of disappearing. Taking writing as a continuation of a conversation inaugurated by specific movement performances, Townsend and Cvetkovich issue an invitation to their readers to keep that conversation going. I'm not much of a dancer but I try to respond to invitations. So, inspired by Townsend's generative vagueness and Cvetkovich's passionate historical chronicle, here's a try:

> The night dripped through the music like ice through coke
> and I tasted your thigh as it pivoted on mine.
> Salsa to tango to samba to disco to go-go
> the pulse between us like airplanes touching down:
> whoosh, whoosh, glide, slide.

> I missed your show in Paris, was sick when you played Ann Arbor.

> Farther away now I remember the way the music slowed and the engines went idle. Your hands, my eyes. Melodies color memories of the first night, the first flame, the little table, the soft curtain. Coming. Going.

> (*There is in me sometimes a loneliness that makes me mute. But even in that silence my skin whispers the secret of that first dance. A hand more eloquent than the waking sun. Hips that rotate through streets that can be mapped by no city. Sweat soaking us with elixir even now I thirst for.*)

> I read your letters. They are full of names: Loie, Gaby, Allison, Kathy, Lauren, Julie, Ann. The music had words but from here I

can only hum the opening lines. Was it Bebop? Hip-Hop? Smoke
and scotch undid me.
But God what I do remember.

Your words like kisses swiveling in the half-light of our half-opened
lips.
Tonight my lids drooped down before you rendered me nothing
but thought.

Hooded. The curtain closed on that and opened on this.

NOTES

1. Luce Irigaray, *Ce sexe qui n'en est pas un* (Paris: Éditions de Minuit, 1977),
and *This Sex Which Is Not One,* trans. Catherine Porter with Carolyn Burke
(Ithaca, N.Y.: Cornell University Press, 1985).

2. See Cathy Caruth, ed., *Traumas: Explorations in Memory* (Baltimore,
Md.: Johns Hopkins University Press, 1994), for an excellent discussion of
trauma and latency.

16

Gesture, Ephemera, and Queer Feeling: Approaching Kevin Aviance

José Estéban Muñoz

This chapter has two beginnings. One is a story culled from personal memory, and the other is a poem by a prominent twentieth-century North American poet. Both openings function as queer evidence, an evidence that has been queered in relation to the laws of what counts as proof. Queerness has an especially vexed relationship to evidence. Historically, evidence of queerness has been used to penalize and discipline queer desires, connections, and acts. When the historian of queer experience attempts to document a queer past, there is often a gatekeeper, representing a straight present, who will labor to invalidate the historical fact of queer lives—present, past, and future. Queerness is rarely complemented by evidence, or at least by traditional understandings of the term. The key to queering evidence, and by this I mean the ways in which we prove queerness and read queerness, is by suturing it to the concept of ephemera. Think of ephemera as trace, the remains, the things that are left, hanging in the air like a rumor. Jacques Derrida's idea of the trace is relevant here. Ephemeral evidence is rarely obvious because it is needed to stand against the harsh lights of mainstream visibility and the potential tyranny of the fact. (Not that all facts are harmful, but the discourse of the fact has often cast antinormative desire as the bad object.) Ephemera are the remains that are often embedded in queer acts, in both stories we tell each other and communicative physical gestures like the cool look of a street cruise, a lingering handshake between recent acquaintances, or the mannish strut of a particularly confident woman.

In this writing I want to approach the idea of queerness and gesture. How so much can be located in the gesture. Dance is an especially valuable site for ruminations on queerness and gesture. This theoretical work will be anchored to a case study, a living body, a performer who is a master of the pose. Kevin Aviance is a mainstay of New York City's club world. He is something of a deity in the cosmology of gay nightlife. He is paid to perform— to sing and to move—at clubs in New York City and the world. He has been flown all over North America, Europe, and Asia and has performed for devoted cognoscenti, men and women who share a global sphere of queer knowing, moving, and feeling. At the center of that international sphere of queer experience is gesture, Aviance's resonant poses, and the force of queer ephemera.

This chapter builds on and speaks to themes that animate at least three other chapters in this book. Like Johnathan Bollen (chapter 9), I look at the dance floor as a stage for queer performativity that is integral to everyday life. I am on the same page as Bollen when he considers the dance floor as space where relations between memory and content, self and other, become inextricably intertwined. Furthermore, I also align my project with Bollen's Maurice Merleau-Ponty–inspired proposition that the dance floor increases our tolerance to embodied practices. It may do so because it demands, in the openness and closeness of relations to others, an exchange and alteration of kinesthetic experience through which we become, in a sense, less like ourselves and more like each other. In my analysis this does not mean that queers become one nation under groove once we hit the dance floor. I am in fact interested in the persistent variables of difference and inequity that follow us from queer communities to the dance floor, but I am nonetheless interested in the ways in which a certain queer communal logic overwhelms practices of individual identity. And I am also interested in the way in which the state responds to the communal becoming. To this end I consider Paul Siegel's contribution to this book, "A Right to Boogie Queerly: The First Amendment on the Dance Floor" (chapter 8), a valuable resource for students of queer dance who wish to understand not only the social significance of queer dance but the various ways in which a repressive state apparatus counters queer movements both literal and symbolic. Siegel's essay discusses the ways in which First Amendment discourse has ultimately served queer dance movements. Yet his chapter does not consider recent developments in New York City, like the Giuliani administration's reanimating of archaic cabaret license laws that have been used as a tool to shut down and harass various queer and racial minority bars in New York City. Those bars that survive display large signs that read "No Dancing—by Order of the New York City Department of Consumer Affairs." This edict has not been repealed and in this insistence the optimistic appraisal of the juridical sphere that Siegel drafts does not hold. Nonetheless, the stories of queer legal victory he recounts serve as a valuable resource for hope. In a similar vein Paul Franklin's historical account of Charlie Chaplin's dance, chapter 1, also stands as an incredible analysis of how queer movement, despite dominant biases against queer dance, nonetheless provides us with a narrative of queer iconicity's force within popular culture. While Kevin Aviance and Charlie Chaplin are an unlikely match, one a little white tramp and the other a big black queen, both are masters of the historically dense queer gesture.[1] Aviance, like Chaplin before him, calls upon an expressive vocabulary beyond the spoken word. For both men, the body in motion is the foundation of a visual lexicon in which the gesture speaks loud and clear.

Dance studies has focused its attention on the idea of movement. While a movement analysis of Kevin Aviance's work could certainly be elucidating, this chapter is instead a gesture analysis. I am not as interested in what the queer gesture means as I am interested in what such gestures perform. Such an analysis is inspired by what Elin Diamond has attempted to articulate, after Brecht's notion of *gestus*, as gestic feminist criticism. There is certainly something quite gestic about Aviance's performance practice, one that I argue does attempt to show its material conditions of (im)possibility and historical positionality. But while *gestus* suggests a lot more than *gesture*, I wish to concentrate my focus on the precise and specific physical acts that are conventionally understood as gesture, like the tilt of an ankle in very high heels, the swish of a hand that pats a face with imaginary makeup, and so many more precise acts. These acts are different but certainly not independent from movements that have more to do with a moving body's flow. Concentrating on gesture atomizes movement. These atomized and particular movements tell tales of historical becoming. Gestures transmit ephemeral knowledge of lost queer histories and possibilities within a phobic majoritarian public culture.

BEGINNING ONE: MEMORY

I'm young, maybe five or six. Our house is crowded by relatives who have just arrived from Cuba via a brief stopover exile in Spain. They arrived like my family did a few years earlier, without anything. Thus the little south Florida house that barely held five is now occupied by eleven. The only television set is in the family room. The boy cousins, my brother, my father, and my uncle are watching boxing on television, perhaps one of those early matches between Cuba and the United States in which none of the recent refugees feels comfortable taking a side. I'm bored. By this time it's clear that the culture of men and sports holds absolutely no allure for me. (Women's tennis is another matter altogether.) I walk across the red-brick floor and momentarily cross the screen. Then my oldest cousin calls out, "Look at the way he walks, how he shakes his ass. I wish I had a girlfriend who walked like that!" The other men and boys in the room erupt into laughter. I protest: "What is wrong with the way I walk? I don't understand." The taunts continue and I'm flushed with shame. I rush to my room to hide from this mockery, which I find amazingly painful.

My family has always been one that showed affection by mocking and joking. It's just our dysfunctional little way and, as those people with whom I live my emotional life today can attest, I am very much a child of that home. So it was odd that reaction I had. I would usually have retorted by commenting on my cousin's newest and shiniest zit. This was a different wounding, one that I had no defense for because I knew something was there, something I did not quite understand but felt at my core. This proto-homophobic attack made me sit down and think about my movement, to figure out what it was about the way I moved that elicited such mockery and such palpable contempt from a room full of males. I wanted—no, needed—to know what was it about my body and the way I moved it through the world that was so off, so different. I studied movement from then on, watching the way in which women walked and the way in which men walked. I looked at the ways in which men steered a sidewalk and tried to understand how women did it so differently. I noticed a stiffness in the men around me and a lack of stiffness in the women next to them. I studied all this and applied it to my own body. I began a project of butching up, even though that is not what I understood it to be back then. I tried to avoid the fact that I was studying something that came very naturally to other boys. I avoided the fact that heterogender was a space I was strangely on the outside of. I was a spy in the house of gender normative and, like any spy, I was extremely careful and worried that my cover would be blown. I did not understand that as long as I tried to ape the movements of heterosexuality, hardly anyone would even try to see through the facade because those around me did not want to believe in fairies. As long as I played the game, I was relatively safe. This is not universal; other boys cannot or will not straighten their gesture, and for them childhood is often a degraded zone of random violence and constant policing.

Sometimes I would slip and be called out. I remember a fey boy who was part of my mother's car-pool system. He took me aside in junior high and told me that I pulled my books too close to my chest like a girl. I started carrying my books to the side, just like a little man. Every so often a boy would tell me my slip was showing, would caution me to straighten up, as though my gesture could ruin it for everyone. Part of me wants to encounter him again, now in a gay space, a march, a club, a bathhouse, and embrace him like a fellow survivor, somebody else who made it through. Yet I imagine him at home, in Miami, with a wife who might remind him every once in awhile how he should position his legs when he sits down while visiting his in-laws.

That butching-up practice had a serious effect on me. Today I'm not often accused of flaming. I am considered mildly butch for a gay man of my age. Yet the older I get, the more I enjoy camping it up with my nellier friends. And now I can only enjoy performing masculinity in the company of my butch female friends because something about being boys with them feels weirdly liberating. I take further pleasure in talking about being a guy with my friend A., who is currently crossing and becoming a man. As I notice his voice deepen, his body bulk up, and his already butch mannerisms continue to evolve, I feel some kind of sweet revenge on gender.

When I encounter accomplished drag, I feel this revenge again. I am drawn to Justin Bonds Kiki, a strung-out aging showbiz personality who is really a young white man in his early thirties but plays a grizzled show business veteran in her late sixties. She is accompanied by Herb, who is actually Kenny Mellman, an attractive gay Jewish man in his thirties, who plays her homosexual accompanist, a gray little old man.[2] Kiki cavorts and staggers as she does Loungey-Punk hybrids of contemporary pop songs and old standards. The drink in her hand is ever present as she stumbles from table to table. Often, she will mount the table of an unsuspecting guest, throw his cocktail to the floor, and demand that the patron sitting at the table lick her fishnet stocking because she is on fire, as intimated by the song she is singing, P. J. Harvey's "Rid of Me." The fishnets cover a dancer's set of gams, muscles that get exercised when Kiki does a fast and frantic tap number, competent and exaggerated at exactly the same time. She is visibly winded after finishing this self-consciously old-school number. She closes that component of the cabaret act with the lines "Ladies and Gentlemen! I started as a burlesque dancer in Baltimore in the fifties and I still got it!" This line conjures a lot of showbiz divas on the decline. That tap dance number itself indexes a sick camp aesthetic that the fans of Kiki and Herb love. Their camp celebrates virtuosity while reveling in an antinormative degeneracy. In this instance camp works as an index to a shared aesthetic and a communal structure of feeling. The dance is over and seemingly gone, but it lives as an ephemeral happening that we remember, something that fuels anecdotes we tell each other. Because the show is weekly, the devoted go week after week and it takes on the feel of a ritual. It lives, then, after its immediate dematerializations as a transformed materiality, circulating in queer realms of knowing and becoming.

The story with which I began this section functions that way too. It is an ephemeral proof. It does not count as evidence in some systems of reading and understanding proper documentation and knowing. Making a case for queer evidence in theory seems to beg the use of such evidence.

BEGINNING TWO: POETRY

Here is one of my favorite poems and a second opening:

ONE ART
The art of losing isn't hard to master;
so many things seem filled with the intent
to be lost that their loss is no disaster.

Lose something every day. Accept the fluster
of lost door keys, the hour badly spent.
The art of losing isn't hard to master

Then practice farther, losing faster:
places, and names, and where it was you meant
to travel. None of these will bring disaster.

I lost my mother's watch. And look! my last, or
next-to-last, of three loved houses went.
The art of losing isn't hard to master.

I lost two cities, lovely ones. And, vaster,
some realms I owned, two rivers, a continent,
I miss them, but it wasn't a disaster.

Even losing you (the joking voice, a gesture
I love) I shan't have lied. It's evident
the art of losing's not to hard to master
though it may look like (*Write* it!)   like disaster.[3]

The parenthetical remarks within the poem are most interesting for my purposes. I suggest that these remarks are graphically differentiated through grammatical devices so they might connote a different register than the majority of the poem. The parenthetical remarks communicate a queer trace, an ephemeral evidence. I want to read these remarks, words that evoke the idea of gesture, as gestures. Interest in these specific lines should not derail interest in the poem in its entirety. "One Art" offers the attentive reader a theory of the materiality of performance and ephemera. It has become somewhat axiomatic within the field of performance studies that that act exists only during its actual duration. I have been making a case for a hermeneutics of residue that looks to understand the wake of performance. What is left? What remains? Ephemera remain. They are absent and they are present, disrupting a predictable metaphysics of presence. The actual act is only a stage in the game, it is a moment, pure and simple. There is a deductive element to performance that has everything to do with its conditions of possibility, and there is much that follows. The poet, Elizabeth Bishop, asks the forgetful person to not become upset about the loss of certain objects because they seem filled with the intent to be lost—their loss is no disaster.[4] She asks us to accept the fluster of loss and understand that it is not a disaster. Something is embedded within those acts, traces that have an indelible materiality. The poet is inviting us to more than simply accept this loss—to embrace it and to perhaps not even understand it as loss but as something else. She is, within a parenthetical phrase in the poem's last line, asking us to "Write it!" The word *write* is not only in parentheses but italicized, more than doubling its emphasis. This command to write is a command to save the ephemeral thing by committing it to memory, to word, to language. The poet instructs us to retain the last thing through a documentation of our loss, a retelling of our relationship to it. Thus her mother's watch now exists, or perhaps has found an afterlife, in its transformation and current status as residue, as ephemera. It partially (re)lives in its documentation.

And while we cannot simply conserve a person or a performance through documentation, we can perhaps begin to summon up, through the auspices of memory, the acts and gestures that meant so much to us. The poem clearly has an addressee, who is a "you." Now, we ask, who is that "you"? If we were to lean on biography—something I always caution my students against—it would be Lota de Macedo Soares, Bishop's estranged Brazilian lover who committed suicide. Much would suggest that (the joking voice, a gesture I love). The parenthetical remark contains queer content, queer memory, a certain residue of lesbian love.

One temptation is to say Bishop was in the closet and, furthermore, that she gives frightened and furtive little signs of her lesbian desire. But this is a mistake and not what I mean by traces of queer desire. As the North American poetry scholar Katie Kent has suggested to me in a correspondence, calling Bishop's work closeted is a mistake: I am wary of calling her work more or less closeted. I think it reinforces this trajectory to her life that only right before she died did she claim her sexuality in her poetry and in any other way, whereas if you read her poems expecting to read about queerness, it is there throughout. A lot of the biographers and critics impose the closet on her as a way, I think, of not having to talk about the role of queer identity and queer sex play throughout her work.

Kent's suggestion, that we read with queerness as an expectation, challenges the reader to approach the poet with a different optic, one that is attuned to the ways in which, through small gestures, particular intonations, and other ephemeral traces, queer energies and lives are laid bare. The parenthetical remark in Bishop's "One Art" is a queer gesture, one that accesses the force of queer ephemera and is utterly legible to an optic of feeling, a queer optic, that permits us to take in the queerness that is embedded in gesture. The poem's narrative instructs us as to the transience of things filled with the intent to be lost, and as it does so, it retains a queer trace that lingers, tragically and lovingly, within the hold of parentheses. This poetic gesture in Bishop's masterful text is not unlike the moves on a dance floor or a stage that a queer artist can conjure. The gesture summons the resources of queer experience and collective identity that have been lost to us because of the demand for official evidence and facts.

We can understand queerness itself as being filled with the intention to be lost. Queerness is illegible and therefore lost in relation to the straight minds' mapping of space. Queerness is lost in space or lost in relation to the space of heteronormativity. Bishop's poem should be read as a primer for queer self-enactment or queer becoming. To accept loss is to accept the way in which one's queerness will always render one lost to a world of heterosexual imperatives, codes, and laws. To accept loss is to accept queerness. Or, more accurately, the loss of heteronormativity authorization and entitlement. To be lost is not to hide in a closet or to perform a simple (ontological) disappearing act; it is to veer away from heterosexuality's path. Freedmen escaping slavery got lost too, and this is a salient reverberation between queerness and racialization. At this historical moment, one that can be described as being characterized by encroaching assimilationist ideology in the mainstream gay and lesbian movement, some gays and lesbians want to be found on a normative map of the world. Being lost, in this particular queer sense, is to relinquish one's role (and subsequent privilege) in the heternormative order. The dispossessed are appropriately adept at critiquing possession as a logic. To accept the way in which one is lost is to be also found and not found in a particularly queer fashion.

A BODY: APPROACHING AVIANCE

This section's subtitle is meant to connote a few things. I invoke the phrase "approaching Aviance" because I want to cast a picture from life, the scene of Aviance's being approached. To travel through the gay world of New York City with Kevin Aviance is certainly to call attention to one's self. Aviance is sixty-two, bald, black, and effeminate. In or out of his unique drag he is immediately recognizable to anyone who has seen his show. To walk the cityscape with him is to watch as strangers approach him and remark on one of his performances. They often gush enthusiastically and convey how much a particular performance or his body of performances means to them. One will hear things like "I'll always remember that one show you did before they shut the Palladium down," or "You turned it out at Roxy last week." Kevin will be gracious and give back the love he has just received. His work, his singing and his movement, is not the high art of Bill T. Jones or Mark Morris, but I would venture to say that more queer people see Aviance move than have witnessed Jones's mas-

terful productions. I don't mean to undermine the value of
Jones's work. I only want to properly frame the way in which
Aviance's nightlife performances matter. The gestures he performs matter worlds to the children who comprise his audiences.
Aviance is something of a beacon that displays and channels
worlds of queer pain and pleasure. In his moves we see the suffering of being a gender outlaw, one who lives outside the dictates
of heteronormativity. Furthermore, another story about being
black in a predominately white-supremacist gay world ruminates
beneath his gestures. Some of his other gestures transmit and amplify the pleasures of queerness, the joys of gender dissidence, of
willfully making one's own way against the stream of a crushing
heteronormative tide. The strong influence of vogueing practice
in his moves affirms the racialized ontology of the pier queen, a
personage who is degraded in New York City's above-ground gay
culture. Often, one gesture will contain both positive and negative polarities simultaneously, because the pleasure and pain of
queerness are not a strict binary. The conversations that ensue
after his performances, the friends and strangers that approach
him on the street, the ads in bar rags, the reviews in local papers,
the occasional home video documentation, and the hazy and
often drug-tinged memories that remain after the actual live performances are the queer ephemera, that transmutation of the performance energy, that also function as a beacon for queer possibility and survival.

To understand the lure of Aviance's performance it is useful to
describe a performance from Montreal's Red and Blue party. The
Red and Blue is part of the circuit-party system. The circuit is just
that, a loosely aligned social circuit of dance parties that happen
throughout the year in major cities throughout North America.
Aviance was invited to perform at Montreal. Another drag performer, a black queen in traditional illusionist drag, appears on
stage and introduces the fierce and legendary Kevin Aviance.
Aviance emerges from behind an ornate red curtain with gold
trim. He is wearing a fantastical suit that features puffy, exaggerated purple shoulders that rise to the length of his ears. As he
sings his first club hit, his microphone emerges from his lapel,

permitting his hands total freedom to move in gestures that are familiar to those conversant with vogueing and break-dancing styles. In the middle of the song his entire body becomes involved as he feigns cold robotic motions. The monster walks. He then sings his club hit "Cunty."[5] He sings, "Feeling Like a Lilly / Feeling Like a Rose" and as he stands in place, his body quivers with extravagant emotion. He stands center stage, and as he screams, he quivers with an emotional force that connotes the stigma of gender ostracism. His gender freakiness speaks to the audiences that surround him. His is an amplified and extreme queer body, a body in motion that rapidly deploys the signs, the gestures, of queer communication, survival, and self-making. Spectators connect his trembling with the ways in which he flips his wrist and regains composure by applying imaginary pancake makeup.

By this juncture in the performance, the jacket is removed and the silky pants are removed. He is revealed in a body-embracing prismatic body stocking. He begins to bound around the stage, offering the audience a particular version of runway—the vogueing practice of walking as though one were a supermodel. One particular Aviance gesture worth noting is the way in which his ankles fold or crack as he walks, or rather stomps, the runway. This gesture permits him to be quicker and more determined in his steps than most high-heeled walkers. This gesture connotes a tradition of queenly identification with the sadism of female beauty rituals. The move—to walk with heels in such an unorthodox fashion—constitutes a disidentification with these traditions of gay male performances of female embodiment. Aviance's refusal to wear wigs is a further example of this disidentificatory dynamic. The determined walking is replaced by a particular swayback walk in which his buttocks and chest are both outstretched, in this instance exaggerating the features of a racialized body. To do so, I want to argue, is not to play the Venus Hottentot for a predominately white Canadian audience; it is, instead, to insist on the fact of blackness in this overwhelmingly white space. Aviance then throws himself into the audience and is held aloft by a sea of white hands. He is lost in a sea of white hands; this being lost can be understood as a particularly queer mode of performing the self. This is how the performance ends. This amazing counterfetish is absorbed by the desiring masses. He has opened in them a desire or a mode of desiring that is uneasy and utterly important if he is to surpass the new gender symmetry of the gay world.

Aviance's biography is, in and of itself, a testament to queer survival. He grew up as Eric Snead in a large family in Richmond, Virginia. His first experience in drag was in the seventh grade. As a youth he escaped the narrow confines of the small town and moved to the nearest gay metropolis, Washington, D.C., where he worked as a hairdresser, did drag as an amateur, and developed a disabling drug habit. He eventually overcame crack with the help of the House of Aviance. The House of Aviance is not exactly like the vogueing houses of Jennie Livingston's film *Paris Is Burning*, inasmuch as it does not compete. The House of Aviance is something of a queer kinship network in which members serve as extended, pretended, and—some would argue—improved family that supports and enables its members. Kevin Aviance was the name he took after initiation. He eventually landed in New York City, where he first made a name for himself at the now legendary Sound Factory, a queer club that began as a predominately Latino and black space. He distinguished himself on the dance floor, grabbing the attention of major DJs and nightlife promoters, and soon became a professional performer. Today he is one of a handful of New York drag performers who can distinguish himself as living solely off his performance. He forsook traditional drag and the world of wigs early in his career. His look is reminiscent of the legendary group of black soul divas called LaBelle, the group that wrote the almost perfect disco hit, "Lady Marmalade."[6] I think of Aviance's look when I study the album cover for LaBelle's phenomenal 1974 album, *Nightbirds*. All three women, dressed in metallic outfits, are portrayed as swirls of space-age Afro glamor. LaBelle's Afro futurism was a strategic move to make the group look freakish and alien, to make blackness something otherworldly and uncanny. Aviance, like LaBelle, reconstructs blackness as a mysterious Lost-in-Space aesthetic. Other comparisons can be drawn between the punk performance style of Klaus Nomi, the deranged disco divinity of Grace Jones, the insane and beautiful drag of the late performer Leigh Bowery, and the spaced-out elegance of the hip-hop artist Missy Misdemeanor Elliot. But Aviance's look is definitely his. I have seen him in many outfits, including fantastic gold lamé jumpsuits, sheer polka-dot minidresses, and leopard-skin body stockings. While he does not wear wigs, he sometimes adorns his bald head with a hat.

Both his appearance and his performances are in no way attempting to imitate a woman. He is instead interested in approximating a notion of femininity. Queer theory has made one lesson explicitly clear: the set of behaviors and codes of conduct that we refer to as feminine or masculine are not slaves to the biological.[7] Women, straight and gay, perform and live masculinity in the same way as many a biological man inhabits femininity. Sometimes technology aligns people's gender identity and their biological self. Others relish the antinormative disjuncture between their biological gender and their performed or lived gender. Aviance's masculinity, partially informed by his biological maleness, is never hidden—he wears no wig and he does not tuck (conceal or hide the male genital bulge while in drag). Indeed, in his performance we see a unique cohabitation of traditional female and male traits.

To perform such a hybrid gender is not only to be queer but to defy troubling gender logics within gay spaces. Bollen's chapter on queer performativity and the dance floor (chapter 9) catalogues different dancing styles—such as girly poofter, Australian slang for campy and feminine male dancing, and the standard macho style of dancing that dominates many gay dance venues. Bollen notes but does not delve into the femmephobia apparent on many queer dance floors, where those who break the gay clone edict to act like a man are de-eroticized and demoted to second-class citizenship. I observe this tension when I find myself at the Roxy, the sceniest place to be for a certain stratum of New York gay men. I am overwhelmed by the throngs of shirtless dancers with gym-crafted bodies. Their dance style is aggressive yet rigid; the moves they make are meant to show off the rewards of hours of gym workouts. They do not spread out but instead dance closely together, almost in packs. They are often awash in the effects of club drugs, like ecstasy and special K, and huddle together as they dance. For the most part, they do not let themselves flow and keep close to each other, enjoying the ways in which their gym-sculpted muscles rub up against those of the next clonish dance-floor compatriot. Through the mist of the smoke machine I watch Aviance elevate himself above the crowd. He is dancing on a small platform that is about five feet high, the kind of mini-istage usually occupied by a gym-built go-go boy. Go-go boys mostly just bump and grind. There isn't much room for steps and Aviance doesn't need them. This particular dance is about his hands. His hands move in jerky, mechanical spasms. They frame his face and his outfit. He dances to the house music that the DJ is playing especially for him. He is elevated from the dance floor but also surrounded by dancers who are now dancing with him. He is both on stage and one of the throng, one with the music. It makes sense that he is elevated. He is there not because he is simply a better dancer than the other club goers around him (he is) but because he is the bridge between quotidian nightlife dancing and theatrical performance.[8] He defies the codes of masculinity that saturate the dance floor. His gestures are unapologetically femme. His fingers swiftly minister to his face, as though applying invisible makeup. His movements are coded as masculine (strong abrupt motions), feminine (smooth flowing moves), and, above all, robotic (precise mechanical movements).

What does it mean that in this space, where codes of masculinity dominate, Aviance is a local deity? What work does his performance do in this venue? Furthermore, what about his blackness in this space that is overrun by sweaty and shirtless white torsos? One response would be that he is a fetish in this space, a magic juju that lets white and antifeminine gay men be fabulous while not being progressive around gender, race, and sexuality. Such a reading would miss the point. Aviance is extremely aware of the audience, and when the time comes to play the race man/woman, he will certainly do so. I've seen this occur on stage on many occasions. At La Nueva Esculeita, a Latino queer space in midtown, I have seen him convert the dance club's stage to a pulpit between musical numbers and witnessed him denouncing the fascist regime of the city's mayor and his racist police force. Aviance speaks out regularly at venues both white and racialized. He has also read the racism of New York's privileged gay community. Aviance is conscious about the ways in which he can be made into a fetish, but he disidentifies with such a role in very particular ways.[9] Marxism tells us the story of the commodity fetish, the object that alienates us from the conditions of possibility that brought whatever commodity into being.[10] The fetish, in its Marxian dimensions, is about occlusion, displacement, and concealment—illusion. Some drag artists prefer the gender title of illusionist. Aviance does not work in illusion. He becomes many things at once. His performance labors to index a fantastic female glamor, but his masculinity is never eclipsed. If the fetish is about illusion, Aviance disidentifies with the standard notion of the fetish and makes it about a certain demystification.

When he is on that stage, he performs gestures that few others can perform. His gestures are not allowed in the strict codes of masculinity that habitués of most commercial queer dance spaces follow. Paul Franklin's chapter on Charlie Chaplin's gestures (chapter 1) speaks to the fear of effeminacy that has haunted the history of the male dancer in the West. This anti-effeminate bias has, ironically, resurfaced in many gay male dance spaces. As an icon, a beacon above the dance floor, Aviance uses gestures that permit the dancers to see and experience the feelings they do not permit themselves to let in. He and the gestures he performs are beacons for all the emotions the throng is not allowed to feel. These pumped-up gym queens started out, in most cases, as pudgy or skinny sissy boys who attempted to hide their gestures. Many of them, like the *I* from my earlier autobiographical account, attempted to walk like men and hide the telltale queer gesture. This culture needs to be critiqued for the normative gender paradigms to which it subscribes as well as the exclusionary logics it applies to people who do not make its normative (often white and decidedly masculine) cut. Nonetheless, while this symbolic violence is not justifiable, one can certainly understand this desire to be masculine. These men did not stop at straightening out the swish of their walk; they worked on their bodies and approximated a hypermasculine ideal.

I do not want to extend energy in moralizing against this route to survival in a heteronormative world. It makes sense, especially when we consider that they came into masculinity as they were surrounded by the specter of the AIDS pandemic. The AIDS catastrophe provides a lot of reasons to build up the body. But imagine how hard it must be to try to look and act so butch all the time. Indeed, these men become their own fetish of masculinity insofar as they hide the conditions of possibility that lead to their becoming butch. Aviance reveals these conditions. This is the function of the counterfetish. He performs the powerful interface between femininity and masculinity that is active in any gender, especially queer ones. In this fashion he is once again a counterfetish, elucidating the real material conditions of our gender and desire. Imagine the relief these gym queens feel as Aviance lets himself be both masculine and feminine, as his fabulous and strange gestures connote the worlds of queer suffering that these huddled men attempt to block out but cannot escape, and the pleasures of being swish and queeny that they cannot admit to in their quotidian lives. Furthermore, imagine that his performance is something that is instructive, that recodifies signs of abjection in mainstream queer spaces—blackness, femininity/effeminacy—and not only makes them desirable but something to be desired. Imagine how some of those men on the dance floor might come around to accepting and embracing the queer gesture through Aviance's exemplary performance. More important, imagine what his performance means to those on the margins of the crowd, those who have not devoted their lives to daily gym visits and this hypermasculine ideal. To those whose race or appearance does not conform to rigid schematics of what might be hot. Those on the margins can get extreme pleasure in seeing Aviance rise from the muscled masses, elevated and luminous.

For the racialized cognoscenti, his gestures function like the sorrow songs of W. E. B. DuBois's *The Souls of Black Folk*. In that paradigm-shifting text DuBois meditates on the power of Negro music and the embedded and syncretic meaning found in these testaments to the culture of slavery. What are these songs, and what do they mean? I know little of music and can say nothing in technical phrases, but I know something of men. Knowing them, I know that these songs are the articulate message of the slave to the world. They tell us that life was joyous to the black slave, careless and happy. I can easily believe this of some, of many. The Old South cannot deny the heart-touching witness of these songs. They are the music of an unhappy people, of the children of disappointment; they tell of death and suffering and unvoiced longing toward a truer world, of misty wanderings and hidden ways.[11]

I risk sounding a bit overdramatic by using this analogy. I nonetheless invoke this classic text in African American letters for the express purpose of calling attention to the pathos that underlies some of these gestures. Vogueing, for instance, is too often considered a simplistic celebration of black queer culture. It is seen as a simple appropriation of high fashion or other aspect of commodity culture. I am proposing that we might see something other than a celebration in these moves—the strong trace of black and queer racialized survival, the way in which children need to imagine becoming Other in the face of conspiring cultural logics of white supremacy and heteronormativity. The gesture contains an articulate message for all to read, in this case a message of fabulousness and fantastical becoming. It also contains another message, one less articulated and more ephemeral but equally relevant to any understanding of queer gestures, gestures that, as I have argued, are often double- or multivalenced. So while the short-sighted viewer of Aviance's vogueing might see only the approximation of high fashion glamor as he moves and gestures on the stage, others see/hear another tune, one of racialized self-enactment in the face of overarching opposition.

CONCLUSION: THE NOT-VANISHING POINT

Even New York clubs eventually close for the night; most close the next afternoon, but they do close. The performances come to an end. Club kids stumble into taxis in broad daylight, and Aviance and other performers pack up their outfits and makeup and go home for a restorative nap. Is this performance's end? That moment when the venue closes? Has the vanishing point been reached? In her influential book of dance criticism, *At the Vanishing Point: A Critic Looks at Dance*, Marcia Siegel provocatively links dance to the notion of a vanishing point: dance exists as a perpetual vanishing point. At the moment of its creation it is gone. All the years of training in the studio, all the choreographer's planning, the rehearsals, the coordination of designers, composers, and technicians, the raising of money and the gathering together of an audience—all these are only a preparation for an event that disappears in the very act of materializing. No other art is so hard to catch, so impossible.

Seigel certainly knows that every vanishing point signals a return, the promise of the next performance, of continuation. She argues that dancers and audiences must have been aware of this ephemerality and used it. I agree with the revered critic. Queer dance is hard to catch, and it is meant to be hard to catch—it is supposed to slip through the fingers and comprehension of those who would use knowledge against us. But it matters and takes on a vast material weight for those of us who perform or draw important sustenance from performance. Rather than dematerialize, dance rematerializes. Dance, like energy, never disappears; it is simply transformed. Queer dance, after the live act, does not just expire. The ephemeral does not equal unmateriality. It is more nearly about another understanding of what matters. It matters to get lost in dance or to use dance to get lost. Lost from the evidentiary logic of heterosexuality.

For queers, the gesture and its aftermath, the ephemeral trace, matter more than many traditional modes of evidencing lives and politics. The hermeneutics of residue for which I have called are calibrated to read Aviance's gestures and know these moves as vast storehouses of queer history and futurity. We also must understand that after the gesture expires, its materiality has transformed into ephemera that are utterly necessary.

NOTES

I am grateful to Carol Martin and Jane Desmond for excellent editorial advice. Fred Moten provided brilliant feedback from which I benefited immensely. Ari Gold is my Beatrice who leads me into the inferno of clubland with great patience. Kevin Aviance has been helpful and generally divine.

1. By "historically dense queer gesture," I mean a gesture whose significance and connotive queer force is dense with antinormative meanings.

2. That Kiki would be in her late sixties seems a bit unlikely because, according to the oral biography that Kiki and Herb recite during their performances, they began performing during the Great Depression. When I asked Bond about Kiki's age, she explained that her "official age" is sixty-six.

3. "One Art" from *The Complete Poems: 1927–1979* by Elizabeth Bishop. Copyright © 1979, 1983 by Alice Helen Methfessel. Reprinted by permission of Farrar, Straus and Giroux, LLC.

4. In some ways this echoes Peggy Phelan, who has famously argued that disappearance is the very ontology of something like performance.

5. The word *cunty* is black gay slang that describes a certain performed mode of femininity. While its misogynist implications cannot be underemphasized, it should be understood that the term *cunty*, unlike *cunt*, is not meant to be derogatory. A good queen strives to achieve a high level of "cuntiness."

6. The members of LaBelle were Patti LaBelle, Nona Hendrix, and Sarah Dash.

7. While I could plug in many an example here, especially most of Judith Butler's important oeuvre, I take this opportunity to refer readers to Judith Halberstam's important study, *Female Masculinity* (Durham, N.C.: Duke University Press, 1998).

8. I argue for the notion of resistance through dance/nightlife culture in the introduction that Celeste Fraser Delgado and I wrote for our edited volume, *Everynight Life: Culture and Dance in Latin/o America* (Durham, N.C.: Duke University Press, 1998).

9. For more on the process I describe at length as disidentification, see my book *Disidentifications: Queers of Color and the Performance of Politics* (Minneapolis: University of Minnesota Press, 1999).

10. Marx articulates the theory of the commodity fetish in his famous *Das Kapital*, vol. 1, pt. 1, chap. 1, sec. 4.

11. W. E. B. DuBois, *The Souls of Black Folk* (New York: Bantam, 1989), 179–80.

CONTRIBUTORS

INDEX

JONATHAN BOLLEN completed his dissertation, "Queer Kinesthesia: On the Dance Floor at Gay and Lesbian Parties, Sydney, 1994–1998," at the University of Western Sydney, Nepean, Australia. He is the author of "Sexing the Dance at Sleaze Ball 1994," *TDR: The Journal of Performance Studies* 40/3 (1996) and "'What a Queen's Gotta Do': Queer Performativity and the Rhetorics of Performance," *Australasian Drama Studies* 31 (1997).

JENNIFER DeVERE BRODY is an associate professor in the departments of English and African American studies at the University of Illinois at Chicago. Her essay here is part of a larger project entitled *The Style of Elements: Politically Performing Punctuation*. She is the author of *Impossible Purities: Blackness, Femininity and Victorian Culture* (1998).

RAMSAY BURT is senior research fellow in dance at De Montfort University, Leicester, U.K., and the author of *The Male Dancer: Bodies, Spectacle, Sexualities* (1995) and *Alien Bodies: Representations of Modernity, "Race," and Nation in Early Modern Dance* (1998).

ANN CVETKOVICH is an associate professor of English at the University of Texas at Austin. She is the author of *Mixed Feelings: Feminism, Mass Culture, and Victorian Sensationalism* (1992) and *An Archive of Feelings: Trauma, Sexuality, and Lesbian Public Cultures* (forthcoming).

JANE C. DESMOND is an associate professor of American studies at the University of Iowa, editor of *Meaning in Motion: New*

Cultural Studies of Dance (1997), and author of *Staging Tourism: Bodies on Display from Waikiki to Sea World* (1999).

JANE FEUER is a professor of English and film studies at the University of Pittsburgh. A specialist in media and cultural studies, she is the author of *The Hollywood Musical* (1993) and *Seeing through the Eighties: Television and Reaganism* (1995).

SUSAN LEIGH FOSTER is professor of dance at the University of California campuses at Riverside and Davis. She is the author of *Reading Dancing: Bodies and Subjects in Contemporary American Dance* (1986), *Choreography and Narrative: Ballet's Staging of Story and Desire* (1996), and the forthcoming *Dances That Describe Themselves: The Improvised Choreography of Richard Bull.* She is also editor of *Choreographing History* (1995), and *Corporealities: Dancing, Knowledge, Culture, and Power* (1995).

JULIA L. FOULKES is a core faculty member at the New School in New York City where she teaches history. She is the author of *Modern Bodies: Dance in American Modernism* (forthcoming) and "Angels 'Rewolt!' ": Jewish Women in Modern Dance in the 1930s," *American Jewish History* (forthcoming). She was a Rockefeller Foundation Postdoctoral Fellow at the Center for Black Music Research, Columbia College Chicago (1997–98) and the winner of the 1996 Selma Jeanne Cohen Graduate Student Award of the Society of Dance History Scholars.

PAUL B. FRANKLIN received his doctoral degree in art history from Harvard University. He resides in Paris where he is managing editor and director of research for *nest*, a cutting-edge shelter magazine. He is coeditor of *Fieldwork: Sites in Literary and Culture Studies* (1996) and the author of numerous articles, including "Object Choice: Marcel Duchamp's Fountain and the Art of Queer Art History," *Oxford Art Journal* 23, no. 1 (2000) and "Beatrice Wood, Her Dada . . . and Her Mama," in Naomi Sawelson-Gorse, ed., *Women in Dada: Essays on Sex, Gender, and Identity* (1998).

DAVID GERE is an assistant professor in the Department of World Arts and Cultures at the University of California, Los Angeles. He is coeditor of *Looking Out: Perspectives on Dance and Criticism in a Multicultural World* (1995) and is writing a book on dance and corporeality in the AIDS era.

KEVIN KOPELSON is an associate professor of English at the University of Iowa and author of *Beethoven's Kiss: Pianism, Perversion, and the Mastery of Desire* (1996). His article on Nijinsky is excerpted from his latest book, *The Queer Afterlife of Vaslav Nijinsky* (1997).

SUSAN MANNING is an associate professor of English, theater, and dance at Northwestern University and author of the award-winning *Ecstasy and the Demon: Feminism and Nationalism in the Dances of Mary Wigman* (1993). Her latest book is *Making an American Dance* (forthcoming).

GAY MORRIS has been an art and dance critic for a number of years, writing for such publications as *Artnews, Dancing Times, Dance Ink, Dance View, Christian Science Monitor, New York Times*, and the *International Herald Tribune*. She was a corresponding editor for *Art in America* from 1987 to 1996. She is the editor of an anthology, *Moving Words: Rewriting Dance*, and is currently a doctoral candidate in sociology at Goldsmiths College, University of London. Her dissertation is a sociological study of American avant-garde dance in the postwar years.

JOSÉ ESTÉBAN MUÑOZ is an associate professor of performance studies at the Tisch School of the Arts, New York University. He is the coeditor of several anthologies, including *Pop Out: Queer Warhol* (1996) and *Everynight Life: Culture and Dance in Latino/a America* (1998), and author of *Disidentifications: Queers of Color and the Performance of Politics* (1999).

PEGGY PHELAN is a professor of performance studies at the Tisch School of the Arts, New York University. She is the author and editor of several books, including *Unmarked: the Politics of Performance* (1993) and *Mourning Sex: Performing Public Memories* (1997).

PAUL SIEGEL is a professor of communication arts at Gallaudet University where he writes in the areas of communication law and political communication. His collection of edited readings on the Clarence Thomas hearings is *Outsiders Looking In* (1996). He is also the author of dozens of law review articles and book chapters, and as well as the forthcoming textbooks, *Communication Law in America* and *Cases in Communication Law*.

JULIE TOWNSEND is a doctoral candidate in comparative literature at the University of California, Los Angeles. As this book went to press, she was completing her dissertation, "The Choreography of Modernism: Dancing across Aesthetic Borders." Her work on Loie Fuller was supported by a 1996–1997 fellowship at the Paris Critical Studies Center. She is the author of "Staging the Spectator: The Erotics of Performance in Colette's *La Vagabonde* and Fuller's *Danse Serpentine*," in Annette Jael Lehmann's forthcoming edited collection, *Un/Sichtbarkeiten der Differenz Beiträge zur Gender-Debatte in den Künsten*.